Edith Stein
The Life of a Philosopher
and Carmelite

Sr. Teresa Benedicta, late 1938
(donning Teresa R. Posselt's scapular)

Edith Stein
The Life of a Philosopher and Carmelite

**Authorized and Revised Biography by Her Prioress
Sister Teresia Renata Posselt, O.C.D.**

(Text, Commentary and Explanatory Notes)

*Compilation and Commentaries
by Susanne M. Batzdorff, Josephine Koeppel, John Sullivan
in collaboration with Maria Amata Neyer, Cologne Carmel*

ICS Publications
Washington, D.C.
2005

© Washington Province of Discalced Carmelites, Inc. 2005
ICS Publications
2131 Lincoln Road NE
Washington, DC 20002-1151
800-832-8489
www.icspublications.org

Typesetting by Stephen Tiano Page Design & Production
Typeset and produced in the U.S.A.

Library of Congress Cataloging-in-Publications Data

Teresia de Spiritu Sancto, Sister, O.D.C., b. 1891.
[Edith Stein, Philosophin und Karmelitin. English]
Edith Stein : the life of a philosopher and Carmelite : authorized and revised biography by Her Prioress / Sister Teresia Renata Posselt ; text, commentary and explanatory notes by Susanne Batzdorff, Josephine Koeppel, John Sullivan ; in collaboration with Maria Amata Neyer, Cologne Carmel.
    p. cm.
Includes bibliographical references and indexes.
ISBN 0-935216-36-7 (alk. paper)
1. Stein, Edith, Saint, 1891-1942.   2. Christian philosophers—Germany—Biography.   3. Carmelite Nuns—Germany—Biography.
4. Christian martyrs—Germany—Biography.   5. Catholic converts—Germany—Biography.   6. Philosophers—Germany—Biography.
I. Batzdorff, Susanne M.   II. Koeppel, Josephine.   III. Sullivan, John, 1942-   IV. Title.
BX4705.S814T47 2004
282'.092—dc22

                                  2004020303

Contents

Part 2
". . .in the harbor of the divine will."

Foreword

News of a fresh English translation of the first biography of Edith Stein was very welcome to me. The translators, Susanne M. Batzdorff, a niece of Edith Stein, and my Sister and Brother in Carmel, Sr. Josephine Koeppel of the Carmel of Elysburg, PA, and Rev. Dr. John Sullivan Chairman of the Institute of Carmelite Studies, ought to assure excellent results. In Germany, and in many other countries too, this long-out-of-print book is sought after again and again. It was written in 1947 by Teresia Renata of the Holy Spirit (Posselt), once novice mistress of Edith Stein, who then became prioress in 1936 and died in 1961. At first it was not at all easy to find a publisher for this slight volume, but finally Glock and Lutz of Nuremberg published it at Christmas 1948. The author is the only one of several biographers who have since written other fine biographies, who personally knew Edith Stein, Sr. Teresia Benedicta a Cruce, and knew her as a Carmelite.

This personal connection is evident in this little book. It is written very warmly and allows you to experience the loving relationship between the writer and our sainted Sister. At the time, however, the author had no reliable sources to help her. Edith Stein's belongings, including all her writings, were in the Netherlands and not accessible to Sr. Teresia Renata. She was exclusively dependent on the recollections of the Sisters in Cologne and Echt and on her own memory. Besides, one cannot ignore the fact that her memory played her many a trick and sometimes totally abandoned her. True, the uninformed reader did not notice this in the early editions of the biography: by nature the author did not allow those mistakes to bother her at all, even when they were gross errors, as when she ascribes to Edith Stein a book that in reality Hedwig Conrad-Martius had written. This did not diminish her enthusiasm. Other errors that pertained to the Stein family had already been noted early on by Dr. Erna Biberstein, née

vii

Stein, Edith's slightly older sister, but unfortunately in vain. We don't know whether the publisher had difficulty with altering several pages or whether Teresia Renata was not interested in making the changes – at any rate, from then on several bits of misinformation began to circulate around the world.

The book's first edition had the simple title *Edith Stein*; its subtitle was *The Life of a Philosopher and Carmelite*. Within just a few years the book reached seven editions. Its contents expanded considerably. Again and again relatives, friends and acquaintances came forward, former students and colleagues of Edith Stein, who were able to contribute reminiscences, letters, and photos. The translators have decided to use the fifth edition, that is considerably enlarged compared to the earlier ones. It also includes a final chapter entitled "Postscript."

I would underscore two particulars about the book by Teresia Renata Posselt, newly translated into English. Beginning with the fifth edition, the motto of this work was changed. Originally it said, "To be an image of the eternal, the spirit must be directed toward the eternal. It must embrace the eternal in faith, retain it in memory, and lovingly seize it with the will." (See Edith Stein, Collected Works 9, *Finite and Eternal Being*, 456). It now reads:

> In other words, what did not lie in my plan lay in God's plan. And the more often such things happen to me the more lively becomes in me the conviction of my faith that – from God's point of view – nothing is accidental, that my entire life, even in the most minute details, was pre-designed in the plans of divine providence and is thus for the all-seeing eye of God a perfect coherence of meaning. Once I begin to realize this, my heart rejoices in anticipation of the light of glory in whose sheen this coherence of meaning will be fully unveiled to me.
> (See Edith Stein, *Finite and Eternal Being*, 113)

The book, published by Glock und Lutz, was preceded by an introduction that includes the following quotation from a letter by Prof.

Martin Grabmann, then at Munich: "The desire arises spontaneously that she [Edith Stein] may radiate through beatification and canonization as a shining example of knowledge and love of God, and one may ask for her intercession." The Cologne Carmel considered this purely as a private statement. We had lost our monastery in the war, we lived in rented quarters, and we could not even dream of tackling the extra work that such a process would involve. Only in 1962 did Cardinal Frings, responding to the requests of many Catholics and especially of the Association of Catholic German Women Teachers, open the first part of this process with interviews of witnesses.

Only after the end of the war, reliable inquiries, even through official search organizations, had become possible. In March 1948 we received information from Echt about a report from the Joodsen Raad in Amsterdam, that the group including Edith Stein had, with certainty, been killed in a camp in Poland soon after their deportation. When the Red Cross of the Netherlands confirmed the murder of the missing on 9 or 10 August (today the 9th is accepted as the most reliable date) we arranged for a solemn requiem to be sung and the Office for the Dead to be recited in the temporary chapel of our interim Carmel in Köln-Junkersdorf.

At that point, putting together an obituary would have been appropriate, as is customary for any deceased community Sister. But there were problems with that. Edith Stein, Sr. Teresia Benedicta a Cruce, had been highly esteemed as one of our Sisters both in Cologne and in Echt. The many years of worrying over her fate had increased that devotion. In the meantime, innumerable requests for information pouring in literally from all over the world strengthened the idea that it was impossible to do justice to Edith Stein's exceptional personality, her stirring life story and her shattering end, by an obituary of just a few pages.

Our prioress, Teresia Renata, became persuaded, despite the heavy burden of having to supervise the construction of a new monastery, to write a book. I can still see one of the older Sisters stand guard in front of the prioress's cell door, to turn away anyone who came to her with a question or other concerns. Teresia Renata did not want this book to be seen as a biography in the true sense. For that, experts would be found later. She only wished to braid a "wreath of memories." The success of her little book surpassed all expectations.

The material that Sr. Teresia Renata had collected for this purpose formed the basis for the Edith Stein Archive, for which Sr. Teresia Margareta [Drügemöller] obtained a file cabinet from her relatives, because we did not have that type of furniture on hand. As a matter of fact, at that time most of our belongings were still stored in boxes. In the fall of 1949, we were able to move into the first part of the new Carmel next to the former Carmelite Church "Maria vom Frieden." At the time no one in Carmel seriously thought of an ecclesiastical process for the canonization of our venerable deceased, with the exception perhaps of Sr. Teresia Margareta, who wrote a booklet entitled *Edith Stein - A Saint?* The title was formulated as a question and the author, as a prophet in her own land, was at first not taken too seriously. No one doubted that Sr. Benedicta, who at first had lived as a seeker for truth and the meaning of life, later in intimate connection with God until her terrible end, had now entered God's eternal life. But a process for beatification we imagined to be something very time-consuming and expensive, and we could not afford either of these.

The book jacket of the seventh Glock & Lutz edition stated, "There is probably no book that has occupied radio and the press so intensively, both in the Old and the New World, as this biography. After four years, it is already available in six languages. High statesmen and princes of the Church, highly respected journals and large organizations, international universities and likewise broad masses of people respond to the fascinating image of her personality." What seemed to us at first to be an exaggeration, has in the meantime become reality. In our archives are long rows of file folders containing texts and pictures of institutions and events, works of art, and organizations named after Edith Stein. Secondary literature and dissertations on themes that are related to her life and work fill entire bookshelves. A Complete Edition (Edith Stein Gesamtausgabe, ESGA), meeting scholarly standards, was begun in 2000 and is currently being published by Herder-Verlag, Freiburg.

Pope John Paul II beatified Edith Stein in Cologne in 1987 and canonized her in Rome in 1998. In 1999 he declared Edith Stein, together with Bridget of Sweden and Catherine of Siena, as patron saints of Europe. It is the devout wish of the editor and the translators that Sr. Teresia Benedicta a Cruce, Edith Stein, may be a role model of awe for God and love of truth, justice and peace, not just for Europe but also for all the world, especially for young people whose task it will be to build the future. May she become ever more widely known and honored.

Sr. Maria Amata Neyer, O.C.D.

Introduction to This Edition

Sr. Maria Amata Neyer describes in masterful fashion above the genesis and nature of Sr. Teresa Renata Posselt's biography of Edith Stein. Her pages set out clearly the author's original intent. Few persons alive today have such a broad and incisive familiarity with Edith Stein' own writings and personal history as Sr. Amata. She also knew personally Sr. Teresa Renata Posselt, or "P", since she joined the Carmelite community in Cologne soon after World War II.

Some further remarks explaining the appearance of a new American edition of the biography, and its particular features, will complement Neyer's informative account. The translated biography, titled simply *Edith Stein*, went out of print soon after its appearance; still, it has influenced English-speaking readers for fifty years. Comparative study shows that subsequent authors relied on it extensively as they crafted their own narratives. Much of the published knowledge of the person, life's activities, and spiritual heritage of Edith Stein can be traced to the assertions in this book created by her beloved prioress from Cologne.

In the half-century that has followed publication in English in 1952, scholarship has advanced, happily deepening our understanding of the life and times of the sainted protagonist of *Edith Stein, The Life of a Philosopher and Carmelite*. The decade between Edith Stein's beatification in 1987 and her canonization in 1998 indicated the time was ripe to re-present P's text to a new readership.

Comparison of the present English-language volume with its predecessor will show how it differs in two significant ways: first, the chapters are recast in a text that follows P's German original more closely; secondly, the biographical data laid out are now broadened by contextualizing notes, commentaries, and bibliographical information.

Fuller access to Edith Stein's legacy, possible only now, is drawn from increased availability of her writings. Nine volumes to date form

the English-language series of "The Collected Works of Edith Stein";
and ever-increasing accuracy, as well as growing completeness, mark
the German edition found in the recently launched "Gesamtausgabe
Edith Steins" or ESGA that Herder Publishers of Freiburg has been
issuing at the rate of several volumes per year (eleven by mid-2004).
To illustrate St. Edith's presence in this biography we place direct quotations of her words always in italics.

Furthermore, contextualizing features have been introduced to assist
readers: a detailed chronology of Edith's life; photographs of her times;
indexes; and a map of the major locales she visited.

A team of three authors (of translations and commentary volumes
alike) strove to bring to bear on P's work their own knowledge and experience of at least three dimensions of Edith Stein's fascinating life story:
that of her family in Silesia, her years as a professional laywoman, and
her dedicated service as a Carmelite religious. Mrs. Susanne Batzdorff,
a niece of Edith Stein, was directly responsible for the initial six chapters, then Chap. 13 of Part One; also the final two chapters in Part
Two. Fr. John Sullivan, O.C.D. worked on Chaps. 7 through 12 of Part
One. Sr. Josephine Koeppel, O.C.D. handled Chaps. 14 through 21 of
Part Two. All three of them have visited archives in Europe and interviewed persons mentioned in the book. The frequent exchanges of insight and interpretation they conducted as work progressed brought their
individual evaluations and assertions into clearer focus; they also assured
greater accuracy of detail. They have composed commentary statements
or "Gleanings" and indicated them within the chapters of the text by
markers within brackets thus, "[G 1]" etc. They have placed together at
the back of the book passages they believe do not belong in Posselt's text,
marking them in the chapters as "[T 1]" etc. All the scholarly work they
invested in providing this renewed portrait of Edith Stein was guided by
helpful assistance from Sr. Maria Amata Neyer, O.C.D. in Cologne.

We hope that the availability of this memoir of P will extend knowledge of Edith Stein, "child of the Jewish people. . .[and] also a child of
the Catholic Church," as she identified herself to a modern pope. We

also like to believe that our ever cordial collaboration on this important testimony to the "Fräulein Doktor" of Breslau will form a latter-day tribute to someone who dreamt of harmony between peoples of diverse faiths. May everyone who uses the volume find in her a guide to accepting life's often sharp challenges with serenity, relying on the light of God's faithful providence.

John Sullivan, O.C.D.

Publisher, ICS Publications

Publication Sequence of the Biography

German Editions

First .... December 1948 (4,000 copies)

Second 1949

Third .... Summer 1949 (5,000 copies)

Fourth 1950

Fifth 1950

Sixth 1952

Seventh 1954

Eighth [paperback] 1957

Ninth [paperback] 1963

English Edition

First and only edition from Fifth German 1952

   [U.S. and U.K. editions]

Chronology of Saint Edith Stein's Life

1891 Oct. 12   Born in Breslau

1897 Oct. 12   Entered Viktoria School in Breslau

1908-1911   Attended the Oberlyceum of Viktoria School

1911   *Abitur* (Comprehensive final exam) in Breslau, with distinction

1911-1913   Studies at University in Breslau, German Studies, History, Psychology, Philosophy

1913-1915   Studies at University in Göttingen: Philosophy, German Studies, History

1915 Jan.   State Examination in Göttingen, with distinction

1915   Volunteer nursing service with German Red Cross at a Military Hospital in Mährisch-Weisskirchen

1916   Substitute teaching in Breslau

1916   PhD examination in Freiburg, *summa cum laude*

1916-1918   Assistant to Prof. Edmund Husserl in Freiburg

1917   *On the Problem of Empathy*, Doctoral Dissertation, Halle, 1917.

1919-21   Various scholarly writings, unsuccessful attempts to get a university appointment

1921   Completes reading of the *Life* of St. Teresa of Avila at the home of her friend, Hedwig Conrad-Martius in Bergzabern. Decision to become a Roman Catholic.

1922 Jan. 1   Baptism and first communion in the parish church St. Martin in Bergzabern.

Feb. 2   Confirmation in the private chapel of the Bishop of Speyer

1923-1931   Teacher at a girls' high school and teachers' training institute of the Dominican nuns of St. Magdalena, Speyer. Translations and other writings

	Lectures at educational workshops and congresses in Aachen, Augsburg, Bendorf, Berlin, Essen, Heidelberg, Ludwigshafen, Münster, Munich, Paris, Salzburg, Speyer, Vienna, and Zurich
1932-1933	Lecturer at the German Institute for Scientific Pedagogy, Münster
1933 April	Dismissal from position as lecturer at the Institute by government decree under Nazi regime.
1933 Oct. 14	Entry into Carmelite monastery of Cologne
1934 Apr. 15	Clothing ceremony as Sr. Teresia Benedicta a Cruce
1935 Apr. 21	Temporary vows. Profession for three years
1938 Apr. 21	Final vows
May 1	Ceremony of the veil
Dec. 31	Transfer to Carmelite monastery in Echt, Netherlands
1934-1942	Work on her most important books, *Finite and Eternal Being,* and *The Science of the Cross,* as well as many smaller writing projects.
1942 July 26	Pastoral letter condemning deportation of Jews was read from all pulpits in Dutch Catholic churches
Aug. 2	Reprisal: Arrest of all Catholics of Jewish descent, 300 in number, including Edith and Rosa Stein. Transfer to transit camp Amersfoort, then camp Westerbork
Aug. 7	Deportation from Westerbork toward the East
Aug. 9	Arrival in Auschwitz, gassing in Birkenau
1962 Apr. 1	Opening of the process for the beatification of Edith Stein by Josef Cardinal Frings, Archbishop of Cologne
1972 Aug. 9	Conclusion of the complete diocesan process by Cardinal Höffner at a commemoration of the 30th anniversary of Edith Stein's death in the Cologne Carmel; subsequent transmittal of all documents to Rome
1987 May 1	Beatification of Edith Stein by His Holiness Pope John Paul II in Cologne, Germany

1997 Apr. 8   Vatican announced that the pope had officially recognized the miraculous cure of Teresia Benedicta McCarthy, the final step required for canonization of Edith Stein

1998 Oct. 11   Canonization of Edith Stein by Pope John Paul II in Rome

1999 Oct. 1   Pope John Paul II declares three new patronesses of Europe: St. Bridget of Sweden, St. Catherine of Siena, and St. Edith Stein

2003 Feb. 15   Vatican releases letter written by Edith Stein to Pope Pius XI in April 1933

Main Abbreviations

ESGA *Edith Stein Gesamtausgabe*, or Collected Works of Edith Stein: current revised edition began in 1999; 25 volumes expected as of 2004

ESW *Edith Stein Werke*, or Edith Stein's Works: series of 17 volumes edited by Dr. Lucy Gelber and two Discalced Carmelite friars Father Romaeus Leuven, then Father Michael Linssen from 1952-1994. Now being superseded and re-arranged in the ESGA series.

H/N English language edition of Posselt's work, *Edith Stein*, trans. Cecily Hastings and Donald Nicholl. New York and London: Sheed and Ward, 1952.

  Also indicates the translating team of C. Hastings and D. Nicholl

ICS *The Collected Works of Edith Stein,* series begun in 1986 and current.

  – used often in this volume, from the English-language edition, are

   Life vol. 1 *Life in a Jewish Family*

   Letters vol. 5 *Self-Portrait in Letters*

P Sister Teresia Renata of the Holy Spirit Posselt, O.C.D., author of the biography

Part 1
In the Flow of Time

1

Home[G 1]

Week by week, usually on Friday morning, there was a knock at the door of my cell. At my "Come in," Sr. Benedicta would enter with a letter addressed to "Frau Auguste Stein, Breslau, Michaelisstrasse 38." These few words summed up everything that was dearest on earth to Edith Stein: Her mother's house,[1] her hometown, and the name of the woman who had brought her into the world.

Edith Stein traveled widely, saw her own era with a clear vision and formed her judgment and intellect through contact with many people, but it was her home that was, and remained, the soil that nourished her heart. While that house on Michaelisstrasse was not actually the place of her birth, it was the focus of family life and the place to which Edith returned for vacations regularly.[2] It was a solid stone-built house with a plain and unadorned exterior.[3][T 1] The whole house, down to the smallest articles of furniture, bore evidence of a highly cultured and decorously stable pattern of life.[T 2] The vast spaces of the living rooms, with elaborate parquet floors and stucco-decorated ceilings,[4] were too big to be really comfortable. This was the home of Frau Auguste Stein, née Courant; here it was her outlook, her taste, and her spirit that reigned. Frau Stein was Jewish and proud of the fact. She set an irreproachable example in her Jewish observance, and saw to it that her children strictly followed her example.[5][T 3] And so a reverent fear of God formed a deeply serious background to the children's natural gaiety.

Frau Stein had not found it at all easy to achieve this comfortable and cultured lifestyle for her family. She had been thrown early into the hard struggle for survival. Her marriage with Siegfried Stein had been cut short.[T 4] [G 2] Edith, the youngest of her seven children, was only three years old[6] when the sudden death of her husband – he died of sunstroke when away on business – left her to take care of the

family and the growing lumber business. We may catch a glimpse of
what Frau Stein accomplished during those early years of widowhood
from the following description by Frau [Katharina] Rubens,[7] Edith's
godchild, that also throws a significant light on young Edith:

> *Wer einmal lügt, dem glaubt man nicht,*
> *Und wenn er auch die Wahrheit spricht.*
>
> One who lies once is never believed,
> even when speaking the truth!

I can still hear young Edith saying that; she would
then have been in her fourth year at the most; she and
her sister Erna, eighteen months older,[8] were speaking
as one. It was Erna who was my real friend at that time.
We were just the same age, and regarded little Edith,
"Jitschel"[9] as she was called, with proper contempt.
Besides, she was much too small and pale and delicate,
and since Erna and I were often complimented on being big and strong for our age, we behaved condescend-
ingly toward her. I did not even know, then, that
"Jitschel" had another name. The reason why I remember this moral lesson administered by the two sisters so
clearly is that I strongly resented it because it was thoroughly unjust. I had *not* told a lie.

Our mothers came from the same little town in Upper Silesia, Lublinitz, and had been girlhood friends.
After their marriages, they met again in Breslau, but
their relationship was polite rather than intimate. Their
children, on the other hand (I had a brother and sister
much older than myself, just as Edith's brothers and
sisters were much older than she) became close friends
and even for a time inseparable.

We lived very close together, "just round the corner" in the same part of the town,[10] and at that time we
used to play together a lot. My mother used to go for a
walk with me every afternoon, usually on the "Prom-
enade," the old crumbling ramparts, beautifully land-

scaped, that encircled a large part of the center of the town. But poor Frau Stein, a widow with seven children, ambitious, compelled by necessity to continue managing her late husband's lumber business, and occupied over and above this with baking bread and a thousand other household matters, could find no time to take her two small daughters for walks. One morning my mother had promised me some little hike that I found especially appealing. She then sent me to play with Edith and Erna, and in my excitement I told them about this expected treat, asking them if they would like to come too. They would. I told them we would be leaving at three o'clock, and ran off home. But they didn't come, and I said nothing about it to my mother. But when I came to see the Steins next day, I was greeted with the accusation I have already quoted. They had waited all afternoon, dressed up in their best clothes, and had been so disappointed. And the worst accusation was the one my mother made when she heard what had happened: "Poor Frau Stein, she had to waste all that time getting the children ready."

This remark shows how overworked Edith's mother was at that time. All her children except the eldest boy, who was probably serving his apprenticeship,[11] and Else, who left school to help take care of her younger sisters, were still at school, and of little help to her.[12] Everything rested on her seemingly fragile shoulders. She must have been extraordinarily capable.[G 3]

She was the first person I knew to install a telephone for business purposes and the glorious thing was that she let me use it, and I made my first telephone attempts under her supervision. By that time things were improving for her. She had taken her eldest son into the business, and had moved to a new lumberyard for the third time. And this one was a really large yard.[13]

Oh that lumberyard! It was heaven for us children. What games we could play there! Edith was then perhaps about eight, or a little less. We no longer lived so close together, and, more important, we did not go to the same school.[14][T5] The two of them now had a very high opinion of themselves. Meanwhile Edith's whole character had developed clearly.

As she was the youngest member of a large family, it was not surprising that she was a precocious child. She read a great deal, and the great mental stimulus provided by her reading and the company of her brothers and sisters was probably a desirable thing. A less desirable result was that she acquired an irrepressible ambition, a source of tension liable to break out into tears of rage if she did not get what she wanted and if she did not always prove to be the best, the most capable.[15] And yet her brothers and sisters were in part to blame for this, too, for they made a sort of infant prodigy of her and idolized her. Moreover she was her mother's favorite, though I never noticed that her mother showed this by spoiling her or giving her any special privileges.

At this time I no longer used to go very often to the Steins, but when I did go, she [Edith] used to make much of me, and never refused me anything. But however rare my visits were, I never missed one of the birthdays. Birthdays at the Steins were a very special kind of festival. They had a host of relatives in town, all with several children. All these children were invited, and even though these parties were of the very simplest, none of the children gave that a moment's thought: They were all aching for the games to begin. Lotto was one of our favorites. Edith preferred those games that gave an opportunity to show one's brilliance, such as "How, where and why?" For this you had to be pretty cunning and skillful, in order to find out what the object was, if you were sent out of the room, or to conceal it with clever answers, if someone else was supposed to guess it.[16] Afterwards we got our prizes, that meant more fun. In fact it was all pure bliss, and I am certain that is how we all felt.[17]

Then came the day when my parents transferred me from my old school, and I went into the same class as Edith. She was an excellent student, and I must say that it was her real interest in the subject that made her so attentive and hardworking. But like every human being she had her limits, and I shall never forget how deadly pale and worried her face used to become during arithmetic exams. During the last three years (at school) we always sat together. We were now Seniors, and Seniors did not have to sit at benches like "little ones," but at real, slope-topped desks with chairs. There were three pupils to a desk, whereas the benches were always for two. As she was now always second and I third in class, until I left school, we were always next to each other.[18] Now I was just as bad at languages as I was good at arithmetic and science, while with her it was the other way round. So we quite spontaneously began a sort of (illicit) cooperation, in which each of us was prompted by the other, or copied from the other whatever she did not know. We formed a perfect team. But we were both equally good at German, and did not write our essays together.

However, though our intellectual concerns brought us together in this way, we no longer met socially. It may partly have been because of the great distance between our two homes – we had moved to a suburb that lay in a diametrically opposite direction.[19] And things were now going so well with Frau Stein that the house she lived in was her own, and she probably also owned the site of her greatly expanded lumberyard. I never saw this, the last of her houses in Breslau.[20]

[But the estrangement was due more to Edith's character, that was so dominated by fierce ambition that it left no room for warm feeling. She was obsessed with the aim of being first – an aim, moreover, that she never reached during the time I was at school with her. The fact that she never realized it was perhaps due less to

her than to a certain latent anti-Semitism from which
even then our German schools were not free. Edith herself assumed that our Headmaster, Professor Roehl,
whom we always called "Rex," was an anti-Semite, and
I am glad that I remember the following little scene,
that probably took place about 1904. Prizes were distributed to celebrate the centenary of Schiller's death.
Edith was doing particularly well at this time, and everyone expected her to get the prize. But instead of her,
it was given to one Martha Ritter, the head of our class.
(She was always first and also, as it happened, the daughter of a widow.) We took Geography with Rex, at which
I was especially good. I was also personally in high
favor with him. So it was not a very heroic act [for me]
to come forward and ask why Edith Stein had not got
the prize, when the whole class considered that she
rather than Martha Ritter deserved it. He laughed, but
with the faintest touch of embarrassment – of course it
was quite impossible that "Rex" should really be embarrassed – and said that the head of the class had to
have it. It was the rule. There was, of course, no such
rule, because it was an altogether exceptional occasion,
since Schiller anniversaries were not regular events –
but Edith's honor was saved!][21]
    It was with tears of bitter regret that I eventually
left school, after reaching Class I B. I had loved school
passionately.

There is little to add to this very vivid account. We are introduced
to the strenuous and courageous struggle of the young widow, who
succeeded in spite of her difficulties in providing for her young family a childhood filled with sunshine and warmed by genuine motherly
love. She had always been the pivotal point for the whole family, and
after the father's death she had become the undisputed authority to
whom everyone submitted. She undertook the management of the
business in a spirit of virile determination and devout trust in God.

A quick look at the books showed her that the business was not in good shape financially. But she was undismayed and had the strength and energy to surmount this crisis. She made several trips to the Silesian countryside, in order to renew and maintain her personal contacts with business friends. She had acquired such specialized knowledge that she had only to pass by a wood to make an accurate estimate of its value as timber. She bought up whole forests in Silesia,[22] had the wood sawn up on the spot and then brought to Breslau as it was needed. Her untiring diligence, judgment and competence brought the business added prestige.

At the same time, the valiant services of the eldest sister, Else, ought not to be overlooked. Having only just left school, she alone shared the endless worries of the early years. While her mother took charge of their complicated business affairs – an impossibility according to everyone else in the family – Else kept house and looked after the children. Previously their father had used to travel to the forest every Monday; now it was the mother who had to go, leaving everything in charge of this slip of a girl.[T 6] [G 4]

In this way Else became attached to her two youngest sisters like a second mother; as a matter of fact, that heavy responsibility had been laid upon this mature child on the very Day of Atonement that Edith was born. Her father had come to her with the good news during the night, and had brought along Erna, then aged eighteen months[23]; Erna had been used to sleeping with her mother and was now so upset that nothing Else said could comfort her. Else was probably the person who influenced the development of the two children most directly. She herself says of Edith:

> We used to stick together a great deal, and she was also
> more like me than any of my other sisters and brothers.
> Her first introduction to literature she received from
> Paul; holding her on his arm he used to cram her with
> poets' names, their dates and their main works, from

his new illustrated history of literature. I can still see
her as she used to sit upon the large table at which her
elder sisters and their friends used to play *Dichterquar-
tett*.[24] Every now and again they used to shoo her away
for butting in, "You can't join in, little Edith, you can't
read yet!" But why did she need to? While the rest of
them were puzzling out the answer she would reel it off
by heart. (I became indignant when some people considered her too forward.) Her first literary venture was
made under my direction when she was ten years old, a
composition in honor of Paul's marriage. The following example shows how different those two inseparable
youngsters [Erna and Edith] were: After leaving school
and before attending teachers' college I had spent four
years helping my over-burdened mother; consequently,
despite being also first in my class, I was trembling at
the thought of my teacher's examination. I had promised Edith that if I passed I would register her at our
Viktoriaschule, even though it was October and the
middle of the school year. But in my excitement I probably had also once said, in front of the children, "If I
don't pass, I shall jump into the Oder!"[25] It was late in
the evening when I arrived back home after the last day
of examinations, and Erna lay fast asleep in bed. Edith
had gone to sleep in Mother's lap. Mother now woke
her: "Edith, darling, Else has failed!" She leaped up
immediately and put her arms round me: *"But you won't
jump into the Oder!"* (I cannot give you any idea of the
tone in which she said it.) Mother now set her down
beside Erna and said: "Erna, darling, Else has failed."
Back came the sleepy reply, "A likely story!"[26]

For me, Mother had the photograph of the little ones
made.[27] It was during my first teaching job in Preussisch-
Oderberg[28] and I had pleaded with Mother to come and
bring "our two little ones" for a visit.[29] Instead, she came
alone for just one day, but to make up for my disappoint-
ment at not seeing the children she proudly brought me
this delightful picture of them.[30]

The family reached a level of prosperity that the children, indeed, attributed rather to their mother's goodness than to her efficiency in business. The poor craftsmen and other people without means could all have told stories of how Frau Stein used to sell them the wood they needed and then not infrequently return the purchase money. She bought up whole stands of timber to donate as winter fuel to the poor. Frau Stein handed on this characteristic of warm neighborly love especially to Edith, over whose development she had watched with devoted care. *"In our family,"* Sr. Benedicta was later to say, *"it was not strictly a matter of education. As children we read proper conduct in our mother's example as if in a mirror of virtues."*[G 5] There was only one thing that this God-fearing Jewish woman tried to impress deeply in her children's hearts: an abhorrence of sin. When their mother said "That is a sin," they all knew that she meant to convey the idea of all that is ugly and unworthy. Edith was the acknowledged favorite of this serious, austere woman, who abhorred all vanity. Frau Stein felt that the fact that she had brought this child into the world – on one of the Jewish High Holy Days – was an especially favorable portent for the future of this daughter.[31]

2

School

Judging from the photographs, Edith must have been a most attractive child. She was naturally vivacious, with a quick intelligence and a precocious critical faculty. Her sister Erna, who was her inseparable playmate, tells us:

> Overburdened with activity as she was, Mother could devote little of her time to us. We two little ones were quite used to getting along by ourselves and keeping ourselves occupied, at least in the mornings before the older ones came back from school.
>
> So far as I know, from what my mother and family have told me and from my own recollection, we were fairly well-behaved and seldom quarreled. One of my earliest memories is of my eldest brother Paul carrying Edith round the room on his arm and singing student songs to her, or showing her pictures in a history of literature and lecturing her on Schiller, Goethe etc. She had a tremendous memory and forgot nothing of all this. Several of our numerous [G1] aunts and uncles[1] used to tease her and try to trip her up, trying to convince her that Goethe wrote *Maria Stuart*, for instance. It was always a total failure. She began to get a grasp of literature when she was between four and five years old.[2]

It was no wonder that such a precocious child should have wished to go to school along with her beloved elder sister as soon as the latter began to attend. But in this, alas, her mother refused to allow her to have her way. Pleading and tears were of no avail. The only consolation granted the four-year-old was a promise to send her to a day care facility. But to this proud little girl, eager to learn, whose life-long desire for knowledge was already awakened, such a solution was an intolerable insult. She tried everything she could think of to alter her

12

mother's decision. But Frau Stein was firm. The dreaded first day arrived. It was pouring rain. Edith made a desperate attempt by declaring energetically, *"I can't go to child care, my shoes will get dirty."* No use. Paul, who was to accompany her, picked up his baby sister and firmly carried her off to the nursery school. But the experiment was soon abandoned, for Edith was so inconsolably unhappy and so far ahead of all the other children that there was obviously no point in keeping her there.

[T 1] [G 2] After this, Edith looked forward to the 12th of October, since her sister Else had promised her that, after passing her examination, she would arrange for Edith's acceptance to *Viktoriaschule* in the middle of the school year. "And I kept my promise, writes Mrs. Gordon, "despite my shyness and reserve."

> At first Professor Dr. R.[3] was reluctant, because Edith was conspicuously small. But when he saw my sadness, he said, "Since she is **your** sister, I'll take your word for it and try it. If it doesn't work by Easter, she'll simply have to repeat the grade." Now I smiled happily, and Edith started school on her sixth birthday, 12 October 1897.

As it was not the custom in those days to begin the school year in autumn, she spent only six months in the lowest grade. All the same, she was one of the best by Christmas. She was hard-working as well as gifted, and possessed an iron will. She was, however, never a "go-getter" in the bad sense, always friendly and helpful.

This is from Erna, who goes on:

> Though she continued to shine throughout her school years, and we all assumed that she would, like me, go on from the Girls' School to complete the newly-introduced *Realgymnasium* courses at *Viktoriaschule*, in order to qualify for university, she surprised us by deciding to leave school. As she was still undersized and delicate,

my mother consented and sent her, partly for a rest and
partly as "help," to my eldest sister, Else, who had married Dr. Max Gordon of Hamburg and had three small
children. She stayed there ten months[4] and carried out
her tasks conscientiously and tirelessly, though housework was not to her taste.

When, after about six months, my mother went to visit them, she
hardly recognized Edith. She had grown a lot and looked radiantly
healthy. But she confided to my mother that she had changed her
mind and wanted to go back to school, in order to be able to attend
university. She came back to Breslau, worked at Latin and Mathematics
with two students to tutor her, and passed the entrance examination
brilliantly.[5]

A girl who was at school with her at this time writes:

> Edith Stein was my fellow-student in the Breslau Girls'
> *Gymnasium*, and as we used to walk to school together
> for a long time I got to know her well. Though at that
> time the Girls' *Gymnasium* was closed to less gifted girls
> due to the stiff entrance examination, and most of the
> students were extremely talented, she was way above the
> others in ability and knowledge. She was a diligent stu-
> dent, without being an overly ambitious go-getter. Even
> then she already possessed great modesty.[G 3] [T 2] As
> a matter of fact it was only when I saw this sketch of her
> life that I realized that she was the same age as myself; I
> had always believed that she was our superior in age as
> well as in knowledge, probably just because she was more
> mature and serious than the rest. I remember her as a
> quiet, withdrawn, and at the same time very lovable per-
> son. One thing she said I shall never forget, when she
> once gave her reason for an unfavorable criticism of a
> very free translation: *"A translator must be like a pane
> of glass, that lets all the light through but is not seen
> itself."* It was a very characteristic saying.

Erna's account concludes as follows:

For the rest, nothing remarkable happened during her time there. As always, Edith was at the head of her class and was excused from the oral examination *viva voce* at the *Abitur.*[6] At the graduation ceremony, the Director in his address spoke about the individual personalities of the graduates who were going on to the university, trying to characterize them in an apt phrase. When it came to Edith's turn, he said, after a moment's thought, punning on her name, "Strike the stone[7] and wisdom gushes out." Outside of school she always took a lively part in social entertainments; she was never a spoilsport. You could trust her with all your troubles and secrets, she was always ready to advise and help, and anything was safe with her. Our years there (I had begun to study medicine in 1909, while Edith was studying German language and literature) were a time of serious work, but also of wonderful conviviality."[8]

3

The Student: Breslau and Göttingen [G 1]

Among the lecturers in the Philosophy Seminar in Breslau at that time were Professor Hönigswald,[1] a man of outstanding intellect, [G 2] and Professor Stern,[2] an experimental psychologist.[G 3] Both were of Jewish origin. [Edith Stein writes *"Stern and Hönigswald were barred from advancement in their academic careers because of their Jewish descent."*][3] Of one of them Edith herself says, *"As I was the only female student, the Herr Professor once said smirkingly in the middle of his lecture, 'When I say "Gentlemen," that, of course, includes that lady there!'"*

Frau Stein had followed her youngest daughter's intellectual development with justifiable pride, but also with a secret anxiety. Edith was intelligent, but not pious. Up till now she had not acknowledged any religious convictions, and she showed little interest in Judaism. She herself said she was an atheist until her twenty-first year, [G 4] being unable to believe in the existence of God. She was also at that time a thorough-going feminist.[4] During vacation, it is true, she went with her beloved mother to the synagogue whenever her mother desired. But more impressive to her than the religious ceremonies was the deep devotion of her mother, who used to lose herself completely in God. Frau Stein feared that the study of philosophy, to which Edith wished to devote herself exclusively would sweep her child more and more into the liberal current and thus away from her religious influence.[G 5]

This fear was probably not unfounded. Sr. Benedicta said later: *"To study philosophy is to walk perpetually on the edge of the abyss."* Frau Stein at first offered some opposition to her daughter's plans. But in this battle, too, Edith won out over her mother's wishes. For two years she studied at the university in her hometown, and then transferred to Göttingen, that she herself so charmingly describes.

4

My First Semester in Göttingen[G 1]

I had been studying for four semesters at the university in Breslau. Few students had taken such an active part in the life of this "Alma Mater" as I had, and it might have seemed as though I had grown into it so much that I could not break away of my own free will. But now, as so often in later years, I was able to snap seemingly secure ties with one easy movement and to fly off like a bird from a snare. I had always intended to study at some other university. While I was at secondary school, my plan had been to go with Erna for my first university semester to Heidelberg, whose magic is so enticingly evoked by the old student songs. This plan did not materialize because Erna was in the middle of her preliminary exams in medicine during that semester and so could not leave Breslau. The next summer it was the same; she was too near her State Examination and must therefore stay at home. A more powerful attraction, no doubt, was Hans Biberstein; he had been studying in Freiburg-im-Breisgau during the summer before my matriculation and would not be going away again. I realized now that I could not make my plans dependent on my sister. Nor did I wish to delay and find myself having to stay just because of my own examination schedule. During my fourth semester I got the impression that Breslau had nothing more to offer me, and that I needed some fresh stimulus. Objectively, this was by no means true. There were more than enough unexplored possibilities, and I would still have been able to learn a great deal. But something was drawing me away. However, the poetry of the student-songs no longer played the decisive role in my choice of a university; a quite different factor was determining that clearly.

During the summer of 1912 and the winter 1912-1913 Stern's seminar was devoted to problems in the psychology of thought, mainly with reference to the works of the "Würzburg School"[1] (Külpe, Bühler, Messer, etc.). In both semesters I undertook to write a paper, and time and again as I was poring over the treatises I had to study in preparation, I came across references to Edmund Husserl's Logische Untersuchungen (Logical Investigations). *One day, as I was working on my thesis in the Psychology Seminar, Dr. Moskiewicz came up to me. "Leave all that stuff alone," he said, "and read this; the others get their ideas only from here." He handed me a thick book – it was the second volume of Husserl's* Logische Untersuchungen. *I could not delve into it immediately because the semester's program did not allow me enough time, but I noted it for my next vacation reading. Mos knew Husserl personally, having studied under him for a semester in Göttingen, where he was always longing to return.*

"In Göttingen you do nothing but philosophize – day and night, at meal-times, on the street, everywhere. You just discuss 'phenomena' all the time."²

One day the illustrated magazines showed a picture of a Göttingen woman student who had won a philosophical award – it was Husserl's extraordinarily gifted student, Hedwig Martius. Mos knew her as well and had heard of her recent marriage to Hans Theodor Conrad, an older student of Husserl's. When I came home late one evening I found a letter for me from Göttingen on the table. Not long before, my cousin Richard Courant had become a Privatdozent [lecturer]³ there in mathematics. He had just been married to his fellow-student Nelli Neumann from Breslau, and this letter was from Nelli to my mother, thanking us for our wedding-present. After a description of the young couple's new life, the letter went on: "Richard has brought a lot of male friends into our married life but very few young ladies. Could you not send Erna and Edith here for their studies? They would balance things a bit." After this letter I did not need any more persuasion. The next day I informed my astonished family that I wanted to go to Göttingen for the coming summer semester. Since they did not know what had previously been going on in my mind, the announcement came like a bolt from the blue.

My mother said, "If it is necessary for your studies, I shall certainly not stand in your way." Nevertheless, she was sad – much sadder than the separation for a short summer semester warranted. "She doesn't like being with us any longer," she once said to little Erika⁴ in my presence. The child was very attached to me, and loved to sit beside me in the room as I was working. I used to sit her down on the carpet and give her a picture-book, then she would keep herself quietly occupied and not disturb me. You could give her the very best books – she never damaged one. And she did not need entertaining, but sat there contented and peaceful until someone took her away.

The first step toward putting my plan into operation was a postcard to my cousin asking for information about the lectures to be given by the Göttingen philosophers during the next semester. Soon afterward he sent me the proof-sheets of the lecture-program. I used the Christmas holidays to study the Logische Untersuchungen; *since it was then out of print, however, I had to use the copy in the Philosophy Seminar, and there I spent my days. Professor Hönigswald often used to come in and eventually he asked me one day what I was studying so eagerly throughout the whole vacation. "Well! Nothing less than Husserl!" was his exclamation when I informed him. Then my heart beat faster. "In summer I shall be going to Göttingen," I told him, my eyes shining with joy, "oh, if only I were far enough along to work along those lines myself." He was rather taken aback. That winter, it was the first time that he gave a lecture on the psychology of thought; it was his first attempt to make an assessment of phenomenology of which he later became a resolute opponent. At that time his disapproval was not so marked, but he was not altogether pleased to discover one of his students going over to that camp with flying colors. I had scarcely thought of it in that way, for, despite admiring Hönigswald's acute mind, it had never struck me that he would dare to set himself on a level with Husserl – so sure was I that Husserl was* **the** *philosopher of our age. From then on, whenever phenomenology was being discussed in Hönigswald's seminar I was always called upon as "the expert."*

On New Year's eve Lilli Platau and Rose and Hede Guttmann recited some humorous rhymes. About each of us they had composed a verse to the well-known refrain, "Wouldn't that make you stand on your head?" They sang from behind a screen above which only their heads were visible; but each time they came to the refrain they would bob down, and up would come a pair of feet (actually they were stuffed shoes and stockings fitted over their hands). The verse for me said:

> *Many a maiden dreams of "busserl" [kisses]*
> *Edith, though, of naught but Husserl.*
> *In Göttingen she soon will see*
> *Husserl as real as real can be.*

But a deeper note was struck in our New Year's Eve party newsletter that contained a fairy tale about a little blue "stone": its tender symbolism revealed to me how deeply my relatives and friends had felt my pursuit of pure learning as their loss of my companionship. It had been written by Lilli.

Gradually all my preparations for leaving were completed, but, once my own summer semester in Göttingen was arranged, a new idea had occurred to me. Göttingen was a paradise not only for philosophers but also for mathematicians. So I suggested to Rose that she should come along. Of course my suggestion appealed to her greatly, but she had to think it over to see if she could afford it. She used to pay for her own studies by private tutoring; this was out of the question at a strange university, where she would have to use every minute to drink in the new material that it had to offer. That was precisely what I wanted for Rose. This constant strain on someone so young in years[5] worried me, and I would have been very glad to take her away from all these concerns, if only for a couple of months. One day, when I was alone with my mother, I asked her jokingly, "Mama, are you a rich woman?" In the same tone she replied, "Yes, child; what would you like?" Immediately I confessed what was at the back of my mind, that perhaps she could provide Rose with the means to study for a semester in Göttingen. She agreed right away to do so. When I passed the news on to my friend, she decided to go with me; then, after discussing it with her family, it turned out that she could manage on her own and did not need to rely on Mother's generosity. Our decision also clinched Georg Moskiewicz's plans for going back to Göttingen once more. This was very pleasant for us, since he already knew his way around and could introduce us to the circle of phenomenologists.

I had never thought of staying there for more than one semester. If it was an inexpensive treat in those days to study at one of the smaller universities, still it did cost more than living at home. And the habits of economy that had been bred into me since childhood never even allowed me to entertain the wish to accept such an outlay for a longer period. Therefore my mother's sadness over the impending separation seemed to me exaggerated. In the depth of my heart, I had, however, a secret premonition, as she did, too, that this separation was going to go deeper than appeared. Almost as if to counteract this half-conscious suspicion, I did something that would compel me to come back: I went to Professor Stern to ask him for a topic for a doctorate in psychology. The reason why I went to him, rather than to any other professor, was because my previous dealings with him had made me imagine he would be most likely to give me a free hand. There I was mistaken. In his seminar he had accepted our criticism of his methods in a kindly fashion and without the least resentment; but his ideas were so rigidly fixed that nothing could move him from them; moreover he wished to use his students' work as a basis for his own research. That became very obvious to me after our conversation. He received me as kindly as ever and also agreed readily to my request, although I was still very young.[6] But I could not take seriously what he suggested to me: Amplifying the thesis that I had written during the winter, I should work out the development of child-thought, and that, indeed, by means of those very experimental interrogations with which poor, tormented Mos had been forced to struggle for years. Since I planned to travel to Göttingen by way of Berlin and Hamburg, I should pay a visit to the Institute of

Applied Physiology in Klein-Glieneke near Potsdam; there Stern's collaborator, Dr. Otto Lipmann could show me whatever pictures he had on hand, to see if they contained anything suitable for my work.

The visit to Klein-Glieneke was the only step I ever took toward my dissertation in psychology. Since Moskiewicz was friendly with Dr. Lipmann, he sent word that all three of us (himself, Rose and I) would come for an afternoon. Our host and his charming little wife received us with cordial hospitality and invited us to stay for coffee and dinner. After being introduced to the sweet children, we were given a tour of the whole house and then went for a beautiful stroll along the Havelsee on which the town was located. In between, we had been taken to look at the brightly-lit basement rooms in which the "Institute" was housed. The collection of pictures, that was kept in a file cabinet, did not prove in the least enticing, and the shrewd Dr. Lipmann confirmed to me that there was nothing there worth working on. I took away with me the memory of a nice afternoon and the conviction that nothing would come of that project. It had been wrong from the start to think of a thesis in psychology. All my psychological studies had only led me to the realization that this science was still stuck in its infancy, that it still lacked the essential, clear, basic concepts, and that it was in no condition to achieve these basic concepts.

And what I had so far learned about phenomenology had delighted me precisely because it consisted of this work of clarification, and one could fashion for oneself the very conceptual tools one needed. For a time, when I was first in Göttingen, the thought of my dissertation in psychology would occasionally burden my mind, but I soon shook it off.

Dear old Göttingen! I do believe that only someone who studied there between 1905 and 1914, during the short flowering of the Göttingen school of phenomenology, can appreciate what that name conjures up for us.[7]

I was twenty-one years old, and keyed up in anticipation of what was to happen. During the vacation I paid a visit to Hamburg. No lectures were held before the end of April, although the semester offi-

cially began on the 15th, when all the university offices opened for business. I was able to take care of registration and other incidentals and could get down to work as soon as the lecture-rooms came alive. And so I left Hamburg on 17 April. My brother-in-law, Max, was a bit worried at the thought of sending me off alone into strange surroundings, and asked whether I could not stay with the Courants, for the first night at least, rather than at the students' lodgings that they had booked for Rose and myself. Of course I declined the suggestion. I simply informed them of my arrival, and Richard picked me up at the station, although he was suffering from an injured foot. It was already evening as he led me through the darkened streets to my new home. Rose was not due to arrive from Berlin until a few days later. I was overjoyed when the door was opened for me by a young woman with a pretty, friendly face. Later she admitted that she was herself pleasantly surprised at my own appearance, because this was the first time she had taken in female students, and she had thought that they were all old and ugly. Almost all the households in Göttingen took in students, but many landladies refused to take female students on principle. Some had moral scruples, others feared that their kitchens would be commandeered for washing, cooking and ironing or that spirit stoves would be set up and ruin their rooms. It was very unpleasant to go searching for rooms and be met by a surly face that squinted through an opening in the door and muttered a few words of refusal. Therefore we had been in luck. The house was situated in a narrow small-town alley, the Lange Geismarstrasse, that led out from the center of the town to the Albanikirchhof – "Kirchhof" is the name given in Göttingen to the church-square – and our lodging was No. 2, immediately next to the square.[8] The Albanikirchhof lies on the boundary of the old city, and beyond it is the residential area where the professors' homes and elegant guest houses are located.

St. Albani is the oldest church with a perfectly smooth façade and a massive tower. Three times a day the bells used to ring out the Angelus, that sign of its Catholic past that I heard but did not understand.

*On the very day following my arrival I set off on a tour of discovery.
Ever since my earliest childhood it had given me great joy to go ex-
ploring. Whenever Erna and I went out for a walk in Breslau or Hamburg on our own, I used to say, "Today let's go where we have never
been before."*

*And now I had a whole city to conquer, as well as the surrounding
countryside! There was certainly enough to see. You need only go down
the Lange Geismarstrasse, turn right at the corner, and there you were
at the marketplace. Facing you was the beautiful Gothic town hall, at
the windows blossoming red geraniums that stood out so merrily against
the old gray stones. In front stood the charming Goose-Girl fountain
by Schaper. Nearby in a side street was the loveliest old house in Göttingen, the "Mütze" (the cap) as it was called [G 2] an old-German
inn with half-timbering and bull's-eye windowpanes. Leading directly
northward from the marketplace to the Weender Gate ran the main
street of the city, the Weenderstrasse, where in the afternoon the
"Bummel" took place, crowds of pedestrians strolling about. On the
right-hand side toward the middle rises the great church-tower of St.
James, the very symbol of Göttingen. When viewed from a distance,
this tower, along with the two less stately towers of St. John's, characterizes the image of the city. On the opposite side of the street is the
famous Konditorei (café) Kron and Lanz, where the best pastries are
to be had, and where professors and students (providing their budget
permits) take their afternoon coffee and read the newspapers. The last
building on the right-hand side right at Weender Gate is the
Auditorienhaus with the lecture halls, the center of university life. It is
by no means a great monument and cannot be compared either with
our old Leopoldina in Breslau or with the splendid modern buildings
in Jena or Munich; a simple, modest building, rather, with simple,
modest workrooms. It is set back a little from the street and is shel-
tered by landscaped grounds, where the students wander during re-
cess between lectures, smoking their cigarettes. The adjacent Seminar
building, both more modern and more elegant, is located to the right,*

*around the corner on Nikolausbergerweg; at the time, it was com-
pletely new. Most of the seminars took place there, with the Philosophy Seminar right up under the roof, where I have found it in almost
every other university I know.*

*The Psychology Institute was entirely separate, being situated near
St. John's church, a little west of the marketplace; it was an old house
with worn steps and narrow rooms. This spatial separation in itself
indicated clearly that in Göttingen philosophy and psychology had
nothing to do with each other. The Nikolausbergerweg runs eastward
from the city out of the Weender Gate and winds its circuitous way up
the mountainside. Once you have the last houses of the city behind
you, the charming little hamlet of Nikolausberg is visible above you
on the mountaintop. Those in the know could tell you about the wonderful waffles that were baked by the hostess of the inn; if you let her
know beforehand, you could walk up there after a day's work and find
a steaming dish waiting for you. This I discovered only much later. To
the left of Nikolausberg there rose a bare hill with three wind-swept
trees, that always reminded me of the three crosses on Golgotha. All
this I caught a glimpse of during those first days, but on my first walk
I was not able to go up the mountain; instead I turned off to the side
and wandered through the meadows, and got to know the peculiar properties of the Leineberg soil; for you seldom return from there without
thick lumps of clay sticking to your shoes. Even the paving in the streets
is peculiar – a sort of asphalt that is alternately softened by the sun or
the rain, more often by the rain, for it rains a great deal in Göttingen.
At that time, the population was about 30,000. There were no trolleys.
Until the outbreak of war, their introduction was constantly under discussion. After that, it was out of the question. The city's life centered in
the university and the students; it was a genuine university city, and
not, like Breslau, a city that, amongst other things, had a university.*

*I was very much struck by the memorial plaques that were at-
tached to almost every old house. They tell of previous famous inhab-
itants. At every step one is reminded of the past; the Brothers Grimm,*

the physicists Gauss and Weber and the others who belonged to the "Göttingen Seven,"[9] [G 3] all who ever lived here and made their mark, are constantly brought to the attention of the later generations. Also the ancient city ramparts have survived, planted with mighty, tall linden-trees; in the summertime, their fragrance wafts into the lecture-rooms (the lecture-hall being immediately next to the ramparts). And when-ever I heard Heine mentioned in the lecture-hall, it reminded me of how he himself had once sat on these very benches, and how the ramparts of Göttingen must have come before his mind's eye when he spoke in his poetry about the "Ramparts of Salamanca." I was always glad to go for a walk along the ramparts; there was such a lovely view on one side toward the old houses within the city, and on the other side toward the villas and gardens stretching farther outside. At one spot on the wall stood the little log cabin in which Bismarck had lived as a student.

A few days after my arrival Rose also came, and we arranged our accommodation. Between us we had two rooms, one in which we both slept and a larger one that we used as a common living room and study. In the morning our landlady used to bring us hot milk and fresh rolls, and we made some cocoa for ourselves. We would meet again for lunch, that we usually took in a vegetarian restaurant kept by a South German lady and her three nice daughters. It was very popular. Several tables were pushed together to make one long table at which the English and American students sat; their noisy yet innocent exu-berance used to dominate the whole place. After the lectures, whoever of us arrived home first in the evening would prepare a meal of tea and sandwiches, and so the one who came late would find the table set for her. I do not remember a single occasion during that whole summer of living so close together when any quarrel or disagreement sprang up between us. So far as her time allowed, Rose used to attend my philosophy lectures, and I did a little mathematics with her. Still, our schedules were very different. In Göttingen it was a tradition to have no lectures on Wednesday and Saturday afternoons, because the stu-dents, and occasionally even the professors and their daughters, used to go dancing at Maria Spring.[10] Only the philosophers, Nelson and Husserl ignored this tradition. On Wednesday afternoon Husserl held his seminar, but on Saturday afternoon even we were free. All the same we did not go to Maria Spring but out into the country, weather permitting. Beforehand we would write our weekly letters home and take turns writing to the friends we had left behind. If it was nice weather on Sunday, we would spend the whole day outdoors, sometimes staying there from Saturday noon till Sunday evening.

That summer, we wanted to get to know the countryside of central Germany, and Göttingen was a wonderful starting point. On the southeast side the city nestles against a hill crowned by the Bismarck tower. Beautiful parkland stretches from the edge of town and gradually turns into the Göttingen forest; one can walk for a whole day through the forest without coming to the end, and mostly without meeting another soul. The people of Göttingen do not go in for long walks. When we were setting off on a Sunday, we would see them pouring forth in large numbers, but their destination was no further than one of the two large coffee-houses that lay a suitable distance apart on the broad sweep of the hillside, "Rohns" and "Kehr"[11] [G 4] as they were called. One could easily distinguish the townspeople from the students because they always wore hats, whereas the students went bareheaded. Besides, the townspeople were all loaded down with big parcels of cake. If they wished to go further than Kehr's, they would drive out in carriages. Because everyone took their cake out with them, the inns did not provide any, and one had to be content with coarse country-bread and Göttingen sausage.

On longer excursions we took our provisions with us in a rucksack and picnicked in the woods; a loaf of black bread, a container of butter, a slice of cold meat, fruit and chocolate, it tasted better than a dinner in a restaurant. Göttingen is also surrounded by woods and hills in other directions. There are beech-woods that used to glow red and gold in autumn when we returned for the winter semester. And from the surrounding hills the ruins of old castles look down into the valley. I had a special liking for the "Gleichen," twin peaks standing close together, each of them crowned with the ruins of a castle. On the ridge between the peaks was a modest inn with a chronicle of the Counts von Gleichen, who had once dwelt up there. Whenever I looked down into the valley I used to feel that I was in the very heart of Germany; a lovely landscape, the fields on the slopes carefully cultivated, the neat little villages and around them a wreath of green woods. It was almost as if any moment a wedding procession might emerge on the edge of the wood, as in Ludwig Richter's paintings.[12]

On our longer outings we got to know Kassel, the Weserland, Goslar and the Harz Mountains. At Pentecost we spent several days wandering through Thuringia. From Eisenach we climbed up to 'he Wartburg, went through the Dragon's Gorge to Hohe Sonne and later up the Rennsteig to Inselsberg. On some stretches we took the train in order to be able to cover more ground in those few days. Of course Weimar was included in our program, and that visit we were supposed to end by touring the Free School Community of Wickersdorf. For the first few days we had glorious weather, and then on the third day (if I remember correctly) it began to rain in the evening.

We had been on the road since morning and we wanted to reach Ilmenau, our last stop before Weimar, before nightfall. The rain came down harder and harder, the road stretched out farther and farther in front of us, our feet were refusing to go another step, and there was no sign of habitation. Rose was silent and depressed from sheer weariness, and so I did everything I could to remain in good humor. It must have been easily eight o'clock by the time we eventually reached a long strung-out village. Judging by the guesthouses on the roadside it seemed to be a summer resort, but wherever we knocked it was the same – there was no room for us to stay. At every house I screwed up my courage to repeat our request, but each time in vain. We must have spent a good half hour there going through the village, before we finally found a hotel that could take us in. The guest rooms were actually in a separate building opposite the hotel itself. While the beds were being made up we went to the dining room, where a hearty, hot meal revived our spirits. We asked our friendly host where we actually were. The name of the little village was Manebach. Manebach – it sounded so stretched-out, like the endless rain and the endless road. Already we had re-gained sufficient good humor to have a hearty laugh over it. As soon as our rooms were ready we slipped out of our sopping clothes into the warm beds. Now a new battle plan would have to be worked out. We pulled out Richard's beautiful military map – the relic of troop-maneuvers in Thuringia – that until this evening had guided us superbly. Whereabouts was Manebach? Yes, there it was. We were only one rail-way station distant from Ilmenau. But we could not make up the loss of time any more, and so we decided to skip Ilmenau and the Gickelhahn, and take the train to Weimar the next morning. Having our railway timetable with us, we were able to look up the schedule for the next train.

In Weimar we visited the stately Goethehaus at the Frauenplan and the enchanting garden cottage at the Stern, and finally Schiller's house with the heart-rending miserable little room in which he died. It was a Sunday, and crowds of hikers were flocking out. As we were rather beat and footsore from the previous day's hike we thought we were crawling like snails, but, all the same, we soon left the citizens of Weimar far behind us. In the beautiful park of Tiefurt we had to sit down on a bench in order to transact the not–so–poetic business of counting our cash. Before setting off, I had drawn enough money out of the bank to last me for this trip, but Rose had wanted to save herself the errand, and so had not brought enough cash with her. Now we reckoned that our combined resources would not suffice for a visit to Wickersdorf, so we had to telegraph to cancel it. With what was left we had just enough to travel to Jena that evening and return straight to Göttingen the following day.

I was very thrilled at getting to know Jena, and felt much more at ease than in Weimar. You could seek out its memorable places in com-plete peace; everything was less obtrusive here, and you did not, at every turn, run into groups of boarding-school girls in devout amazement. When we went to return his military map to Richard, we, of course, had to give an account of our wanderings. We would have gladly kept quiet about the ignominious ending, but Richard asked immediately about our visit to Wickersdorf. He had an uncanny knack of always asking about whatever we did not want to mention.

Rose and I had ventured on this trip on our own. On other occasions we almost always had a companion with us, Dr. Erich Danziger, an assistant in the Chemical Institute. Rose had made his acquaintance during her chemistry studies in Breslau, that was his hometown. He was a small, plain and somewhat awkward man, but Rose said that he had the most skillful hands in the whole Institute, and his help was always asked for whenever something required especially delicate handling. There was always an oppressed atmosphere about him, the result, no doubt, of the very sad circumstances of his family life; his mother had been in a mental hospital for many years, that meant that he and his only sister had grown up almost like orphans. Now he doggedly attached himself to us, since he had scarcely any other contacts. He was a good-hearted and faithful soul. It always depressed him a little that he had no entry into the philosophical world in which we lived.

Georg Moskiewicz arrived somewhat later than we. He was considerably older than we; in May we celebrated his thirty-fifth birthday together. Instead of living in student digs, he rented two spacious and well-furnished rooms in the quiet Kirchweg near the clinics; that befitted his status as doctor of medicine and philosophy, and as a budding Privatdozent (lecturer). For him [as for Erich Danziger] we provided some moral support. He seldom joined us on our excursions, because such ventures involved making decisions, and he did not find it easy to do that. When he did come with us, however, he was as merry and exuberant as a little boy, and it was very obvious that he had conceived a deep affection for Rose. But how could he ask her to attach herself to him when his own future was so uncertain? He and I were connected by a cordial friendship and similar philosophical interests.

After many digressions, I have at last come to my main reason for coming to Göttingen: phenomenology and the phenomenologists. In Breslau they had given me this piece of advice: "When you arrive in Göttingen, you go first of all to Reinach;[13] *[G 5] he 'll take care of all the rest." Adolf Reinach was a Privatdozent in Philosophy. He and his friends, Hans Theodor Conrad*[14] *[G 6] Moritz Geiger*[15] *[G 7] and several others, had originally been students of Theodor Lipps in Munich. After the publication of Logische* Untersuchungen *they had all insisted on Lipps discussing this work with them in his seminar; and when Husserl was called to Göttingen, the group followed him (in 1905) in order to be initiated by the master himself into the secrets of the new science. Such was the beginning of the "Göttingen School." Reinach was the first of them to qualify as a lecturer in Göttingen, and had thereby become Husserl's right-hand man, acting, above all, as a link between him and the students; for Reinach had a wonderful way of dealing with people, whereas Husserl was pretty helpless at it. Reinach was thirty-three years old at the time.*

I followed Mos's good advice to the letter. The very day after my arrival, I believe, I made my way to No. 28 Steinsgraben; this street takes you right to the edge of the city, and the Reinachs lived in the last house of all. Beyond it lies a great stretch of grain fields through which a narrow footpath leads to the Kaiser-Wilhelm Park, along the route up to the Bismarck Tower and the Göttingen Forest. When I asked for Dr. Reinach, a blond maid showed me into his study and took my calling card before telling him of my arrival. It was a beautiful, large room with two tall windows, dark wallpaper, and brown oak furniture. The two walls to the left of the entrance were covered with bookshelves reaching almost up to the ceiling; to the right, opening into the next room, was a big sliding door with panes of multicolored glass. The large corner between this door and one window was completely occupied by a massive desk. To the right of the desk and opposite the desk chair, easy chairs stood ready for visitors. In the space between the two walls of books there was a cozy corner with a table,

*a sofa, and several easy chairs. Hanging on the wall opposite the
desk chair was a reproduction of Michelangelo's "Creation of Man."
It was the most comfortable and tasteful study I had ever seen. Reinach
had been married some six months previously, and it was his wife
who had lovingly planned the interior design of the spacious apartment, and had the furniture built according to her instructions. Nevertheless I do not believe that I took in all these details on my first
visit, for I had only been waiting a few moments when I heard a voice
calling out in joyful surprise from the end of the long passage. Someone came dashing along, the door opened, and there was Reinach
facing me. Barely medium-height, not heavy, but broad-shouldered,
he had a beardless chin, a short, dark mustache and a broad, high
forehead; through his rimless pince-nez, his intelligent and very kind
brown eyes looked at you. He greeted me with warmth and gracious-
ness, helped me to a seat, and then took a seat at his desk diagonally
across from me.*

*"Dr. Moskiewicz has written to me about you. You have already
studied a bit of phenomenology?" (He spoke with a pronounced Mainz
dialect.) I responded briefly. He was immediately ready to let me take
part in his "Exercises for advanced students," but could not give me
any more precise information about the day or the hour, because he
wanted to arrange that with his students. He promised to mention my
name to Husserl. "Would you like to meet some of the people in the
Philosophical Society? I could introduce you to the ladies." I asked
him not to put himself out on that score, because Dr. Moskiewicz would
introduce me. "Right! Then you will soon get to know them all."*

*After this first conversation I was very happy and filled with deep
gratitude. It seemed to me that no one had ever received me with such
sheer goodness of heart. The affection displayed by close relatives
and friends, who have known me for years, seemed to me a matter of
course; but here was something quite different. It was my first glimpse
into a completely new world. A few days later I received a postcard to
say that the exercises had been set for Mondays between 6 and 8. Unfor-*

tunately I had already scheduled something else for those hours that I did not wish to miss, Max Lehmann's history seminar. Therefore I had to decline, though very reluctantly.

I did not immediately pay a call to Husserl's home, because he had put up a notice on the board to say that he would be holding a preliminary discussion in the philosophical seminar, that newcomers were expected to attend. There, for the first time, I saw "Husserl as real as real can be." There was nothing striking or overpowering about his appearance; he was a typical distinguished professor. Of average height and dignified bearing, with a well-shaped, impressive head, his speech betraying his Austrian origins (he came from Moravia and had studied in Vienna). His cheerful kindliness also had something of old Vienna in it. He had just reached the age of fifty-four.

After the general discussion he called the newcomers up to him, one by one. When I told him my name, he said, "Dr. Reinach has spoken to me about you. Have you already read some of my stuff?" –

"*The* Logische Untersuchungen."
"*The whole of* Logische Untersuchungen?"
"*The whole second volume.*"
"*The whole second volume? Really! That is heroic,*" he said smilingly.

That's how I was accepted.

Shortly before the beginning of the semester, Husserl's great new work appeared, Ideas: General Introduction to Pure Phenomenology ("Ideen zu einer reinen Phänomenologie und phänomenologischen Philosophie").[17] *It was to be discussed in the Seminar, but, in addition, Husserl announced that he would be "at home" regularly one afternoon each week, so that we could come and address our questions and concerns to him. Of course, I bought the book immediately (i.e., the first volume of the "Jahrbuch für Philosophie und phänomenologische Forschung;" it was the lead article of this Yearbook, that was founded in order to publish the collected works of the phenomenologists).*

For the first "at home" I happened to be the first arrival, and stated my concerns. Soon others began to appear, all of them bursting with the self-same question. The main reason for the tremendous excitement caused by the Logische Untersuchungen *had been its apparently radical departure from Critical Idealism, either of the Kantian or the neo-Kantian variety. It was regarded as a "new Scholasticism," because it turned attention away from the "subject" and toward things themselves: perception was once more a process of reception whose laws were derived from objects, and not, as in Criticism, the imposition of laws upon objects. All the young phenomenologists were confirmed Realists. The* Ideen, *however, contained certain passages that strongly suggested that the "Master" was tending toward a return to Idealism. Nor did his explanations in the subsequent discussion relieve these suspicions. It was the beginning of that development in Husserl's thought that led him to regard what he called "Transcendental Idealism" (not to be confused with the "Transcendental Idealism" of the Kantian School) as the kernel of his thought, and to the implications of which he devoted all his energies. This was a path on which, to his sorrow as well as their own, his old Göttingen students could not follow him.*

Husserl owned a house on the Hohen Weg, on the edge of town, on the road leading up to the "Rohns" (the "Rohns" played an important part in his philosophical discussions, for the place often had to serve as an example when Husserl was talking about how we perceive things). The house was built to meet the needs of the family, in accordance with his wife's instructions. Upstairs was the Master's study, that opened out onto a small balcony where he used to retire to "meditate." Its most important piece of furniture was an old leather sofa that he had purchased with a stipend he had received while a Privatdozent in Halle. Usually I had to sit at one end of the sofa; and later, in Freiburg, our conversations about Idealism used to flow back and forth between one corner of that sofa and the other.

Among his students, he was known as "the Master;" he was aware of this title and didn't like it at all. His wife, we called, among ourselves, by her poetic name Malwine. She was small and thin, her shiny black hair was smoothly parted, and her lively brown eyes, full of curiosity, would always gaze out onto the world with a certain astonishment. Her voice sounded sharp and hard, always as if she were calling you to task; yet signs of good humor were rarely lacking, and this was reassuring. But in her presence you were always a bit apprehensive about what might happen next, for she frequently said something embarrassing; and people whom she could not stand fared very badly. She also developed a pronounced liking for some people, however, and I personally have never experienced anything but sincere friendliness from her. How I came to deserve it, I do not know. In later years it might perhaps have been attributed to the valuable services I was able to render her husband; but as a matter of fact she had always treated me kindly, even when I was an insignificant little student. When I was with her husband, she used to come in midway through my visit and say she just wanted to say hello.

She attended Husserl's lectures regularly, though she later admitted to me that it was in order to count the students (a fact of which we had long been aware); philosophy left her cold.[18] She considered philosophy the greatest misfortune of her life, because Husserl had had to live as a Privatdozent in Halle for twelve years before receiving a professorship. And even then, what he received was not a regular chair in Göttingen, but a special position created for him by Althoff, the Minister of Culture, a far-seeing and energetic but somewhat self-important man; consequently Husserl's position on the faculty was extremely awkward.[19] On account of these experiences Frau Malwine was determined to keep her three children away from philosophy. The oldest of them, Elli, was about my age. She studied art history; in appearance she resembled her mother, but her manner was much gentler and more tender. Gerhart became a lawyer, but in later years did not let himself be cut off from philosophy. Wolfgang was still in high school at that time. He had an exceptional linguistic ability and intended to study languages. He was his mother's favorite. Later on, after his untimely death – he was killed in Flanders [in World War I] as a volunteer at the age of only seventeen – one gained an insight into her heart when she spoke about him. She once told me that she had never worried about Wolfgang's future, because she had always known that, wherever he went, he would bring happiness to those around him.

Both the Husserls were Jewish by birth, but had become Protestants early in life. Their children were brought up as Protestants. The story goes – though I cannot vouch for it – that, when Gerhart was six, he attended school together with Franz Hilbert, the only child of the great mathematician; Gerhart asked his little classmate what he was (i.e., which denomination he belonged to). Franz did not know.

"If you don't know, then you must certainly be a Jew." The conclusion was incorrect, but very typical. Later Gerhart used to refer to his Jewish origins quite openly.

During that summer Husserl lectured on "Nature and Spirit," examining the foundations of the natural sciences and the humanities. He was to deal with the same subject in the second part of his Ideen, *that had not yet been published. The Master had already drawn up a rough outline of the second part at the same time as he did the first part, but had put off the job of preparing it for publication to give himself time to bring out the new edition of the* Logische Untersuchungen. *This was urgently needed, since the book had been out of print for years and was in constant demand.*

Soon after Moskiewicz had arrived in Göttingen, the Philosophical Society held its first meeting of the semester. This was the more select circle of Husserl's actual students who gathered one evening a week to discuss specific problems. Rose and I had no idea how bold it was of us to join this select group immediately; but since Mos took it for granted that we should go with him, we thought the same. Other-

wise it might have taken many semesters before one learned about this institution, and even then, after being admitted, one would listen in silence for months before daring to open one's mouth. But I chirped up straight away. Since Moskiewicz was by far the oldest, the chairmanship was entrusted to him for this semester, but no one in the whole circle felt himself less suited than he. At the meetings it was obvious how unhappy he felt in this role; true, he did preside at the table, but it was never long before he lost control of the discussion. Our meeting place was the home of Herr von Heister, a young landowner who delighted in living in Göttingen, attending philosophical lectures and enjoying personal contact with the philosophers. He was very pleased to have us in his home, and not in the least disturbed that his own contributions to the discussion were ignored because they were irrelevant. His delicate, blond wife was far more popular with all of us. She was a daughter of the Düsseldorf painter Achenbach. Numerous paintings by her father adorned the house. Whenever we arrived – often enough in a genuine Göttingen rainstorm – with wet coats and shoes, the butler would help us off with our clothes in polite silence; but it was perfectly obvious that he was secretly shaking his head over these strange guests. He must have noticed many unusual incidents, as he was serving tea or wine (according to our preference) in the elegant dining room. I shall never forget how Hans Lipps, during a heated discussion, kept knocking his cigar ash into the silver sugar bowl, until our laughter startled him.

None of the founders of the Philosophical Society attended its meetings any more at that time. Reinach had not been coming since he had become a lecturer and got married. Conrad and Hedwig Martius, were living alternately in Munich and Bergzabern (Palatinate) since their marriage. Dietrich von Hildebrand[20] [G 8] had moved to Munich; Alexander Koyré[21] to Paris; Johannes Hering[22] wanted to take his State Examinations sometime the next summer and had withdrawn to his home in Strasbourg in order to be able to study undisturbed. However, some people still remained who had worked alongside these outstanding people for many semesters and who were able to hand on the tradition to us newcomers. A leading light was Rudolf Clemens, a philologist. His dark blond beard and his neckties, his soft voice, and eyes that were both soulful and mischievous, all reminded one of the Romantics. His manner was friendly, but it was a friendliness that did not inspire complete confidence. Fritz Frankfurter, a native of Breslau, was studying mathematics. His brown eyes expressed his child-like openness, innocence and goodness. The pure delight most of us felt in philosophizing was most apparent in him. Once while telling me something about Husserl's lecture on Kant, that I had not yet heard, he suddenly stopped himself and said, "No, what comes next is too delicious for me to tell you in advance. You must hear it for yourself."

But the one who most deeply impressed me was Hans Lipps.[23] [G 9]
He was then twenty-three years old, but looked much younger. He was very tall and slim, but strong, and his handsome, expressive face was as fresh as a child's, as well as serious, and his large round eyes were questioning like a child's. Normally he expressed his view in a brief but very decisive sentence; and, if asked to amplify his statement, he would say that there was nothing more to be said, since the matter was self-evident. We had to be satisfied with that, and we were all convinced that his insights were both genuine and profound, even when we were not in a position to follow his train of thought. Though he had difficulty in expressing himself in words, his eyes and his animated, spontaneous facial expressions spoke all the more eloquently. That summer he could not attend our meetings regularly, because he was both taking his preliminary medical examinations and completing his doctorate in philosophy with a dissertation on plant physiology. He was taking medicine and natural science in order to fill in the hours when philosophizing was not possible. He already had a varied career behind him. He had started out as an interior decorator and craftsman, but that could not satisfy him. Still he continued to enjoy tinkering, and a distinct artistic bent was part of his personality. While doing his year's military service as a dragoon in the Leibgarderegiment (Body

Guards) in Dresden, he had become acquainted with the Logische Untersuchungen, *and that meant the beginning of a new life for him. That was what brought him to Göttingen. He was the only one in our circle who occasionally got together with poor Mos and liked him. The others would secretly make fun of Mos's insecurity and his eternally unsolved problems.*

For those mentioned so far, philosophy was the essential element in their lives, even though they were also studying other subjects. For some others the reverse was true; their own particular field had priority, but it was substantially enriched by phenomenology. For instance, there were the Germanists, Friedrich Neumann and Günther Müller, who were later to receive chairs in their specialty comparatively early.

For several semesters, the Philosophical Society had also included two ladies among its members, Grete Ortmann and Erika Gothe. They were considerably older than myself, both of them having spent some time teaching before deciding to come to the university. Both came from Mecklenburg. Fräulein Gothe's home was the city of Schwerin and Fräulein Ortmann's a country estate; she was a short, frail creature, but she had such a ponderous tread that her coat was usually splattered high up with mud from the streets of Göttingen. Similarly weighty strokes punctuated her conversation, but her remarks often seemed trivial to me, even though they sounded like solemn proclamations. However, she rarely spoke, usually listening both in the seminars and in the Philosophical Society with an expression of enraptured devotion in her big blue eyes. In her, this seemed to me comical, though by contrast I found Erika Gothe's attitude of reverent silence quite attractive.

Fräulein Ortmann immediately made it clear that she did not like me. Later, she once told me in a moment of confidentiality that Reinach had once had a serious talk with her and asked why she behaved in such an unfriendly way towards Fräulein Stein, who was so nice. The reason she gave, "She always simply joins in the discussion. And these are such difficult matters!" Even worse, Mos had asked me right at the first meeting if I would take minutes, that I accepted without a second thought. None of the others seemed to take offense at my doing so. They were always friendly toward me and took my remarks in the discussion seriously. Nevertheless Fräulein Ortmann's behavior had the effect that at first my social contacts with the whole circle remained rather restricted, because she and Erika Gothe seemed to be inseparable and it should have been up to these ladies to draw me more closely into the group. I did not miss it that summer, because my Breslau acquaintances supplied my need for personal contacts. Besides it was only later that I learned of the activities outside the Philosophical Society and the university, and so I could not tell that I was being excluded.

There were other recent new arrivals to the circle besides Rose and myself. Betty Heymann was a Jewish student from Hamburg, small and somewhat stunted in her growth, her fine, delicate face somewhat spoiled by oversized teeth; her beautiful eyes were uncommonly intelligent and clear. She was a student of Georg Simmel[24] and intended to do her doctorate under him, but had at first come for just one semester to get to know Husserl. Fritz Kaufmann,[25] [G 10], too, already had a philosophical past to which he looked back with a certain pride. He had been studying under Natorp[26] in Marburg and already had so much neo-Kantianism in his system that he found difficulty in adjusting to the phenomenological method. He was the eldest son of an obviously very wealthy Jewish family with a business in Leipzig. Since he had two younger brothers who could take over the family business, he could devote himself entirely to philosophy and aim directly for an academic career. He was probably the only one of us who had no need to plan his studies with an eye to earning a living. In a circle such as ours, where no one bothered much about appearances, his elegant clothes were very conspicuous. We were all secretly amused once, when his neighbor in the seminar, an American, vigorously squirted the ink out of his fountain pen, and Kaufmann was visibly concerned for his light gray suit. He spoke faultless high German without the slightest trace of Saxon dialect, whereas Lipps, to his great distress, betrayed his

Saxon origins with his very first words. (He absolutely denied being a Saxon, but always insisted instead that he was Prussian, since he had inherited Prussian citizenship from his father.)

The day that we had our preliminary discussion with Husserl, Rose and I set off in the afternoon for the Bismarck tower for the first time. As we were eagerly picking violets along the way, Kaufmann caught up with us; he recognized us from our meeting in the morning and greeted us in a friendly way. "There are plenty of violets here." So we began our first conversation. I was amazed when he informed me that on his first visit Reinach had "almost thrown him out," and had firmly refused to admit him to his "exercises." Until then it had never occurred to me that the kindliness with which he had received me might be a personal favor. When I later took part in Reinach's "exercises" I found the explanation. For all his kindness and friendliness, Reinach was really revolted whenever he encountered signs of arrogance, and Kaufmann might have introduced himself with some self-importance. This attitude and a certain affectation in his speech hurt him in his relationships with almost everyone, but I noticed fairly quickly that this was only superficial. So I made a point of teasing him mercilessly and ignoring the dignified façade that he presented to the world. Then he would look startled as if something highly unusual had happened, but it seemed to be good for him; for he gradually thawed out and his tone became quite unpretentious and warm.

There were also people in Husserl's seminar who were studying with him but did not join the Philosophical Society. Soon after the semester began, I was invited one evening at the Courants, when Richard said, "If you are in Husserl's seminar then you must have met Bell."[27] [G 11] He was a Canadian. I had indeed noticed some Americans and Englishmen, but did not know which one he meant. "He is the nicest student in Göttingen. You will certainly discover him." Some time afterward I saw a student standing on the ramp in front of the lecture hall; wearing sports clothes and hatless, he seemed to be looking out for someone. There was something very attractive in his free and easy attitude, and I thought, "That is Bell." And so it was. He did not often get together with the other phenomenologists, because the American and English students in Göttingen formed their own colonies and stuck closely together. Besides, he had a circle of friends who did not all specialize in his own subject. My cousin was one of them. From him I learned of Bell's previous history. A native of Halifax, he was originally an engineer, but during voyages to the Arctic Ocean, he had started philosophizing. He had gone to study first in England and then in Germany. He told me once that a review by Moritz Schlick [28] called his attention to the Logische Untersuchungen, and drew him to Göttingen. By now, he had already been there three years and was working under Husserl on his doctoral thesis about the American philosopher Royce. Although thirty-one years old, he looked much younger.

In the Philosophical Society that summer we chose as our subject for discussion the second major work that had appeared in the "Jahrbuch," and that had perhaps exercised a more powerful influence upon recent intellectual life in general than Husserl's Ideen. This was Max Scheler's[29] [G 12] work on ethical formalism (Der Formalismus in der Ethik und die materielle Wertethik). The younger phenomenologists were strongly influenced by Scheler; some, like Hildebrand and Clemens, followed him rather than Husserl. Scheler's personal life was in a very sad state at the time. His first wife, from whom he was divorced, had involved him in a sensational trial in Munich. The damaging facts that came to light caused the university to withdraw the "venia legendi" (his teaching privileges) from him. Besides, he was left without any steady income, and was living on his writing – most of the time in a modest boarding house in Berlin, with his second wife (Märit Furtwängler), though he was frequently away on travels.

For several weeks each semester, the Philosophical Society used to invite him to lecture in Göttingen. But he was not permitted to talk in the university, nor were we even allowed to publicize his lectures on the bulletin board. We could only pass the information by word of *mouth. We had to book a meeting room in some hotel or café. At the end of the semester Scheler came once again. Originally his lectures were scheduled for several evenings a week, but since he did not know how to organize his time, at the end there was so much material left to cover that we had to meet every day. When the official part was over, he used to remain in the café for hours and hours talking to a smaller group. I only took part in these nocturnal sessions once or twice; for, despite my eagerness to seize on every stimulating thought, something about them put me off; it was the tone in which they spoke about Husserl. Scheler was, of course, strongly opposed to the turn toward Idealism and spoke almost with condescension on the subject; but many of the younger students also indulged in ironic remarks, and such disrespect and ingratitude outraged me.*

Relations between Husserl and Scheler were not altogether smooth. At every opportunity Scheler insisted that he was not a disciple of Husserl, but had discovered the phenomenological method for himself. Certainly he had not attended Husserl's lectures as a student, yet Husserl was quite convinced of his dependence. They had known each other for many years. While Husserl was still a Privatdozent in Halle, Scheler was living in nearby Jena, and they frequently met and carried on a lively exchange of ideas. Anyone who knew Scheler, or had read his works closely, would know how open he was to suggestions from other people. The ideas flew in and worked within him without his being aware of the influence; and so he could say with a clear conscience that it was all his own property. In addition to this dispute over primacy, Husserl had a serious concern for his students. He took the greatest pains to instill in us precision and thoroughness, to cultivate a "radical intellectual integrity." Scheler's way of throwing out stimulating suggestions, without ever following them up systematically, had something dazzling and seductive about it. In addition, he was always discussing questions of vital importance to each individual personally, and especially calculated to impress young people, while Husserl dealt with sober, abstract matters. Yet in spite of this tension, caused by their professional rivalry, they still maintained friendly relations at that time in Göttingen.

The first impression that Scheler made was one of fascination. Never again in any man have I experienced so purely the "phenomenon of genius." Out of his big blue eyes shone the light of a higher world; his face was handsome and his features noble, although life had left devastating traces upon them. Betty Heymann used to say that he reminded her of the picture of Dorian Gray; that mysterious portrait in which the dissolute life of the original draws its disfiguring lines, while the man himself retains his unspoiled youthful beauty. Scheler spoke with great insistence, sometimes with dramatic liveliness. He dwelt reverently and tenderly upon certain words of which he was particularly fond, e.g., pure Washeit *("pure whatness"). If he was arguing with his presumed opponents, he would adopt a contemptuous tone. Just then he was dealing with questions that were also the theme of his recently published book,* On the Phenomenology and Theory of the Feelings of Sympathy. (Zur Phänomenologie und Theorie der Sympathiegefühle). *These were of particular interest to me, because I had just begun to deal with the problem of "empathy."*

In practical matters Scheler was as helpless as a child. I once saw him standing in the cloak-room of a restaurant and gazing at a row of hats; he did not know which was his. "You're missing your wife right now, aren't you?" I said smiling. He nodded in agreement. When one saw him like that one could not be angry with him – not even when he had done something that one would have condemned in other people. Even the victims of his aberrations used to stand up for him.

His influence, beyond the bounds of philosophy, was of great importance during those years, for myself as for many others. I do not know what year Scheler returned to the Catholic Church, but it cannot have been long before that time. In any case, this was the time when he was overflowing with Catholic ideas and when he was pleading them with all the brilliance of his intellect and his eloquence. This

*was my first contact with a world that had so far remained entirely
unknown to me, and even though it did not lead me to the faith it did
open up for me a whole range of "phenomena" that I could no longer
blindly pass by. Not in vain were we continually being admonished to
look at all things without prejudice and to cast aside all "blinkers."
The barriers of rationalist prejudice of which I had been unaware, fell
away, and the world of faith suddenly rose up before me. In that world
lived people with whom I was in contact every day and whom I admired, and therefore it must at least be worthy of serious consider-
ation. Yet I did not make any systematic inquiries into questions of
belief, because my mind was occupied with so many other things. I
contented myself with accepting suggestions from my surroundings
without resistance, and being transformed by them almost without
noticing it.*

*In describing my early days in Göttingen, I left out details about my
relationship with my relatives. My cousin Richard Courant was then
twenty-five years old, had recently become Privatdozent and also been
married. His wife, Nelli Neumann from Breslau, was a little older than
he; she had studied mathematics with him, had earned her doctorate
in that subject and passed her State Examination. Justizrat (Council-
lor) Neumann [her father] had hesitated for a long time before entrusting his only child to this young man without a secure income.
Father Neumann was a thoroughly kind and noble man, his very appearance distinguished and inspiring confidence. Tall, slim, with light
blond hair and blue eyes, he did not give the impression of a Jew from
Posen (which he was) but rather of a Teutonic aristocrat. Since Nelli's
mother had died, when Nelli was only two years old, he had been both
a father and mother to her; he surrounded her with the tenderest affection and worked with her like a comrade. Their blissful life together
was only disturbed by his mother-in-law, whom he had kept in the
house after his wife's death, although she was constantly tormenting
him and the child with her moods. She died only after Nelli was married. I have previously mentioned my cousin's sad and difficult early*

years.[30] *He had risen entirely by his own energy, and all of us har-*
bored a profound admiration for his extraordinary gifts and his char-
acter. His wife's fortune afforded him an opportunity of a worry-free
existence and a youthful, untroubled life for the first time.

   Like Anne Reinach, Nelli had taken the greatest care to have beauti-
ful and comfortable furniture custom-built. The little house in the Schiller-
strasse, where they occupied two stories, lay on the southern edge of
the city, with gardens and fields stretching behind it. Their lovely home
was open for informal hospitality. Richard loved to bring home unex-
pected guests. He had a very large circle of friends among both lec-
turers and older students. He would even bring some of his students
home with him when there was something they wanted to discuss. It was
Nelli who had suggested my coming to Göttingen and she welcomed
me warmly. Once in a while I was invited to dinner; and the bath was
placed at my disposal whenever I wanted it, for Nelli's greatest joy was
to let others share the luxuries she possessed. She was cheerful and
talkative, and yet the sort of person who really wants to get to the root
of things. Ethical questions interested her particularly, and she never
undertook anything without carefully weighing the pros and cons. She
still attended occasional lectures. Once a week we attended the same
course and afterwards would walk home together. On the way she would
inquire about all my activities, eagerly following the progress of my
studies and visibly rejoicing that here was someone pursuing the career
for which she was cut out. Being a housewife did not suit her; her whole
upbringing had not prepared her for it. A few months after her wedding,
when she went to Breslau for her grandmother's funeral, she recounted
with great humor all sorts of mishaps in her housekeeping, explaining
that, "Things become more complicated the further removed they are
from mathematics, and housekeeping is the furthest removed of all."
Richard used to banter with her in that teasing manner so typical of
him. He and I were united by our close kinship, because, although he
would never admit it, he was very much attached to the family, and was
always inquiring about all the relatives. He also liked to talk to me

about his worries about his parents, just as he had used to ask advice of my mother in Breslau. He, too, showed a lively interest in the progress of my studies.

I had come to Göttingen for the sake of philosophy and wished to devote most of my time to it; but since I intended to stay only that one summer, I wanted to utilize it also to get acquainted with Germanists and historians other than those I had known in Breslau. Richard Weissenfels' course on "Börne, Heine, and Young Germany," proved more recreation than work. I also enjoyed the strict and dreaded Eduard Schröder as a "phenomenon," without worrying about him. He was a large, powerful man with a wide, greyish, beard, parted in the middle. It was his boast that he could speak a "grown language" – that of his native Hessen: though I myself thought it even more fitting for him to speak Middle High German or Old High German, and was always pleased whenever he read us a sample text. Like his brother-in-law Roethe in Berlin, he was opposed to women studying and had so far refused to allow any women into his seminar, but I was present at his "conversion." At the beginning of that semester he distributed the meeting room keys to the members. Each of us had to approach him individually and solemnly promise him with a handclasp never to take a book home from the seminar library. And now he announced publicly that from now on he would admit ladies to the senior level of his seminar; they had earned it by their industriousness and their excellent performances. Besides, he was an emotional person; once in a lecture, when he recalled a deceased colleague, he had tears in his eyes.

Another philosopher with whom I took a course, apart from the phenomenologists, was Leonard Nelson.[31] He was still young – scarcely over thirty – but he was already famous, or rather notorious, throughout Germany for his book on "the so-called problem of knowledge." In this book he had "liquidated" every outstanding spokesman for modern theories of knowledge by incisively proving them all guilty of formal contradictions. When I attended his course on the "Critique of Practical Reason," his procedure was no more lenient. He had two schematic diagrams to show the typical contradictions; they were drawn on the board almost every period for some new victim, and were described by his students as "the guillotine." The only survivor on the battlefield was the Kant disciple Fries,[32] after whom Nelson named his own philosophy. His ethics culminated in a derivative of a somewhat modified categorical imperative. His every lecture was primarily an unbroken series of deductions from several postulated theses, and although his conclusions were very difficult to refute, I always had the impression that his presuppositions contained errors. The great danger arose from the fact that, what he derived theoretically in his ethics, he unhesitatingly put into practice and demanded the same of his students.

He had gathered around him a circle of young people, mainly from the youth movement, who allowed him to lead them and who shaped their lives according to his axioms. Richard Courant, who had been strongly influenced by him at one time, used to say, "Just as the fraternity brothers go for their morning beer, so the Freischärler (fellows from the volunteer corps) go to Nelson's lectures." He was a born leader; his solid character, his unbending will and the silent passion of his ethical idealism gave him power over others. There was nothing enticing about his appearance. He was big and broad-shouldered, and walked ponderously; the lids of his light blue eyes were heavy; even his speech sounded heavy and rather weary despite the decisiveness and emphasis with which he expressed himself. His face was ugly yet attractive; his handsomest feature was his thick, wavy blond hair. His speech was quite sober and dry. He used to sketch his main line of thought on the board, and both his handwriting and his diagrams showed that he had an artist's touch.

There were few people whom he deemed worthy of his company, unless they subscribed unconditionally to his philosophy and lifestyle. Among these few was Rosa Heine, a Russian Jewish woman who had been studying psychology in Göttingen for years. I had met her in the Psychology Institute, and one day, as I was walking down the street with her, we met Nelson. She greeted him, introduced us, and then said

*that he and I must have a talk, at that point she took off and left us to
go on alone. Nelson knew me by sight from his course and wanted to
hear what I thought of it, because he knew that I was a Husserl student, and it was not often that anyone drifted over to him from that
camp. He himself did not know Husserl's writings in detail. As he explained, it would take too much time to get accustomed to his difficult
novel terminology. I asked him whether he had not discussed these
matters with Reinach, because that would be simpler. "Reinach is
clearer, but also less profound," came the terse reply. With that, our
conversation was over, because we had arrived in front of his destination, the publishing house of Vandenhoeck and Ruprecht. Not until
years afterwards did I meet him again.*

*At the Psychology Institute I was taking a course with Georg Elias
Müller³³[G 13] on "Psychophysics of Visual Perception." He was a
veteran of the old school that followed the way of purely natural sciences. It had a precision that attracted me and seemed more depend-
able than what I had learned from Stern; but this was a subject that I
only enjoyed the way I enjoyed theoretical physics or mathematics: I
was glad of the instruction but knew that the work offered no scope for
me personally. Müller was a rabid opponent of phenomenology, because for him nothing existed but empirical science. Husserl on the
other hand recommended that we take Müller's course, because it was
important to him that we should be familiar with the methods of the
positive sciences. David Katz,³⁴[G 14] who was working as a Privatdozent in the Institute alongside Müller, had devoted some time to phenomenology in his student days, and from his lectures one could tell
that he had benefited from this exposure. I came to know him personally through Moskiewicz and Rosa Heine (whom he later married).*

*The atmosphere in the Institute was most peculiar. Müller had a
whole string of students who wanted to earn their doctorates under
him, although this was no easy matter. Sometimes, months went by
before you had accumulated the schedule of experiments and the necessary apparatus. No one divulged to anyone else what sort of work*

they were doing, and they would tinker secretively over their machines in the laboratories of the old building in Paulinenstrasse. At one time I served as "guinea pig" for a Danish psychologist. I sat in a darkened room in front of a tachystoscope while various green, illuminated shapes were quickly passed in front of my eyes; and then I had to describe what I had seen. Consequently I knew that it had something to do with recognizing shapes, but I was never given any further explanation. We phenomenologists used to laugh at this secrecy and were always glad about the freedom with which we exchanged ideas; we were not worried that one of us might steal the results of another's project.

Apart from philosophy, studying under Max Lehmann was the most important work I did in Göttingen. In Breslau I had plodded through his great study on Baron von Stein[35][G 15] and was glad to meet Lehmann in person. I attended his major course on the Age of Absolutism and Enlightenment, as well as a one-hour lecture on Bismarck, and enjoyed his European outlook, a legacy from his eminent teacher, Ranke,[36] and it made me proud to become Ranke's scholastic quasi-granddaughter. Yet I could not agree entirely with his viewpoint; as a former citizen of Hannover he was strongly anti-Prussian, and his ideal was English liberalism. This was especially apparent in his lecture on Bismarck. Since one-sidedness always prompted me to do justice to the opposite view, I became more conscious of the merits of Prussian qualities than I had been at home, and was confirmed in my Prussianism.

I have already mentioned that I renounced Reinach's exercises in order to go to Lehmann's seminar, that met at the same time. However, I almost regretted it, when I discovered how much work it involved, because, while in Göttingen, I had no desire to devote that much time to History. Our task for the entire semester was to compare the German Constitution of that time with the Draft Constitution of 1849. The most essential books for this research had been assembled for us in a little study next to the large study hall. I spent many an hour there. But, most disconcerting of all, every newcomer had to undertake to write a term paper. The subjects were handed out in our very first period in such a way that two people (preferably a man and a woman) were to work on the same subject. Even the due date was set at once. Our essays were discussed at the seminars during the second half of the semester. On these occasions, the two victims had to take their places at the large U-shaped table, facing Lehmann, and defend their thesis. This was his chance to get to know each of us thoroughly. His eyes were very weak, so that he could not see us if we sat some distance away. At the beginning of every semester he used to have diagrams made of the table, showing the name of each student at his designated place. That way he came to know us by the seating order, that we were not permitted to change. My subject was, "The Realization of the Party Program in the Draft Constitution of 1849."

My partner and I had our turn at the very end of the semester. Previously we had not known each other, but now that we were groaning under the same burden, he accompanied me home a few times, so we could talk our troubles over on the way. He was an intelligent and industrious person; I had great confidence in his work. Ours was a painstaking task. One had to obtain precise information about the line-up of the parties in the Frankfurt National Assembly and get copies of their programs. Not all of them were easily accessible, even though most of them had been published in a handy collection. But there was one which I only obtained in an old newspaper volume of 1848 from the Heidelberg library. And only then the job of comparing began. During the whole semester that project oppressed me. Finally the session arrived at which Lehmann would have us under fire. However he always did so in a most friendly way and this time, too, declared himself very satisfied with the course of the discussion. But a tragicomical difficulty arose – he had been unable to decipher my essay completely, because the ink was too pale for his weak eyes. An older colleague (a teacher doing graduate study) gave me the good advice to visit Lehmann and ask him whether I might not hand in a typewritten copy of my paper. So I made my way to his house on Bürgerstrasse, an older house surrounded by a garden. There I was shown upstairs, where even the hallway leading to his study was filled with bookshelves. Lehmann welcomed me most pleasantly. No, it would not be necessary to have my essay copied; he had gathered enough from the discussion and was very satisfied. As for the ladies altogether! What would his seminar be like without the ladies, who are so industrious and able! This seemed to me rather exaggerated and I felt obliged to stand up for my male colleagues, saying that some of the men also performed well. He was somewhat surprised by this reply, but then agreed, "Oh, yes, a few. Your partner, for instance, also turned in a good essay." But now came a great surprise. Lehmann revealed to me that he considered my essay good enough to be acceptable as a thesis for the State Examination;[37] I would only need to amplify it here and there. This was not an exceptional privilege, because Lehmann used to allow good seminar essays to be submitted for the State Examination; but I knew nothing of this, since up to now I had paid no attention to the examination process in Göttingen. First of all, I had always thought of the State Examination as something very remote, because I intended to do my doctorate first. Besides, I had only come to Göttingen for that summer and counted on doing my State Examination in Breslau. Yet, the closer we got to the end of the semester, the more impossible seemed the idea of leaving Göttingen and not returning. These last months had not just been an episode but the beginning of a new phase of my life. Help had now come from a quarter whence it was least expected. After all, you could hardly abandon a completed thesis acceptable for the State Examination – even my folks at home would see that. I believe that my plans were already finalized on the way home from this momentous visit.

First of all I had to sort out my relationship with Professor Stern. I gave him an account of this semester: I had done no work for my psychology thesis; on the contrary I had become more and more absorbed in phenomenology, and now my urgent desire was to continue studying with Husserl. His response was very kind. If that is what I wished, then he could only advise me to earn my doctorate with Husserl. Nor did my relatives offer any objections. Now came the decisive step. I went to Husserl and asked him for a subject for a doctorate. "You mean you're ready for that?" he asked in surprise. He was accustomed to people studying under him for years before they dared to embark on an independent project.

All the same he did not refuse me outright; he simply pointed out to me all the difficulties before me: He demanded very high standards for a doctorate and reckoned on its taking three years. If I had the State Examination in mind, then he would strongly advise me to take that first, otherwise I would get too far away from my specialty. He himself considered it very important to achieve something worthwhile in a specialized subject. It was no good just to philosophize, because this demanded a solid familiarity with the methods of other disciplines. That really threw over my cherished plans and depressed me a little; however, I did not let myself be deterred, and was willing to agree to any condition.

With that "the Master" became rather more accommodating. He would not object to my choosing a subject and beginning to work on it. Then, when I was far enough advanced in my preparations for the State Examinations, he would be glad to pose my task for the State Examination in such a way that it could be developed into a doctoral dissertation. The only question was what I wanted to work on. I had no difficulty with that. Husserl, in his course on Nature and Spirit, had maintained that an objective external world can only be experienced intersubjectively (i.e., by a majority of perceiving individuals) who are in a position mutually to exchange information; accordingly, the experience of other individuals is a prerequisite. Husserl, following the work of Theodor Lipps,[38] named this experience "empathy," but did not elaborate about what it consisted of. Here was a gap to be filled; I wanted to examine the nature of empathy. This did not displease the master, but at the same time he gave me another bitter pill to swallow. He demanded that I should carry out this thesis as an analysis of the work of Theodor Lipps.

He was very keen for his students in their work to clarify the relationship between phenomenology and the other important philosophical movements of the day. He was not inclined to do this himself, being too preoccupied with his own thought to spend time commenting upon other people's. But this demand evoked no more sympathy in us either. As he used to remark smilingly, "I train my students to become systematic philosophers, and then I am surprised that they don't like to work on the history of philosophy." But at first he was adamant. I had to swallow the bitter pill, i.e., apply myself to studying the lengthy series of works by Theodor Lipps.

This visit to Husserl once again had momentous consequences. Totally new plans had to be drawn up, but it did not take me long to do that. If I had to pass the State Examination before my doctorate, then I would get it out of the way as soon as possible. I had already completed five semesters, but, since the prescribed minimum was six, that did not qualify me to apply for the examination. But that regulation harked back to earlier times when there was less material to be covered, and nowadays most people took eight to ten semesters. For me, that was out of the question. My mind was made up: In the coming winter I must have the outline of my work on empathy completed, and must be sufficiently prepared for orals to apply for the exam by the end of the semester.

5

Assistant to Husserl

After the summer vacation Edith returned to Göttingen without Rose[1] Guttmann. In the course of the following semesters, her relations with Erika Gothe seem to have become friendlier, and here is what Erika Gothe says, reminiscing about the lovely time that she and Edith spent together:

> We went on many hikes together and Edith was a quietly happy companion. We talked philosophy together and often touched upon religious matters, being specially motivated by the fact that our teacher, Adolf Reinach, had converted to Christianity during the war and had mentioned in various writings that henceforth he would only teach philosophy in order to show people the way to faith.
>
> Besides, the Munich phenomenologist Max Scheler was at that time giving evening lectures in Göttingen on religious questions, including one on the essence of holiness. They were a real event in the little university town and must have given an impetus to the movement toward the Catholic Church that was then unmistakably taking place in the circle around Husserl and Reinach. This affected us a great deal, but both of us were still children of the secular world, and we never discussed conversion. Nevertheless for me, and probably also for her, this was the first impetus toward conversion.[2]

Edith's sister Erna's description tempers somewhat the almost frightening picture of the strenuous study program that the young student, in her thirst for learning, had imposed upon herself in her first semester in Göttingen:

> In Breslau we had both made a lot of friends of both sexes, with whom we used to spend our leisure time and our vacations in what was, for that time, great free-

dom from restraint and conventions. We had discussions about scientific or social matters in larger groups or in the more intimate circle of our friends. Edith was our authority because of her infallible logic and her great knowledge of literary and philosophical matters. During our vacations we used to go into the mountains, full of the joy of life and adventure.

When later she went to Göttingen to study history and philosophy, she made friends there, too, many of whom remained her friends for life. But our old group remained always the same for her and she remained loyal to it.[3]

After our State Examination in medicine my friend Hans Biberstein (now my husband) and I decided to visit Edith and Rose in Göttingen. It was an unforgettable time of lovely excursions and happy hours, while they tried to show us their beloved Göttingen and its beautiful surroundings at their best. We finished with a glorious hike through the Harz mountains.

Edith threw herself into these pleasures and recreations with her whole soul; in fact, with her sensitivity she knew how to heighten them. Thus she was a splendid companion, loyal, understanding, sympathetic, helpful to the point of self-sacrifice, but with a strong sense of identity. Edith Stein had only one love: Knowledge. She had only one passion: Books to deepen her knowledge. Her library had expanded so much in the course of years that, even after everything unsuitable to the Carmel had been eliminated, she entered the convent with six huge boxes of books as her "dowry." But for now, any such thought of monastic life was still a long way off for her.[4]

The world war[5] broke out. The lecture halls grew empty. Professors and students hurried to enlist. While Erna, who had begun her medical residency in Breslau early in 1914, merely transferred to another clinic, Edith felt compelled by sheer patriotism to discontinue her studies and volunteer for the Red Cross.[G 1] After the required training she was sent to the contagious diseases ward of the military hospital in Mährisch-Weisskirchen. There, as everywhere, she threw herself into her work with her whole soul and her unique selflessness, and was popular with the sick and wounded as she had been with her fellow-students and teachers.

In 1916 Edmund Husserl was called from Göttingen to a full professorship at the University of Freiburg. He chose Edith Stein, his most discerning and therefore his favorite student, as his private assistant; she had received her doctorate from him *summa cum laude.* Her doctoral dissertation appeared in 1917; it dealt with the problem of empathy.[T 1] [G 2]

Edith now went to work in Husserl's seminar in Freiburg, where her first job was to organize "the Master's" manuscripts and to summarize them, that involved an almost superhuman effort. As is well known, Husserl's habit was to think stenographically, i.e., to write down his train of thought in shorthand.[6] As a result, tens of thousands of shorthand manuscripts lay waiting for the young assistant to transcribe, interpret, and arrange. Heidegger and Koyré were both there to help her, but according to Frau Reinach, no one knew so well as Edith how to find her way quickly around these mountains of manuscripts and, with the expert's sure eye, dig out the hidden treasures. She found things there that Husserl had once labored at and long since forgotten, but whose importance she at once recognized; off she went with them to "the Master," placed them on his desk and "ordered" him to continue to work on them.[G 3] With her unique receptivity and her capacity for adapting herself to intellectual climates she soon recognized the difference in the level of preparedness between the philosophy students in Freiburg and those in Göttingen, who had long been accustomed to Husserl's phenomenological method. Husserl himself would hardly have thought of smoothing his new students' introduction into his world of ideas. But Edith appreciated the difficulties and started introductory courses that would permit their members to follow the lectures more easily and grasp them better. This accounts for an anecdote, passed on by Frau Reinach, that nicely illustrates Edith's good-natured wit.

Someone asked Edith Stein, "I hear that you are running a philosophical preparatory seminar in Freiburg?" to that she replied, *"No, I'm running a philosophical kindergarten."*[T 2] [G 4]

Only after leaving Husserl's service could Edith Stein devote time and energy to her own work.[8] In those years she completed "Contributions to Philosophical Foundation of Psychology and the Humanities."[9] It was a delight for her crystal-clear and penetrating intellect to glide amidst the profound and complicated reflections of phenomenology. Her mind was at home there, as if in its proper element. The springs of this world's wisdom were opened up to her, and she drank of them in full measure. Did this still her thirst for truth? Perhaps it only became more tormenting through the knowledge that even philosophy is in no position to give unassailable answers to the ultimate questions.

In order to make up in part for the two years' interruption of her studies, Edith denied herself the joy of going home for her vacations in 1917 and 1918. But she was amply compensated by the visit of her sister Erna and Rose Guttmann.[10] Together, they went on hikes in the glorious Black Forest.

A friend who took part in these excursions says:

> Though the war was weighing heavily on us all, and short rations might have detracted from our good mood, we were for the most part extremely cheerful. Sometimes we attended Husserl's lecture in the morning and then spent the night in the mountains. Once we were taken in by a farmer on the Feldberg, and it made a deep impression on us when this Catholic master said his prayers with his men in the morning and shook hands with each of them before they went out haying.[G 5]
>
> Living at close quarters with Edith, I often admired the way she was always cheerful, remaining unruffled when annoying things happened, and not getting angry, for instance, when we overslept and missed a beautiful sunrise; or once on a walk to the Bodensee,[11] when we went via the *Hohentwiel*, and on the island Reichenau

we were terribly hungry, because we couldn't buy anything with our ration cards. Edith took great pleasure
in the splendors of nature. She was absolutely enraptured by the masses of flowers on the *Belchen* and the
many multi-colored butterflies. On the *Blauen* she was
delighted because even at night from her bed she could
look over the Rhine valley all the way to the lights of
Basel in the distance and the shimmering stars
overhead.[G 6] Unfortunately we could not climb the
tower, because of wartime restrictions."

Frau Reinach had invited Edith to Göttingen and requested her to
arrange the philosophical papers left behind by her late husband. Edith
was ready to do so immediately, but was afraid of entering the Reinach
home now that it had been robbed of [Adolf] Reinach's presence, who
had filled it with sunny warmth and overflowing kindness. Even more
she feared to find Frau Reinach, whom she had only known as this
fine man's radiantly happy wife, transformed into a broken, despair-
ing widow.

However, it turned out quite differently. What the atheist Edith Stein
could only regard as a shattering blow of fate had been accepted by the
Christian Frau Reinach as part of her Master's holy Cross. It was true
that every fiber in her sensitive soul had been shaken by profound sorrow, but this sorrow had at the same time laid bare the deepest sources of
her being, so that ardent faith, gratitude, and the spirit of sacrifice welled
up and surrounded Him who drew her closer by means of the Cross.

The healing Cross and its secret blessing had transfigured the sorrowful features of this remarkable woman.

Edith never spoke to her about it, but the impression left on her by
this experience could never be effaced.

> *This was my first encounter with the Cross and the di-*
> *vine strength that it inspires in those who bear it. For*
> *the first time I saw before my very eyes the Church,*
> *born of Christ's redemptive suffering, victorious over*

the sting of death. It was the moment in which my unbe-
lief was shattered, Judaism paled, and Christ radiated
before me: Christ in the mystery of the Cross.

Sr. Benedicta revealed all this to a priest shortly before her death, ending with these words: "*Therefore at my clothing I could express no other desire than that of being called in the Order, 'of the Cross'.*"[12]

It is surprising that the course of Edith Stein's later life did not lead her to the Protestant Church to which both Frau Reinach and Edith's friend [Hedwig] Conrad-Martius belonged. It almost seems as though she contemplated this course until a second experience in Bergzabern led her to a clear religious decision.[G 7][13]

6

The Good Aunt

W ithin her own family Edith gave and received as much love and warmth as in the circle of her friends. A visit from her was an event, especially for the growing number of nephews and nieces. For them Aunt Edith was the essence of all that was kind and good. No one was so expert at inventing fascinating games, no one could tell a story so suspensefully or, when necessary, intervene so effectively between them and their stern grandmother. Dr. Bienias tells of what happened when she went to visit Edith at the Stein home. With joyous shouts of "Auntie, Auntie," one of her little nephews was running down to the bottom of the stairs where Edith was waiting for him with arms outstretched. Then she led him to the newly arrived visitor, introduced him to her with every formality, giving his full name, all with an affectionate motherliness that Dr. Bienias had never suspected in her fellow-student.[1]

At the end of the war, Erna Stein became engaged to her fellow-student, Dr. Biberstein, and Edith, of course, came to Breslau for the celebration. At the engagement party, one of Aunt Edith's small nephews asked her gravely whether she would become engaged to him. Then, he added quickly, they would have to share everything they had. His kind aunt understood at once, took her bridegroom-to-be on her knee and gave him the piece of cake to which she had just been helped. The rascal ate it up with enjoyment, but when he had finished he was smitten with doubt. Hadn't he said they would *share* everything? But he soon consoled himself, saying, "Well, we weren't engaged yet." However, from then on he regarded his Aunt Edith as his fiancée, until his father corrected his impression.

One of the other young nephews became ill. Aunt Edith was sitting in his room doing some writing when his mother came in to see whether

her darling needed anything, to which she received the unexpected reply, "I don't need Mother or any nurses. Aunt Edith's enough for me." When Erna got married in December 1920 [G 1], Edith composed poems for all her nephews and nieces, reviving all the joyous memories of their childhood and youth.

These small details, often provided by Edith herself, show how close she felt to her family.[2] Of her brothers and sisters, Paul had gone into banking, Arno into his mother's business. Though both had long headed their own families, their strong mother, in true Old Testament fashion, subjected all her children, both sons and daughters, to her matriarchal dominance. None of them would think of doing or not doing anything important without asking and receiving their mother's opinion. Apart from Edith, only the eldest daughter, Else, lived away from Breslau. Edith tells us that of all her pretty sisters Else was the real beauty. She lived with her husband, Dr. Gordon, in Hamburg, where she never came to feel at home, but consumed herself in longing for her dearly beloved mother. Frieda had also married, but did not find the happiness she had hoped for with her husband, Herr Tworoger.[3] After only a year, she was divorced and returned to her mother's house with her little daughter Erika. Rosa had no wish to get married. She stayed with her mother and in keeping with her loving nature, gently and diligently relieved her of the cares of the household. But even in her old age Frau Stein remained actively at the head of her flourishing business. Even at eighty she still kept all the business correspondence under her control. Her children and grandchildren looked up to her with reverent awe and adoring respect.

It must have been a most strong and tender affection that united such a mother and such a daughter. And yet! Did Frau Stein, with her long life experience and penetrating knowledge of human beings, see nothing of the change that was slowly taking place in her child's soul? Did she not realize where the philosophical studies of her "Fräulein Doktor," of whom she was so proud, might lead her?

7

The Convert

At this time Edith's friend, Frau Hedwig Conrad-Martius, suggested that she should write an essay ("Plant soul – animal soul – human soul") that was to cause a sensation among her colleagues.[G 1] The whole work was an ascent, an acknowledgment of God, that seemed to show that she was already converted.[1] Such was the opinion of her friends, but Edith was not convinced. Did she ever pray for the grace of faith? She herself said later, "*My longing for truth was a prayer in itself.*"[G 2]

Her work and study with Hedwig Conrad-Martius and her husband had developed into a real friendship between them, that often led Edith to make longer or shorter visits to Bergzabern, where her friends were running a large fruit-farm. Edith, who never shrank from practical work, found the fruit-picking, packing, and grading a valuable mental relaxation. She threw herself into whatever was going on. During the day they worked; in the evening they talked philosophy.[G 3]

It happened, however, that during one of these vacation-time visits both husband and wife had to go away. Before their departure Frau Conrad-Martius took her friend over to the book case and told her to take her pick. They were all at her disposal. Edith herself tells us:

> *I picked at random and took out a large volume. It bore the title* The Life of St. Teresa of Avila, *written by herself.[2] I began to read, was at once captivated, and did not stop till I reached the end.[3] As I closed the book, I said, "That is the truth."*[G 4]

Day was breaking. Edith hardly noticed it. God's hand was upon her and she did not turn from him. In the morning she went into the town to buy two things: a Catholic catechism and a missal.[G 5] She studied them until she had mastered their contents. Then for the first time she went into a Catholic church, the parish church at Bergzabern, to hear mass. Edith said later:

> *Nothing was strange to me. Thanks to my previous study, I understood even the smallest ceremonies. The priest, a saintly-looking old man,[4] went to the altar and offered the holy sacrifice reverently and devoutly. After mass I waited until he made his thanksgiving. I followed him to the presbytery and asked him without more ado for baptism. He looked astonished and answered that one had to be prepared before being received into the Church. "How long have you been receiving instruction and who has been giving it?" The only reply I could make was, "Please, your reverence, test my knowledge."*

This was the start of a theological discussion ranging over the entire doctrine of the Catholic Church.[G 6] Edith never failed in her answers. The priest, astonished by what he saw of the workings of divine grace in Edith's heart, could not refuse her baptism. The formalities were arranged between them. Who would be her sponsor? Edith asked her friend Hedwig Conrad-Martius to do her this service. They fixed her baptism for New Year's Day 1922. The joyful catechumen kept vigil during the preceding night and in the early hours of the New Year the miracle of baptism was performed in her. As a thanksgiving she chose the name of Teresa.[5][G 7] On the next day she received the Sacrament of the altar, the bread of the strong, that from now on was to be her daily food.[6] Now she was a Christian, a child of Mother Church.

And her mother, Auguste? The joy of conversion had not blinded Edith to the heartbreak she would cause. She went cold with fear whenever she thought of how she must reveal her new life to the woman she loved so much – a new life that threatened to swallow up everything bright and warm and joyous in her previous existence. And it was she, she herself, who had opened up this gulf. But there was no help. Edith did not choose to escape by a written explanation.[7][T1] [G8]

She stayed in Breslau six months.[T 2] [G 9]   As before, she went with her mother to the synagogue. On the Day of Atonement, that the elderly lady spent as usual in the synagogue without taking either food or drink, Edith even kept this strict fast with her.[T 3] [G 10]

On Candlemas Day 1922 she had received the Sacrament of Confirmation in the housechapel of His Excellency Dr. Ludwig Sebastian.[8] There in Speyer she got to know Canon Schwind, who introduced her to his family and took care of her like a father.[9] Canon Schwind, a fervent and learned priest, was her director during these first years after her conversion.[G 11] God had appointed him to guide the convert's fiery zeal into the paths of prudence, and to warn her against unconsidered excesses. It was necessary. The divine riches that the Church poured over her often carried her away with the serene rapture of the Holy Spirit.

She no longer felt at ease in Freiburg. Her innermost desire impelled her to the final surrender of a life devoted to God. But Canon Schwind, her spiritual adviser, would not hear of her entering an order for the time being.[10] However, he gladly offered to find her a peaceful occupation that would allow her to live in conventual surroundings, where she could apply herself undisturbed to her studies and at the same time deepen her spiritual life.[G 12] He introduced her to the Dominican convent school of St. Magdalena in Speyer.

8

"Fräulein Doktor"

How must she have felt upon entering the wide gate and then crossing the threshold of this ancient building's convent? From above the enclosure door, she was greeted by the single word *"Veritas,"* the Dominican motto.[G 1] Among the kind Sisters in their timeless white habits she seemed to have been transported into a world that was not of this earth. Her soul breathed deep a sigh of relief in the hallowed atmosphere of composure and silence now all around her.[1] This was the right framework for the new life that she had resolved to begin.[2] It was to be divided between God and the duties she now undertook toward her pupils. But she had in mind a work to occupy her free time that was to bring immeasurable profit to her soul, now at last really hungering after salvation: the study of St. Thomas Aquinas.[3][G 2]

She came to an arrangement with the Dominican Mother Prioress by which she would have a quiet room,[4] a modest salary, and the ordinary convent food.[5][G 3] That would satisfy her needs. The Sisters themselves regarded her as an angel sent to their rescue in their hour of need:

> We had just opened the new daughter-house in Mannheim, the first one to have high school classes. These were to open immediately after Easter 1923. The principal of the teachers' college was transferred there. We could find no suitable substitute to take the German classes that she had taught.[G 4] Along came Fräulein Stein. She took over the German classes in the teachers' college and in the girls' school, and guided her pupils calmly and safely through to their final [comprehensive] examinations.[6] Her educational work was very fruitful; she quickly won the hearts of her pupils. To all of us she was a shining example whose effect we still feel today. In humility and simplicity, almost unheard and unnoticed, she went quietly about her duties, always serenely friendly

66

and accessible to anyone who wanted her help. And not a few did. She took an interest, too, in the convent's rising generation, and gave the young Sisters and postulants private lessons to prepare them for their *Abitur* examinations.[7] And then she was always busy with her scholarly work.[8][G 5] God alone can know to how many people she gave her help, advice and direction, how often she came as an angel of charity to the relief of spiritual and bodily need. The pressure on her was often great. Her correspondence was very extensive.[G 6]

But she always had time for others. She was acting on a principle that she once expressed thus in a letter: *"As to one's relationship with people: our neighbor's spiritual need transcends every commandment. Everything else we do is a means to that end. But love is the end itself, for God is love."* The Fräulein Doktor kept entirely to the daily routine and way of life of the nuns. She had her place in the choir of the convent's church that she occupied often and for long periods at a time. She had a good eye for opportunities of giving welcome assistance where it had not even been asked. On great feasts, for instance, when the nuns were all much in demand, she used to go into the kitchen to help the maids with washing up the dishes.[G 7] So the years went by, every day filled to the very brim.

The philosopher, then, had become a teacher.[9][G 8] But a teacher in the widest sense of the word. Her ideal was that the children should receive from their convent education the strength to live their lives in the spirit of Christ. She wrote about this to a nun:

> *Surely it is most important that the teachers truly have this [Christ's] spirit themselves and vividly exemplify it. At the same time they also need to know life as the children will find it. Otherwise there will be a great danger that the girls will tell themselves: "The Sisters have no notion about the world; they have been unable to*

*prepare us for the questions we now have to answer";
and the [danger] that then everything might be thrown
overboard as useless. . . You personally, though, have
the advantage of not having entered too soon and of
having belonged to the youth movement. That gives you
access to much that others lack. However, it is necessary to keep up contacts. Today's young generation has
passed through so many crises – it can no longer understand us, but we must make the effort to understand
them; then perhaps we may yet be able to be of some
help to them.[10]*

And what did she want helping to mean? An example will show
how wisely she was able to give encouragement without in any way
compromising the truth. She writes to a student:

*The most helpful thing, in the present situation, will be
if I tell you frankly what I think of your abilities. You are
not outstandingly gifted like your sisters. And of course
it is a little oppressive to have such people always at
your side. But you have a good mind, to which, in principle, everything is open. Only you process things slowly
and are awkward in expressing yourself, so that you will
never achieve brilliant success – especially in examinations. But you will always produce something useful. You
need not measure what you understand by what you
are able to say. What you have taken in does take root,
and is fruitful both for yourself and others, even if you
can put none of it into words. But you will gradually
learn to express yourself more easily. If we put ourselves
entirely in God's hands, we may have confidence that
He can make something of us. It is for Him to pass judgment. We do not need to examine and weigh ourselves.
And believe me, those people whom you "were privi-
leged to know," who seem to you so much nearer to the
ideal of a Christian, seen from within, are just as
wretched, just as unsure of themselves as you.[11]*

Just as she knew how to encourage the timid she had the happy knack of suggesting valuable lessons to the youthfully self-confident. One of her pupils says:

> I had just passed my final school examinations, I was very sure of myself and had a great opinion of my own ability. For the oral examination in German a small, modest young woman came in, made me read and summarize a set text and then began a searching examination on it of a kind that I had never experienced. I failed completely and grew very silent. My feeling as I came out was "You've never met anything as clever as *that* before."

She must have been most deeply loved by her pupils. Let us listen to one of her youngest "children":

> Unfortunately, I was only at St. Magdalena's for one year. We were seventeen years old, and the Fräulein Doktor taught us German. She really gave us everything. We were still very young, but none of us has forgotten the magic of her personality. We saw her every day at mass up front in the chapel on her kneeler, and we began to get an inkling of what it means to bring faith and conduct into perfect harmony. To us at that critical age she provided an example simply by her bearing. I would not be able to repeat a single thing she said, not so much because it has not stayed in my memory as because she was a still and silent person who led us only by what she **was.** And how she came down to our level in class so as to introduce us to everything involved in the study of German. "First weigh, then dare"; "Character is destiny"; "I am not a book to be read and understood, I am a human being with all its contradictions" – these were the essay-subjects she gave us and illumined for us from the vantage point at which she stood.[12][G 9] In her criticisms she was a perfect combination of kindness and

fairness. We never saw her other than calm, gentle, and quiet. That is how she always came into the classroom, and how she bore herself every week, during a recreation hour that otherwise we spent with the Sisters of the boarding school. She wanted to be with her pupils during their free time, too – though she probably had to take this hour from her own free time that she must have needed for her own relaxation. And how cheerfully she would then give in entirely to whatever games we wanted to play! Silly games of forfeits, such as we at our age loved. I can still see the sweet, courteous, motherly smile on her face as she joined in our childish high spirits. But no one was disobedient, even in thought, when she was there. It was she who, in her generosity, won for us strictly-controlled girls our first visit to the theater. It was Shakespeare's *Hamlet*.[13] We saw the play through her eyes, for she had thrown open the great English dramatist's world to us. Her heart stood wide open for everything noble and beautiful to take its place beside her union with God. That is how she stands before us still.

And another:

I saw Fräulein Dr. Stein for the first time in March 1926. She tested me in grammar for the teachers' college entrance examination. She asked me if I was more familiar with the Latin terms. However, I was not familiar with grammar at all, because it was already nine years since I had left elementary school. I did my test very badly, but she remained absolutely calm and friendly all the same. She made a very deep impression upon me; her appearance was refined, delicate, and womanly. Not until many weeks later did I learn more about her life, from the pupils in the top class. Everyone loved her and considered her the best and cleverest teacher in the school, as well as the fairest. One of the older pupils put it to me in this way: "You can't tell any longer what kind of temperament she has, because she has become perfectly balanced." Actually, she had an excitable temperament, because on one occasion – about four years later, I imagine – she left our class before the end of the period because we were unable to construe a phrase. We were left utterly baffled. Nor could she understand why we were so unversed in the Old Testament. We had only been given the contents of the *Eck Bible*.[G 10] She herself had the whole of the scriptures at her fingertips, and every day she used to say the office. As we knew, she came into our church through studying the works of St. Teresa for whom her admiration and devotion were plainly visible. I was often amazed at the profound humility of her fine mind, and even more at her noble, modest, and unruffled friendliness toward everyone. Before I had moved up into her class I fell ill and was in bed near her room; and although only the nursing Sister was supposed to visit me, Fräulein Doktor came to give me Meschler's *St. Aloysius* and Eichendorff's immortal *Taugenichts* to read.[G 11] On one outing I had the good luck to be sitting opposite her; she peeled an orange and offered me a half with the utmost kindness. Apart from a card that she wrote to me later, these were the only occasions when I had personal dealings with her.

There was something about Fräulein Doktor that made her difficult to approach, she was too distant – perhaps too intelligent and distinguished, that made us rather shy of her. Yet I trusted her implicitly as my teacher; in my schoolwork, so long as only she saw it, I had no hesitation in setting down my personal viewpoints and innermost feelings. I felt very deeply: Here you could say everything without being misunderstood. When correcting our essays she was extremely painstaking as well as strict; the discussion was very instructive and interesting, and went into great detail without ever becoming pedantic, for she never hurt or humiliated anyone. Those periods with Dr. Stein are among the dearest memories of my stay in the teachers' college; my life was full of sorrow at that time, but her lessons were like rays of light in the darkness. And when I had to leave for a new school what I missed most were my classes with her.

Fräulein Doktor was a personality, a human being in the fullest sense, nothing stunted or twisted. Her natural, moral and religious endowments had all been integrated in complete harmony. May she, who has become perfected, pray for us, that we may live up to her example and labor for our unhappy Fatherland that she loved truly with all her heart.[14][G 12]

The last witness to be called is a young teacher from Speyer:

I saw the Fräulein Doktor for the first time from my classroom window as she went across the courtyard into the seminar with a pile of books under her arm. I was so struck by her personality – though I did not know in the least who she was – that I have never forgotten that first impression. Later on I entered St. Magdalena's and therefore had the chance of going to the conferences that she gave to the Sisters. Later still I got to know her personally and spent many happy hours with her, as she gave me Latin lessons and some instructions in English and French. In good weather we used to meet in the convent garden – a flag at her window that I could see from the novitiate corridor let me know that she was waiting for me out of doors. With very few words – just by her personality and everything that emanated from her – she set me on my way, not only in my studies, but in my whole moral life. With her you felt that you were in an atmosphere of everything noble, pure, and sublime that simply carried you up with it.

To see her praying in church, where she often knelt motionless for hours at a time, besides the times of the services, was an impressive sermon. And with it all she

was so plain and so simple. There were always great
goings-on in her room before Christmas. There was a
surprise for everyone in any way connected with her,
all beautifully wrapped up. And what big parcels found
their way secretly to the poor in the town![15] I do not
know how she got hold of the addresses for it. It was
the Sister who looked after her room who told me about
it. Before the feast of Christ the King was kept for the
first time, she translated the new Office and read it out
to the assembled nuns. That was an unforgettable hour
of celebration.[16]

She visited me once in Würzburg. Together we attended matins at the Carmel. When I could no longer
kneel and had to sit down, she knelt through the whole
long office without flinching.[17]

Edith Stein had retired, then, from public life into the quietness of
a provincial town and the limitations of a round of everyday duties.
Was that what God wanted of her? Looking back on these days in
1928,[18] she wrote:

*That it is possible to worship God by doing scholarly re-
search is something I learned, actually, only when I was
busy with [the translation of] St. Thomas Aquinas' "Quaestiones de Veritate" from Latin into German]. . . .Only
thereafter could I decide to resume serious scholarly
research.*

*Immediately before, and for a good while after my
conversion, I was of the opinion that to lead a religious
life meant one had to give up all that was secular and
to live totally immersed in thoughts of the Divine. But
gradually I realized that something else is asked of us
in this world and that, even in the contemplative life,
one may not sever the connection with the world. I even
believe that the deeper one is drawn into God, the more
one must "go out of oneself";[19] that is, one must go to
the world in order to carry the divine life into it.*

Working with St. Thomas, then, according to her own words, built a road for her back to philosophical work. She found herself resolving the tension between the intellectual world of Thomas and the intellectual world that had hitherto formed her thinking. This tension produced an essay in Husserl's *Yearbook*: "Husserl's Phenomenology and the Philosophy of St. Thomas Aquinas. Dedicated to Edmund Husserl in Commemoration of his Seventieth Birthday" (Verlag Niemeyer, Halle, 1929).[20]

As a return gift Husserl sent her his *Formal and Transcendental Logic* during the summer vacation time of 1929. But it was only in the spring of 1930 that she was able to settle down to study it in conjunction with her own work; by that time she had already visited Husserl personally. It was the first time since her conversion; in between lay the significant changes of the past eight years. She herself writes of this first re-encounter with her revered "Master":

> *I was able to be totally frank. His wife was present, and every time she made a remark that was totally lacking in understanding, he responded with such depth and beauty that I scarcely needed to add anything at all. But I believe one must be on one's guard against illusions. It is good to be able to speak to him so freely about the last things. But doing so heightens his responsibility as well as our responsibility for him. Prayer and sacrifice are surely much more important than anything we can say to him and therefore – I have no doubt about this – they are very necessary.*
>
> *There is a real difference between being a chosen instrument and being in the state of grace. It is not up to us to pass judgment, and we may confidently leave all to God's unfathomable mercy. . . .After every encounter in which I am made aware how powerless we are to exercise direct influence, I have a deeper sense of the urgency of my own "holocaustum." And this awareness culminates increasingly in a "hic Rhodus, hic salta!"[21]*

> *However much our present mode of living may ap-*
> *pear inadequate to us – what do we really know about*
> *it? But there can be no doubt that we are in the here-*
> *and-now to work out our salvation and that of those*
> *who have been entrusted to our souls. Let us help one*
> *another to learn more and more how to make every day*
> *and every hour part of the structure for eternity – shall*
> *we* [do so] *by our mutual prayers during this holy*
> *season?*[22][G 13]

But the world had not forgotten Edith Stein. The Catholic world, in particular, had begun to notice this young convert and her published writings.[23] She was urged on all sides to undertake lectures on educational, philosophical, and religious subjects. Her lecture in Ludwigshafen on "The Proper Dignity of Woman and its Importance in the Life of the Nation" laid the foundation for her fame as a speaker.[24] In Heidelberg she delivered a lecture (very well received) on a theme from St. Thomas.[25] She was invited to Freiburg, Munich, Cologne, Zürich, Vienna [T 1].[26] Her greatest success was at the meeting of the Akademikerverband in Salzburg in 1932 [*sic*], where she spoke so convincingly about woman's vocation that this evening was described as the climax of the whole congress.[27] She made two friends on this occasion who remained faithful to her even unto death: Dr. Waitz, Prince-Bishop of Salzburg, and Professor Peter Wust.[28] The extraordinary modesty of her bearing was an occasion of astonishment as soon as she appeared, and sometimes the organizers of these lecture-meetings even considered it necessary to announce that the audience must not be misled by the youthful appearance of the lecturer, who was in fact thirty-six [*sic*] years of age.[29] Indeed, the bearing of her slim figure, the soft coloring of her fine face, her thick hair plainly parted and gathered into a knot in back of her neck, and, above all, the light in her dark eyes would have done credit to a twenty-year-old.[T 2][30] She dressed to suit the occasion, but always with simplicity. She would stand at the rostrum, quietly confident, speaking in a clear voice using no gestures, no special effects, as though teaching in class.[T 3][31] But while everyone was still speaking about her and the newspapers publishing her speeches, she would be back at Speyer, sitting over her pupils' exercise books, as though nothing had happened. The center of her life was in God, and could not be disturbed by human praise or blame. Those who spoke to her felt that she would dedicate herself entirely to God.

Since her conversion the monastic life had been the silent desire of her heart. But on every occasion that she raised the matter in her confidential talks with Canon Schwind, he advised her that the time was not yet ripe. She believed him, and left her direction in his hands.[G 14] What a hard blow it must have been for her childlike trustful heart when one mellow autumn evening the news ran like wildfire through Speyer that Canon Schwind, the Vicar General, was dead.[32] That evening, as usual, the Vicar General had set off for the cathedral to hear confessions. In the confessional he had a stroke that caused his sudden death. How deep her affection and gratitude toward him had grown comes out in the obituary notice that Edith Stein published in the *Innsbruck Clergy Review.*[33]

> *Our Reverend Father, Canon Schwind, whom the Eternal High Priest has taken to Himself after fifty-one years of richly blessed service in the priesthood, always had great faith in the powerful inspiration that souls derive from reading vivid descriptions of saintly lives. . .though even when the word was not describing a saint, so long as it lit up the secret riches and profound temptations of human beings, his experience and love of mankind enabled him to draw out its treasures.[G 15] He and I used to find relaxation sometimes in reading together during our scant leisure time, and the last book we were going through was Grisar's "Life of Luther."*
>
> *He was always glad whenever he came across some fresh observation to fill in his picture of "Dr. Martinus." He looked upon this book as a masterpiece precisely be-*

cause it contained a wealth of apparently trifling, yet concrete, facts that brought Luther vividly before one's eyes.

More than once Cardinal Newman has emphasized that it is relatively easy for us to develop one aspect of our Christian life, strictness, gentleness, seriousness or cheerfulness. But truly Christian perfection is only attained when these contrasted virtues are exercised in unison. Canon Schwind satisfied this condition in full measure. I have heard it said that he had a reputation for being just, but strict – a judgment that immediately astonishes anyone who knew him well. Yet, if one reflects for a moment one can understand it. From youth onwards the guiding thread of his life was the strict fulfillment of duty; he had the very highest conception of the priesthood and never spared himself in his faithfulness to that ideal. No doubt he fulfilled his office as Vicar General with this ideal in mind, for he certainly never deviated one hair's breadth from his principles; and it is quite likely that anyone with different opinions would consider his attitude unbending and strict. But, equally certainly, whenever he had to hurt anyone by a word of blame or by refusing them something, it was only after he had tormented his own gentle heart, as anyone knows who went to him with some request. And how he gave you his undivided attention, listening to every word that you said! If it was a question of making the right decision in a difficult situation, a picture would immediately spring before his mind's eye of the person involved, whom he had never seen; and his advice nearly always hit the nail on the head. If there seemed any chance that he might help in the matter, he would do so without being asked. Nor did he expect to be thanked: And if one ever ventured to do so, the reply would come "I am doing no more than my duty and, as far as I can see, not even that." And he was ready to help everyone, without exception, including people unknown to him personally, whose need or distress he had heard of at second hand.

In his spiritual direction he was calm, firm, and prudent. He relied upon his deep knowledge of human beings and his years of apostolic experience, yet his penetration remained gentle through utter reverence before the workings of God's grace in the soul. Whenever he found a soul responsive to God's demands he would show boundless trust, leaving it alone and refusing to interfere. In such cases he would even encourage proposals that from outside must have seemed audacious and questionable. He possessed an unshakable confidence in the ways of divine Providence and the power of prayer; therefore in situations where every human suggestion was inadequate he could always strengthen souls, bringing peace and consolation.

His own soul was securely rooted in eternity; it seemed that he scarcely knew how to view things other than "sub specie aeternitatis" ["seen from the perspective of eternity"], that endowed his personality with a deep and saintly gravity. You could see this from his tall dignified figure and the recollection in his impressive face when you met him in the street or visited his study. Yet as soon as he recognized anyone, a warm, cheerful smile would light up his serious features. And his childlike gaiety used to sparkle whenever he was entertaining guests at his table; with infectious spontaneity he would tell stories about his student days as if they had happened only yesterday; and how intensely absorbed he would listen whenever some widely traveled, intelligent man was describing the ebb and flow of events in the wider world. Many a Sunday, if he was not on duty, he was still to be found chatting over the coffee table when it was time for dinner.

Strict and kind, serious and gay, dignified and humble, his soul brought these many contrasting shades of character into harmony because they reflected his pure love of God. To be a servant of God; that expressed his purpose in life, the nobility and responsibility of which he was always conscious. He prayed his office joyfully and devoutly, never curtailing it no matter how busy he was. Also he used to introduce lay folk to the office when he found them in love with the beauty of the liturgy and longing, like him, to share more intimately in the life of the Church. Daily meditations upon divine truth and good spiritual reading contributed indispensable nourishment for his interior life; this nourishment he gladly shared with others, and his well-stocked library was open to all who could use it. No other book was so dear to him (apart from the Scriptures and the Breviary) as the "Imitation of Christ."

With the death of Canon Schwind a good and faithful servant has entered into the joy of his Lord. In the "Kirchenverordnungsblatt" a tribute from his bishop has already appeared, full of gratitude for the departed canon's services. The Theological Faculty and the seminary in Innsbruck may well be proud to count this noble soul and model priest among their former pupils (1873-75). May he be a model for the younger generation, and for all of us a faithful intercessor with the Father. "In pace Christi vivat." ["May he live in the peace of Christ."]

But God did not leave Edith Stein without a director for long.

9

Beuron

The blossoming of the liturgical movement had brought the Abbey of Beuron to her notice; following a suggestion from her friend Father Erich Przywara, S.J., she had gone there for Holy Week and Easter in 1928.[1] With all the capacity of her sensitive nature she had contemplated and lived through the marvelous mysteries of the Passion and Resurrection of Our Lord. She was given great graces about which she would never speak. She gave thanks to God with the decision to go every year for Easter to this hallowed spot, so long as she was able. Beuron became her spiritual home.

At her first visit she asked for a short interview with Abbot Raphael Walzer. This meeting proved to be of decisive significance. In the young Abbot, who with his monastic *hilaritas* [upbeat pleasantness], was the embodiment of the joy of the religious life, Edith saw the ideal type of Benedictine monasticism.[2] He recognized her for "one of the greatest women of our time" and later wrote this testimony of her:

> I have seldom met a soul that united so many excellent qualities; and she was simplicity and naturalness personified. She was completely a woman, gentle and even maternal, without ever wanting to 'mother' anyone. Gifted with mystical graces, in the true sense of the word, she never gave any sign of affectation or a sense of superiority. She was simple with simple people, learned with the learned yet without presumption, an inquirer with inquirers, and I would almost like to add, a sinner with sinners.[3]

This is a judgment of the greatest value, because Edith allowed no other priest to see so deeply into her interior life, nor confided her aspirations to any other with the same childlike openness as to Abbot Raphael.[G 1] She thought of herself as his daughter, and would often say jokingly that she would have liked best to become a Benedictine.

Abbot Walzer, for his part, would assure her that he already had in mind where he would send her in that event. Seriously, however, the Lord Abbot set himself firmly against his spiritual daughter's ever recurring longing for the monastic life.[4] As he saw it, her task was to use the rich talents the Lord had given her in the commerce of life, making them fruitful for the benefit of many.[G 2] So he spurred her on to refuse none of the opportunities for this that might be offered. Lectures, publications,[5] commitments, travels, and papers multiplied accordingly, and one wonders how this woman, who also devoted a great part of her day and night to prayer – she recited the Office daily from the time of her conversion – could carry out such a program.[6]

She herself gives the answer:

I use no special means to increase my working time. I do as much as I can. One's capacity plainly increases with the number of things to be done. When there is nothing urgent on hand, the limit comes much sooner. Heaven surely understands economy. That things do not in practice run smoothly according to the laws of reason is due to the fact that we are not pure spirits.[7]

The only essential is that one finds, first of all, a quiet corner in that one can communicate with God as though there were nothing else, and that must be done daily. It seems to me the best time is in the early morning hours before we begin our daily work; furthermore, it is also essential that one accepts one's particular mission there, preferably for each day, and does not make one's own choice. Finally, one is to consider oneself totally an instrument, especially with regard to the abilities one uses to perform one's special tasks, in our case, e. g., intellectual ones. We are to see them as something used, not by us, but by God in us.[8] [G 3]

The Abbey of Beuron was for Edith Stein the "quiet corner" where her soul could draw breath. It was there that the substance of her being came most clearly into the light. Without exaggeration, Father Damasus

Zähringer describes this essential character of her life as *ecclesia orans*.[9]
He writes:

> When I saw her for the first time in a corner of the
> entrance to the Beuron monastery, her appearance and
> attitude made an impression on me that I can only com-
> pare with that of pictures of *ecclesia orans* in the old-
> est ecclesiastical art of the catacombs. Apart from the
> arms uplifted in prayer, everything about her was remi-
> niscent of that Christian archetype. And this was no
> mere bizarre fancy. She was in truth a type of that
> *ecclesia*, standing in the world of time and yet apart
> from it, and knowing nothing else, in the depths of her
> union with Christ, but the Lord's words: "For them do
> I sanctify myself; that they also may be sanctified in
> the truth."[10]

Ecclesia orans. The classic phrase is indeed the most concise way
of expressing the essence of Edith Stein. She was the embodiment of
the Church's prayer. No happier theme could have been offered her, to
touch the deepest springs of her heart, than that set her by the Academic Union of St. Boniface: The Prayer of the Church. In 1936 she
contributed an essay under that title to a symposium on "The Life-
stream of the Church" (Bonifatius Verlag, Paderborn). The thoughts
she there expresses are the precious fruits of her own enlightened
devotion.[11]

Edith experienced the rise of that most welcome and quickly-grow-
ing movement, the liturgical revival. But she was quick to recognize
the danger of an over-emphasis on the community idea and a conse-
quent one-sidedness in the life of prayer. She considered it an error to
describe interior prayer, without set traditional forms, as "subjective
piety" in opposition to the "objective prayer" of the Church's liturgy.
She thus touched on a hotly disputed question, then seriously agitat-
ing souls and troubling religious communities. The swelling flood of
liturgical enthusiasm was threatening to sweep away respect for silent

prayer of the heart.[G 4] In that essay Sr. Benedicta faces this question and writes with the wise assurance of practical experience:

> *All authentic prayer is prayer of the Church. Through*
> *every sincere prayer something happens in the Church,*
> *and it is the Church itself that is praying therein, for it*
> *is the Holy Spirit living in the Church that intercedes for*
> *every individual soul "with sighs too deep for words."[12]*
> *This is exactly what "authentic" prayer is, for "no one*
> *can say 'Jesus is Lord' except by the Holy Spirit."[13] What*
> *could the prayer of the Church be, if not great lovers*
> *giving themselves to God who is love! The unbounded*
> *loving surrender to God and God's return gift, full and*
> *enduring union, this is the highest elevation of the heart*
> *attainable, the highest level of prayer. Souls who have*
> *attained it are truly the heart of the Church. . .[14]*

Whoever reads this, can discern that Sr. Benedicta here opens the carefully guarded door to the sanctuary of her soul and lets us glimpse a little of her intimacy with God, kindled to a flame of love by the Holy Spirit in the *opus Dei* and in contemplation.[15] Many people who were not very close to her were disappointed when Edith Stein chose to enter the contemplative order of Carmel rather than a liturgical order. But anyone who reads her article *The Prayer of the Church* will unhesitatingly include her among the great men and women of prayer from whom she there quotes, and will realize that this soul, inclined to contemplation by nature and grace, by inclination and vocation, could only become a Carmelite.[16]

True, she was as yet far from this goal. Any temporary stay in the cloister was all the more a joy to her, especially in her beloved Beuron.[17]

"She could pray for hours before the picture of Our Lady of Sorrows," writes a Swiss lady. "I could never understand it, for medieval and Beuron-style art had no attraction for me. But now I have come to think that Edith Stein not only prayed to have sufferings, but also had intimations that she was to travel the road of suffering."[18][G 5]

In support of this opinion let us quote the poem that was found among Sr. Benedicta's posthumous papers:

Good Friday 1938

Juxta Crucem Tecum Stare!

(Standing with you at the Cross)

Today I stood with you beneath the Cross,
And felt more clearly than I ever did
That you became our mother only there.
Even an earthly mother faithfully
Seeks to fulfill the last will of her son.
But you became the handmaid of the Lord:
The life and being of the God made man
Was perfectly inscribed in your own life.
So you could take your own into your heart,
And with the lifeblood of your bitter pains
You purchased life anew for every soul.
You know us all, our wounds, our imperfections;
But you also know the celestial radiance
That your son's love would shed on us in heaven.
Thus carefully you guide our faltering footsteps,
No price too high for you to lead us to our goal.
But those whom you have chosen for companions
To stand with you around the eternal throne,
They here must stand with You beneath the Cross,
And with the lifeblood of their own bitter pains
Must purchase heavenly glory for those souls
Whom God's own Son entrusted to their care.[19]

Maria Schäfer describes in a letter her memories of the lovely days of Holy Week and Easter that she and Edith Stein spent together in Beuron:

I can only say "together" in the sense that we stayed in immediate proximity to each other and took part in the services together. Apart from this the holy events of these days passed in absolute solitude. Edith Stein was always the first to appear in choir, usually before four in the morning. During those days, she spoke hardly at all. But her greetings and good wishes on Easter morning, radiant and full of warmth, made you feel how deeply she must have descended into the godforsakenness and sufferings of the God-man, so as to shine with such Easter brightness.[20] She seemed during those days to live more than usually in the spirit; she seemed even more pale and delicate-looking than usual; only her eyes and features betrayed something of her *compassio*.[21] To me it was, at times, a criterion of her very holiness that there were sometimes people, and devout people, who did not restrain their criticisms even in the face of her unassuming ways. "Must Dr. Stein always have the first place in Church and hold on to it so obstinately?" Or people would interpret the selection of dishes at mealtime as demanding; that she used to leave table early out of arrogance; and maintain strict silence, out of pride.[G 6] They had, probably, no inkling that this future Carmelite was already guiding her life in the world by the principles of Carmel. And these people had no final knowledge of the reality that is sung in the words of the psalm: "*Quam dilecta tabernacula tua Domine virtutum: concupiscit et deficit anima mea in atria Domini*" ["How lovely are your dwelling places, Lord of Hosts; my soul yearns and pines for the halls of the Lord."][22]

Yes, her soul longed for a hidden life in a cell in the house of the Lord. But Abbot Walzer would not hear of it. On the contrary, he persuaded her at last to give up her all too modest position at St. Magdalena's.

Edith Stein herself had already considered giving up teaching school, as she explains in a letter of 10 December 1930: *"Salzburg has created astonishing ripples. I have to show up as speaker here, there, and everywhere. In between, there are mountains of essays. . .I*

*will chuck school at Easter. . .and after that I don't know yet. I have
put aside – as useless and a waste of time – all reflection about it until
the Christmas vacation."*[23]

She spent Christmas in Beuron where she had the prospect of the
baptism of a young Jewish woman, a special joy because *"I was in a
small way instrumental in it as a* causa secunda."*[24][G 7] After an interview with the Lord Abbot she realized that she could no longer com-
bine her lectures with teaching school. Some time after leaving Beuron
she confided her decision to the Reverend Mother of St. Magdalena.
"In full understanding of my situation, she released me."[25] It was kept
secret until the end of the semester.[G 8] *"It caused great consterna-
tion when, suddenly, on the last day of school, I said farewell. The children and most of the Sisters had no inkling beforehand. The few initiates
helped, with touching sisterly love, to complete the whole of my packing in the short time there was outside of school, so that I was able to
escape to Beuron as soon as school closed."* [26]

From Beuron she wrote to a friend:

> *. . .on Thursday I took leave of St Magdalena's. St. Thomas
> [her translation] is no longer satisfied with my spare time,
> he demands all of me.*[27]
>
> *On the Tuesday after Easter, I have to go to a con-
> ference in Munich (student teachers from all over Bavaria
> and some fifteen from the Palatinate will be coming)
> From there I will go to Breslau for a while, in order to
> have the quiet in which to carry on with a major work I
> have begun. . .That this will enable me, once more to be
> at home for a longer period is surely very good. My sis-
> ter [Rosa] seems to be especially in need of my pres-
> ence now.*[28][G 9]

10

In the Service of Scholarship [G 1]

The work [G 2] of which Edith Stein was here speaking was the translation of St. Thomas's *Quaestiones disputatae de Veritate*, that came out in two volumes in 1931 and 1932.[G 3] Martin Grabmann wrote a preface to give the book a send-off.[2] A translation of this kind could only be achieved by someone who was "at once at home in the world of Scholastic thought and understood the language of contemporary philosophy." Edith Stein had both qualifications, having "taken up the study of Scholasticism after being immersed in the currents of contemporary philosophy. So equipped, she has undertaken the translation of the *Quaestiones disputatae de Veritate*[3] and made this basic work of Aquinas available for the first time in German. Without obscuring the character of Thomistic terminology she has clothed Thomism in modern speech and translated its thought processes into current German." And Father Erich Przywara wrote of it:

> The astonishing thing about this work is the fact that for the first time it strikes the perfect balance: On the one hand, here is German through which shines the simple clarity of Aquinas' Latin with almost immediate lucidity; on the other, everything, not only in the rich annotations but in the matter of the translation itself, has become living up-to-date philosophy. It is St. Thomas and nothing but St. Thomas throughout; but he is brought face to face with Husserl, Scheler, and Heidegger. Phenomenologist terminology, that Edith commands as a philosopher in her own right, has nowhere replaced Aquinas's own language, but the transition from one to the other can now be made smoothly. This is surely the most significant feature of this important work: that in the German footnotes the basis is laid for an exposition of Thomism in German, i.e., in terms of living, present-

day philosophy. Edith Stein, in her comparative treatment
of St. Thomas and Husserl, has written something in the
nature of a program. It would be a blessing for German
Catholic philosophy if it were receptive to it in time.[4]

Such were the judgments made in 1931.[G 4]

The name of Edith Stein was becoming well known. Therefore friendly
parties suggested that she should apply for a position as a lecturer at
Freiburg University. She had mentioned this suggestion when she was
talking to the Lord Abbot in Beuron during the Christmas holidays, because she did not wish to take it up without his approval.[5] Back in Speyer
once more she had written immediately to Prof. Finke[6] asking whether
she might have an interview with him in Freiburg on either 24 or 25
January to discuss the matter. The answer was slow in coming. "There
has been no answer to that yet," she wrote on 19 January 1931:

> *(Without word from him, of course, I would not come.)*
> *If the situation is completely without any prospect - and*
> *expert opinion assures me of this – he would surely pre-*
> *fer not to have to tell me so in person. You could make*
> *him understand that the whole thing does not affect me*
> *inwardly, and that, if nothing comes of it, I shall nei-*
> *ther be disappointed nor saddened.[7]*

Eventually Prof. Finke referred her to Heidegger, whom she visited in Freiburg on the date arranged. The account of it written on 26
January, runs:

> *As soon as I rang the doorbell at Rotebuckweg 47 there*
> *was a clatter down the stairs to the door, indicating that*
> *someone had been waiting for that signal. It was the*
> *eldest boy, who had obviously been instructed to re-*
> *ceive me, and did so faultlessly.[8] It was a very friendly*
> *beginning. Heidegger was not at all astonished by my*
> *request; he said that he had no objections at all, either*
> *professionally or personally. But he would only be able*

to give an endorsement when he had learned from the
governing board whether he could get a fellowship for
me. From that I perceived he thought I intended to get
it in his department. I considered how I might begin to
dissuade him. But he came to my aid: Were I thinking of
a Catholic appointment, it would be very impractical for
me to seek it through him. And a grant would be obtained
much more easily by other means. The governing board
would hardly be able to refuse Honecker, just on the basis
of parity, for he did not have anyone [as assistant] so far.
I was very amazed to find myself back on the street [in
so short a time]. Honecker was much more reluctant in
the beginning. But in the end he, too, declared himself
willing to present the matter to the faculty, making only
a stipulation that his own candidate be not eliminated.
On his next trip to Karlsruhe he would talk to them there
about a fellowship.

There was great surprise and joy at the Husserls'
over the outcome. What's more, I only left at 5:30 p.m.
If need be, I could still have made the earlier train; that,
however, would have meant dashing away as soon as
we got up from dinner and, after all, I could not do that
to the old folks. This way they could have their after-
noon nap – I, too, was made to lie down on a sofa – and
then we could talk at leisure for a while longer. Frau
Husserl took me to the train.[9]

With her lectureship in mind Edith Stein had taken advantage of
the remaining six weeks before leaving Speyer in order to begin elabo-
rating a philosophical work that she had been planning for a long
time.[10][G 5] It had already assumed the proportions of a bulky manuscript when a fresh possibility presented itself. This was due to two
people, Prof. Dr. Steffes, the head of the theological faculty in Münster
and Principal of the German Institute of Scientific Pedagogy,[11] and Maria
Schmitz, President of the German Association of Catholic Teachers.[12]
They were trying to persuade Edith to move to Münster and become a

lecturer at the Institute, where she would give lectures and exercises on education for girls and women.[G 6] With her usual calmness Edith Stein just let things take their course, and carried on with her work undisturbed. She writes from Breslau:

> *I would prefer to come to Freiburg only when my work is completed. When that will be, I do not know. And were I to receive my appointment to the P.A. (Pedagogical Academy)[13] before [it is finished], I might forego the habilitation completely. Once I had begun the work, it immediately became more important to me than any other purpose that it might perhaps serve. God knows what He has in store for me. I do not need to concern myself about it.[14]*

Suddenly another quite different possibility was opened up in Breslau itself. We hear about it in a letter of Edith's on 28 June 1931:

> *My brother-in-law [Hans Biberstein] meets regularly with a group of other professors [at the university of Breslau], including several Catholic theologians. One of these (Koch) has inquired repeatedly about his sister-in-law (especially since Salzburg).[15] Recently he said that, in Rome, he has heard some very favorable comments about me (i.e., about my "Thomas")[16] and would be very happy to make my acquaintance: he asked whether I would not like a habilitation here.[G 7] Thereupon I asked my mother, first of all, whether it would be all right with her if I were to engage, publicly, in a Catholic enterprise here in town. To my great surprise, it developed that she would make allowance for anything that would keep me in the area. On Tuesday, my relatives [Hans and Erna] invited Professor Koch and me [for dinner]. He would welcome it greatly if I could teach phenomenology (with my modification) here and has, meanwhile, begun to work along those lines on Professor Bauer, the Catholic head of the faculty for philosophy.[17] Tomorrow, I'm to come with Bauer to Professor Koch for coffee. I am going to just*

*let the matter run its course, waiting to see what will
come of it.*

*My work cares little about where it can be used. It
has already grown into a monster and gives no sign of
coming to an end. I want to keep at it until autumn,
without interruption if possible. For the month of October, the Academic Society has concocted a lecture cir-
cuit for me throughout the Rhine-Westphalian industrial
belt.[18] So far, fourteen chapters have signed up for it.*

*On 22 November, I'm to give the principal address
in Heidelberg's Catholic community, meeting in the
large town hall for the Jubilee of St. Elizabeth [of Thur-
ingia]. . . And for the second half of January, I've been
engaged [in Zürich] to give four lectures, twice, before
an audience of Catholic women. I do not know yet where
I shall spend the time in-between. That will depend on
what happens in the matter of the habilitation.[19]*

Prof. Koch has given us this reminiscence of their first meeting in
Breslau:

> I was sitting with Dr. Biberstein, his sister-in-law, his
> wife, and her mother, Frau Stein. Then the door opened
> and Edith came in. I can remember very vividly the
> plain, light blue dress she was wearing, and how I was
> struck with her simplicity. She had already made a name
> for herself but she showed no trace of posing. The eyes
> with which she calmly surveyed the visitor had an ex-
> traordinary charm that I cannot forget. Nor can I forget
> something she said. It was her brief but exact descrip-
> tion of Heidegger's philosophy as "the philosophy of a
> bad conscience."[20][G 8] The phrase says so much for
> her knowledge of humanity, and for her integrity when
> truth was in question.

11

In the Service of Love

B esides the great "work," as Edith Stein herself called it,[T 1] God had called her back to Breslau for another heavy task. Edith referred to this in a sentence, quoted above, in a letter of 28 March 1931, saying *"My sister[1] seems to be especially in need of my presence at home."*[2][G 1]

In Speyer and Freiburg Edith Stein had already had opportunities of helping young people in their effort to reach the Christian faith from Judaism. In fact she had dedicated herself to this task, with thoroughgoing devotion, inexhaustible patience, and exquisite understanding. God blessed her zeal with abundant success.[G 2] Many times she had the privilege of [T 2] acting as godmother to the happy catechumens when they were baptized: amongst others, Dr. Ruth Kantorowicz, Alice Reis, Hede Heß [Spiegel] and her childhood friend Katharina, later Doctor, Rubens.[3][G 3] The latter describes Edith's part in her conversion in the continuation of her narrative, quoted earlier in this book:

> I never lost interest in my childhood companion. I heard of her going over to Catholicism. That was amazing news. I knew that Frau Stein was anything but tolerant. [4] I knew, moreover, how passionately attached Edith was to her mother, no less than her mother was to her. I knew, too, how indifferent Edith had been to religious matters. During the religious instruction class – that was, it is true, exceedingly bad – she even lost her desire to shine.[5] How she must have changed! But I did not meet her again – not until 1931 or 1932; it must have been early in the summer.[6] I had heard that she was in Breslau to see her elderly mother.[7] I myself was struggling with light and faith. I rang her up. She was at once ready to come to me, and we met often, near where she lived, where one could take beautiful walks. Once, when I could not

give her a definite time for an appointment, I suggested that I should come and fetch her. But she objected: "My mother knows that your husband has gone over to Catholicism. She has her own idea, of course, of what we talk about, and she would not want to see you."
Her mother was then already an octogenarian. But it was amazing how she [Edith] herself had changed. Where there had been ambition, there was now only tranquil poise; where there had been egoism, there was only understanding and kindness. She discussed things with me with endless patience, as well as consoling me in personal matters and discussing questions of faith, philosophy and everything that affected us.[8] We came very close to each other. She was my godmother, too, and we parted from each other in deep and genuine love. To the last, up to the outbreak of war, she wrote us frequent and affectionate letters in South Africa and told us of the fullness and perfection of joy that she found in Carmel.[9]

Dr. Albert Rubens, missionary doctor and District Surgeon in Tweespruit, South Africa, fills out his wife's account:

I met Edith Stein only a few times in all. The first was when I was just emerging from a severe crisis in my life. I had not, of course, entirely recovered my equilibrium. She sat opposite me in my wife's room, her slim figure almost lost to sight in the big easy chair. I have never forgotten that picture. Why? In a short time I was completely defeated and outstripped in the discussion; for in her quiet fashion, never raising her voice even for a moment, with nothing affected in her perfect style of speaking, she presented me with one inexorable truth after another.
Once, probably in 1932, she visited us in the medical missionary institute in Würzburg. But all I know of this is that Msgr. Becker, professor and director of the institute, a Salvatorian, was deeply impressed by her.[10]

The last time I spoke to her was in December 1933, through the grille of the Carmel in Cologne. It was cold and she was wearing a thick coat.[11] I have forgotten the content of our conversation. In part, of course, it revolved round our departure to the mission. I revered her greatly. I have in my missal her definition of the Church of Christ. I have never found a more beautiful one. Her fate is an indication of how far removed men are from it.

So God blessed her apostolic zeal. But in her own family, where she so deeply longed for it and so unceasingly and passionately prayed for it, she found little interest in Christ.[G 4] Only her thoughtful sister Rosa opened her heart to grace, and would gladly have followed her younger sister's example. But could they inflict this fresh hurt on their beloved mother, now very elderly, and not yet recovered from the first blow?[12] Edith was usually away from home, but Rosa was constantly at her mother's service. In such close coexistence, conflicts would surely arise. So Rosa had decided to delay her baptism till after their beloved mother's death.[13] This sacrifice to filial piety afforded her no escape from the conflict in her heart, and it was Edith alone who could bring harmony out of her painful doubts, torn as she was between duty and love:

> *These years of 1930-31 made Rosa's position harder than ever:*
>
> *It does seem there's a very critical situation in Breslau right now. For some months my sister [Rosa] has been suffering a great deal; Erika's [Tworoger] increasingly pronounced Jewish leaning and her interference in running the household are becoming almost unbearable for Rosa. So far she has avoided any arguments in order to spare my mother. Now she has entrusted her secret to Erika herself, and it is not apparent yet what consequences that will have. For the moment, I can see hardly any other possibility than to help by prayer, and so I want to call upon all my auxiliary troops.[14]*

They were blessed hours for Rosa when Edith was at home and spoke to her of Jesus, or prayed with her, or kept her dear mother company so that Rosa could pay a secret visit to the church.[G 5] Such a happy time was the summer of 1931, with Edith in Breslau, except for a lecture trip to Vienna,[15] where she stayed with Dr. Rudolf Allers.[16][G 6]

Toward the end of autumn she came back to Freiburg and stayed at St. Lioba,[17][G 7] happy to have found a home in a religious house once more and to be praying the monastic office [whereas she wrote that in Breslau she did]:

> . . . *return to the silent liturgy that is my portion here. Even this way one can be richly supplied with what one needs. I experience that daily. But only when, once again, I am able to live in fullness, do I realize how I thirsted for it. When I decided to leave Speyer, I knew it would be very difficult not to be living in a convent any longer. But I would never have imagined that it would be as difficult as it has proved to be in these first months. For all that, as I cannot doubt that things are as they should be, I have never for a moment regretted making the move.[18]*

Countess Tes von Bissingen[19] tells of the impression that she left behind in St. Lioba:

> She was so extraordinarily modest that one hardly noticed she was there. She never put herself forward, always stayed in the background. And yet from the first moment one felt as it were spellbound by the great sanctity that emanated from her quiet nature. There was never any drifting along with her – nothing but strict self-discipline and striving toward God. But she exercised the greatest gentleness toward others – and the more wretched a poor creature was, the more touching would be her joy in seeking in such people the favorites of

God, just where the rest of us really saw wretchedness and nothing else. Of course she took a very serious view of our attitude toward God. She could not conceive how it was that some of our party – I mean, during the winter in the little house of St. Lioba – only rushed off to vespers when they were sung, and otherwise took the time off. From the way she spoke one had the impression that she had lived just as seriously and ascetically before her conversion as after. I even think that her conversion had actually made her more gentle toward herself, since her inclination was to be too severe. This great sanctity of hers gave me a slight sense of awe. A deep affection bound her to Beuron, but even more to Carmel, and she was obviously delighted when she met someone who shared and understood her predilection.

Maria Schäfer,[20] who was staying at St. Lioba at the same time as Edith Stein, had the joy of reading the proofs of St. Thomas's *De Veritate* with her.

We read them in her little room, just opposite my own, sitting side by side at her desk. She would go very gladly into the questions that occurred to me during the reading; and how clear her answers were. An old carved crucifix that lay on the table kept catching my eye, or were they drawn to it rather by the loving glances that Edith Stein would give it from time to time? Though her time was very full and she made a strict allocation of it, she always found an hour or two to talk to me about her small book *Ethos der Frauenberufe*,[21] or we would read some poems from Przywara's *Karmel*, or discuss *Die Letzte am Schafott*[22] or *Marie de la Trinité*. [G 8] At that time I was deeply under the spell of her radiant, simple, completely unassuming personality. For me she was the very model of the *vita contemplativa*. The Reverend Mother Prioress of St. Lioba once said that she would sometimes go to the chapel very early in the morn-

ing, but she was never the first, Edith Stein was always
there before her. She would hide her knowledge and
ability in simplicity. I was often touched by it; I even
had the impression that she chose her unassuming dress,
her old-fashioned, much-mended undergarments in a
spirit of holy poverty. Her work too went forward so
quietly and unobtrusively; I sometimes wondered how
it was that she had so few scholarly reference materials
at hand.

During this winter, from 18 to 28 January 1932, she gave a series
of lectures in Switzerland.[23] After this she spoke at Septuagesima at
the great Cantonal Celebration of St. Elizabeth at Zürich.[24] From this
period dates the article "Ways to Interior Silence," that has fortunately
been preserved. It was written for the *Societas Religiosa*, a society of
professional women, living according to a rule. Maria Buczkoska had
asked her to write it.[G 9] Similar "monthly letters" were intended to
stimulate their readers toward self-improvement in a certain way. Maria
Buczkoska had proposed the theme in connection with the lecture that
Edith Stein gave at Bendorf in November 1930. What she recommends
in this article is obviously the result of years of faithful practice in
self-discipline.[25]

"WAYS TO INTERIOR SILENCE"

St. Lioba, 12 January 1932

*In the talk that I gave in November 1930 in Bendorf
concerning the foundations of woman's education, I
tried to draw the picture of woman's soul as it would
correspond to the eternal vocation of woman, and I
termed its attributes as expansive, quiet, empty of self,
warm, and clear. Now I am asked to say something regarding how one might come to possess these qualities.*

*I believe that it is not a matter of multiplicity of attributes that we can tackle and acquire individually; it
is rather a single total condition of the soul, a condition*

that is envisaged here in these attributes from various aspects. We are not able to attain this condition by willing it, it must be effected through grace. What we can and must do is open ourselves to grace; that means to renounce our own will completely and to give it captive to the divine will, to lay our whole soul, ready for reception and formation, into God's hands.

Becoming empty and still are closely connected. The soul is replenished by nature in so many ways that one thing always replaces another, and the soul is in constant agitation, often in tumult and uproar.

The duties and cares of the day ahead crowd about us when we awake in the morning (if they have not already dispelled our night's rest). Now arises the uneasy question: How can all this be accommodated in one day? When will I do this, when that? How shall I start on this and that? Thus agitated, we would like to run around and rush forth. We must then take the reins in hand and say "Take it easy! Not any of this may touch me now. My first morning's hour belongs to the Lord. I will tackle the day's work that He charges me with, and He will give me the power to accomplish it."

So I will go to the altar of God. [Ps 43:4] Here it is not a question of my minute, petty affairs, but of the great offering of reconciliation. I may participate in that, purify myself and be made happy, and lay myself with all my doings and troubles along with the sacrifice on the altar. And when the Lord comes to me then in Holy Communion, then I may ask him, "Lord, what do you want of me?" (St. Teresa) And after quiet dialogue, I will go to that which I see as my next duty.

I will still be joyful when I enter into my day's work after this morning's celebration: my soul will be empty of that which could assail and burden it, but it will be filled with holy joy, courage, and energy.

Because my soul has left itself and entered into the divine life, it has become great and expansive. Love burns in it like a composed flame that the Lord has enkindled, and that urges my soul to render love to inflame love in others: "flammescat igne caritas, accendat ardor proximos." [Let charity be inflamed with fire, and ardor enkindle our neighbors.] And it sees clearly the next part of the path before it; it does not see very far, but it knows that when it has arrived at that place where the horizon now intersects, a new vista will then be opened.

Now begins the day's work, perhaps the teaching profession – four or five hours, one after the other. That means giving our concentration there. We cannot achieve in each hour what we want, perhaps in none. We must contend with our own fatigue, unforeseen interruptions, shortcomings of the children, diverse vexations, indignities, anxieties. Or perhaps it is office work: give and take with disagreeable supervisors and colleagues, unfulfilled demands, unjust reproaches, human meanness, perhaps also distress of the most distinct kind.

It is the noon hour. We come home exhausted, shattered. New vexations possibly await us there. Now where is the soul's morning freshness? The soul would like to seethe and storm again: indignation, chagrin, regret. And there is still so much to do until evening. Should we not go immediately to it? No, not before calm sets in at least for a moment. Each one must know, or get to know, where and how she can find peace. The best way, when it is possible, is to shed all cares again for a short time before the tabernacle. Whoever cannot do that, whoever also possibly requires bodily rest, should take a breathing space in her own room. And when no outer rest whatever is attainable, when there is no place in which to retreat, if pressing duties prohibit a quiet hour, then at least she must for a moment seal off herself inwardly against all other things and take refuge in the Lord. He is indeed there and can give us in a single moment what we need.

Thus the remainder of the day will continue, perhaps in great fatigue and laboriousness, but in peace. And when night comes, and retrospect shows that everything was patchwork and much that one had planned left undone, when so many things rouse shame and regret, then take all as it is, lay it in God's hands, and offer it up to Him. In this way we will be able to rest in Him, actually rest, and begin the new day like a new life.

This is only a small indication how the day could take shape in order to make room for God's grace. Each individual will know best how this can be used in her particular circumstances. It could be further indicated how Sunday must be a great door through that celestial life can enter into everyday life, and strength for the work of the entire week, and how the great feasts, holidays, and penitential times, lived through in the spirit of the Church, permit the soul to mature the more from year to year to the eternal Sabbath rest.

It will be an essential duty of each individual to consider how she must shape her plan for daily and yearly living, according to her bent and to her respective circumstances of life, in order to make ready the way for the Lord. The exterior allotment must be different for each one, and it must also adjust resiliently to the change of circumstances in the course of time. But the psychic situation varies with individuals and with each individual in different times. As to the means that are suitable for bringing about union with the eternal, keeping it alive or also enlivening it anew – such as contemplation, spiritual reading, participation in the liturgy, popular services, etc. – these are not fruitful for each person and at all times. For example, contemplation cannot be practiced by all and always in the same way.

It is important to each case to find out the most efficacious way and to make it useful for oneself. It would be good to listen to expert advice in order to know what one lacks, and this is especially so before one takes on variations from a tested arrangement.[26]

If we meditate upon the road God's mother followed from Candlemas to Good Friday, we shall find roads through her to interior silence.[27]

Now and again criticisms were leveled at her lectures, on the ground that she overstressed the supernatural.[G 10]

> *But if I could not speak about that, I would probably not mount a lecturer's platform at all. Basically, it is always a small, simple truth that I have to express: How to go about living at the Lord's hand. Then when people demand something else from me and propose very clever themes that are very foreign to me, I can take them only as an introduction in order to arrive at my "Ceterum censeo". [All the same my opinion is.] Perhaps that is a very reprehensible method. But my entire activity as lecturer has hit me like an avalanche, so that I have been unable as yet to reflect on it in principle. Most likely, I will have to do that some time.*[28][T 3][29]

12

Lecturer in Münster

This last stay at St. Lioba also meant good-bye to Freiburg.[T 1][1] She had not obtained a university position either there or in Breslau. Early in 1932 she accepted a call to the faculty of the German Institute for Scientific Pedagogy at Münster.[2][T 2] She took up residence in the Collegium Marianum, basing her way of life, as always, on simplicity.[3] Her name went like wildfire through Münster, arousing curiosity particularly among the numerous women students, religious and lay, who lived in the Collegium Marianum. Her appearance at lunch on the first day was awaited with keen anticipation, after it had been indicated that Dr. Stein would take her meals in common with the students, and not alone in her room. When she did arrive, excitement changed to astonishment. A little inconspicuous woman came in, her dress almost exaggeratedly simple, with nothing whatsoever remarkable in her appearance.[G 1] Nevertheless, even this first encounter made a deep impression. We learn this from Dr. Schweitzer, who was then studying in Münster:

> Her very being radiated concentrated energy. Her every act revealed an inner disposition such as one only finds in those people who live a rich spiritual life, molded by intellectual discipline and held in perfect control. The kind and noticeably modest way in which she returned our greeting bore witness to a state of soul where humility and dignity were combined with a humanity that would display itself in some such a characteristic whenever one met her.

Another student writes:

> Edith Stein had a large and beautiful room, provided for her by the Sisters of Notre Dame who were in charge of the Marianum. But the students were none the less

astonished at a lecturer in an academic institution with such modest requirements. By the standards of that time it was extremely unassuming to be content with a single bed-sitting room.[4]

Another tells us:

> My friend Helene (later a Carmelite) and I had our little rooms just facing hers. Until late at night we used to see the light on her desk, that stood by the window. But next day she would be first in the chapel, before any of the nuns, as they themselves told us.[5] She seldom went out of the house, and was hardly ever even in the garden. Her life was all prayer and work. She thought little of her own output.[G 2] Once Johann, the handyman of the house, had made a little rock garden in the courtyard with flowers in bloom. She said "How quickly he has made something so lovely, and how little do we achieve with our work."
>
> Normally we only saw each other at meals. Even at that time she did not eat meat. We used to guess why not – whether it was because of a digestive complaint or out of asceticism – and we never found out.[6] She ate very little altogether, that astonished us, considering the intensity of her intellectual work. She had a wonderfully harmonious character, always gentle, kind, and so unpretentious.

Apparently Edith Stein was, during her short stay in Münster, an object of pious curiosity to the nuns sent from various teaching orders to study there. It was known when she got up and went to bed. "The Fräulein Doktor got up long before wake-up time." "When I put out my light late at night, there still would be a light burning in Edith Stein's room." She was observed at prayer and at work, during recreation and in private conversation:

> In spite of her frail constitution Edith Stein kept a strict fast even though engaged in strenuous intellectual work.

She already practiced monastic asceticism. If she could arrange it so that she could attend three masses in succession, she could be seen throughout them all kneeling reverently upright, never leaning, never sitting. And at every mass she followed every prayer of the priest with the greatest devotion. During the day, too, she would visit the Savior in the Eucharist.

She affectionately devoted her free time to the young students. They loved to listen to her lectures,[7] and willingly accepted the encouragement and advice she gave them for living exemplary Catholic lives. She saw this work for young people as a God-given task, and sacrificed to it her longing to devote herself entirely to God in the religious life. She was always ready to give her time to the student Sisters, too, for answering questions about religion or their academic work.[8] She was an example to us all of sheer, noble humanity and deeply Christian conviction. She understood so charmingly how to hide her enormous knowledge under her equally great, always helpful modesty.

The same student continues:

We liked to be with her. She was interested in all our affairs, our studies, our students' association, and also in the political questions that we were then getting heated over. It was the time when National Socialism was already spreading among students. We organized a student meeting against the A.N.S.T. (Study Group of National Socialist Women Students), at which Helene Weber spoke and some of the National Socialist students behaved very badly. Dr. Stein also came to this meeting and spoke in the discussion. What she had to say was essential, but it had little effect. Her voice was low and almost disappeared in the big hall.[9][G 3]

Her personality had a much stronger effect in a small group. She loved to join in our small parties and celebrations in the house and at the students' association. In the winter of 1932 we had a celebration for St. Nicholas. After a visit by St. Nicholas, played by one of us, we sat down together in our common room in front of a plate and an innocent glass of punch. She had put a small card of the Immaculate Conception from Beuron beside each plate. It was December 8th. We sang Advent songs, and she was just like one of us.

There are one or two other traits that show what she was like. It was summer, and strawberry time. At the midday meal we were talking of our homes, and I was strongly regretting that I could not be at home now, where there were lots of strawberries in the garden. Since students are notoriously short of cash, however, I had to do without such expensive fruit. In the afternoon there was a knock on the door of our room. Unsuspectingly I opened it, and there was Edith Stein with a bowl of strawberries, that she handed to me with a smile, and vanished. Helene and I were really moved as we intently ate the expensive fruit, sitting on the edge of the bed.

Another little incident. At the end of October 1932 there was a rather hard frost. Then the heating system in the Marianum broke down and had to be repaired. It took several days. We shivered with cold in our rooms. Edith Stein sat well wrapped up before her books and worked as usual. We asked her if she were not cold. Frozen blue, but smiling, she said, *"So long as my head doesn't freeze up, it's all right!"*

In the summer of 1933 there were quite a lot of students living at the Marianum, about ten. Among them was one enthusiastic National Socialist, who praised Hitler's *Mein Kampf* at table as the greatest revelation of the world's history. Though Dr. Stein was very restrained in all her dealings with people, a certain antipathy was discernible in her attitude toward this student. Once during a meal the conversation turned on women smoking.

The student in question smoked like a chimney. Edith
Stein made some spiteful remark in this connection,
that I am afraid I have forgotten. She liked a little play-
ful malice, and once said, *"Malice is witty and wit is
malicious."* Later on I was sitting with her, and she
suddenly asked, *"Was what I just said too spiteful?"*
To that I was able to assure her that it had given us
some satisfaction to see that young lady catch it for
once.[G 4]

Edith Stein was often merry and cheerful like a child,
but mostly serious and thoughtful. Especially when the
persecution of the Jews began, she got more and more
grave when she thought of her family.[10] You never heard
her complain, but it was shattering to see her quiet face,
drawn with pain. Already her features showed a glim-
mer of the mystery that was to be expressed in her religious name, "of the Cross." Even today I can hear her
saying, *"All this will be avenged some day,"* and I don't
doubt that she even then saw our poor people's bitter
punishment on its way.[G 5]

It was a comfort to her sister Rosa that Edith was again able to spend
her autumn vacation in Breslau, where they celebrated their mother's
eighty-third[11] birthday:

> *My mother is in good spirits most of the time, but some
> effects of old age can no longer be denied.[12] Things seem
> to be somewhat better for my sister now. She laments a
> good deal over the difficulties of living together with
> relatives whose thinking differs so much from hers (surely
> you can readily understand her feelings). And obviously
> I cannot even think of having her join me at any fore-
> seeable time. As things are now, one has to be glad just
> to have the Institute continue in existence.*
>
> *I have to put up quite a struggle to justify my schol-
> arly existence – not with any of the people, since they
> do all they possibly can to help me – but with the situa-*

tion created by my ten-year exclusion from the continu-
ity of [academic] work and the lack, rooted so deeply
within me, of contact with the contemporary scene. What
is good is that gradually I am establishing rapport with
the faculty members as well as with the [women] stu-
dents. (That it is gradual is my doing, since I am still
unable to devote more time to it.)

Two Catholic student societies and the academic
Conference on Elizabeth had their emissaries visit me
to ask me to visit them. With the first of these I recently
held an evening discussion program on the status of
women – it became very lively. I believe this is a way in
which the female students at the university could be
attracted to audit courses at the Institute (at future lec-
tures). That would be a gain for both sides.[13]

That was how she saw things at the beginning of June; looking
back at the end of August her hopes are confirmed:

For me the final weeks of the [summer] semester were
very fruitful. Above all, I have already won amazingly
good rapport with the women students (not only with
those who attend my lectures but those from the univer-
sity), and also with the Sisters from the Marianum who
are students. I expect that in winter the best part of my
audience will come from these two groups, and so will
no longer consist principally of women teachers and
candidates for school administration.

On 24 and 25 July I attended a very enjoyable con-
vention for young girls in Augsburg. At the leadership
meeting I had to give a talk on "The Task of Woman as
Guide of Youth to the Church."[14]

On 2 September, she set off for a week's visit to her friend Koyré,[15]
"getting to know a bit of Paris and gaining much profit for my study
of Scholasticism."[16] The Société Thomiste had invited her to Juvisy

on 12 September for a conference on "Phenomenology and Thomism."
Also invited, Professor [Bernhard] Rosenmöller writes:

> The idea was to have an exchange of opinions on phenom-
> enology, on the trend in philosophy given by Husserl, first
> when he was at Göttingen, then when he was at Freiburg.
> Noel von Lo[e]wen took the chair. The foremost philos-
> ophers of France, among others Maritain and Berdiaev,
> were there. From Germany there were Father Mager,
> O.S.B., Father Daniel Feuling, O.S.B., [Fritz-Joachim]
> von Rintelen of Munich, Professor Sölingen of Bonn
> who went on to Braunsberg, then later back to Bonn,[17]
> Edith Stein and myself. Father Feuling gave the lecture.
> The discussion was dominated entirely by Edith Stein.
> Certainly she had the best understanding of Husserl, hav-
> ing been for years his assistant in Freiburg, but she de-
> veloped her thoughts with such clarity, in French when
> necessary, that she made an extraordinarily strong impres-
> sion on this learned company of scholars.[18]

One of those taking part in the congress, Father Daniel Feuling,[19]
recalls Edith Stein well in his recollections of this meeting:

> Life has twice brought me into contact with Sr. Benedicta.
> The first was a remarkable meeting. I came back one
> Monday morning from the Schwarzwald [Black Forest],
> where I had been discussing my forthcoming lecture
> on phenomenology with Professor Martin Heidegger.
> We had talked of Edith Stein, whom I did not yet know
> personally, though her name was well known to me. I
> was having considerable linguistic difficulties over my
> lecture. Both Husserl, the founder of phenomenology
> and formerly Edith Stein's master, and more precisely
> Heidegger, wrote in a highly individual idiom, and it
> was not easy to render the German expressions intelli-
> gibly in French. When I spoke about this to Heidegger
> he told me that the Russian Professor Koyré, who had

been one of Husserl's assistants along with Heidegger and Edith Stein, had edited some of his (Heidegger's) works in French.

As Heidegger did not have these books with him in the mountains, he suggested I might go to see Koyré in Paris, and acquaint myself with his translation work. But I did not know how I was going to do this, since I was not going to stay in Paris, but some distance away, with the Dominicans at Juvisy, where the congress was to be held. With this problem in my mind I came back to Neuberg Abbey.

That Monday afternoon I had something to do at the monastery gate. While I was there the brother doorkeeper handed me a visiting card. He thought it was something special that might concern me. To my surprise, I read "Dr. Edith Stein." Of course, I asked at once "Is she here? I must speak to her!" She was; and she had come out from Heidelberg with her friend Dr. Hedwig Conrad-Martius to see a friend, Father Peter Jans. Dr. Hedwig Conrad-Martius had been ill in Heidelberg, and Edith Stein had come to visit her. We were all delighted, for, as a philosopher in Glasgow once said to me, "Philosophers are all brethren." And we talked for a good while on matters of common interest. I soon asked whether she knew where in Paris I could find Koyré, and repeated what Heidegger had told me about his translations. To that Edith Stein replied, "I am going to Paris on Wednesday to stay with Professor Koyré." And she promised to bring the things out to Juvisy. I traveled on Saturday to Paris and covered the extra twenty-four miles beyond the city to Juvisy. That afternoon, as I was crossing the great courtyard of the Dominican Priory, I saw a lady coming toward me. It was Edith Stein who had come out by train to bring me what I wanted. On Sunday I was able to compare my translations with Koyré's.

On Monday, the day of the congress, I met and talked to Edith Stein again. Koyré had come with her. On Tues-

day afternoon I went out to have a philosophical discussion with them both. We sat together for hours. Then
Koyré took us up to the [basilica of] Sacré Coeur, Mont-
martre, where we prayed for a time. On the way the two
of them spoke together of various things, especially of
Jewish philosophers – Husserl, too, had Jewish blood in
him, as did Henri Bergson and Meyerson in Paris. "He
is another of ours" was the constantly recurring phrase.
It amused me a little to hear the way Koyré and Edith
Stein, speaking of Jews and Jewish matters, would say
simply "we." I had a vivid impression of that blood-
brotherhood that was so strong in Edith, as formerly in
St. Paul, who spoke with such pride and emphasis his,
Hebraei sunt – et ego. ["They are Jews, I am too."] Then
I was a little naughty, and asked on a serious tone, "And
where are you placing *me*?" They looked at me in great
concern, and asked "Are you one of us, too?" until I
assured them otherwise.

Toward evening Professor Koyré took us to another
part of Paris to see the earlier mentioned philosopher
Meyerson. There we had more discussions over our cups
of tea. Edith Stein had to bear the brunt of this hour's
talk and give the answers; I was so exhausted by the strain
of all this discussion that by this time in the evening I
couldn't put my thoughts together any more. Later still
that night we had a meal together. Then we parted, and
I went back, late, to Juvisy.

[T 3][20] In October 1932 she traveled from Münster to Aachen:

The Educational Council of the Catholic Women's Soci-
ety had a public discussion on "The Spiritual Charac-
ter of the Young Generation," with its keynote address a
lecture by Prof. Aloys Dempf, from Bonn, on Saturday
evening. He's a superb person, an Upper Bavarian,
blunt, and thoroughly honest.[21] He himself was in the
first wave of the Youth Movement before the war, and
belonged with Professor Platz of Bonn and with Brüning

*to the first Liturgical Circle in Germany. All this con-
tributed to making things very lively.*

*Of the leading women of the Rhineland who were pres-
ent, there are, of course, many known to me from earlier
events. With some others I have strong bonds merely through
common interests, not through close personal relationships. One of these, above all, is Annie Bender. . .*[22] *A
friendly relationship has now been established with several others who showed me such strong opposition that
time in Bendorf,*[23] *although the differences of opinion keep
turning up repeatedly in such discussions. They are after
all persons with very serious intentions who invest their
entire personalities in their positions, and one has to respect that. Besides, I understand very well now how much,
at that time, I must have displeased people who live very
much in the midst of things. For I notice only now since
I, too, am in that situation, how far I stand outside the
world, how completely estranged from it I have become,
and what a struggle it is for me to get back into the
stream. I doubt that I shall ever succeed entirely.*[24]

Did her audiences also appreciate how much it cost her to "stand
outside," as she expresses it? Let us listen to the words of one member of the audience:

In my last term at Münster I attended Edith Stein's lectures on "The Structure of the Human Person" at the
German Institute for Scientific Pedagogy.[25] My recollection of her is still fresh in my mind, for I was deeply
impressed by her simplicity and modesty. She spoke
slowly and calmly, without gestures but with great clarity and intensity. She was said to be "among the faculty,
the most uncompromising representative of the Catholic point of view," and everyone who heard her endorsed
this judgment. Frequently I came across her in the chapel
of the Marianum sunk deep in prayer. It was a moving
experience to see her there, so completely absorbed in
God that nothing could disturb or distract her. But when

one went to have a word with her she was unassuming
and always ready to help in an unobtrusive manner.

Again, one of her colleagues who met Edith rather more frequently
because she had charge of the Institute library, writes:

> She stood head and shoulders above the other tutors on
> account of her incisive thought, her broad culture, her
> masterly exposition and her self-assurance or steadi-
> ness of bearing; in fact, to compare her with all the rest
> of us who were employed there one would have to use
> some entirely different standard of measurement. Even
> at that time her essential saintliness displayed itself. I
> am quite convinced that she was fully aware of her
> neighbors' many human weaknesses, yet she never ac-
> cused anyone, but went so steadily and graciously along
> her way that we, with our worldly notions, often did not
> understand her modesty.

Nor was it only her humility that struck one – her love of poverty
and of the poor also was enough to astonish anyone who had taken a
vow of poverty. One Sister from the Marianum writes:

> It was during the very cold winter of 1932-33. One day
> we were discussing the poverty-stricken condition of some
> of the residents in a certain hamlet I knew, who still con-
> tinued to go regularly to mass despite the church being
> so distant and the weather so bitter. Not long afterwards
> Fräulein Stein came up to me, her arms full of warm
> clothing and undergarments, and asked me to send them
> to the needy folk of the hamlet. When I suggested that
> she should think a little about protecting herself from
> the cold, she replied that she could easily spare these
> things, and that I should send them on, which I did.

With good deeds and charity Edith Stein prepared especially carefully for Christmas during this Advent. In response to an invitation

from the Reverend Mother of the Ursulines in Dorsten, whom she profoundly admired, she kept the feast in the silence of their convent.[26] Mother Petra [Brüning] tells us:

> On Christmas Eve she joined with us in singing matins; then we went to rest for a few hours until midnight. When I returned to the church I found her kneeling motionless in the same position as we had left her; she then attended mass and sang the office of lauds with us. When I asked her later whether she had not been weary, her eyes lit up and she replied: *"How could this night make one weary?"*

In the course of the following months the National Socialists strengthened their hold over the German people and began to show their hand. Even Edith Stein was affected by the laws excluding non-Aryans from public office. She was abruptly suspended from teaching at the very moment when she was preparing an extensive reform of higher grade teaching that had been most promising. Although the Berlin authorities had cooperated with her in these plans, they were abandoned when she was suspended. Though full of sorrow at the suffering that was being imposed on her Jewish brethren she accepted her own fate with complete composure.[G 6] Her work as an instructor in the German Institute of Scientific Pedagogy at Münster came to an end on 25 February 1933, the day she gave her last lecture.[27]

13

The Road to Carmel[1]

How I Came to the Cologne Carmel
(Fourth Sunday in Advent, 18 December 1938)[G 1]

*P*erhaps I shall leave this house soon after Christmas. The circumstances that have forced us to initiate my transfer to Echt (Holland) are strikingly reminiscent of the situation at the time of my entrance into Carmel. It is likely that there is a subtle connection between the two.

When the Third Reich was established early in the year 1933, I had been an instructor at the German Institute for Scientific Pedagogy in Münster, Westphalia for about a year. I lived in the "Collegium Marianum" amidst a large number of nuns who were students and who belonged to the most diverse orders as well as a small group of other women students, lovingly taken care of by the Sisters of Notre Dame.

One evening during the vacation I returned late from a meeting of the Katholische Akademikerverband [Society of Catholic Academics]. I don't know whether I had forgotten to take my house key or whether there was a key stuck in the lock from the inside. At any rate, I could not get in. I tried to lure someone to the window by ringing the bell and clapping hands, but in vain. The women students who lived in the rooms facing the street were already away on vacation. A passerby asked whether he could help me. When I turned to him, he bowed deeply and said, "Dr. Stein, I didn't recognize you." He was a Catholic teacher who was a participant in a workshop sponsored by the Institute. He excused himself for a moment to tell his wife, who had gone ahead with another lady. He exchanged a few words with her and then returned to me. "My wife would like to invite you to spend the night at our house."

That was a good solution, and I accepted gratefully. They took me to a simple house typical for a Münster middle class dwelling. We sat down in the living room. The amiable lady of the house put a bowl of fruit on the table and left in order to prepare a room for me. The man began a conversation in which he related what American newspapers had reported concerning cruelties to which Jews had been subjected. They were unconfirmed reports; and so I do not wish to repeat them. I am only interested in the impression I got that evening. True, I had heard of rigorous measures against the Jews before. But now it dawned on me that once again God had put a heavy hand upon His people, and that the fate of this people would also be mine. I did not allow the man who sat opposite me to notice what was going on inside of me. Apparently he did not know about my Jewish descent. In similar cases, I would usually enlighten the others immediately. This time I did not do it. It would have seemed to me like a breach of their hospitality if I had disturbed their night's rest by such a revelation.

On Thursday of Passion Week, I traveled to Beuron. Since 1928 I had spent that week and the Easter holiday there each year, and had quietly held my own private retreat. This time a special reason drew me there. During the past weeks I had constantly given thought to whether I could do something about the plight of the Jews. Finally I had made a plan to travel to Rome and to ask the Holy Father in a private audience for an encyclical. But I did not want to take such a step on my own. Years ago, I had taken private vows. Since I had found a kind of monastic home in Beuron, I was permitted to regard Archabbot Raphael[2] as "my abbot" and to put before him all important problems for his judgment. It was not certain, however, that I would find him there. In early January he had gone on a trip to Japan. But I knew that he would do his utmost to be at home during Passion Week. [G 2]

Although it suited my nature to make such an overt move, I sensed that this was not yet "of the essence." But I did not yet know what this "essence" really was. I interrupted my travels in Cologne from Thursday afternoon until Friday morning. I was instructing a catechumen there, and had to devote some time to her at every possible opportunity. I wrote and asked her to find out where we could attend the Holy Hour in the evening. It was the eve of the First Friday in April, and in this Holy Year 1933[3] the memory of the passion of Our Lord was being observed with particular solemnity everywhere. At eight o'clock in the evening, we arrived for the Holy Hour at the Cologne-Lindental[4] Carmel. A priest (it was Father Wüsten,[5] Vicar at the Cathedral, as I learned later) gave a sermon and announced that from then on this worship service would be held there every Thursday. He spoke beautifully and movingly, but something other than his words occupied me more intensely. I talked with the Savior and told Him that I knew that it was His Cross that was now being placed upon the Jewish people; that most of them did not understand this; but that those who did, would have to take it up willingly in the name of all. I would do that. He should only show me how. At the end of the service, I was certain that I had been heard. But what this carrying of the Cross was to consist in, that I did not yet know.

Next morning I continued my trip to Beuron. When I changed trains that evening in Immendingen, I met Father Aloys Mager.[6] We spent the last part of the trip together. [G 3] Soon after we said hello, he reported, as Beuron's most important news item: Father Archabbot had returned from Japan that very morning in good health. So that, too, was in order.

Through my inquiries in Rome I ascertained that, because of the tremendous crowds I would have no chance for a private audience. At best I might be admitted to a "semiprivate audience," i.e., an audience in a small group. That did not serve my purpose. I abandoned my travel plans and instead presented my request in writing. [G 4] I know that my letter was delivered to the Holy Father[7] unopened;[8] some time thereafter I received his blessing for myself and for my relatives. Nothing else happened. Later on I often wondered whether this letter might have come to his mind once in a while. For in the years that followed, that which I had predicted for the future of the Catholics in Germany came true step by step.

Prior to my departure I asked Father Archabbot what I should do if I had to give up my work in Münster. He found it totally unbelievable that that could happen. On my return trip to Münster I read a newspaper article about a big National Socialist teacher's meeting in which the religious teachers' organizations were also forced to participate. It became clear to me that in the field of education one would least tolerate influences that were contrary to the ruling policy. The institute in which I worked was purely Catholic, co-founded and supported by the Catholic Teachers' Organization. Thus its days were probably numbered. All the more I would have to reckon with the termination of my short career as a college instructor. On 19 April I returned to Münster; next day I went to the institute. The director was on a vacation trip in Greece. The administrator, a Catholic teacher, took me into his office and told me his troubles. For weeks he had been involved in upsetting negotiations; he was totally worn out.

"Imagine, Doctor Stein, somebody even came and said, 'Dr. Stein isn't going to continue teaching, is she?'"

He considered it best if I would refrain from scheduling any lectures for this summer and just do some quiet research in the Marianum.[9] By autumn the situation would settle down, perhaps the Church would take over the institute. In that case nothing would prevent me from resuming my activities. I accepted this information very calmly. I attached no importance to the hopes he held out.

"If I can't go on here," I said, "then there's no possibility for me in Germany any more." The administrator expressed his admiration for me for seeing things so clearly, even though I lived as a recluse and paid no attention to worldly matters.

I felt almost relieved that I was now caught up in the common fate. I had to decide, however, what I should now do with myself. I consulted the opinion of the chairwoman of the Catholic Teachers' Organization.[10] It was at her suggestion that I had come to Münster. She advised me to spend at least the summer in Münster and to continue working on a research paper I had started. The Organization would pay my subsistence, because the results of my research would be useful to them. If it should be impossible to resume my work at the Institute, I could, later on, look into opportunities abroad. Very soon thereafter, I did in fact receive an offer from South America.[11] But by that time, a very different path had been revealed to me.

About ten days after my return from Beuron, the idea occurred to me: Might not now the time be ripe to enter Carmel? For almost twelve years, Carmel had been my goal; since summer 1921 when the "Life" of our Holy Mother Teresa had happened to fall into my hands and had put an end to my long search for the true faith. When on New Year's Day 1922, I received the Sacrament of Baptism, I thought that this was merely the preparation for entering the Order. But a few months later, when for the first time since my baptism I stood face to face with my dear mother, it became clear to me that she would not be able to withstand this second blow for the time being. She would not die of it, but it would fill her with such bitterness that I could not take the responsibility for that. I would have to wait patiently. My spiritual counselors assured me of this over and over. Lately this waiting had become very hard for me. I had become a stranger in the outside world. Before I began my job in Münster and after the first semester I had urgently pleaded for permission to enter the Order. It was denied me[12] with reference to my mother and because of the effectiveness that my work had had in Catholic circles in recent years. I had yielded. But now the walls that had stood in my way had crumbled.[13] My effectiveness was at an end. And surely my mother would prefer me to be in a convent in Germany rather than a school in South America. [G 5] On 30 April – it was the Sunday of the Good Shepherd – the Feast of St. Ludger was observed in St. Ludger's Church with thirteen hours of prayer. I went there late in the afternoon,[14] and said to myself: "I'm not leaving here until I have a clear-cut assurance whether I may now enter Carmel." After the concluding blessing had been pronounced, I had the assurance of the Good Shepherd.

That very evening I wrote to Father Archabbot. But he was in Rome, and I did not want to send the letter out of the country. It had to wait in my desk drawer until I could send it to Beuron. It got to be the middle of May until I received permission to take the preliminary steps in preparation. I did this immediately. Through my catechumen in Cologne[15] I asked Dr. Cosack[16] for an appointment to talk to her. We had met in Aachen in October 1932. She had introduced herself to me because she knew that I felt an inner bond with Carmel, and she had told me that she had close ties to the Carmelite Order, and especially to the Cologne Carmel. I planned to get information from her concerning the possibilities there. She sent word that the following Sunday (it was Rogation Sunday) or on Ascension Day she could give me some time. Saturday, I received the news in the morning mail.[17] At noon I traveled to Cologne. I telephoned Dr. Cosack, and we agreed that she would pick me up for a walk the following morning.

So far neither she nor my catechumen knew for what purpose I had come. The latter accompanied me to the Carmel for the early morning mass. On the way back, she said to me: "Edith, while I knelt next to you, the thought occurred to me: 'She wouldn't be thinking of entering Carmel now, would she?'" At that point I did not want to keep my secret from her any longer. She promised to keep it confidential. A little bit later, Dr. Cosack appeared. As soon as we had turned toward the Stadtwald, I told her what I had in mind. I immediately added what might be held against me: My age (42), my Jewish descent, my lack of means. She did not consider any of it important. She even held out hopes that I might be accepted here in Cologne, because, due to the founding of a new Carmel in Silesia, vacancies would occur. A new Carmel outside the gates of my hometown Breslau – was that not a sign from heaven?

I told Frau Dr. Cosack enough about my background for her to form an opinion about my vocation as a Carmelite. She then proposed on her own that we should pay a visit to the Carmel. She was especially close to Sr. Marianne (Countess Praschma),[18] who was to go to Silesia to found the new convent. She would first talk to her.

*While she was in the parlor, I knelt in the chapel, close to the altar of
little St. Thérèse. I experienced the serenity of someone who has reached
her goal. The talk took a long time. When Miss Cosack finally called me,
she said confidently "I believe something will come of it." She had talked
with Sr. Marianne, then with Mother Prioress (at that time M. Josepha of
the Blessed Sacrament), and had paved the way for me well. But now the
monastic schedule did not allow any more time for the parlor. I was told
to return after vespers. Long before vespers, I was back in the chapel and
participated in the Vesper prayer; after that, May devotions were held
behind the choir grille. It was about 3:30 when I was finally called into
the parlor. Mother Josepha and our dear Mother (Teresia Renata de
Spiritu Sancto,[19] then sub-prioress and novice-mistress) were at the grille.*

*[G 6] I explained once more by what road I had reached this point, how
the thought of Carmel had never left me; I spent eight years as a teacher
with the Dominican nuns in Speyer, was intimately connected with the
entire convent, and yet was unable to enter; I considered Beuron the
antechamber of heaven, yet it had never entered my mind to become a
Benedictine nun; it always seemed to me that the Lord was saving something for me in Carmel that I could find there and nowhere else.*

*That made an impression. Mother Teresia had only one hesitation:
Could she take responsibility for removing someone from the outside
world who could yet accomplish much there?[20] I finally was told to
come back when Father Provincial was there. They expected him soon.*

*That evening I returned to Münster. I had accomplished more than
I had expected when I arrived in Cologne. But Father Provincial kept
me waiting a long time. During Pentecost I spent most of my time in
the Cathedral in Münster. Encouraged by the Holy Spirit, I wrote to
Mother Josepha and pleaded urgently for a prompt answer, because
in my uncertain situation I had to find out what exactly I had to reckon
with. In reply I got an appointment in Cologne. The Vicar for Religious would see me. They (the nuns) no longer wanted to wait for
Father Provincial. This time I was to meet the Chapter nuns who would
vote on my admission.*

Again I went to Cologne from Saturday afternoon until Sunday night. (I believe it was 18-19 June.) I talked to Mother Josepha, Mother Teresia and Sr. Marianne before my visit to Monsignor, and had the opportunity to introduce my friend. On the way to Dr. Lenné I was caught in a thunderstorm and arrived totally soaked. I had to wait an hour before he appeared. After greeting me, he passed his hand over his forehead and said,

"What was that again that you have come to see me about? I have completely forgotten."

I replied that I was applying for admission to Carmel and that I had an appointment with him. Now he knew and stopped addressing me with the familiar "Du." I realized later that he had been testing me. I had swallowed it without flinching. He made me repeat everything he already knew, told me what objections he wanted to raise against me, but comforted me with the assurance that the Sisters rarely let his objections deter them and that he usually struck a friendly compromise with them. He then dismissed me with his blessing.

This time, after vespers, all the Chapter nuns approached the grille. Tiny Sister Teresia, the community's oldest member, came very close to the grille so as to be able to see and hear clearly. Sister Aloysia, a liturgy enthusiast, wanted to hear all about Beuron. On that score I could oblige her. Finally I had to sing a song. I had been warned about that the day before, but I had assumed it was a joke. I sang "Segne, Du Maria," [Bless us, Mary] a bit shyly and softly. Afterwards I said that that had been more difficult for me than addressing a thousand people. As I was to find out later, the Sisters didn't understand that reference, because they did not yet know anything about my activities as a lecturer. After the Sisters had withdrawn, Mother Josepha told me that the vote could not take place until next morning. Thus I had to leave that night without knowing.

Sr. Marianne, to whom I talked privately at the end, promised to notify me by telegram. And indeed, the next day, the telegram arrived. "Joyful assent. Regards, Carmel." I read it and went into the chapel to give thanks.

We had already made plans. By 15 July I wanted to wind up everything in Münster, and on the 16th I planned to take part in celebrating the Feast of the Queen of Carmel (with the Sisters in Cologne). After that I was to live for one month as a guest in the extern quarters. In mid-August I would travel home on a round trip ticket and be admitted into the enclosure on 15 October for the Feast of our Holy Mother. Beyond that it was planned to transfer me later to the Silesian Carmel.

Six large cartons of books traveled to Cologne ahead of me. I had written to them that it was not likely that any other Carmelite had brought such a dowry with her! Sister Ursula took them under her care, and took great pains to keep theology, philosophy, philology, etc., apart. (This was the way the boxes were labeled). But in the end, everything got mixed up.

Few people in Münster knew where I was going. I wanted to keep it as secret as possible as long as my family was not informed. Among the few who knew was the Mother Superior of the Marianum. I had confided in her as soon as the telegram came. She had worried about me a great deal and was very glad now. Shortly before my departure, a farewell gathering was held in the music room of the house. The lay students – all women – had prepared it with much affection, and the nuns took part as well. I thanked them briefly and told them that later, when they would find out where I had gone, they would rejoice with me. The Sisters of the Order gave me a cross, a relic that the late Bishop Johannes von Poggenburg[21] had given them. Sr. Prioress brought it to me on a paten, covered with roses. [G 7]

Five students and the librarian of the institute accompanied me to the train station. I was able to take huge bouquets of roses along for the Feast of the Queen of Carmel. Less than eighteen months earlier, I had gone to Münster a stranger. Aside from my professional activities, I had lived in monastic seclusion. Nevertheless I now left a large circle of people who were bound to me in love and loyalty. I have always held the beautiful old town and the Münster countryside in fond and grateful memory.

To my family I had only written that I had found a place to stay in Cologne with a group of nuns and would move there for good in October. They wished me good luck as one would for a new job.[22]

The month in the extern quarters was a very happy time. I took part in the entire daily routine, worked during the hours outside of prayers, and was allowed into the parlor now and then. All questions that came up I submitted to Mother Josepha; her decisions always coincided with what I would have done on my own. This inner agreement made me very happy.

My catechumen came to see me often. She wanted to be baptized before my departure, so that I could be her godmother. On 1 August, Prelate Lenné baptized her in the Cathedral Chapter Room, and the following morning she received her First Holy Communion in the convent chapel. Her husband was present at both celebrations, but he could not make up his mind to follow her example. On 10 August, I met Father Archabbot in Trier and received his blessing for the difficult journey to Breslau. I contemplated the Holy Robe (of Trier) [G 8], and prayed for strength. I also knelt for a long time at the shrine in St. Matthias Church, where many favors had been granted. That night I found hospitality at Cordel,[23] *where our dear Mother Teresia Renata had been Mistress of Novices for nine years, until she was called back to Cologne as subprioress. On 14 August, my godchild and I went to Maria Laach for the Feast of Our Lady's Assumption. From there I continued on to Breslau.*

At the train station, my sister Rosa was waiting for me. Since she had felt herself a part of the Church for a long time and was in full agreement with me, I told her right away what my plans were. She showed no surprise, and yet I noticed that not even she had had an inkling of it. The others asked no questions at all for about two or three weeks. Only my nephew Wolfgang (then twenty-one years old) inquired immediately, as soon as he came to welcome me, what I was going to do in Cologne. I answered him honestly but asked him to keep it confidential for now.

*My mother suffered greatly under the political conditions. She
became upset again and again over the fact that "there are such wicked
people in the world." Added to that there was a personal loss that
affected her badly. My sister Erna was to take over the medical practice of our friend Lilli Berg, who was going to Palestine with her family. The Bibersteins[24] had to move into the Bergs' apartment in the south
of the city and leave our house. Erna and her two children were a
comfort and joy to my mother. Having to miss her daily contact with
them was very bitter for her.[G 9] But despite all these depressing
concerns, she revived when I came. Her cheerfulness and her humor
came through once again.*

*When she got home from work, she liked to sit down next to my
desk with her knitting and to talk about all her domestic and business
worries. I also let her tell me again her reminiscences of the past, as a
foundation for a family history that I started at that time. This cozy
togetherness was really good for her.[25] As for me, I kept thinking: If
only you knew!*

*It was a great comfort to me that at that time Sr. Marianne was in
Breslau with her cousin, Sister Elisabeth,[26] in order to prepare for the
founding of the new convent. They had left Cologne for Breslau prior to
me. Sr. Marianne had visited my mother and brought her my regards.
During my stay in Breslau she came to our house twice more and became quite friendly with my mother. When I visited her at the Ursuline
convent on Ritterplatz where she lived, I could speak freely and vent my
true feelings. On the other hand, I was told about all the joys and troubles
of the founding of the convent, and once I was allowed to accompany the
two Sisters to the construction site in Pawelwitz (later Wendelborn).*

*I helped Erna a lot with the move. During a trolley ride to their
new apartment, she finally put the question about the situation in Cologne. When I answered, she grew pale, and there were tears in her
eyes. "How dreadful life is!" she said. "What makes one person happy
is for another the worst blow imaginable."*

She did not try to dissuade me. A few days later she told me on behalf of her husband that, if worry about my livelihood were a contributing factor in my decision, then I should know that I could live with them as long as they still had anything. (My brother-in-law in Hamburg had said the same thing.) Erna added that she was obliged to give me this message, even though she knew very well that such reasons would carry no weight with me.

On the first Sunday in September, my mother and I were alone in the house. She was sitting at the window knitting a sock. I sat close by. All of a sudden came the long-expected question: "What will you do with the Sisters in Cologne?" "Live with them." Now there followed a desperate denial. My mother never stopped knitting. Her yarn became tangled; with trembling hands she sought to unravel it, and I helped her as our discussion continued.

From now on all tranquillity had vanished. A cloud lay upon the entire household. From time to time, my mother attempted a new assault. Quiet desperation would follow. My niece Erika, the most observant Jew in the family, felt an obligation to influence me. My brothers and sisters did not try, since they considered it useless. It got even worse when my sister Else arrived from Hamburg for Mother's birthday. While my mother usually controlled her emotions firmly when she was with me, she got very upset in talking to Else. My sister related to me all these outbursts, because she thought that I was unaware of how my mother felt.

Aside from this, the family experienced severe economic problems. The business had been doing very badly for some time. Now, too, that half of the house, that the Bibersteins had inhabited, stood empty. People came to look at it every day, but no deal was ever concluded. Among the most eager aspirants was a Protestant congregation. One day when, once again, two of their clergymen appeared, my mother asked me to go with them into the empty apartment; she was already sick of it.

*I managed to get to the point at which we formulated all condi-
tions. I reported back to my mother and in her behalf wrote to the
head pastor,[27] asking him for his written assent. Indeed it was given.
Nevertheless the entire affair threatened to come undone shortly before my departure. I wanted to take at least this worry off my mother's
shoulders and therefore called upon the clergyman in his place of
residence. It seemed hopeless, but when I turned to go, he said, "Now,
you look so sad. I'm sorry."*

*I told him that my mother had so many worries at this time. He
asked me compassionately, what kind of worries these were. I spoke
briefly about my conversion and my monastic plans. That made a big
impression.*

*"I want you to know before you go there, that you have won a sympa-
thetic heart here." He called his wife, and after some deliberations they
decided to call another board meeting and to bring the matter up once
more. And before my departure, the head pastor came to our house with
his colleague to conclude the deal. In parting he whispered to me,
"God bless you."*

*Sr. Marianne had another private talk with my mother. It accom-
plished little. Sr. Marianne was not willing to try to deter me (as my
mother hoped). And any other consolation was unacceptable. Of course
(while they refused to dissuade me) the two Sisters would not have
presumed to reinforce my decision further by their encouragement.
The decision was so difficult that no one could tell me with certainty
which was the right path. Good reasons could be cited for both alter-
natives. I had to take that step in the complete darkness of faith. During those weeks I often thought: Which of us two will break down, my
mother or I? But both of us managed to persevere to the last day.*

*Shortly before my departure I had a dental checkup. While I sat in the
dentist's waiting room, the door opened and my niece Susel entered.
She blushed with pleasure. Unbeknownst to us, both our appointments
had been made for the same time.*

*We both went into the office, and afterward she accompanied me
home. She hung on my arm and I took the child's brown hand in mine.
Susel was twelve years old at that time, but mature and thoughtful
beyond her years. I had never been permitted to talk to the children
about my conversion, but by now Erna had told them everything; for
this I was grateful.*

*I asked the child to visit Grandmother often after I was gone. She
promised to do so.*

"Why are you doing this now?" she asked.

*I understood very clearly what kind of parental discussions she
had witnessed. I gave her my reasons as if she were an adult. She
listened thoughtfully and understood.*[28]

*Two days before my departure, her father (Hans Biberstein) came
to see me. He felt obliged to state his objections, even though he saw
no hope for success. What I was planning appeared to him to draw the
line between myself and the Jewish people more sharply than before,
and that just now when they were so sorely oppressed. The fact that I
saw it very differently, he could not understand.*

*My last day at home was 12 October, my birthday. It coincided with a
Jewish holiday, the end of the Feast of Tabernacles. My mother attended
services in the synagogue of the Rabbinical Seminary. I accompanied
her, because we wanted to spend as much of this day together as possible. Erika's favorite teacher, an eminent scholar,*[29] *gave a beautiful sermon. On the way there on the trolley we had not talked very much. In
order to comfort her a little, I had said that at first there would be a
probationary period. But that was no help. "If you take on a probationary period, I know that you will pass." Now my mother asked to walk
home, a distance of about forty-five minutes, and this at eighty-four years
of age! But I had to consent, for I knew well that she wanted to talk with
me undisturbed a little longer.*

"Wasn't it a beautiful sermon?"

"Yes, it was."

"It's possible then to be devout as a Jew also?"

"Certainly, if one has not come to know anything else."

Now she replied, sounding desperate: "Why did you have to come to know it? I don't want to say anything against him. He may have been a very good man. But why did he make himself into God?"

After lunch she went to the office, so that my sister Frieda would not be left alone during my brother's lunch time. But she told me she would come back soon, and she did (solely for my sake; on other days she still spent all day at work).

Many visitors came that afternoon and evening; all the brothers and sisters, their children, my women friends. That was good, because it was distracting. But as one after another said good-bye and left, it became difficult. Finally my mother and I were left alone in the room. My sisters were still busy with dishwashing and cleanup. Then she covered her face with her hands and began to weep. I stood behind her chair and held her silvery head to my breast. Thus we remained for a long while, until she let me persuade her to go to bed. I took her upstairs and helped her to undress, for the first time in my life. Then I sat on the edge of her bed till she herself sent me to bed. . . I don't think either of us found any rest that night.

My train was due to leave at about 8 a.m. Else and Rosa wanted to accompany me to the station. Erna had also wanted to come, but I begged her to come to the house early instead and stay with my mother. I knew that she would best be able to calm her. We two youngest ones had always retained our childish tenderness toward Mother. The older siblings were embarrassed by it, even though they surely did not love her any less. At half past five I left the house as usual to attend early mass at St. Michael's Church. Afterwards we gathered around the breakfast table. Erna arrived about seven o'clock. My mother tried to eat something, but soon she pushed her cup aside and began to cry as on the previous night.

I returned to her and put my arms around her until it was time to go. I motioned to Erna to take my place. I put on hat and coat next door; then came the good-bye. My mother embraced and kissed me warmly. Erika thanked me for all my help (I had helped her prepare for her exam as a middle school teacher; as I was packing, she still kept coming to me with questions). In the end she added, "May the Eternal be with you." When I embraced Erna, my mother wept aloud. I left quickly; Rosa and Else followed. When the trolley on which we were riding passed our house, there was no one at the window as on other occasions to wave a last farewell.

At the station we had to wait a short while for the train to arrive. Else clung to me. After I had saved a seat for myself, I went to the window and looked down at my sisters. I was struck by the difference in the two faces. Rosa was so serene as if she were going along into the tranquillity of the convent. Else on the other hand, in her grief suddenly resembled an old woman.

Finally the train began to move. Both waved as long as we could get even a glimpse of each other. At last they left. I could now withdraw to my seat in the compartment. So what I had scarcely yet hoped for would now become reality. I could not feel any wild joy. The scene I had just left behind was too terrible for that. But I felt a deep peace, in the harbor of the divine will.

I arrived in Cologne late at night. My godchild had asked me to spend one more night at their house. I was not supposed to be received within the enclosure until the next day after vespers.

In the morning I announced my arrival by telephone at the convent and was permitted to come to the grille for a welcome. Soon after lunch we were back again to attend vespers in the chapel; first vespers of the Feast of our Holy Mother. Earlier, while kneeling in the sanctuary, I heard someone whisper at the sacristy turn, "Is Edith outside?"

Then a bunch of big white chrysanthemums was delivered to me. Teachers from the Palatinate had sent them in welcome. I was supposed to see the flowers before they were used to decorate the altar.

After vespers we were asked to have coffee. Then a lady arrived, who introduced herself as the sister of our dear Mother Teresia Renata.

She asked which one of us was the postulant; she wanted to offer some encouragement. But there was no need of that. This sponsor and my god-child accompanied me to the door of the enclosure. At last it opened, and in deep peace I crossed the threshold into the House of the Lord.

Stein Family Montage including
Father, Siegfried Stein (d. 1893)

Mother Auguste Stein and Susanne Biberstein

Edith Stein in 1921

Lecturer in Vienna

Fräulein Doktor

Sr. Teresa Renata Posselt
Prioress of Edith Stein

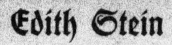

Edith Stein

Schwester Teresia Benedicta a cruce · Philosophin und Karmelitin · Ein Lebensbild, gewonnen aus Erinnerungen und Briefen durch Schwester Teresia Renata de Spiritu Sancto

In Dankbarkeit gewidmet
Schw. Teresia Renata,
Priorin

Köln, 30. I. 1949

BEI GLOCK UND LUTZ IN NÜRNBERG

First German edition, gift copy sent by
Teresa Renata Posselt to Erna Stein Biberstein

Rosa Stein and Sr. Teresa Benedicta at Echt monastery

Biberstein and Batzdorff Families in U.S. (Autumn 1944)

Back row, l. to r.: Dr. Erwin Batzdorff, Ersnst Ludwig Biberstein
(U.S. Army uniform), Ulrich Batzdorff, Susanne Batzdorff, Alfred Batzdorff
(U.S. Navy uniform) Front row, l. to r.: Lotte Batzdorff,
Dr. Erna Stein Biberstein, Dr. Hans Biberstein

Part 2
". . .in the harbor of the divine will."

14

The School of Humility

*"It always seemed to me that our Lord was keeping something for
me in Carmel that I could find only there."*

In these words[1] this outstanding philosopher and famous lecturer,
already revered as a saint by many people, acknowledged that something was lacking before she could be completely happy and fulfilled.
We ask ourselves: What could this be? And what is this Carmel from
which she expected this final fulfillment that the Lord had saved up
for her as the best?

Carmel presents a mystery that cannot be taken in at a glance. Even
those intimately acquainted, like Edith, with Carmelite spirituality
through reading the works of its great exponents can scarcely avoid
shrinking when for the first time they begin to breathe the dry air of
Carmel. They soon have a sense that they have been set in a trackless
desert, a waterless land that only slowly surrenders its secrets.

Carmel is circumscribed by two words: the Nothing and the All.[G 1]
They are the eternal poles around which the Carmelite world revolves.
The hidden force of this paradox startles outsiders when they encounter
it for the first time; they react like a person suddenly seeing an abyss on
either side of him. Yet, for those called to it, Carmel's "Nothing" is not an
empty concept and the "All" is for them a sacred name. The nothingness
of this solitude encompasses a boundless expanse and its rhythm is contemplative silence. It is not only external freedom from needs and poverty. What matters is conscious striving after voluntary emptiness in
thinking and in willing, in comprehension and enjoyment, for then God's
presence can come pouring in without hindrance into this emptiness and,
if one may say so, penetrate it with more abundant fullness.

The solitude of Carmel is filled by God, in face of Whom every
desire is quenched and every voice sinks into silence, in that stillness

empty of everything save God. God alone is all in all. It is an emptiness overflowing with His life.

In this sense, Edith Stein was a Carmelite even while she was in the world.[G 2] But her significant position in this world, the demands and tasks of the day, the interests of the persons in an extensive circle around her kept drawing her soul out of her own life element. Now the Lord was drawing her into His solitude that there at His feet with Mary she might find that better part that would never be taken from her.[T 1] [G 3]

Only in Carmel, moreover, was she to find something else that our Lord had been saving for her. As we can infer from her own account, God had shown her His Cross in a vision [G 4] as the Cross under which her own people were suffering. At the same time He had requested her to carry her allotted share in this Cross, as the innocent Lamb of God had taken it upon Himself in the name of all, for them and for their salvation. Edith had courageously responded by declaring herself ready for this sacrifice but she wrote, *"In what the bearing of the Cross was to consist I did not yet know."*

But God knew of the essential uniqueness of Carmel and its basic action by which the contemplative soul is led back to her nothingness, thereby opening her completely for the One who with overflowing love wished to become her All. And God knew it was the only action capable of giving this chosen one that resemblance to the divine Sacrificial Lamb that he wanted to achieve in her to such a degree that she was conformed even with His Son's violent death for the salvation of the people.

The first phase of such resemblance had to be the imitation of a humble descent into abasement. In all actuality, for Edith Stein entrance into Carmel was a descent from the height of a distinguished career to the depth of insignificance. Maybe she herself did not perceive this as we see it. But when she left behind the world at her crossing the threshold of Carmel, did not everything that gave her prominence in that world sink with it and lower her to the level of the humanly commonplace? She was received into the Cologne Carmel as just another postulant. Most of the Sisters had not even heard of her before. None of them was aware of her public activities; very few would have been able to follow her if she had tried to introduce them into her own intellectual world. But no one thought about this – least of all Edith herself. Everyone assumed, quite naturally, that she should undertake the thousand and one little tasks that a postulant has to get used to from the first day. And it was moving to watch the childlike way in which Edith struggled to fall in with the regulations of the house at every point, promptly responding to all requests and trying to accustom herself to this new mode of life.[G 5]

It did not come easily, even with the best will in the world. "Does she sew nicely?" The searching question came from one of the older Sisters, and it helps one to appreciate the standard of values applied to the new postulant.[G 6] Unfortunately Edith sewed very badly; worse, it was positively painful watching her trying to do housework, at which she was so clumsy and unskilled. But she always bore with good humor the humiliations arising out of these deficiencies, no matter how they affected her inwardly. Later she wrote to one of her pupils[2] who had followed her into Carmel and was experiencing the same difficulties in the *Arbeitsdienst*.[3] In the letter she said how well she understood her friend's feelings, because she had *"always been in the same position. Never was there anyone so useless in a kitchen."* But she added that it all formed part of the school of humility and was good for someone who had been excessively praised all her life. In Carmel no one thought for a moment of revering this new postulant, though she had made herself loved by her disarming friendliness; and Edith saw to it that no one noticed how she outstripped them all intellectually.[G 7]

A few days after she had entered she wrote to her colleague Dr. Hans Brunnengräber,[4] *"Now I am at the place where for the longest time I felt I belonged. Far be it from me to reproach those who have opened the way for me – even though that was not their intention."* And to a nun in an active Order, "*We too are 'in via,'* [on the way] *for Carmel is a high mountain that one must climb from its very base. But it is a tremendous grace to go this way. And, believe me, in the hours of prayer I always remember especially those who would like to be in my place. Please help me that I may become worthy to live in the inner sanctum of the Church and to represent those who must labor outside.*"[5]

From the time when St. Teresa reformed the Order and very wisely limited the numbers in each convent on the ground that the medieval communities had been too large, every Carmelite convent has formed an intimate little family of twenty-one members. Eighteen of these are choir-Sisters and three of them lay–Sisters [G 8], though a fourth lay-Sister is allowed if one of them is ill or too old. The maximum number was reached when Edith Stein entered, and she could only be accepted because another foundation was being planned in Breslau, to which three of the Sisters from the Cologne Carmel departed in the summer of 1933.[G 9]

In 1894 the Carmelites, who had been driven out of their convent at St. Gereon by the *Kulturkampf* [G 10], returned to Cologne. They were unable to re-acquire their old house, however, because in the meantime it had been turned over to some charitable institution; and they built a modest little church and an intimate convent in a Cologne suburb, at Lindenthal, Dürenerstrasse 89. Attached to it was a lovely but small garden. When Edith entered this foundation it had been standing for about forty years; in 1944 it was completely destroyed by air raids.[G 11] In charge of the convent at this time in 1933, was Mother Josepha of the Blessed Sacrament, the Mother Prioress, while the sub-prioress, Sister Teresia of the Holy Spirit ["P"], was also novice-mistress.

The novitiate then numbered two novices [G 12] who had already made their first (temporary) profession, and one lay-Sister postulant, all nearly twenty years younger than Edith. This was another circumstance that made demands upon the humility, adaptability and constant self-control of the mature woman who had to live with them. Still no one could have guessed that it was proving a source of trouble

or stress to her. She blended into the prevalent mood during their recreation and lent her sympathy to all the sorrows and joys of her young
companions. In return she shared with them her own interests, telling
them about what was happening to her own beloved family. She was a
first-rate storyteller and could turn even the most trivial incident into
a thrilling adventure. She delighted everyone with the witty remarks
she would interject in the conversation.

Besides this attractive and companionable side of her character
she had a great inclination toward the seclusion that is the true life of
Carmel. When she came to her cell [G 13] for the first time her joy
was unmistakable. A happy smile flickered across her face at the sight
of the poverty of the room in which she was to live. It was about ten
feet square, the walls whitewashed, the window looking straight out
into the peaceful convent garden; on the walls a plain wooden cross
without the figure of our Lord, an equally plain holy water stoup, and
unframed pictures of Carmelite saints. On the floor was an earthen-
ware water-jug standing in a basin, on the little table a work box, and
in front of the table a low narrow bench. Her resting place was in a
corner; on a slightly raised board, a straw mattress on which were a
pillow and a few rough, woolen blankets, hidden by the brown woolen
coverlet draped over them. Such is the equipment of a Carmelite cell,
that secret battleground where the nun struggles daily against her self-
love until her nature is wedded to grace and she is free to serve Him
who created her for Himself.

It is possible that even Edith's heart began to beat faster and louder
when for the first time she encountered this harsh and unconditional
poverty in all its nakedness. But this was the Cross she had longed for,
that only Carmel could give to her. Outward poverty is no more than a
symbol for the complete stripping of one's self, giving all to God and
holding nothing back. It expressed a life based upon utter faith, guided
by the darkness infused by light that draws one ever closer to the presence of God. Is such a life of prayer and penance gloomy and boring?
Edith could easily have quelled such a suspicion – and not with words

alone! Her very being and her every act gave it the lie. It was sheer joy to observe her growing younger and more radiant after her first weeks in the enclosure. One might have imagined that Edith herself had forgotten her past, her abilities and her learning, and had retained just one desire, to be a child amongst other children. Excessive intellectual work, fasting, irregular hours of sleep, all these mortifications that she had laid upon herself were abandoned in the name of obedience. To eat sufficiently, to sleep contentedly and to be thoroughly joyous; these are the three recognized signs of a true Carmelite vocation according to our holy Mother, St. Teresa. Edith never found it any trouble to display all these three qualities, and especially the decisive one, joyfulness. How fitting was it that the approach of Christmas tended to bring out this joyful spirit.

Christmas in Carmel! One might say: Heaven on earth![G 14] Edith was now to celebrate it with us, the one night of the year when the great silence in Carmel is lifted, when all the rooms and corridors, the stairs and every part of the cloister echo with music and jubilation, when every nook and corner contains its own little crib, each one lovelier than the last. This holy night when, instead of being wakened by a hard clapper,[6] one wakes to the sound of silver bells and the singing of carols, so that it seems as if one had really been sleeping in Bethlehem and was hurrying into the ante-choir to be there before the shepherds.

Dressed in their white mantles the Sisters stand waiting for the bells to ring for the third time, the sign for them to move into the choir, now blazing with light. Matins are never sung more beautifully than during this sacred night before the Blessed Sacrament exposed on the altar. Soft noises can be heard through the wide-open grille in spite of the curtains over it; indicating that the little chapel is filling with people. Now it is almost midnight. The jubilant sounds of the *Te Deum laudamus* fade away and the Sisters retire to the ante-choir to receive their lighted candles. There in front of the altar, laid upon a silk cushion, is the image of the Christ-child. Carefully the Mother Prioress lifts it and holds it up to the community who now begin to move back into the choir amidst a peal of bells, the youngest Sister at the head of the procession. Complete silence reigns throughout the chapel; everyone is listening to the Sisters singing: "Bethlehem, dost thou hear thy Savior? Let Him in. . ." The Sisters themselves stand on either side of the choir while the Mother Prioress carries the Christ-child to the grotto and lays Him in the crib. And now it strikes twelve. The organ thunders, the priests approach the altar, and the choir intones the eternally beautiful *Dominus dixit ad me: Filius meus es tu.* [*The Lord said to me: You are my son*-Ps. 2:7.] What the Sisters have symbolically represented by their play in the choir is now going to take place in reality. The Christ-child is coming into the world, descending upon the altar, finding a crèche in our hearts. *Ave Jesu!* The priest is giving the Christmas blessing. The servers are coming away from the altar. There follows a second, then a third mass. Now the congregation takes up the melody and bursts forth into the old, familiar Christmas carols so dear to the music-loving people of Cologne. To hear them once is to remember them always. After the last *Amen* the chapel slowly empties.

There is a stir again in the choir; the Sisters are intoning Lauds. The Brides of Christ hardly wait for the liturgy to come to an end before they sing aloud their hearts' love in their German mother tongue, accompanying themselves on the flute and the lute. Who thinks of sleep? or of bodily refreshment? Until finally the Mother Prioress singing the invitation – the well-known carol – "Oh, come, little children. . ." gives the sign to disperse.

Edith Stein was at home in the conventual family from the beginning. She used to laugh and joke like a child with the other Sisters until the tears ran down her cheeks. She used to declare that she had never laughed so much in all her life as during recreation in Carmel. Everyone was at their ease with her. Soon after she herself had entered the Cologne Carmel she was given the wonderful experience of bringing in one of her young friends through her own example. This is what she wrote about it. *"When we now stand facing each other in choir or walk together in procession I am struck more than ever by the*

wonderful ways of God. Naturally, in our seclusion we have a beauti-
ful and silent Advent. How much one longs to send some of it to very
many of those in the world. . .I believe that it would do them untold
good to learn more of the peace of Carmel."[7]

An even deeper impression emerges from another letter of about
the same date:

> *My deepest thanks for your greetings on the anniver-*
> *sary of my Baptism that of course I have celebrated*
> *this year as never before. The fact that you have not*
> *received any word from me in Carmel and that I could*
> *not send you any visible token even at Christmas should*
> *not make you imagine that I do not have permission to*
> *write. In fact I am allowed very wide freedom in main-*
> *taining my old contacts. But each day is so ordered that*
> *one has to concentrate upon doing whatever happens*
> *to be most urgent. I need your prayers for my mother as*
> *much as ever, since she is not one whit more reconciled*
> *to the situation than before. Meanwhile our little Carmel*
> *in Breslau-Pawelwitz continues to flourish. Recently I*
> *heard from my sister Rosa that she had just paid her*
> *first visit to this little convent, and she will be very happy*
> *to slip away there whenever she can, but she finds it*
> *rather difficult to manage. The two children (Susel and*
> *Ernst Biberstein) know quite well where their aunt has*
> *gone. Apparently Susel is greatly impressed because she*
> *writes to me more often than she used to. She is serious*
> *beyond her years, having matured very rapidly through*
> *hearing so much political talk and through having to*
> *suffer, as she has, at school. So far my brother-in-law*
> *cannot make up his mind to let the children change*
> *schools. In her last letter, however, my sister wrote that*
> *they might perhaps send Susel to a Catholic high school,*
> *where Jewish children are still somewhat better treated.*
> *The child did not yet know anything about it. Of course I*
> *am aware of all those on the outside; it must be difficult*
> *to be in the teaching profession. As I stand in our peace-*

ful choir I cannot thank God enough for having lifted me
out of the whirlwind and set me in this profound peace,
that I have done nothing to deserve. I have never cele-
brated Advent and Christmas as I did this year.[G 15]

In this way Edith's six months of probation passed quickly. On 15 February 1934, following the custom of the Order, she knelt before the assembled community [G 16] and asked to receive the habit of Our Blessed Lady of Mount Carmel. She was granted her request on 15 April. During the two months that she was preparing for her clothing she grew in love and gratitude toward her superiors and her sisters. It was not easy for her to grasp that, as the "bride-to-be," she should be the object of so much attention and solicitude on the part of her Sisters. Everyone was busy helping her to prepare for her clothing as it drew nearer. Besides the bridal dress all the clothes she would need in the convent had to be made -- a long white tunic of wool, a pair of rope sandals, a rosary with big beads and a coarse brown handkerchief.[G17] She had to go from one workroom to another to try on first one thing and then another; and though nothing more was done for her than for anyone else, she accepted each service as though it were a special token of love for herself.

15

The Novitiate[1]

E dith had announced the big event to her family. When she had presented herself at the Carmel in the previous summer, as soon as the conversation turned toward her mother she had asked for just one exceptional permission: that she might write her a weekly letter. This had been her lifelong practice and if letters had suddenly stopped arriving, her aged mother would have been cut to the quick. The kind and understanding Prioress gladly granted the postulant her request in view of her unusual family circumstances. So even in Carmel Edith continued to write her regular weekly letter to her mother. But the maternal reply that had previously come just as regularly now ceased. Frau Stein could not bring herself to send letters to her daughter in a convent. Rosa therefore undertook to act as intermediary, and to keep them in contact with each other. Full of joy on hearing the news of the forthcoming clothing she lovingly inquired whether she herself could contribute anything to her sister's wedding feast. When Edith asked her for the bridal dress Rosa sent some heavy white silk material that is still in the Carmel, having since been made into a Mass vestment.[2][G 1]

On 15 April 1934, Good Shepherd Sunday, Edith Stein was clothed in the habit of Our Blessed Lady of Mount Carmel and received a name that she herself had suggested, Teresia Benedicta a Cruce.[3][G 2] It was a feast such as the Cologne Carmel had never seen. The generous bouquets of flowers given by many friends and acquaintances lent the little church a most marvelous beauty.

Everyone had expected a lot of people to be present at the ceremony but they still were surprised at the great throng that did come. It was an overwhelming testimony to the high esteem, the veneration, and the love that Edith had enjoyed in the world. It hardly affected Edith. The equilibrium of soul she had gained was not to be unbalanced by this evidence of universal admiration.[T 1]

An hour before the ceremony began she left the enclosure "as a Bride adorned for her Husband" to receive the guests of honor in the reception room.[4][G 3] These included the Most Rev. Archabbot of Beuron, who was to celebrate the Pontifical Mass; the Most Rev. Father Provincial of the Carmelites, Fr. Theodore of St. Francis from Regensburg, who was to perform the clothing; her highly respected last employer, Prof. Johann Peter Steffes from Münster, Professors Dr. Alois Dempf, Dr. Adolf Donders, Dr. Wilhelm Neuss, Peter Wust, Dr. Bernhard Rosenmöller, Dr. Hans Brunnengräber and many more. Nor was her godmother, Frau Dr. Hedwig Conrad-Martius, missing.[5][G 4]

Especially numerous were the representatives of the Catholic Women's League, Frau Dr. Gerda Krabbel, Annie Bender, Dr. Elisabeth Cosack, and many of her fellow students [G 5] and of her students from Freiburg, Speyer and Münster. Representatives from many different religious orders had also come. Known or unknown, they all passed in line to offer their good wishes. For each one of them she had a friendly word, but when the ringing of bells [G 6] signaled the beginning of the ceremony, she breathed with relief.

At the head of the procession of clergy coming from the sacristy, dressed in his liturgical attire, was the Most Rev. Archabbot who received Edith at the church door and led her toward the altar. There she knelt at the prie-dieu[6] to follow the liturgy of the mass that was rendered even more beautiful by the singing of a choir of Third Order Dominicans.

After the High Mass the celebrant delivered an address that again severely tried the humility of our unassuming Bride of Christ. Then her Carmelite superior, Fr. Theodore,[7] moved toward her, and there followed a dialogue that has remained unchanged for centuries, in which the postulant bears witness in clear, unambiguous words, before Holy Church and the whole world, to the strength and freedom of the incomparable love that has drawn her and will keep her forever behind the high convent walls in that "enclosure" valued above all else.

"What do you ask for?" Calmly and distinctly audible to everyone present, came the answer from Edith's lips. *"The mercy of God, the poverty*

*of the Order, and the company of the Sisters." "*Are you resolved to persevere in the Order until death?" *"Thus do I hope and desire, through the
mercy of God and the prayers of the Sisters."* With the closing blessing,
"May the Lord who has led you to us divest you of [G 7] your former self
together with all its works," her superior left her side.

Edith Stein rose, took the lighted candle in her hand and approached
the convent door as it opened before her. Awaiting her inside the enclosure were the veiled nuns standing in two ranks, each of them holding a lighted candle. One of the Sisters, stepping forward, held up the
crucifix. Edith sank on her knees before it and kissed it. She crossed
the threshold and the door closed behind her.

While the congregation now pressed toward the wide-open grille
in the church and the Sisters threaded their way through the cloisters
singing "*O gloriosa Domina*,"[8] Edith Stein hurriedly removed her secular adornment. Over her shoulders was laid the coarse habit. The bridal
veil and myrtle-wreath gave place to the nun's habit and helping hands
changed her pretty shoes for a pair of rough sandals.[T 2] [G 8] When
the procession drew into the choir at the last verse of the hymn, the
transformation was complete and she and the Reverend Mother came
in together, the last pair in the procession.

The novice knelt on the carpet before the grille; lying on a foot-
stool nearby was the rest of her Carmelite habit. "May the Lord
clothe you with the new self, created in God's image, in justice
and holiness of truth." The Mother Prioress, standing on the novice's left, took the leather cincture, [G 9] handed one end of it to the
novice-mistress standing on the right, and together they fastened
it round her waist. "When you were younger," said the provincial,
reminding her of her absolute obedience, [G 10] "you girded yourself and walked where you would; but when you shall be old, another shall gird you. In the name of the Father and of the Son and
of the Holy Spirit." Taking the blessed scapular, the Reverend
Mother, together with the novice-mistress, laid it on the shoulders
of the kneeling novice. "Receive the sweet yoke of Christ and His

burden that is light. In the name of the Father and of the Son, and of the Holy Spirit," prayed her superior [G 11], indicating evangelical poverty. Now the two Sisters put the white mantle and veil on the Novice while the provincial referred to the voluntary commitment to chastity as he prayed: "Those who follow the Lamb without stain shall walk with Him in white garments. Therefore let your vesture be ever unspotted in token of interior purity."

The clothing was now over. While everyone knelt and the provincial intoned the hymn *Veni Creator Spiritus* (Come, Holy Spirit) the new Carmelite prostrated herself on the floor in the form of a cross, the symbol of the mystical death her nature must die. She remained thus until the novice-mistress gave her a sign, her call to rise to the higher life of grace.

The new Sister was led by the novice-mistress to the Mother Prioress to kiss her hand as a pledge of her grateful submission. Then she embraced all the other Sisters while the chantresses [G 12] joyfully sang, "Behold how good and how pleasant it is for brethren to dwell together in unity."[Ps. 133] Slowly the choir emptied. Those in front of the grille looked and listened until they heard nothing anymore but the suppressed cry of their own heart[9] [T 3] that suddenly they longed to follow, while a secret fear held it back. They returned to their everyday lives, that for the moment seemed to them a poor thing whereas this freely surrendered one had in truth come into possession of the precious pearl of the Gospel.

Some days later the following article by Professor Peter Wust was published in the *Kölnische Volkszeitung:*

FROM HUSSERL TO CARMEL [G 13]

In the small, inconspicuous chapel of the Carmel at Cologne on Sunday the 15th of April, a circle of intellectually interested people assembled to celebrate together an out-of-the-ordinary occasion. A bride was led to the altar whose life might be taken as a symbol of the intellectual movements of the last decade. It was no earthly bridegroom to whom she committed herself. She did wear a wreath and veil, it is true, and carried a lighted candle in her hand when we greeted her before she proceeded to the altar. But at the end of the ceremony we took our leave of a nun dressed in the Carmelite habit. And no longer did the newly clothed novice bear the name of the philosopher, the disciple of Husserl, by which we had known her and admired her in the world. She now bore the very plain name of "Sister Teresa Benedicta."

Many years earlier, her path through life had led her to the founder of phenomenology. For a time she was assistant to Husserl and was thus enabled to develop a deep insight into the life's work of this thinker, who, since the appearance of his *Logische Untersuchungen* [*Logical Investigations*], has provoked a revolution in the philosophy of the current era. From the very beginning there must have been something mysterious hidden in the intention of this new philosophical movement, a longing to regain the objective, to reach for the sacredness of being, for the purity and chastity of things, for "the things themselves." Because, although in the case of Husserl himself, who was the father of this whole school, the modern curse of subjectivism could not be completely overcome,[10] that openness to the object that is this school's own original intention drove many of his disciples farther down the road toward [the] things, toward the actual facts, toward being itself, yes, even to that predisposition [*habitus*] of the Catholic person for whom nothing serves more appropriately as a standard for the perceptive spirit than the standards of the eternal.

It is a known fact that Max Scheler, too, was one day carried away by phenomenology into the objectivity of Catholic thought and how – at least for a time – this thought transformed this thinker who was always so inclined to follow his emotions. But, unfortunately, he was swept again into the relativistic counter-current of the age that led him to abandon completely, once more, the path he had for a time walked with such happiness and such promise.

On the other hand, Edith Stein, Husserl's assistant referred to above, and who is now the Carmelite Sr. Benedicta, had the good fortune to continue more consistently along her way. To begin with, like Scheler and the others, she, too, was drawn into the great silence of the "Una Sancta." But with this conversion she had not yet attained the final goal. At first she remained true to philosophy, and especially to that philosophical movement for which she had been won by her master, Husserl. But it soon became obvious that she was extraordinarily serious about the elements of objectivity inherent in phenomenology. Shut off from all the secular noise of that age, she plunged herself into the ontological thought of Aquinas. She did this by translating his comprehensive work the *Quaestiones Disputatae de Veritate* [*Disputed Questions on Truth*] page by page in such a way as to give the impression that she was holding up the work of this greatest of the phenomenologists of the Middle Ages so filled with the joy of living, as if it were a clear mirror image of her own idea before the eyes of the phenomenologists of our age who are still cramped by their subjectivism.

Evidently, though, the spirit and language of this thinker for whom being was so deep-seated rubbed off so much on this disciple of Husserl as she worked on this translation that not only did her whole character become ever more quiet, more simple and more child-like but undoubtedly, one day, the mystical background of the world of ideas of Aquinas became perceptible and palpable for her. So her way led her on, further and further into the actual reality of being, into the reality of the supernatural in the sense of those great figures who, in Carmel, stand as the classical exponents of the mystical life of prayer, in the sense then of a St. Teresa of Avila and a St. John of the Cross.

Surprised and stunned, one followed at this Clothing Ceremony each individual stage of the liturgical journey

to the moving final scene, when the new novice embraced her Sisters one after the other during the singing of the *Veni Creator Spiritus* (Come, Holy Spirit).
Now a member of the community, Sr. Benedicta, was
drawn into their midst and moved with them toward
the choir – toward the choir, away from the world – as
"Sr. Benedicta," as the one "blessed" by the Truth, by
the entire abundance of the Truth.

One particular image from this day's festivity remains imprinted before my eyes, a marvelously symbolic image. It was at the leave-taking by Sister Benedicta
at the close of the festivities in the speakroom. On that
side of the grille stood the newly clothed Carmelite and
on this side, the well-known phenomenologist Hedwig
Conrad-Martius, who in her profound study of the metaphysics of time had carried forward the thought of reality to the abyss of the eternal. What a curious play of
chance it seemed that those two outstanding pupils of
Husserl should now stand opposite one another for a
moment under such unusual conditions. The one had
pursued the basic principles of phenomenology to
plumb the depths of metaphysics far more surely than
her master Husserl himself had done; but the other,
seeking for the very ground of being, had attained the
mysticism of Carmel. And Husserl, too, had sent his
cordial best wishes by telegram that morning to the
Cologne Carmel.

For a long time one stood before the grille of the
enclosure recalling the long and so totally symbolic
journey that this novice had made from Husserl through
Thomas to this place – yes, to here and now. Then the
serious rule of the cloister summoned us to the final
leave-taking and our ways separated, harshly and in-
exorably – away *from* the world – in*to* the world.

When he was asked to comment on Sr. Benedicta's vocational decision, Archabbot Raphael Walzer replied as follows:

It is certainly right that I should be called upon to give witness of her, at least of the final years of the departed one. But I cannot fail to remark how difficult it is for me to provide the final answers to questions about her. For one thing, it is not really in accordance with the wishes of this unassuming woman to reveal the deepest secrets of her heart. In addition, in our correspondence, we exchanged or left behind hardly anything worth mentioning. Also, her interior life was so simple and free from problems that, from all my conversations with her, nothing remains in my memory but the picture of a soul of perfect serenity and maturity. *Fuit et quietus* – tranquillity and balance – as we sing of them in the Hymn for Confessors in the monastic breviary, were also her final and highest state. Nevertheless, in spite of all hesitation, I believe that in what follows I shall be able to throw some light on certain aspects of her character.

When Edith Stein first came to Beuron, she was in truth no longer a beginner. She brought so much treasure with her that, while she at once found her true home in the monastic atmosphere of this hidden spot on the banks of the Danube, she needed to make no adjustment, nor to learn anything essentially new. It was a kind of harvest of what others had sowed and she herself had cultivated in a most fruitful soil. In any account of her life this may be brought out as one of the most surely attested facts about her, without any fear of exaggerating the truth. But what was the special attraction for her of Beuron and its liturgies? Certainly not the length of the services. She seems, it is true, to have had boundless powers of endurance. She managed, for instance, to spend the whole of Good Friday from early morning till late at night in the abbey church.

She was like her strict, ascetic Jewish mother in not seeing in this any special "accomplishment." Any form of pious "performance" was as alien to her as was personal comfort or a desire to gain graces and interior joys without sacrifices. She neither had nor sought after any extraordinary exaltation or ecstasy. Neither her intellect nor her senses lent themselves to any such thing. She simply wanted to be there, to be with God, and, as it were, to have the great mysteries there before her, something she could not have either in the open country outside this secluded sacred space or in her quiet cell. I do not think that she made much use in her meditation and prayer of written texts, nor that she went in for biblical exegesis nor thought out intellectual lectures, to which she was always being summoned. Surely innumerable thoughts would mount and descend in her mind, as if on a Jacob's ladder thronged with heavenly messengers; fervent wishes and exalted plans attached themselves. But, like her external, almost rigid attitude, so her interior rested in blissful gazing and rejoicing before God. Ever thankful for the grace of conversion, and happily at home with her Mother the Church, since her liturgical and dogmatic knowledge enabled her to join fully in its psalmody, she acknowledged in the monastic choir the great praying Church.

As Edith saw in Christ the Divine Head of the Mystical Body in uninterrupted prayer before the Father, so for her the supernatural life consisted first and foremost in the official prayer of the Church, in the realization of the apostolic injunction, "Pray without ceasing." She understood this precept at its deepest level, so that no service was too long for her, no effort too great nor did she see it merely as a worthwhile sacrifice. To her faith it was self-evident that one should join in and be submerged in the *laus perennis*. The strict, solemn liturgical form, however long or short, was certainly everything to her, and in a certain sense indispensable. And yet, when she finally entered Carmel, she did not find it difficult to give up the Benedictine way or the opportunity of belonging to the *Ecclesia orans* [*the Praying Church*]. Nor did I try to suggest that she should enter one of the abbeys of Benedictine Nuns dependent on Beuron. Humanly speaking, she would have made a splendid daughter of St. Benedict. It was sufficient for her to choose, as her second name in religion, the name of the Patriarch. Souls like hers, who have grasped the spirit of the whole, can afford to nourish and deepen this same spirit in more specialized forms of religious life as well.

Nor was the beauty of the strict liturgy itself a decisive factor for her mind and heart. It is certainly true which form took a prominent position in her speech, in her vision, and in her creative work. As she almost gave an impression that in her dress and her whole appearance she wanted to attract attention by her simplicity; and as the shape of her round face and regular features revealed a distinct taste for harmony and true art; so she surely found a rare satisfaction in the official prayers and rites of the Church. But nothing of human origin could disturb her in it; neither the somewhat unfortunate architecture of the abbey church of Beuron, nor other imperfections, none of that escaped her notice because of her wide knowledge. The one-sided aesthetic, the "art for art's sake" never tainted her thought or prayer. We hardly ever spoke of the questions then being discussed everywhere that were the product of the aestheticist approach to the spiritual.

Edith was not interested in any of these problems. She kept away from them and did not occupy herself with criticizing or combating them. On this account, too, she had no difficulty in deciding on Carmel. No one saw more clearly than she that she would have to adjust to the poverty and simplicity emphasized there, and that, in doing so, she would encounter much that would go against her own refined taste. Yet not once did she speak of this to the man to whom she spontaneously confided all her secrets. Nor was there any need for me to prepare her for it, in the manner of the Novice Master of the fifty-eighth chapter of the Rule,[11] who must tell the beginner of all the difficulties and annoyances so as to test his vocation. She simply ran to Carmel like a child into its mother's arms, blithe and singing, without ever regretting later, even for a moment, this almost blind eagerness. It was somewhat as St. Benedict describes this way. "Now we must run, and do all that will have value for eternity."

Moreover, I can expressly state that Edith most certainly did not choose Carmel out of ascetic rigorism on account of its liturgically less attractive general attitude, so as to mortify herself with, humanly speaking, more difficult circumstances – an idea that some might attempt to attribute to her. No, she did not spend much time considering her choice. Carmel had for long been her love and her dream. Once the situation in the Third Reich made it impossible for me to deter her any longer from entering, she simply wished to realize this dream. She heard the voice of the All High, followed it, and did not ask for long where the road led.

I considered it almost a duty to prepare the Carmelite beginner for a final difficulty she might meet. But I soon noticed how little she worried about it. Even in this instance she seemed to find everything self-evident. To go over it a second time was unnecessary. If anyone could by all rights be termed an intellectual in the true sense of the word, then Edith was that one. She herself would have considered it presumption and intellectual pride to count herself in this class. But the great St. Teresa recognized only one class of Sisters, usually not more than twenty-one of whom lived together in a kind of religious equality.

Edith certainly did not seek out the small Cologne Carmel in the hope of finding there an academically trained superior or in order to find there such a circle of highly educated Sisters. As far as I know she was the only one who could be counted among the latter. Whether she would be allowed further scholarly activity, or even have it fostered or imposed on her in obedience, were questions about which she never pondered nor did she attempt to gain any assurance in the matter. Not one of the intellectual friends of the former Husserl assistant and lecturer at the German Institute for Scientific Pedagogy in Münster was allowed, as far as she was concerned, to influence her superiors in the Order, either directly or indirectly, in this matter. Not even a shadow of an ulterior motive darkened her noble attitude.

What all of this signified for such a spirit that hungered so for knowledge and research is not hard to imagine. In fact, I myself thought it altogether too risky a venture for even as heroically blessed a soul as Edith Stein to live daily in as close a communion as was demanded in a cloistered Order and in a convent spatially so restricted in the middle of the city and – as was the impression one got – only among non-academic persons. I was completely mistaken. When I was able to see and speak to her alone after the clothing celebration – it was for the last time – I asked her for a very precise and honest answer to the question of how she had settled into the community of Sisters and accustomed herself to the spiritual direction. I found confirmed what I had expected: She felt entirely at home in heart and soul, was the answer she gave with the enthusiasm so much part of her fiery nature. One was not even tempted to think this a particular miracle of grace. It all seemed to be a natural development as part of her supernatural maturing.

So I see her love of the Cross and her desire for martyrdom not as an all too conscious spiritual attitude that expressed itself in formal wishes and prayer intentions, rather it was a readiness deeply rooted in her soul to follow the Lord everywhere. I don't believe she deliberately failed to take the steps early enough to flee to Switzerland in order to escape a horrendous death. In simple obedience she would have accepted such a solution. But on the other hand, she did not trouble herself about carrying out the plan, always being sustained by a holy indifference and abandonment to the Divine Will.

In Freiburg, Husserl, "the dear old Master," was waiting for a report about Edith Stein's clothing, that he had not attended. On the 3rd of May, Sister Adelgundis, O.S.B., also one of his pupils, visited him and read to him a letter from their mutual friend Maria Merz who had attended the ceremony. Husserl listened to it attentively and with devotion. Now and then he would interrupt her to ask some question about the Church's established practices and customs. It afforded him real satisfaction that Edith was also esteemed in the Church and in the Order. This way he gave the impression of an anxious and yet proud father whose daughter – after all, he used to call her his best pupil – is marrying into a new family. With genuine paternal pride he exclaimed: "I do not believe that the Church has any Neoscholastic of Edith Stein's caliber. Thank God that she will be permitted to keep up her scholarly work in the Cologne Carmel." Subsequently he expressed his regret at not having traveled to attend the Clothing Ceremony in Cologne. He said, innocently, "After all, I would have been entitled to be the 'father of the bride'." Then, after a thoughtful pause, "It's possible to be personally fond of one another, even if one has changed one's world view, as in the case of Edith."

And he continued: "She has come to learn sufficiently the clear affiliation of the spiritual and the Scholastic – why is there no trace of this in St. Teresa?" And after hearing the reply: "Every true Scholastic will be a mystic, and every true mystic a Scholastic," he said, "It is remarkable – Edith stands on a summit, so to speak, and sees the furthest and broadest horizons with amazing clarity and detachment, and simultaneously, she looks in another direction within herself with equal penetration. Everything in her is utterly genuine, otherwise I would say: this is contrived and artificial. But – in the Jew there is radicalism and love for martyrdom." He had them show him pictures of St. Teresa because they portrayed the Carmelite habit, and he kept a photo taken at the Clothing as a memento.

After the celebration of Edith's Clothing Ceremony, the Father Provincial held his canonical visitation [G 14] of the Cologne Carmel. In his interview of Sr. Benedicta Father Theodore inquired in detail about her activities since her entry, and about her philosophical work. One of the things that Sr. Benedicta brought with her when she left the world was a voluminous work entitled *Potency and Act*, that, in her own opinion, and as she herself said in line with her newly acquired knowledge, needed to be entirely reworked. Father Provincial now arranged that Sr. Benedicta should be relieved of all other duties so as to have enough time for this work.

It was not long before literary requests from outside as well as inside Carmel were made of her, and these she gladly filled in her free time. To begin with, she translated for a Clothing Ceremony and then for the Veiling of a novice the customary prayers and prepared a version for printing, with the Latin and German side by side. This booklet was followed by a small brochure of about sixty pages: a biography of St. Teresa of Avila that can rightly be called a gem precisely because of its brevity, while at the same time it presents all the essential features of the saint and her work. Kanisiusverlag published it in 1934.[12]

Teresia Margareta Redi, a young Carmelite saint canonized that same year, formed the subject of a second and similar character sketch that Rita-Verlag, Würzburg, published.[13] The Akademische Bonifatius-Einigung asked her for the contribution *Das Gebet der Kirche* [*The Prayer of the Church*] for their anthology, *Ich lebe und ihr lebet* (*I live and you live*). In Fr. Eugen Lense's book *Die in deinem Hause wohnen* (*Those Who Dwell in Thy house*) appeared her biography of Katherina Esser, the distinguished native of Cologne, who in face of unspeakable odds managed to refound the Cologne Carmel in 1848, the first contemplative convent established in Germany since the secularization.[G 15]

All this work was crammed into Edith's very rare periods of leisure. Most of her energy was devoted to the difficult task of preparing the index for her translation of St. Thomas, that was eventually brought out early in 1935 by Borgmeyer after months of weary proof-correcting. Sr. Benedicta herself writes: "*It cost a great deal to get it into a satisfactory form.*"[14]

At the same time she was carrying on with the history of her family that she had begun in the world. She received permission to do so because it acted as a relief from the intellectual strain of her learned work. And so Sr. Benedicta followed in the footsteps of her predecessors who, in the caves of Mount Carmel, had worked and prayed in order, as Jacques de Vitry (*ca.* 1190) puts it, "to live as bees of the Lord, preparing a honey whose sweetness is wholly spiritual."

Sr. Benedicta also had learned, with diligence like that of the bees, to let no minute pass unused. No matter how necessary it might have seemed for her to have uninterrupted time to work, her love of the Rule led her to adhere strictly to the daily *horarium* [G 16] with inflexible fidelity. It is evident how hard it was for her to be drawn out of her concentration time and again from her comment that the severest penance in Carmel for her was this constant change due to monastic practices. One had hardly warmed to one's task when it was time to give it up in order to begin something else. Not to have more than two hours without interruption was as good as nothing for someone with her eager perseverance. But she recognized in this provision the wisdom of the great reformer of the Order[15] who did not wish that the spirit and heart of her daughter should become attached to any activity, and so she gladly submitted to the regimen.

Even as a Carmelite, Sr. Benedicta was not deprived of an intimate connection with the world, that is, with those whom she had loved in the world, and whom she had left only for the sake of Jesus. This does not mean that she longed to have her friends and relatives visit her: She knew well enough that the noise of the world and all its bustle must be silenced at the threshold of the *hortus conclusus* [locked garden] where rests the Beloved who allows himself to be found only in the silence and recollection of soul. But she was already so much a daughter of St. Teresa, who never ceased during her lifetime to share in her family's joys and sorrows and whose heart overflowed the more with love for them the more it was detached from earthly ties, that Edith followed the fate of her friends' lives with affectionate concern and devoted herself to her visitors with a supernaturally natural warmth.

> "*Most of the Sisters consider it a penance*," she wrote shortly before her clothing, "*to be called to the speakroom. It is, after all like a transition into a strange world, and we are happy to flee once more to the silence of the choir, and, before the tabernacle, to ponder over those matters that have been brought to our attention. But I still receive this peace, daily, as an immense gift of grace that has not been given for one's own exclusive benefit. And when someone comes to us worn out and crushed and then takes away a bit of tranquillity and comfort, that makes me very happy.*
>
> *Of course it is hardly possible to think individually of every intention that is commended to me from so many different sides. All one can do is to try to live the life one has chosen with ever greater fidelity and purity in order to offer it up as an acceptable sacrifice for all those with whom one is connected. The confidence placed in us, the almost fearfully high opinion that so many outside have of our life, is a constant stimulus for us.*[16]

In the first year, of course, only her friends visited her, especially her godchild Hede who, with her husband, Dr. Spiegel, came to gain strength for her newly found faith from Edith's maternal instruction. One frequent visitor was Peter Wust, professor at the University in Münster who was insatiable in expressing his feelings of insignificance as a self-taught philosopher in the presence of Sr. Benedicta's greatness. Other visitors who kept her abreast of the most important contemporary issues were Fr. Petrus Jans, O.S.B. and Fr. Erich Przywara, S.J., neither of whom had been able to come to her clothing.

Gertrude von le Fort came once in order to discuss her book *Die ewige Frau* [*Eternal Woman*]. She had just begun to work on it at the time, and she later said that it was Sr. Benedicta who inspired the most beautiful section of her book that describes the significance of the veil. During the writing of the book, the author had kept, on her desk, a photo of Sr. Benedicta in her bridal dress.

Referring to this visit somewhat later Sr. Benedicta wrote:

> [T 4]*What you wrote me about your impression of her* [Von le Fort's] *evening lectures was important to me. When Gertrud von le Fort visited us in November I realized more clearly than ever how terribly trying this delicate creature must find it to be so much in the public eye, and to be always traveling about. And I began to wonder whether the results in any way corresponded to the sacrifice. Your report now was a "yes" to this question. Gertrud von le Fort is also going to visit my relatives in Breslau. "Nonni" (the famous Icelandic storyteller, Fr. Jon Svensson, S.J.) who was here in December also promised to visit my relatives if he got to Breslau.*[17][G17]

Through such messengers, Edith tried to reach her family whom she had left out of love. Her mother did not know that she had now taken the Carmelite habit; her sisters had all sent their greetings for the occasion. It grieved Rosa that she had not been able to witness the feast, particularly after she heard the enthusiastic descriptions of it that some of those present had sent to her. Month after month she set her hopes on visiting Cologne but she could not have left her mother for any length of time without causing suspicion. So Sr. Benedicta contented herself with writing to her beloved mother week in and week out, without ever receiving an answer. The year of novitiate that was to serve as the final test of Sr. Benedicta's vocation and as preparation for her profession of vows was nearly over.

On 11 February she wrote to her late spiritual director's nephew, Dean Konrad Schwind:

> *Please remember me, especially, during the coming months. I hope to be allowed to make my first profession of vows in April. The question of whether I have accustomed myself to the solitude made me smile. For most of my life I have had much more solitude than I have here. I miss nothing that is outside and have everything I lacked there; therefore I must be grateful for the entirely unmerited, immense grace of my vocation.*[18]

Just as the subsequent development of a human being depends on the direction given the child during his formative years, so from the first years of formation in the monastic life, i.e., the novitiate, to a large extent one can foresee the degree of later zeal and the subsequent striving for perfection. Day after day Sr. Benedicta penetrated more deeply into the spirit of the Order in accordance with that counsel of its holy Foundress to seek nothing in the cloister but God alone and the unreserved submission to His will.

What a profound concept of the religious life Sr. Benedicta already cherished while still in the world is indicated by the following lines, taken from an address to an audience of nuns:

> *The motive, principle and goal of the religious life is to surrender to God entirely in self-forgetting love, allowing one's own life to end in order to make room in oneself for God's life.*
>
> *The more completely this is realized the more is the soul filled with the riches of divine life. But divine life is love, overflowing, undemanding love freely giving itself; love that in compassion bends down to every creature in need; love that heals the sick and awakens the dead to life; love that protects and shelters, nourishes, teaches and shapes us; love that mourns with the mourners,*

rejoices with the joyful, and puts itself at the service of every creature so that each creature may become what the Father wishes it to be – in a word: the love of the Divine Heart. . .

To surrender oneself lovingly to another being, to become wholly the property of another and to possess this other wholly – this is the deepest longing of a woman's heart. This accounts for that specifically feminine quality of concentrating on the personal and on the whole. When this gift of oneself is made to another human being, it is a perverted surrender, an enslavement and at the same time an unjust demand that no human being can fulfill. Only God can accept someone's surrender totally in a manner in which the person does not lose his soul, but rather wins it. And only God can give Himself to a person in a way that He fills that person's being totally without losing anything of His own. That is why the complete surrender that is the principle of the religious life is at the same time the only possible, adequate fulfillment of a woman's longings. . .[19]

There was not the slightest hesitation about admitting her to profession since her life with them had so edified the Sisters. So 21 April, the most solemn Easter Sunday, was chosen for this celebration. Sr. Benedicta's happiness and gratitude knew no bounds. She had always been very modest and composed, but during this Lenten season God seemed to draw her more than ever into herself. On the evening of 10 April she began her retreat in preparation for the profession. She adopted an even stricter silence and seclusion from her Sisters. This was her desert, or rather her fertile oasis in the desert, to which in overflowing bliss she applied the hymn of praise in which St. Jerome speaks: "O desert, adorned with the flowers of Christ! Desert where grow the mystical stones of the Apocalypse, from which the city of the great King is to be built. Holy solitude, wherein to enjoy the intimacy of God! Friend, what are you doing in the world, you who are greater than the world? Why do you dwell beneath the stifling shadows of houses? Why do you remain imprisoned in the golden birdcage that is the city? I know not how, but believe me when I say that I see the light more clearly here. Freed from the weight of the body, the soul takes flight toward heaven."[20]

Did she perhaps in a superabundance of joy, like her sister in the Order, St. Mary Magdalen de Pazzi, kiss the high walls of enclosure that enclosed herself and her Beloved, allowing her to enjoy here below a foretaste of the eternal wedding feast by a union with her Divine Bridegroom that was none the less real for being purely spiritual.

The graces of the profession day remained the secret of the King and His chosen Bride. St. Teresa, in a clause of her Constitutions for which her daughters are ever grateful, wisely ordained that the nuns' profession should take place in Chapter[21] without the presence of prelates or priests, making it an intimate family feast. This Carmelite custom means that no relatives of the Sister being professed are invited on that day. So the expression of sisterly love can be uninhibited on such a wedding day on which the Lord has chosen for Himself a new Bride to join him on the heights of Carmel.

In the early hours of the morning – while the dark of night still reigned – the Easter bells began to ring out in Carmel, ending the silence they had kept during the sorrowful season of Lent.

In solemn procession the community entered the festively decorated choir. Everywhere, amid the first spring flowers the sweet scent of myrtle could be discerned. As the tabernacle was opened, [G 18] the nuns sang the pure-toned *Surrexit Dominus vere, Alleluia!* [The Lord has truly risen. Alleluia!]. At her place in choir Sr. Benedicta stood in the row of novices. How did she participate in chanting this hour of Matins in the penitential monotone of the Carmelites – she who was so accustomed to celebrating the Easter liturgy with all the splendor of monastic ritual in Beuron? The day dawned gradually. Carrying burning candles and with joyful hearts, the community congratulated their Mother and Queen, the Beauty of Carmel on her victory in Jesus over death and the devil: *Regina coeli laetare. Alleluia!* [Queen of Heaven, rejoice, Alleluia!]

The procession of lights moved forward; the chantresses began to intone the great Easter hymn. *Aurora coelum purpurat* [As the rosy dawn] began to stream through the clerestory, the procession went from station to station until it eventually came to the beautifully wrought rock tomb.[G 19] From there they filed back into the choir and assumed their places.

The succeeding ceremony, the taking of vows, was performed with moving simplicity. Mother Prioress had taken up her position on the Gospel side of the choir; Edith knelt before her, folded her hands, and raised them for her superior to clasp while she herself began to recite her simple but weighty promise:

> *"I, Sister Teresia Benedicta of the Cross, make profession of my temporary vows for three years. I promise obedience, chastity and poverty to God, our Lord, to the ever Blessed Virgin Mary of Mount Carmel and to you, Reverend Mother Prioress, and to your successors, according to the Primitive Rule of the Order of Discalced Carmelite Nuns and our Constitutions."*

"Offer a sacrifice of praise to the Lord" came the prioress' exhortation. The voices of the Sisters confirmed it with the cry: "and fulfill your vows to the Almighty."

"I will fulfill my vows to the Lord in the sight of his people, and in the halls of the house of the Lord!" came the calm, firm, answer from Sr. Benedicta. Reverend Mother crowned her with the wreath of white roses that had been prepared. Again the bells accompanied the *Te Deum* [O God, we praise You] sung by the nuns while Sr. Benedicta prostrated herself before the altar in the form of the cross, completing her consecration. It was about six o'clock in the morning.

After the Divine Office, Holy Mass was offered for the intention of Christ's new Bride who was also the first to receive the Lord's Body, taking precedence over the Mother Prioress.

After Mass, however, for all that day, she had to yield to the expressions of her Sisters' joy.[T 5] A few months previously a young

Cologne girl had entered the small novitiate at Lindenthal. Wide-eyed, she had observed Sr. Benedicta and all the happenings on her special day. Now she clung to Sr. Benedicta like a small trusting child and asked, "How does Your Charity feel?"[22][G 20] Sr. Benedicta answered in a tone that cannot be imitated: *"Like the Bride of the Lamb."* An answer that was indelibly impressed in this youthful soul.

A friend, a high school instructor, some days later described her feelings after visiting Sr. Benedicta:

> I shall never forget her radiant countenance and her youthfulness during the week she was professed. It seemed as though she had become twenty years younger and I was deeply impressed by her happiness. She must have received exceptionally great graces from God – like the saints.
>
> But I also want to share what she said to me as she was sitting opposite me, wearing the wreath and her veil drawn back.[23] During our conversation I happened to remark that probably she would be safe here in Carmel. To this she quickly replied: *"Oh no, I don't believe that. Surely they will come and take me out of here. In any case I cannot count on being left here in peace."*[24] She let me know that it was clear to her that she had been called to suffer for her people, that she had a mission to bring many home.

16

Joys and Sorrows of the Bride of Christ

Some time after taking her vows, Sr. Benedicta thought it only right to tell her dear mother in Breslau of the accomplished fact. Her mother's persistent silence had never prevented her from sending off her weekly letter, and her novice-mistress never missed the opportunity of adding a few lines of her own. Who can fathom a mother's heart? And who can describe Sr. Benedicta's intense joy when in Rosa's reply one day she discovered a greeting from her mother. Even greater was her surprise when Rosa reported that one fine autumn day the old lady had gone off alone without saying a word to any of her daughters to pay a visit to the new Carmel in Breslau-Pawelwitz. Did she want to see and hear something of the way of life that her daughter had entered?[G 1] In any case, from now on every letter from Breslau brought with it a few lines from her mother, and one fine day she went so far as to include a return greeting to "Sister Teresa"[1] that was never missing in later letters. This was a great comfort to Sr. Benedicta, who had borne all her sadness without flinching and without ever allowing it to be noticed, but remained constantly warm and friendly.

A woman who knew her well writes in reference to this period, "Later I was able to visit Sr. Benedicta frequently in Carmel and each time it was noticeable how joyful and happy she was, more joyful and happy than I had ever seen her in the world."

The beginning of the year 1936 brought with it a change in the Cologne Carmel. The good Mother Josepha wished to be relieved of her office of prioress that she had held for twelve years. The election took place on 8 January.[G 2] The former novice mistress, Sister Teresa Renata, was elected prioress, and Sister Aloisia of the Blessed Sacrament became sub-prioress. However, Mother Josepha was given charge of the novices and so continued to look after Sr. Benedicta. The change made no difference to Sr. Benedicta, who held both her superiors in equal affection.

Meanwhile she herself had become the senior novice. Her two predecessors had transferred to the community after making their final vows. Three novices and one choir-postulant had joined her.[G 3] She displayed wonderful understanding and sympathy in helping these young souls to take their first steps on the ascent of Mount Carmel with greater ease. It is not seldom that a soul who has made a mighty effort to flee from the world, exhausted by the strain, breaks down once she reaches her goal after passing through the "narrow gate." She feels torn apart inside by a sorrow that St. Thérèse of the Child Jesus described after her own long experience. "I kept asking myself whether I would not die of it! What a time! What a deathly torment! One has to live through it if one is to comprehend it."[2]

Such sufferings are quite sufficient to shake the foundations of anyone who has been so suddenly transplanted into the desert. At first, in fact, many a postulant resembles a convalescent who, if she has not just eluded death itself, has at least escaped from a life that was consuming her. This courageous child has torn the net and liberated herself from the fetters of the world; and now she stands there, empty and weary. And her hands, that only yesterday were filled with the riches of the earth, now have only enough strength left to fold themselves in order to be lifted in prayer to the Lord of Hosts Who is the strength of all the weak.

It is, of course, the novice-mistress's task to inspire souls with temperate steadfastness on the road of self-denial, but how much comfort and help these young souls as yet so inexperienced in the spiritual life, gained from the example and advice of their fellow-novice! One could see plainly that she had found her peace and happiness in God, that her own heart and the rule formed a single unity, and that one could have placed in her mouth the words of the little St. Thérèse: "I busy myself internally solely with becoming more and more united to God, knowing quite well that everything else will then be given to me." It gave Sr. Benedicta great joy to guide others toward the happiness that God had granted to her so undeservedly, as she often emphasized.

For that reason, she strove to have her godchild, Dr. Ruth Kantorowicz,[3] accepted in Carmel. However, her superiors, in view of the unfavorable circumstances at the time, would not consider the candidate. This event along with many others was a wave from the raging seas outside that penetrated the silence of the Cologne Carmel. Sr. Benedicta never deluded herself about what consequences she could expect from the growing anti-Semitism. In the past she had made several contributions to the journal *Die Christliche Frau* [*Christian Woman*], and one of her essays on St. Thomas was due to appear in the December 1935 issue. The proofs arrived, but no review copy was sent. Her friends wished to look into the matter, but she herself guessed what it implied and wrote:

> *My deepest thanks, but please don't go back. After I had sent off a second article to Aachen I suddenly saw the light: neither this one nor the former one would ever appear. G.K. must have realized that the journal should no longer be compromised by my collaboration, but she did not have the courage to write and tell me. All this became clear to me when I learned that I was no longer eligible to vote. So far I have not had any confirmation of this, but I will see that I get it soon. Please do not be disturbed about this. I have been prepared for a long time for much worse.*

And in the same letter:

> *I return your Easter greetings with all my heart. I am overjoyed each day when I recall how long Easter lasts, and that we can absorb ever more of its inexhaustible riches. It is the time in the liturgical year when we are brought closest to heaven. And besides, for me the trees in bloom and the burgeoning bushes in our garden are*

*inseparably bound up with the grace-filled days of my
religious life.*[G 4]

Some weeks later, just before Pentecost, alarming news was brought
from Breslau. For the first time in her life Frau Stein was ill. Sr. Benedicta
immediately feared the worst and said: *"Now she will not see her eighty-
eighth birthday."*[5] She implored the Sisters for their prayers.

In Breslau everything possible was done to alleviate the patient's
suffering, and, in fact, Frau Stein recovered sufficiently to send her last
good wishes to her youngest child. But toward the end of June her suffering increased and it became obvious that it was incurable. The doctor had detected a tumor on her stomach, probably a cancer.

Inwardly Sr. Benedicta must have suffered a great deal, but out-
wardly she was unchanged. Still, we find in a letter she wrote about
this time: *"These summer months have been hard upon my mother
and all those at home, and for me as well."*[6] [G 5]

On 1 September 1936, Sr. Benedicta was able to put the finishing
touch to the huge philosophical work that she had begun at her Provincial's request immediately after her Clothing Ceremony. He gave
the work his approval and Sr. Benedicta sought to arrange for its
publication.[G 6]

Meanwhile, her ailing mother's condition became more and more
serious. The year drew on to the Feast of the Exaltation of the Holy
Cross, 14 September, a very important day in Carmel, since it marks
the beginning of the fast [G 7] that lasts until the day of Our Lord's
Resurrection. Also, in accordance with the seraphic Teresa's instructions all the members of the Order renew their vows. This was the third
time that Sr. Benedicta took part in the ceremony, held at a silent early-
morning hour. Afterward she said to one of her sisters who was spe-
cially intimate with her, *"When it was my turn to renew my vows my
mother was beside me. I felt her presence quite distinctly."*[7] On that
same day a telegram came from Breslau with the news that Frau Stein
had died – at the very time when her daughter was renewing her vows.

This circumstance greatly consoled Sr. Benedicta, who bore up nobly even when the first waves of sorrow were sweeping over her. All the same she did not allow herself any illusions. In the letters of condolence that she received it was frequently suggested that Frau Stein had been converted to Catholicism before she died. Her reply is to be found in a letter dated 4 October, 1936:

> *The news of my mother's conversion is a totally unfounded rumor. I have no idea who made it up. My mother held to her faith to the very last. The faith and firm confidence she had in her God from her earliest childhood until her eighty-seventh year remained steadfast, and were the last things that stayed alive in her during the final difficult agony. Therefore, I have the firm belief that she found a most merciful Judge and is now my most faithful helper on my way, so that I, too, may reach my goal.*[8]

Frieda and Rosa were now alone. According to their mother's wish they were asked to maintain the house at 38 Michaelistrasse as a permanent home for the rest of the family. Already, however, Sr. Benedicta guessed that the political circumstances of the time would soon make this impossible. She had a great desire to speak at last with Rosa – just as Rosa herself felt that she could no longer wait to see her sister. As soon as everything to do with the inheritance had been put in order Rosa began to arrange her trip to the Rhineland. She was expected in Cologne on 15 December that would enable her to experience Christmas in Carmel. But a quite unexpected incident happened beforehand.

It was 14 December, about seven o'clock in the evening. The Carmel lay wrapped in the darkness of winter; and the lights were shining in only one room, the community room, toward which everyone who had finished her evening duties was hurrying to join in recreation. Owing to the shortage of coal the novitiate room was not heated and the "little ones" had to come with their Mother, the novice-mistress, to the "grown-ups."[G 8]

The sub-prioress was missing from the circle. She was making her ten-day private retreat. She was just then praying the stations of the Cross, moving from one station to the next in the dark cloister. Suddenly she heard someone coughing lightly, that is the way Carmelites attract each other's attention during the time or in places of strict silence. "Who is there?" she called into the darkness. There was no reply. But the same sound, now like someone in pain, seemed to come from the direction of the stairs. Quickly she went across to the switch and turned on the lights. A few quick strides and she was up on the landing where she found Sr. Benedicta lying on the floor. She had been feeling for the switch on the wrong side of the door, had stepped too near the stairs and fallen down. With great effort, she was brought to her cell and the community's doctor was called in.

Dr. Eugen Hopmann was soon on the spot, and after examining her foot, that appeared to be broken, ordered the patient to be taken to Trinity Hospital immediately to have her ankle x-rayed and set. This was done as soon as we had received permission from His Eminence [G 9] for her to leave the enclosure. Everyone in Carmel was most concerned about Rosa, who was due to arrive next day and would not find her sister in Carmel, until they suddenly realized: How much better it was that Rosa could visit the patient in the hospital instead of being able to talk to her only behind a double grille.

The same evening Dr. Grüter announced the result of the X-ray: Her left foot and left hand were broken.

Rosa Stein arrived in Cologne the next day. She resembled Sr. Benedicta in appearance, still having beautiful features but, even more noticeably, the same calm gaze in her gentle eyes and the same modesty of speech and manner. She visited her religious [G 10] sister every day and listened to her instructions, because the week leading up to Christmas was to serve as her last preparation for the great day of her baptism. Christmas Eve was the date fixed.

Canon van Aacken was to administer the sacrament of her rebirth in Christ at the lovely church of Hohenlind. The arrangement of these details was undertaken by Heinrich Spaemann,[9] and the sculptress Hildegard Domizlaff[10] [G 11] who were converts themselves.[T 1] [G 12] Everything was in order. But where was one to get a white dress for the candidate? Eventually someone thought of Sr. Benedicta's white Carmelite mantle, a solution with which Rosa was overjoyed. As it happened Sr. Benedicta herself had recovered well enough to leave the hospital on 24 December wearing a walking cast; and her hand was also better. Doctor Hopmann offered to bring Sr. Benedicta back to Lindenthal after making a slight detour to Hohenlind on the way so she was given the wonderful Christmas present of attending her sister's Baptism. The Sacrament was administered at four o'clock in the afternoon. A few hours later, at midnight Christmas Mass, Rosa Stein received the Body of our Lord for the first time.

No one knew about this celebration.[11] The silent witness to the ineffable mystery given by the beautifully decorated baptismal candle[12] that burned at the crib of the newborn Savior aroused the wonderment of those attending the mass.

To celebrate her sister's rebirth by water and of the Holy Spirit, Sr. Benedicta composed the following lines, speaking in the person of Rosa herself.

HOLY NIGHT
IN REMEMBRANCE OF 24 DECEMBER 1936

My Lord and God
You have led me on a long, dark road,
Stony and hard.
Often, my strength was on the point of waning,
And, almost, I no longer hoped ever to see the light.
Yet when my heart was benumbed in the depths of sorrow
A star arose before me, gentle and clear.
Steadily it guided me – I followed it,
Haltingly at first, then ever more surely,

So at last I stood before the door of the Church.
It was opened – I begged to enter –
And from the lips of your priest I received your blessing.

Within shone row upon row of stars
Red Christmas stars,[13]
Showing me the way to you
They led me forward.
The secret of my heart, that for so long I had to hide,
I now proclaim aloud
I believe, I confess!

The priest takes me with him up the altar steps
I bow my head –
And the holy water flows over my head.

Is it possible, Lord, for one to be born again [T 2]
Who has stepped past the midpoint of life?
It is you who said it and for me it became reality.
A long life's burden of guilt and sorrow fell from me.
Standing erect I received the white mantle
That was laid on my shoulders,
The shining symbol of purity!
I carry a candle in my hand,
Its flame announces now: in me your holy Life's aglow.

My heart has now become a crib
That waits for you,
Not for long!
Mary, my Mother and your Mother,
Has given me her name.[14]
At midnight she'll lay her new-born Child
Into my heart.
No human heart could ever conceive
What you prepare for those who love you.

Now I possess you and will never let you go.
For wherever my road of life leads me, you are beside me,
Nothing can ever separate me from your love."

And what happy days of festivity God now granted to the two sisters and to the whole Carmelite community so united with them in love. The happy neophyte returned to Breslau only the day before New Year's Eve; there she received the sacrament of Confirmation on 17 May, Pentecost Monday, 1937, in the crypt of the Kreuzkirche, Church of the Holy Cross.

Looking back on these events Sr. Benedicta wrote:

> *My sister will be confirmed on Pentecost Monday. You*
> *will surely wish to be present with us in spirit.*[T 3] [G 13]
> *She depends on the inner connection with those who are*
> *geographically distant from her. That she feels estranged*
> *from her immediate surroundings is very difficult for her.*
> *But still, we must be very glad that they live together so*
> *peacefully. It is also beautiful that she draws all her*
> *strength and joy from her participation in the life of the*
> *Church. We do everything possible from here to main-*
> *tain for her a sense of belonging.*
>
> *While she was here she was received as one fully be-*
> *longing to our small Carmelite family. Obviously that helps*
> *her a great deal, even more so since they are all very in-*
> *timidated out there, for they can never really know whom*
> *they might still expect to associate with them.*[15] [G 14]

17

Learning and Service of Love [T 1] [G 1]

E ven before the end of 1936 Sr. Benedicta had completed her life's work, the revision of her comprehensive philosophical study called *Potency and Act.*[1] The result was a bulky manuscript of 1,368 single sheets. Because it organically blends the phenomenological way of looking at things with the Thomistic doctrine on being, the work ranks as an important contribution to contemporary inquiries in ontology. She called the revised work: *Finite and Eternal Being: A Survey of the Philosophia Perennis.*[2] [G 2]

By *philosophia perennis* she did not mean a scholastic system, but that unceasing search of the human spirit for true Being. Describing how the book came about, she writes:

> *This book has been written by a learner for those who are fellow-learners. At an age when others may take the risk to call themselves teachers its author found herself having to embark on her way again from the very beginning. She had received her formation in Edmund Husserl's school, and had written a series of papers using phenomenological methods.*[3] *These essays appeared in Husserl's "Jahrbuch," [G 3] and so her name became known at the very time that she abandoned philosophical work and thought of nothing less than of public activity in philosophy. She had found her way to Christ and his Church and was wholly occupied in realizing the practical consequences of this step. As she taught in the Dominican nuns' teacher training college at Speyer she could become thoroughly at home in the Catholic world. As this happened, the desire to examine the range of ideas of this world was soon aroused. Almost inevitably she went first to the writings of St. Thomas Aquinas. By translating his "Quaestiones de veritate"*[4] *she engaged once again in philosophical work.*

*St. Thomas found a reverential, willing pupil – but her
mind was by no means a tabula rasa.*[G 4] *It already had
received a very solid impression that could not deny itself.
The two philosophical worlds that came together called for
analysis. The first expression of this demand was the small
contribution to the Husserl Festschrift: "Husserl's Phenomenology and the Philosophy of St. Thomas Aquinas"[5] written
while the "Quaestiones" were still being translated. Once
the translation was completed and in the press, another
attempt at an analysis was initiated on a larger scale
and with a broader, objective foundation. A comprehensive draft was completed in the year 1931.[6] It centered on a discussion of the concepts of act and potency;
and the title of the whole work was to be based on these
two. A fundamental revision – even then considered indispensable – had to be set aside in favor of different
professional work.[7]*

*After the writer had been received into the Order of
Discalced Carmelites and completed her year in the novitiate she was directed by her superiors this past year
to prepare her old draft for publication. What resulted
was an entirely new version; only a few pages of the old
one have been retained at the beginning of the first part.
The Thomistic teaching on act and potency as the starting point was retained, but only as the starting point. At
the center stands the inquiry into Being. The differentia-
tion between Thomistic and phenomenological thought
on this question results from the objective treatment of
this question. And since both – the search for the meaning of Being and the endeavor to blend medieval thought
with the most vital thought of the present time – are not
only her personal concern but dominate philosophical
life today and are perceived by many others as an inner
need, therefore she considers it possible that her attempt,
as inadequate as it is, may be of help to others.*[8]

Soon thereafter Alexander Koyré,[9] a professor at the Sorbonne, paid
her a visit with his wife on their way to Paris. He took a brief look at

her work, that was later also read by Professor [Alois] Dempf of Bonn. Both these scholars were extremely impressed by Sr. Benedicta's work. Now a publisher had to be found, and this was a difficult undertaking.[10] Wherever Sr. Benedicta turned, whether in Germany, Austria or even Switzerland, it was refused under some pretext. Only the firm of Borgmeyer in Breslau, who had issued her translation of St. Thomas, declared themselves willing to take the risk. On the assumption that Borgmeyer as an experienced businessman had hit upon a way of circumventing the non-Aryan prohibitions, Sr. Benedicta made a contract with him on 22 July 1937.[G 5] Soon the first proofs arrived and Sr. Benedicta was fully occupied correcting them during the ensuing months. The first volume was completely typeset, and the proofs of the second including the two appendices[11] and the notes were ready, when the publisher, through a trusted person, informed Sr. Benedicta that the work was not allowed [T 2] [G 6] to appear under her name but would have to be issued under the name of another Sister, who was a member of the Reich Literary Association. Neither Sr. Benedicta nor the Sister proposed as substitute [G 7] would agree to such a proposal.[12] Under the pressure of these circumstances, Borgmeyer had no choice but to send the manuscript back and stop the printing process once and for all.

It came as no surprise to Sr. Benedicta although it was painful for her. Later, she tried to persuade Borgmeyer to send the type already set to Holland so it might be published there but this plan also proved unworkable.[G 8]

1937 was a year of grace [T 3] for the Cologne Carmel. It was the tercentenary of its foundation. This great jubilee was to be celebrated in grand style and all available talents in the Carmel and the novitiate were to be involved. Sr. Benedicta, who for the first weeks of the year still used a cane, but later walked unaided again, was engaged with all her might in all the preparations.

A *Festschrift*, [G 9] an account of the Carmel of Mary of Peace and the twelve foundations made in the Carmel's 300-year history, was to be written. Sr. Benedicta was the Mother Prioress' right hand in this work, researching the historical sources and obtaining all the necessary documentation for it. She undertook the task, when the manuscript was ready, of shaping it into chapters and paragraphs, and of preparing an exact listing of all the sources as well as a bibliography.

The approaching Jubilee also occasioned Sr. Benedicta's initiation of correspondence with the Carmel at Echt (Netherlands). When the Cologne Carmelites fled to Echt in Holland at the time of the *Kulturkampf*, they took not only themselves but also all the treasures and mementos that had belonged to the original community at Cologne. Now, very generously, the Prioress at Echt sent paintings, chronicles and other documents to Cologne to be copied. Sr. Benedicta assisted with her fluent pen with correspondence or copying, whichever was needed.[G 10]

While the tercentenary festivities took their glowing course there were threats from afar of the storm that was to sweep away so many convents. Sr. Benedicta was able to write from the Cologne Carmel:

> *So far we still live in deep peace, entirely unmolested behind our convent walls. But the fate of our Spanish Sisters* [G 11] *is an indication of what we must be prepared for. And when such profound upheaval takes place in such proximity it is a salutary warning. In any case it is our duty to support with our prayers those who have to perform such pioneer labors.*[13] *We celebrated our jubilee from 30 September to 3 October. The miraculous image of the Queen of Peace from our old monastery-church – Mary of Peace – was present as our principal guest of honor. It was displayed on the beautifully decorated high altar; every morning we had a pontifical High Mass, a High Mass and several other masses; three times daily, a sermon and a large crowd of people. One has to be grateful that something like this is still possible.*

Sr. Benedicta was happy to undertake literary work, inspired by apostolic enthusiasm, but her love of neighbor was not satisfied by merely such works, so easy for her to perform. She would have liked to perform real, practical, works of mercy. Therefore she asked if she might take care of Sister Clara of the Precious Blood who had cancer. Sr. Benedicta was very happy when her superiors allowed her to undertake this labor of love at least for a few months.[14]

In December 1937, she was also appointed under obedience to an important and responsible office in the community, that of Turn Sister [G 12] that had previously been filled by the sub-prioress. In this position, Sr. Benedicta had the duties of seeing to the Sisters' everyday needs, ordering supplies and giving the extern Sisters their instructions as well as announcing the guests and providing for them. All messages going through the grille came into her province.

As our holy Mother [=St. Teresa of Avila] insisted in her Constitutions, it is an office demanding tact, prudence and above all, discretion, virtues that Sr. Benedicta possessed in the highest degree. She behaved with lovingkindness toward the two young girls who used to see to external affairs before extern Sisters were introduced into the Cologne Carmel[15] and who were devoted to her like children.[T 4] [G 13]

18

In the Black Veil[1]

S pring of 1938 brought with it two great feasts for Sr. Benedicta, her final profession and the reception of the black veil, that would mark the end of her formation in the Order.[G 1] The final vows have to be taken on the same date on which, three years earlier, the temporary vows were taken. For Sr. Benedicta it was 21 April, which that year was Thursday in Easter week. She made a ten-day retreat in preparation for her final and irrevocable surrender to Jesus.[T 1] [G 2]

Probably she thought most earnestly about her "dear old Master," now nearly eighty years old, who had recently become ill and who, with clear consciousness and complete peace, looked forward to his imminent death. Sr. Adelgundis Jaegerschmid, O.S.B., a devoted student of his, shared with Frau Husserl in caring for him and she kept Edith informed about the final days of the dear invalid. And so 21 April dawned, the day of perpetual union with Christ for Sr. Benedicta.[T 2]

A few days later Sister Adelgundis sent a detailed account of the almost ecstatically radiant passing away of the revered "Master" that Sr. Benedicta kept as a treasured consolation until her own death.

One final seal had yet to be set upon Sr. Benedicta's marriage to Christ since she still wore the white veil of a novice. At a public ceremony she was to receive the black veil, the symbol of the sacrifice she was now definitely determined on and consecrated for.

Good Shepherd Sunday, 1 May, was the chosen date. Since the Archdiocesan Vicar for Religious, Prelate Dr. Lenné, was prevented from coming, he delegated his friend, Auxiliary Bishop Dr. Wilhelm Stockums to be celebrant.[2]

At nine o'clock Sr. Benedicta's friends were all gathered in the little monastery church. The bride herself was kneeling in the Sisters' choir before the wide-open grille to attend the High Mass and hear the priest who was to preach a special sermon for the occasion. On a rich tray on the altar lay the veil and a wreath of white roses. These were blessed while the Sisters sang *Amo Christum*, "I love Christ whose chambers I have entered; His Mother is a Virgin, His father knew no woman. His instrument – the pipe organ – sings to me in the melodious harmony of its voices. When I love Him, then I am chaste; when I touch Him, I am pure; when I receive Him, I am a virgin. With this ring He has bound me to Himself and has adorned me with treasures beyond price."

Now the Bishop moved toward the grille, calling to the bride: "Come, bride of Christ, receive the crown that your Lord has prepared for you from all eternity." A slight pause ensued. Then Sr. Benedicta rose from her knees and now gave witness of her surrender before all those present: *Suscipe me, Domine...* "Receive me, O Lord, according to Thy Word, and let not my expectations be confounded."

Sr. Benedicta went to the open grille and kneeling again, bowed her head. The Bishop covered it with the black veil, set the wreath of roses on it and said: "Receive the sacred veil, the sign of holy chastity and reverence; carry it before the judgment seat of our Lord Jesus Christ to gain eternal life and to live for ever. Amen." Shrouded in the black veil Sr. Benedicta again withdrew to the middle of the choir and sang, *"He has set his seal upon my countenance."*

Deeply moved, she sank to her knees, while the Sisters continued. "So that I admit no lover but Him." Again she lay prostrate on the floor in the form of a cross, an offering of adoration and love, while the sound of the bells joined with the human voices to glorify God in the [hymn] *Te Deum Laudamus*. After the closing blessing she rose to her feet, dead to this world, but her heart overflowing with that same joy that burst from the heart of her great predecessor, St. John of the Cross, when he sang his great song of triumph:

> Mine are the heavens and mine is the earth; mine are
> the nations, the just are mine, and mine the sinners.
> The angels are mine, and the Mother of God, and all

things are mine; and God himself is mine and for me,
because Christ is mine and all for me. What do you ask
for then, and seek, my soul? Yours is all of this, and all
is for you. Do not engage yourself in something less,
nor pay heed to the crumbs that fall from your Father's
table. Go forth and exult in your glory! Hide yourself
in it and rejoice: and you will obtain the supplications
of your heart.[3]

By making her final profession of vows Sr. Benedicta became a
full member of the community. She was now a member of the Chapter, having both the active and passive right to vote.[G 3] However she
remained what she had always been, a humble and unassuming
Carmelite Sister who carried out all her duties most conscientiously,
living for God alone and in God alone.

Nothing was more painful for her than expressions of admiration.
She once wrote to a lady who admired her greatly:

I do not want to sadden you at all, but I think I must
mention something about your last letter, as about many
previous ones, that caused me some distress. This is
your inference that there is an apparently tremendous
difference between you and me... I should consider
myself a Pharisee if I were to accept such assurances
in silence, because they have no objective foundation.
You are by no means the only person in whom our grille
instills a pious awe. But this grille does not mean that
on that side – "in the world" – everything is wicked,
whereas on this side everything is perfect. We know how
much human poverty still lies concealed below the habit,
and therefore it is very embarrassing for us whenever
we find someone strewing incense. God is merciful and
kindhearted beyond all conception and already rewards
in incomparable measure the mere intention of consecrat-
ing oneself entirely to Him. When you are here you expe-
rience in some way the peace of His House, and this we

are happy to share with you wholeheartedly. But you must
not attribute to a poor human being what is, in fact, God's
gift.[G 4]

News about hostile measures against the Jews increased. Hede Spiegel,[4] the wife of a Jewish attorney, fled to Edith, her godmother, more and more frequently, to pour out her fears and forebodings in the speakroom, and to discuss how she and her elderly parents might avoid the bloody persecution of the Jews then imminent. She was depressed and confused even more by rumors that Hitler was provoking an inevitable war, but Sr. Benedicta's indestructible calm and unshakable faith in God were a rock to which she clung.

It was only natural that in Sr. Benedicta's own mind the thought of emigrating should arise, especially when she heard of people being harassed on account of their association with Jews. This made her fear for the beloved Carmelite family to which she belonged. However, her superior forbade her to mention the matter, so as to avoid disturbing anxious souls before the need arose. And then came the great day of the final decisive election called by Hitler.

Posted on every tree in the Dürenerstrasse at Lindenthal were the sententious words, *"Dem Führer Dein 'Ja'"* or "For the Führer Your Yes!" The previous elections had already provided their own little intermezzo. According to proclamations, non-Aryans were not to take part in the elections. Sr. Benedicta therefore stayed behind while the other Sisters, with the Archbishop's permission, set off for the polls to do what little they could for the just cause. But that same evening, just before the voting closed, two gentlemen appeared in the parlor. Having established that Dr. Stein was the only one in Carmel who had not exercised her right to vote, they assumed it was because she did not feel well enough to go. But they had an auto and would gladly drive her to and from the poll. This was the message brought to Sr. Benedicta and the Prioress by the turn-sister. Since Sr. Benedicta had no mind to declare her ancestry just then, and since there were no other objections, she said very quietly: *"Well, if the gentlemen are so keen to have my 'No' recorded – I cannot bear to disappoint them."* Quickly slipping on her shoes she made ready for the journey.[G 5]

But on 10 April the matter was more serious. Hitler's method of governing and the fundamental teachings of National Socialism had proved to be so clearly hostile to God and Christianity that even the simplest German could no longer be deceived about Hitler's aim. At the same time, the power of the authorities by this time had developed so brutally that everyone was terrified. And so in the Cologne Carmel also, there was much uncertainty about how one should behave. The Gestapo had already forced a lot of religious out of their convents or monasteries without warning and without cause, putting them out on the street without any means of support.[5]

For a long time the Cologne Carmel had been expecting this same fate, that would almost certainly befall them if they attracted the attention of the authorities at this election. Well-meant advice to have nothing to do with the elections was therefore unacceptable.[G 6] Most of the community adopted the attitude that it did not matter how one voted, since the result of the election in any case was a foregone conclusion and the Nazis would make sure that the desired result was achieved in each voting precinct.

Against this view Sr. Benedicta raised her voice with great zeal. She who was generally such a gentle and retiring person was hardly recognizable any more. Repeatedly she implored the Sisters not to vote for Hitler no matter what the consequences to individuals or to the community might be. He was an enemy of God and would drag Germany into perdition with himself. There was great confusion, but it grew even more just before eight o'clock on the morning of the election as the first group of Sisters were getting ready to depart for the polls. Some of the election officials carrying an urn for the ballots were shown into the speakroom of the Cologne Carmel. This was quite unprecedented, and Mother Prioress did not hesitate to express to the gentlemen her displeasure in all frankness. In reply they said they were aware that Carmelites are not allowed to leave the enclosure and so had simply come to oblige the Sisters by collecting their votes. But Mother Prioress insisted that, although voting was a secret act, it was also a public duty that the Sisters had always performed publicly in order to set people a good example in citizenship. The gentlemen were preventing this by coming as they had done. But it was no use to protest, and she had to give in. In alphabetical order, the voting took its course.

At the end the official in charge of the list of voters said, "There are some who have not voted. Anna Fitzeck's one." "She cannot vote," came the curt answer. "Why not?" "Because she is feeble-minded." A short pause and then the dreaded question, "And Dr. Edith Stein? She has not voted either." "She is not entitled to vote." "Certainly she is – year of birth 1891! She is entitled to vote!" The answer was given with iron calm, "She is a non-Aryan." The three of them drew back. Then one of them called out, "Write it down – she is non-Aryan." With all speed they took off and left the Carmel.

When Sr. Benedicta learned all that had happened, she again proposed a transfer. Most of all she would have wished to go to Palestine to the Carmel in Bethlehem that a lay-Sister named Miriam (Mary) of Jesus Crucified, a great servant of God, had founded.[G 7] Most of the Sisters would not believe such a separation was necessary as yet. Then the events of 9 November made it imperative.[G 8] Order was more or less preserved in the quiet suburb of Lindenthal, but the news that synagogues had been burnt, that Jews and their friends had been attacked and their houses wrecked penetrated even into Carmel and filled them all with horror.

Sr. Benedicta herself was almost paralyzed by grief.

> *It is the shadow of the Cross falling upon my people. If only they would understand! It is the fulfillment of the curse that my people called upon its own head.*
> *Cain must be persecuted, but woe to whoever lays hands upon Cain. Woe also to this city and this country*

when God's wrath for what they are now doing to the
Jews descends upon them.[G 9]

Now her fear that her presence was endangering the community
took from her every shred of peace. Since the government in Palestine
refused to admit any more German Jews, Mother Prioress wrote off to
Echt in Holland mentioning that Sr. Benedicta needed a change of air.
The good Sisters understood immediately what "change of air" meant
in this context and warmly invited her to come and join them. And so
Advent was taken up with preparing for the journey and procuring the
necessary papers.

A photo was required for a passport, and so they sent for a photog-
rapher. He came one afternoon and Sr. Benedicta stationed herself by
the open door of the enclosure, since she did not wish to leave the
enclosure on any account until it was absolutely necessary. As usual
she wore her threadbare Carmelite habit. When the Prioress, who was
present, noticed how heavily darned it was, she took off her own scapular and placed it over Sr. Benedicta, who acknowledged the action
with an indescribable look of filial gratitude in her beautiful eyes. The
result was that final photograph that is true to life.

The feasts of Christmas and its octave were saturated that year
with grief at the approaching departure. There certainly were opti-
mists who maintained that the separation would not be for long. And
there were those who were more far-seeing, Sr. Benedicta among them,
who said that it would be forever.

The preparations for the journey were carried out with great caution. In accordance with Sr. Benedicta's own wishes, demonstrative-
ness of any kind was discouraged. Even in the hours just before she
left she remained strong and calm. The first sign of emotion was when
one of the older Sisters, the tears streaming down her face, thanked her
for the good example she had set them from the very first. "*How can
Your Charity say that?*[G 10] *It is I who must thank God for having
allowed me to live with you.*" This was the conviction with which she
had entered the Cologne Carmel and with which she left it.

Paul Strerath, M.D., a friend of the Cologne community and great servant of God, had offered to transport her across the frontier under cover of darkness. Sr. Benedicta had asked if she might have the consolation of praying for a while before the holy statue of the Queen of Peace. This wish being granted, Dr. Strerath drew up at the cozy rectory "Vor den Siebenburgen" where Sr. Benedicta visited the shrine and knelt for the last time at this sacred spot, the cradle of the German Carmelites.[G 11] Four years later, during the year of her death, both the interior of the church and the statue of the Queen of Peace went up in smoke and flames. A last farewell at the hospitable rectory and the car drove away to the Netherlands. At about eight o'clock the travelers arrived in Echt after a comfortable journey. The community had all gathered in the recreation room, and welcomed the poor refugee with the utmost warmth though not, perhaps, without a certain curiosity. "What immediately struck us as so pleasant about Sr. Benedicta was her simple, modest bearing, along with her delicate tact and her warm-heartedness," the Sisters said, when describing her later. "Her features were marked by a deep seriousness, that was very noticeable that evening; evidently due to her grief at having to leave her beloved Carmel in Cologne."

19

In Echt[1]

The little Dutch village of Echt in Limburg [G 1] had offered hospitality to the Cologne Carmelites when they were driven out of Germany during the *Kulturkampf.* Mother Teresia Alberta, the prioress of the community, was able to rent a suitable house until she obtained a plot of land in Boovenste Straat where it was possible to build the church and convent. Since all the Sisters were German it was only natural that most of the vocations to the Carmel were German girls, with the result that for many years German remained the community's everyday language. But as the National Socialist ideology spread, Holland, too, began to reject foreign ways and speech; the Father Provincial of the Dutch Carmelites, therefore prescribed Dutch as the accepted language for prayer, Chapter, refectory reading, and conversation in those communities that came originally from Germany – Roermond, Maastricht and Echt. In other respects, however, the Echt Carmel retained its original German character, largely because the two most influential personalities there were German.

These were Reverend Mothers Ottilia of Jesus[2] and Antonia of the Holy Spirit,[3] one or other of whom was generally either Prioress or Sub-Prioress. When Sr. Benedicta was transferred to Echt the prioress happened to be Mother Ottilia, a mystical person. The sub-prioress was Mother Antonia, a woman according to the heart of St. Teresa of Avila with an enlightened foresight and undaunted energy whom Sr. Benedicta had come to know through the Jubilee correspondence of 1937.[4]

The community numbered thirteen choir-nuns of whom ten were German and four German lay-Sisters. Sr. Benedicta immediately applied herself to the task of learning Dutch, thus adding another to the six languages she had already mastered.[G 2]

> From the very first day she tried to adapt herself to all
> the community's customs. Ever ready to help and wish-

ing to have a share in all the work, she never refused
any favors that were asked of her. Often, in fact, she
even got in the way through over-eagerness, because
with all her good will when it came to practical work,
she could never achieve a real dexterity. Even when she
was sweeping, one saw how unused she was to this
simple household task. The same was true of her needle-
work; she never progressed beyond the beginners' stage.
In recreation she was at once serious and merry. She
could laugh heartily and was always glad to tell stories
about her interesting life.

So runs the Echt Sisters' account of Sr. Benedicta.

Sr. Benedicta had not taken her unfinished family history along to
Echt in order not to give herself away, should crossing the border possibly mean an inspection of her baggage. Now, she would have been
glad to continue working on it and so inquired of Cologne in February, 1939, whether any of her friends there might have the courage to
bring her the dangerous opus. Rev. Dr. Rhabanus, C.M.M., a young
Mariannhill Missionary, offered straight away to undertake this adventure.[5] At the border, his car was stopped and searched. The customs officer came across the voluminous manuscript; flicked through
it and handed it back with the words, " I guess this is your doctoral
thesis." And so, in Echt, Sr. Benedicta was able to continue with this
work, that was so dear to her heart and a true relaxation.[6]

With her charity and unselfishness she did not take long to settle
into the new circle of Sisters, and soon Reverend Mother entrusted
her with a small "office" in the community. She made her assistant to
the portress, Sister Maria Pia, "a genuine Westphalian"[7] as she described
herself the first time they met on New Year's Eve. In Sr. Pia's own words:

> We felt drawn to each other from the start. It turned out
> that we got together sometimes, and we always got along
> splendidly. Later, when Rosa Stein came to live in the
> convent in a room outside the enclosure she also used

to confide in me a lot. One could be well satisfied with
both of them, and what I liked so much was their simplicity, and their unpretentious ways. Sr. Benedicta was
especially modest in regard to eating and drinking so
that Mother Prioress had to warn her occasionally not
to overdo it. Both of them had such tender hearts, even
too tender, perhaps; Sr. Benedicta, for instance, thought
it wrong to kill a mosquito. She found it hard whenever
she heard anyone making remarks about the Jews that
put them in the shade. She would say that almost all
were calumnies, and that, *"just as people will impute
anything at all to the Jesuits, just so is it with the Jews."*

Although Sr. Benedicta, the Carmelite, always remembered her
identity as a member of the Chosen People, it would be a mistake to
imagine that she boasted about her Jewishness. Only with great simplicity would she speak on such matters with persons sensitive to God's
ways who were not inhibited by current opinion. Unhampered by concern for her own self she could quite calmly penetrate to the Source of
all Being, that she saw as necessarily springing from a *Person.* God
answered her cry with the revelation of his triune Personhood and
confirmed her joy at being descended from the people who had always
worshipped Him as the God of Abraham, Isaac and Jacob, the name
by which He wishes to be known to the end of time. This joy used to
radiate like a peaceful light from her beautiful eyes whenever she discussed the Old Covenant, a light that may well have illumined the
road to her own Golgotha. How easily one can understand how she
suffered with her people in these times.

   She would have loved to see once more her favorite sister Erna,
and her family, who left Breslau in 1939 and embarked for America.
Most cordially she invited them to visit her in Echt. But Erna wrote
that, "Having bought tickets to go via Hamburg, and hearing how dangerous it was to cross the Dutch frontier, we decided not to risk it."[8]
Therefore the sisters had to forego even this last farewell.[9]

Sr. Benedicta was all the more pleased, therefore, in the summer of 1940 when her sister Rosa eventually arrived in Echt after several misadventures. Rosa had come to Cologne in 1939 and had been housed in one of the rooms in the extern quarters.[G 3]

She had moved all her household goods and her valuables to Aachen where they were stored, so that she could move from there to Belgium. Moving furniture over the border just at that time, with war imminent, was both difficult and dangerous for a non-Aryan. Finally, it was accomplished with the help of the Cologne portresses.[G 4]

Rosa herself went to Belgium a little later, where, in a small town, she hoped to meet a lady with whom she had been in correspondence for some time. This lady had been advertising in German newspapers to attract members for an Order that she was planning to found, and Rosa wished to join in this worthy cause.

But as soon as she saw the poor and disorderly state the place was in, she realized that she had fallen into the clutches of a swindler, and immediately tried to withdraw. But this seemed almost impossible because she was stranded with no money in a strange land whose language she could not speak. Sr. Benedicta contacted all her own acquaintances to secure a passport for Rosa to come to Holland. These efforts dragged on until the summer of 1940, and even then Rosa received only a personal passport. All her possessions had to remain in Belgium. A certain amount of clothing and linen was all she could bring with her. Everyone was amazed at the equanimity with which Rosa bore the loss of her dearest mementos and the way in which she had surrendered herself to God's will. Thus testify the Sisters in Echt:

> She never allowed a word of complaint to escape from her lips and even joked about how she had become detached from her worldly goods at one swoop! It was all the more admirable since Rosa was a convert of so few years. She possessed excellent qualities needed for running a household and all the people coming to the

monastery appreciated her greatly. In addition she had
a really noble heart, demanding nothing whatsoever for
herself and giving everything she had to others. One of
her outstanding qualities was her sound common sense.
She always worked diligently, got up very early and
spent hours praying in the chapel. In the evening she
would be in the chapel again, holding long converse
with the Eucharistic Savior.[10]

To the relief of all who loved them, both sisters now seemed to be
in safety while in Germany the Church continued to suffer a relent-
less, though secret, persecution. In their concern for the Cologne
Carmel the good Sisters at Echt kept advising the Mother Prioress to
bring the whole community to Holland for safety, saying that Germany was on the brink of a catastrophe. But in Cologne no one would
have dreamed of abandoning the Fatherland in its hour of trial. On the
first of September war broke out with the pillaging of Poland, followed in 1940 by the illegal occupation of neutral Holland.[11] This made
our lively correspondence with Echt more difficult and severely restricted it. Still, we were informed from time to time that Sr. Benedicta
and Rosa Stein were both quite safe and well.

In Echt, too, Sr. Benedicta was allowed to continue with her literary
work. First of all, she compiled a detailed index of subjects and names
for *Finite and Eternal Being* that still exists. She wrote such essays as
"St. Elizabeth as a Spiritual Guide," "Intellectuals," "St. Teresa, the
Teacher," "Love for Love," "The Marriage Feast of the Lamb" and
"The Mystical Sufferings of St. John of the Cross."[12]

Sr. Benedicta's great devotion to the Divine Office induced the
Mother Prioress to entrust the instruction of the younger Sisters on
this subject to her and she also taught them Latin.

For a considerable period she was refectorian as well, that entailed
looking after the refectory and the Sisters' nutritional needs.[G 5]

At the beginning of 1941 Mother Prioress relieved Sr. Benedicta
of her office as turn-Sister to give her more free time for her scholarly

work. She finished her *Ways to Know God.*[13][G 6] But her chief work was *The Science of the Cross,* that she composed during her hours of silence and solitude, for she drew it from the mysterious depths of her intense contemplation and poured it out again in her own crystal-clear language.

In this accomplished interpretation of the sublime mystical teaching of St. John of the Cross she displays a spiritual kinship with that eagle of mystics such as one finds nowhere else except in the saint's greatest daughter.[14] A few sentences from Sr. Benedicta's introduction demonstrate this:

> *In the following pages, an attempt will be made to grasp John of the Cross in the unity of his being as it expresses itself in his life and in his works – from a viewpoint that will enable us to see this unity.*
>
> *This is, therefore,not a biography nor a general evaluative presentation of his doctrine. But the facts of his life and the content of his writings have to be taken into account in order to reach that unity through them. The witnesses will speak in detail, but after they have spoken, an attempt will be made to interpret them and this interpretation will be validated by what the author believes she has gained from a lifelong effort to grasp the laws of spiritual being and life.*
>
> *This holds above all for the expositions on spirit, faith, and contemplation that are inserted at various points, particularly in the chapter: The Soul in the Kingdom of the Spirit and of Spirits. What is said there about the I, freedom, and person, does not spring from the teaching of our Holy Father John of the Cross.*
>
> *Of course there are certain points of departure to be found in him. Expositions on them, however, were far from his main intention and his thought processes. Constructing a philosophy of the person, such as is indicated in the passages named, has, after all, been made a task only in modern philosophy.*[15]

The whole work[16] was produced in 1941-1942 to commemorate the fourth centenary of the birth of St. John of the Cross. Though it was written within the brief period of nine to ten months, Sr. Benedicta had in fact been meditating on it for years. The concept *Science of the Cross* is worked out in its twofold sense, as a theology of the Cross and as a school of the Cross – that is, life under the symbol of the Cross. Therefore this book not only offers a modern exposition of St. John of the Cross but Sr. Benedicta's personal witness.[17]

Sister Pia tells us:

> Sr. Benedicta applied herself so assiduously to writing this book that she seemed to have had a premonition of what was to happen. The last pages were written on 2 August 1942.[18][G 7] Every spare moment of the day and even a part of the night were devoted to it. Yet she never neglected her obligatory prayers [G 8]; in the evenings she was to be heard leaving her cell just before the bell rang so as to be in choir punctually for Matins, and in the morning she got up before the time for rising. Through the open cell-window she could be seen at prayer, on her knees with her arms outstretched. Rosa Stein, who had now been received into the Third Order of Our Lady of Mount Carmel, used, like her sister in the enclosure, to spend many hours of each day praying in the public chapel. Nor were they praying for themselves alone. They clung lovingly to the people from whom they were descended, and as their predecessors Judith and Esther had once offered their prayers and penances to save the people Israel from destruction, so these two apostolic souls were now throwing themselves into the arms of divine justice to obtain salvation and mercy for both persecuted and persecutors.

While the furies of war were claiming their victims on all sides the leaders of Germany calculated that the time had come to release a storm against convents. The Carmelite Order did not escape. The first victims were the Sisters in Luxembourg who were driven out of their monastery in February 1941 so that it could be made into a clubhouse and dance-hall for the B.d.M.[19] Scarcely had these homeless nuns found refuge with their Sisters in Pützchen before this Carmel also, together with the Carmel of Aachen, was dissolved in a space of two hours by the arbitrary power of the Gestapo. Düren followed in August of the same year.

Sr. Benedicta's reflections upon these events are contained in a letter[20] written at the beginning of September 1941: [G 9]

> *Today it is good to reflect on the fact that poverty also includes the readiness to leave our beloved monastery itself. We have pledged ourselves to enclosure and do so anew when we renew our vows. But God did not pledge to leave us within the walls of the enclosure forever. He need not do so because He has other walls to protect us. This is similar to what he does in the sacraments. For us they are the prescribed means to grace, and we cannot receive them eagerly enough. But God is not bound to them. At the moment when some external force were to cut us off from receiving the sacraments, He could compensate us, abundantly, in some other way; and He will do so all the more certainly and generously the more faithfully we have adhered to the sacraments previously. So it is also our holy duty to be as conscientious as possible in observing the precept of the enclosure to lead without hindrance a life hidden with Christ in God. If we are faithful and are then driven out into the street, the Lord will send His angels to encamp themselves around us, and their invisible pinions will enclose our souls more securely than the highest and strongest walls. We do not need to wish for this to happen. We may ask that the experience be spared us, but only with the solemn and honestly intended addition: "Not mine, but Your will be done!"*

With this conviction in mind Sr. Benedicta entered the last stage of her life. The Cologne Carmel was also expecting to be suspended.

Trying to anticipate any eventuality, the Mother Prioress ordered all letters and private notes that might have betrayed the location of Sr. Benedicta's refuge to be destroyed, that accounts for the loss of her very precious letters. The only letter that has been saved was one addressed to a young friend[21] who had entered the Cologne Carmel eight weeks after Sr. Benedicta herself:

Echt, 16 May 1941

I received Your Charity's letter today and am allowed to reply to Y.C. at once. I believe that it is good for Your Charity to work at something definite for there is a strong creative talent there that needs to be directed into a definite channel. It also seems to me that a good beginning has been made. Surely these books did not come "accidentally" into Your Charity's hands. Mother Prioress knows how things happened for me in this respect: how at the appropriate moment it would "occur" to me what I needed at the time, and then it would come to me from somewhere. Your Charity probably knows that there is still a fragment there by our holy Mother on the Song of Songs. The "Spiritual Canticle" will also be very helpful to Your Charity. And surely Your Charity would be glad to take St. Bernard to hand. But I do not know whether there is a translation. Were I there, I would gladly translate everything for Your Charity. A commentary by Fr. Athanasius Miller, O.S.B. can probably give you a bit of an insight into the present interpretation. Surely there are still Fathers coming to the house (P.S.S) [P. Swidbert Soreth, O.P.] who could give you information on sources and provide from somewhere what Your Charity needs. Aside from that, the help of the Holy Spirit is obviously most important. I am very happy to ask for that help with Your Charity and will also be very grateful if Your Charity does the same for me, for I, too, am unable to count on anything else. I am going about my new task [she is referring to *The Science of the Cross*] *like a little child making its first attempts at walking.*

The Holy Spirit must help Your Charity not only at your work, but also in overcoming new crises that may easily arise from it. After all, no spiritual work comes into the world without severe labor pains. It tends to absorb the total person and that, of course, is something we may not permit. On principle, it is very good that the regular schedule and our daily duties bar the door to "letting oneself be devoured"; but the way to achieve this balance annot be found without our being aware of it. I would be very happy were we able to talk about all this sometime. But surely it is not accidental that such an opportunity has been taken from us. So we will be grateful that we are united in the kingdom that knows no boundaries or restraints, no separation and no distance.

Since we have a little postulant in the house again, I think often of our own young days in the Order, and of the wonderful [providential] *guidance that each one's way to Carmel signifies. Perhaps even more wonderful is the story of the souls in Carmel. They are hidden deep in the Divine Heart. And what we believe we understand about our own soul is, after all, only a fleeting reflection of what will remain God's secret until the day when all will be made manifest. My great joy consists in the hope of that future clarity. Faith in the secret history must always strengthen us when what we actually perceive (about ourselves or about others) might discourage us.*

Today is the feast of St. Simon Stock. We sang his High Mass this morning and used the "Flos Carmeli" as the hymn for our May devotion. There are so many promises contained in it.[22]

In Corde Jesu et Regina Carmeli,
Your Charity's faithful, least Sr. Benedicta [G 10]

20

Plans of Escape

With good reason Sr. Benedicta concluded that events in Germany were foreshadowing future developments in the occupied countries. In her account of those days Sister Pia of Echt writes, "She was very concerned about her future, and since she was kept abreast of Jewish affairs by Fräulein Rosa, she herself gave the local authorities all the information she thought was necessary for their security."

Convinced as she was that they could not stay in Holland indefinitely, Sr. Benedicta was not in favor of petitioning Rome to make her a member of the Echt Carmel.[1] Having lived at Echt for three years would have entitled her to that move. Although there had been no legal transfer,[2] the prioress had already granted her the privilege of place and voice in Chapter.[G 1] Instead, Sr. Benedicta wrote to good friends in Switzerland.[3] Fräulein Nägeli and Dr. Vérène Borsinger of the editorial staff of the *Katholische Schweizerin* [*The Catholic Swiss Woman*], Bern, offered to find out whether she could be received into the Carmel of Le Pâquier, near Freiburg, and to handle negotiations with the authorities.[4] The impression that Sr. Benedicta had made in Switzerland, shortly before entering the Order, especially upon the women social workers, remained fresh in their minds. In her lectures at [T 1] Zurich she had talked about Carmel,[5] as she always did, and been instrumental in drawing some new members to the Third Order.[G 2]

Amongst these tertiaries was a great admirer of Edith Stein's whom the Lord led to Le Pâquier Carmel in 1940. When the prioress received Sr. Benedicta's request to be received at Le Pâquier she approached this novice, who had enjoyed a very wide circle of acquaintants in the world, and asked her if the name of Edith Stein meant anything to her. Her enthusiastic reaction to the name was answer enough, and soon the novice was writing with feverish energy to interest all her influential Swiss friends in Sr. Benedicta's fate. It was January 1942. There was certainly no lack of letters of recommendation. In no time Mother Prioress had moved the hearts of her daughters in Le Pâquier and won their support for Sr. Benedicta's acceptance.

Fräulein Dr. Borsinger held out the highest hopes and after some initial astonishment, the Bishop, Monsignor Besson, gave his permission.[6][G 3] Then the difficulties began.[7] On no account would Sr. Benedicta be separated from Rosa, but it would have been impossible for the Carmel to have taken in two foreign Sisters while at the same time they had to refuse young Swiss postulants for lack of space, sending them to Carmels abroad.[G 4]

Once more the generous Mother Prioress mustered her powers of persuasion. She succeeded in convincing the Third Order Carmelites [G 5] to take Rosa in. But the Tertiaries had first of all to obtain permission from their motherhouse in France, all of that meant constant delays.[8] Finally this permission, too, was obtained, but now the civil authorities were making difficulties.[9] Fräulein Dr. Borsinger went from one office to another. The imploring letters from Echt became more and more urgent; the Sisters there feared the worst. Why? What was going on?

After the first welcoming words from Le Pâquier Sr. Benedicta immediately applied for an exit visa to Switzerland. Were the police made aware of her by this action? In any case, Sr. Teresa Benedicta and Rosa received a summons to report in Maastricht. The Dutch Provincial, Father Cornelius Leunissen, O.C.D., intervened and very kindly went to answer the summons himself. He hoped to be able to save them from going in person by insisting on their strict rule of enclosure. But the German police took a dim view of his attempt.[10][G 6] They ordered Sr. Benedicta to appear in person. When she entered the Gestapo office in Maastricht she greeted those present with the words, "Praised be Jesus Christ!"[11][G 7] Startled by this greeting they simply looked up but did not reply. (Later she explained to Reverend Mother that she had felt driven to behave as she had done, knowing well enough that it was imprudent from a human standpoint, because she saw quite clearly that this was no mere question of politics but was part of the eternal struggle between Jesus and Lucifer.) She had to show them her identity card, and as it was not stamped with a large "J" to signify that she was Jewish, nor was her name, Edith, preceded by the name Sara that was prescribed for all Jewish women, they stormed and raged at her.[12] They ordered her to write immediately to the Police Bureau in Breslau and to request "most humbly" that her identity card be modified as required. Afterwards both sisters still had to report to the Joodsen Raad, where they were treated very kindly[13] but were assured that a summons to Amsterdam was certain to come within a few weeks.

Once again a card was sent off to the Cologne Carmel on 9 April (1942). Its calm tone gave no intimation of the storm that was gathering over Sr. Benedicta's head:

> *Dear Sister Maria,*
>
> *Last night I received your kind letter of St. Joseph's feast day* [19 March].[G 8] *I was able to read it without too much trouble* [emphasis is due to her correspondent's distinctive handwriting] *and it made me very happy. Precisely because our ways have to be so diverse, both by nature and by development, it means so much to me when they at times meet at a temporary goal.*
>
> *I have to produce everything with a great deal of effort. To be sure, the building plan is another gift bestowed on me, that is, it unfolds little by little. But I have to quarry the stones by myself, and prepare them, and drag them into place. Besides, while working on this task it often happened when I was greatly exhausted that I had the feeling I could not penetrate to what I wished to say and to grasp. I already thought that it would always remain so. But now I feel I have renewed vigor for creative effort. Holy Father John gave me renewed impetus for some remarks concerning symbols. When I finish this MS I would like to send a German copy off to*

*Father Heribert the German Provincial at the time to
have it duplicated for the monasteries.*[G 9]
　　*The only reason I write so little is that I need all the
time for Father John. Your Charity will understand this
and take my treatises as letters, just as I take Your
Charity's letters as treatises.*
　　　　　　　*Most cordially Your Charity's least Sister
　　　　　　　Benedicta[14]*

Indeed, in May both sisters had to go to Amsterdam for several days to appear before the Gestapo and the Joodsen Raad. They had to stay there for a few days and lived with some Catholic Sisters who were very edified by them. They went from one office to another to answer every possible kind of question, filling in sheaves of forms in triplicate without discovering what is was all about. The Gestapo conducted their inquiries pretty relentlessly, ordering the two sisters, for example, to stand at a distance of three yards during their cross-examinations. In one of these offices, they encountered a kind Gestapo official from Cologne. He told them how the city had been badly damaged by air raids, and confirmed that the church *Maria vom Frieden* along with its miraculous statue had gone up in flames on 28 April 1942.[15]

Among the Jews who had been summoned by the Gestapo was a godchild of Sr. Benedicta's, Alice Reis. Two years after her conversion in 1934, she had come to Leiderdorp, the Dutch provincial-house of the Sisters of the Good Shepherd, recommended by the Sisters in Rastatt [Germany]. Unfortunately she had to leave the Order soon after her clothing because of ill health. Since a return to Germany would have been unwise at that time because of the circumstances, she stayed in Holland serving as a lay helper in various houses of the Order.[16] She and Sr. Benedicta were greatly consoled to see each other again. They had no presentiment that they would soon be united again. Sr. Benedicta's own contacts with the Gestapo had only increased her apprehension. She feared that the Swiss effort to rescue her would not succeed in time, so she also applied to go to Spain.[17][G 10]

In this mood, Sr. Benedicta wrote once more to Cologne in June:

> For months I have been wearing next to my heart a slip
> of paper with the 23rd verse of Mt 10[18] written on it.
> Negotiations with Le Pâquier are still going on, but I
> am so deeply absorbed in John of the Cross that all
> else is a matter of indifference to me.

In Switzerland hopes were running high. During the Ember Days of Pentecost [G 11] one of the most pleasant cells was made ready to receive Sr. Benedicta, that meant that two of the Sisters had to share one cell because the Carmel of Le Pâquier had already reached its complement.[G 12]

Some weeks later the Chapter held a vote and recorded it as follows:

> On Saturday, 4 July 1942, the Chapter nuns of Le Pâquier
> were assembled for a meeting at which the Reverend
> Mother Prioress proposed to them that Sister Teresia
> Benedicta of the Cross, in the world Edith Stein, a pro-
> fessed Sister of the Cologne Carmel who is at present
> in the Carmel of Echt in Holland, be received as a mem-
> ber of the community, either permanently or temporar-
> ily according to circumstances.
>
> In 1938, because of her Jewishness, Sr. Benedicta
> was forced to leave the Carmel where she had made her
> profession. The German authorities who have conquered
> Holland are now compelling her to leave that country. The
> Sister in question has obtained the necessary permis-
> sion for her transfer from the Most Reverend Father
> Provincial in Holland; our Most Reverend Bishop has
> agreed to her reception into our Carmel,[19] and petition
> has been made to our Most Reverend Father General
> for the Indult.[G 13]
>
> On the fifth of the same month, a Sunday, the nuns
> were assembled once again and the Reverend Mother
> Prioress made the same proposal, after which it was unani-
> mously resolved by a secret vote to receive Sister Teresa
> Benedicta into the community for an unlimited time.[20]

We, the undersigned, testify that the above account
is exact,

> Sr. Marie Agnes of the Immaculate Conception,
> Prioress;
>
> Sr. Marie-Françoise of the Most Sacred Heart,
> 1st Clavary [G 14]
> Executed on 5 July 1942, at Le Pâquier.[21]

So the Swiss Carmel had made all preparations, but they were still waiting for the consent of the Swiss civil authorities. Coincidentally, Dr. Etter, President of the Federal Council of Switzerland, paid a visit to the little Carmel at Le Pâquier on 29 July. Reverend Mother seized the opportunity to interest him on Sr. Benedicta's behalf, whereupon he promised to take the matter into his own hands. In her latest letter to the Reverend Mother, Vérène Borsinger had written how depressed she was to see the civil difficulties mount, even though she had replied "Yes" very definitely when the Federal Council had asked whether the non-Aryan applicant stood in danger of her life. Her fear was at its utmost. In fact she had been on holiday at the time but had returned to Bern to speed the negotiations.[22]

In Holland the regulations issued against the Jews grew steadily more fierce. In August 1941, a conflict had already arisen between the Dutch Episcopate and the German authorities. On the Reichskommissar's[23] instruction Professor van Dam had published a decree by which Jewish children were to be taught only by Jewish school teachers. This meant that Catholic children of Jewish parentage were deprived of a Catholic education. Mgr. Johannes de Jong,[24] in the name of all the bishops, protested against this injustice and declared that Catholic educators would never exclude children from school on account of their [racial] origins.

Soon afterwards a proclamation was issued that signs should be posted on all public buildings, "*Voor Joden Verboden.*" ["Forbidden to Jews"]. The Bishops refused this also. Yet the exclusion of Jews from public life was nothing when compared to the mass deportations of men, women and children, indeed of whole Jewish families, that began in 1942. As was generally feared, many of them went to meet certain death in the Polish concentration camps, where they were either gassed or driven to do inhuman work in the salt, lead or tin mines.

On 11 July 1942 the Church communities sent a telegram to the Reichskommissar expressing their anger at these measures, that were totally repugnant to the deepest moral feelings of the Dutch people, and that, above all, defied the divine precepts of justice and mercy. Jewish Christians under these measures were cut off from sharing in the life of the Church. Consequently the Church communities urgently requested that these measures not be carried out.

Replying in the name of the Reichskommissar, General-Kommissar Schmidt, gave an assurance that Jewish Christians who had been members of a Christian community before January 1941 would not be deported.

The Bishop of Roermond wrote at once to Sr. Benedicta, quoting this exception, in order to set her mind at rest.[25] But the favorable decision did not remove the opposition of the churches to the deportation of Jews as such and therefore they resolved to issue a joint protest in writing that was to be read publicly in all the churches on Sunday 26 July 1942.

The proclamation should contain the text of the telegram sent to Seyss-Inquart on 11 July 1942. But even before the day on which it was to be read, Seyss-Inquart and Schmidt found out about the content of this joint letter of the church communities. On 24 July, they attempted to persuade Ds. H.J. Diykmeester[26] of the Nederlandse Herformde Kerk to omit the telegram from the text to be read aloud, alleging that it had a confidential character. The Synod of the Nederlandse Herformde Kerk was prepared to make this concession, but the Gereformerde Kerk (the Calvinist Church) and other church communities refused to agree. The Archbishop of Utrecht also refused on the grounds that he could not countenance a secular power's intervention or attempt to influence a pastoral letter. Besides, from a technical viewpoint it was impossible to make alterations in the pastoral letter that had already been sent off.

Therefore the pastoral letter of 20 July was read in all the Catholic churches on Sunday 26 July.[27]

At the very beginning, the pastoral letter made the following statements:

> We are experiencing a time of great distress, as well from a spiritual as from a material standpoint. But there are two problems greater than any others, that of the Jews and that of those who are deported to forced labor abroad.
>
> We must all become deeply aware of these dangers, and it is the purpose of this joint pastoral letter to make you conscious of them.
>
> Such distress must also be brought to the notice of those who exercise power over these people. Therefore the Most Reverend [Catholic] Episcopate of the Netherlands, in conjunction with almost all the other church communities in the Netherlands, has turned to the authorities of the occupying forces; for the Jews among others, in a telegram with the following content dispatched on Saturday 11 July of this year:
>
> "The undersigned church communities of the Netherlands, deeply shaken by the measures taken against the Jews in the Netherlands that have excluded them from participation in the normal life of the people, have learned with horror of the latest regulations by which men, women, children and whole families are to be deported to the territory of the German Reich.
>
> The suffering that has thus been imposed on tens of thousands of people, the awareness that these regulations offend the deepest moral convictions of the people of the Netherlands, and above all, the denial in these regulations of God's precepts of justice and mercy, force the undersigned religious communities to direct to you the most urgent request that these regulations shall not be carried out. On behalf of those Jews who are Christians we wish to emphasize further that these regulations will cut them off from participating in the normal life of the Church."
>
> As a result of this telegram one of the General-Kommissars in the name of the Reichskommissar has

conceded that Jewish Christians shall not be deported so long as they belonged to a Christian church before January 1941.

Dear Faithful! When we survey the frightful misery of body and soul that has for three years been threatening the whole world with destruction, we cannot help thinking of the event portrayed for us in today's Gospel.

In those days, as Jesus drew near [to Jerusalem] and caught sight of the city, he wept over it, and said: "Would that even today you knew the things that make for peace! But now they are hid from your eyes. For the days shall come upon you when your enemies will cast up a bank about you and surround you, and hem you in on every side, and dash you to the ground, you and your children within you, and they will not leave one stone upon another in you; because you did not know the time of your visitation."(Lk 19:41-44) This prophecy of Jesus was fulfilled to the letter: Forty years later the city of Jerusalem was visited by God's judgment. Unfortunately, it had not recognized the time of grace.

Now, too, everything around us points toward a judgment by God. But, thanks be to God, for us it is not too late. We can still avert that judgment, if we recognize the time of grace, if we will even now see what will serve as our way to peace. And that is only a return to God from whom a part of the world has already turned away for so many years. All human remedies have proved to be in vain – God alone can help anymore.

Dear Faithful! Let us in the first place examine our own selves in a spirit of deep repentance and humility. For do we not share the blame for the catastrophes we are enduring? – Have we always sought first the kingdom of God and His justice? – Have we always practiced our duty of justice and love of neighbor to those around us? – Have we not perhaps nourished feelings of unholy hatred and bitterness? – Have we always sought our refuge in God, our heavenly Father?

When we look inward we must realize that we have all failed. *Peccavimus ante Dominum Deum nostrum;* we have sinned before the Lord, our God.

But we also know that God does not despise a humble and contrite heart. *Cor contritum et humilatum non despicies.* Therefore we turn to Him and, filled with childlike trust, beseech Him for mercy. He himself tells us, "Ask and you shall receive, seek and you shall find, knock and it shall be opened up to you."(Mt. 7:7)

In the Introit of today's Mass the Church calls to us in the words of the Psalmist – "Behold God is my helper: and the Lord is the upholder of my life."(Ps. 54:4). And in the epistle the Church repeats those ever comforting words of the Apostle, "May no temptation come upon you that is beyond human strength. God is faithful and He will not let you be tempted beyond your strength, but with the temptation, He will also provide the way of escape that you may be able to endure it."(1 Cor 10:13)

And so, dear Faithful, let us implore God, through the intercession of the Mother of Mercy, that He may soon grant the world a just peace. That He may strengthen the people of Israel who are being so sorely tested in these days, and may He bring them to the true redemption in Christ Jesus. – May He shelter those whose lot it is to work in a strange land and to live far from their loved ones at home. May He shelter them in body and soul, protecting them from bitterness and loss of courage, keeping them true in the Faith and strengthening their families at home. – Let us implore His help for all those in tribulation, for the oppressed, for prisoners and hostages, for so many over whom hang clouds of threat and the peril of death – *Pateant aures misericordiæ tuæ, Domine, precibus supplicantium* [Open the ears of Thy Mercy, O Lord, to the prayers of those who beseech Thee].

This our joint pastoral shall be read out on Sunday 26 July in all churches within our province and in all

chapels where there is a rector, at every appointed mass
and in the customary manner.

> Given at Utrecht on 20 July
> in the year of our Lord 1942.

This pastoral aroused great excitement in Holland, and the people
became very disturbed and apprehensive over the consequences it was
likely to produce.[28]

In Carmel, however, the oppressed hearts breathed easier again, because Sr. Benedicta had learned from some lines from Bishop Lemmens
that the threatened punishment was now lifted. So she was thought to
be safe, and thanksgiving was offered to God for this favorable turn of
events, that seemed so appropriate to the Liturgy of the day. For it was
the feast of St. Peter's Chains (1 Aug.), about which Sr. Benedicta had
written years earlier:

> *St. Peter in Chains is also a feast I particularly like, not
> as honoring him, but as a commemoration of being freed
> from fetters through the ministry of the angels. How
> many chains have already been removed in this fash-
> ion, and how blessed it will be when the last of them
> falls away.*[29]

Now St. Peter's Chains was to be the last quiet day of Carmelite
life for Sr. Benedicta. Already God had dispatched his angels to end
the exile of this truly free woman whose only remaining attachment to
earth was through her body. While everyone believed that the dreaded
disaster had been averted, the catastrophe was the more unexpected.

On 2 August all non-Aryan members of every Dutch religious community were arrested and taken away.[30] In Echt there was no hint of
what was about to happen. At five in the afternoon the Sisters had
assembled in choir for meditation;[31] Sr. Benedicta was just reading
out the point for meditation when two rings at the turn were heard, the
signal that Mother Prioress was wanted in the speakroom. When she
asked at the turn who wished to speak with her she was told that there

were two officers asking for Sister Stein. So the Reverend Mother signaled for Sr. Benedicta to leave the choir and sent her to the speakroom alone, thinking it was about the exit permit for Switzerland that the two sisters had been expecting daily.

"Two monasteries situated close to each other in the Canton of Freiburg had offered to accept them and on the part of Switzerland, entry permits had been granted[32] so I thought that they could get on without me," reported Mother Prioress. And so she called for Sr. Benedicta to leave the choir and go to the speakroom:

> Rosa was already waiting in the extern part of the speakroom. Standing outside at the window of the choir I said to the community, "Sisters, please pray. I think the Gestapo are here!" Then I stationed myself at the speakroom door to await the result of the conversation. To my horror I discovered that it was something much worse. They were members of the SS. One of them, the spokesman, ordered Sr. Benedicta to leave the monastery within five minutes. She replied, "I can't do that. We are strictly cloistered." "Get this out of the way [he meant the iron grille] and come out." "You must show me how to do it first." "Call your superior." Having heard it all myself I made a slight detour to go to the speakroom while Sr. Benedicta returned to the Choir.
>
> She knelt reverently in front of the Blessed Sacrament and then left the Choir with the whispered words, "Please pray, Sisters!" She signaled to Sister Pia who hurried after her and asked anxiously, "Where to, Sr. Benedicta?" "I must leave the house in ten minutes." "But where to?" "He didn't say.'"

Only then did Sister Pia realize that it must be the SS. Mother Antonia meanwhile had been speaking to the SS man:

> He said, "Are you the Superior?" "Yes." "Sister Stein must leave the monastery in five minutes." "That is impossible." "Then in ten minutes. We don't have time!"

"We have taken steps to have the two sisters received into Swiss monasteries and are only waiting for the permission from the Germans. On the Swiss side everything is already arranged." "That can all be taken care of later, but now Sister Stein must come out. She can either change into something else or come as she is. Give her a blanket, a mug, a spoon and three days' rations." Again the anguished superior protested. The SS man replied, "You can imagine what the consequences will be for you and your monastery if you refuse to send Sister Stein out." Thinking that he was trying to frighten her the prioress said, "Give us half an hour at least." "That's impossible. We don't have the time." Seeing that nothing would move him she said, "If we must give way to force, then we do so in the name of God." She left the speakroom and went upstairs to Sr. Benedicta's cell, where several of the Sisters were already helping her to pack. Sr. Benedicta said quickly, "Please write straight away to the Swiss Consul at the Hague for the travel permits." (We had been in contact with the consul for some time now.)[33] She was still so convinced that the transfer to the Le Pâquier Carmel was a possibility. Then she scarcely spoke again, and her mind seemed to be far away.

Mother Antonia continues:

I went from her cell to the enclosure door, where Fräulein Rosa was kneeling to receive a farewell blessing. A lady, one of her friends, lovingly assisted her. Soon Sr. Benedicta joined them. The other Sisters were running here and there to the kitchen to get her a snack. Sr. Benedicta could only take a few bites because there was no more time.[G 15]

After the two of them had gone outside the enclosure, I could still hear Sr. Benedicta explaining to the spokesman her plans for leaving the country. I did not hear the second officer say anything. While they had been waiting in the speakroom, the two gentlemen had remained perfectly quiet, and we had behaved as calmly as possible in spite of the grief of this mutual farewell.

Of course, the whole street was full of people loudly protesting against this barbarous injustice, for Rosa Stein was very popular and highly respected by the local people.[G16] But whoever wanted to show sympathy came off badly. At the street corner the police van was waiting to move off, having already collected several more victims, among them two boarding students[34] from the Institut Koningsbosch. The two sisters climbed in and then the van drove off, no one knew where.[G 17]

That very day General-Kommissar Schmidt announced in a public speech at 's Gravenhage that this had happened in reprisal against the pastoral letter of 26 July. He ended with these words:

> Even in a few Protestant churches declarations were made in which they took up an unmistakable position. However, the representatives of the Protestant churches have informed us that this announcement was not in accord with their intention but could not be withdrawn in time for technical reasons. Since the Catholic hierarchy, on the other hand, refuses to trouble about negotiations, then we, for our part, are compelled to regard the Catholic Jews as our worst enemies and consequently see to their deportation to the East with all possible speed.[35]

Archbishop de Jong in the name of the hierarchy vigorously protested in writing to Seyss-Inquart, on 23 August 1942, about this statement by Schmidt, with its untruths and misrepresentations. To begin with, various Protestant churches had read out the whole text of the joint letter and had never even considered omitting the telegram of 11 July. Furthermore, this was the first that anyone had heard about these "negotiations with which the Catholic hierarchy would not be troubled."

Neither Ds. (Rev.) Diykmeester nor General-Kommissar Schmidt, at their meeting on 24 July, had breathed a word about the attitude of the Catholic Church or the other religious bodies toward omitting the telegram. At the same time the Archbishop said what he thought of the Germans' pretense that the telegram was "confidential." "There is nothing confidential about a dispatch by telegraph about regulations that are publicly proclaimed and carried out. Moreover, the Catholic population had every right to know what steps their bishops had taken in face of such an important issue as the deportation of the Jews that had upset everyone."

In his deep distress at the Catholic Jews and religious being made the scapegoat, the Archbishop tried desperately to have the same exception applied to them as applied to all other Jewish Christians.[36] This request was repeated in a telegram of 27 August. But Seyss-Inquart made no reply either to the petition or to the telegram.

The one who furnished these accounts, Fr. Horster, S.V.D.[37] of Venlo, adds the comment: "From Commander Schmidt's declaration one can probably conclude that all these religious, both men and women, truly died *in testimonium fidei*, because their arrest was an act of reprisal for the bishops' pastoral letter.[38] It was an attempt to strike at the bishops and the Church by arresting Jewish members of Catholic religious orders."

21

The Way of the Cross

D ays went by. In the Carmel of Echt bitter grief and the torment of waiting prevailed. Had she gone, never to be heard of again? It was on Wednesday, 5 August, that a telegram arrived in the afternoon. It came from Westerbork, a tiny place beside the railway in Northern Holland.[1] The Joodsen Raad [Jewish Council] had sent it at the same time as they sent a similar telegram on behalf of Ruth Kantorowicz to the Ursulines in Venlo, that read: "Send warm clothing, blankets and medication immediately by messenger for Ruth Kantorowicz at Westerbork assembly camp near Hooghalen."

"It was the signal for a positive contest in lovingkindness on the part of the Sisters. Each of them wished to do something for their dear ones, each to sacrifice some object of her own. Everything was collected in the Chapter-room to be packed, so that the whole of this big room looked just like a shop, full of blankets and parcels. Books, candles, edibles and I don't know what all else, ready to go," Mother Antonia reported.

While clearing out Sr. Benedicta's cell they had found a small picture on the back of which she had written down her wish to sacrifice her life for the conversion of the Jews. As it was also sent on to her with the other gifts, this written testimony of her readiness for this heroic sacrifice was unfortunately lost. One precious memento of her is still kept, however, in the Echt Carmel, a used postcard on the back of which Sr. Benedicta had addressed a petition to her prioress as long ago as March 1939. It is a fresh proof of how obediently and loyally she responded to the renewed graces pouring into her soul, of her unconditional wish to pledge her all for the Kingdom of Christ, of how world-inclusive was her love for humankind and how she had looked reality squarely in the face and had foreseen what would come to pass.

She wrote:

> *Passion Sunday, 26 March 1939*
> *Dear Mother, please, will Your Reverence allow me to*
> *offer myself to the Heart of Jesus as a sacrifice of propi-*
> *tiation for true peace: that the dominion of Antichrist may*
> *collapse, if possible, without a new world war, and that a*
> *new order may be established? I would like it [my re-*
> *quest] granted this very day because it is the twelfth hour.*
> *I know that I am a nothing, but Jesus desires it, and surely*
> *He will call many others to do likewise in these days.*[2]

The Sisters' main concern was to find suitable messengers. Two men from Echt said they were willing to deliver the various articles. Early on Thursday morning they set off loaded with cases and parcels.[3] As the camp lay at a considerable distance they blessed their good luck when they were picked up on the way by a truck that was carrying sand to the camp.

Later these men [Pierre Cuypers and Piet O. van Kempen] gave the following account of what happened:[4]

> We arrived at Hooghalen exactly at five o'clock. There we met two gentlemen who had been sent from Venlo by the Ursulines to contact Dr. Ruth Kantorowicz. The camp itself lies about five kilometers away from Hooghalen. In front of the camp's [T 1] barracks,[5] we came to a small building where we had to report to the Dutch police. We gave them the telegram; we offered cigars and cigarettes and were soon chatting to each other in a friendly way. The police did their duty reluc-tantly. When they learned why we were there, they sent a Jewish youngster with the telegram to the barrack where Sr. Benedicta and Rosa were billeted. After a few minutes of suspense, the high barbed-wire fence was opened and immediately, in the distance, we could see the brown habit and black veil of Sr. Benedicta, who was accompanied by her sister.

The Dutch police guards outside the camp were at first greatly surprised to learn that we wished to visit nuns in the camp. They said, "But there are no nuns in this camp!" Only after inquiring did they learn it was true.

Our emotions when we met the sisters were a mixture of sadness and joy. We shook hands and, because they were so happy to see people from Echt again, it was some time before anyone could get any words out. But the ice was soon broken and we handed them everything the Carmelites had given us. Sr. Benedicta in particular was glad and thankful when she heard of her Sisters' greetings and prayers. Through the kindness of the Dutch police she received unopened all that was in writing, even Mother Prioress's letter. Sr. Benedicta told us at once that they found many acquaintances in the camp, even relatives.[6]

On their journey their route had been as follows. In the police van they went from Echt to the headquarters at Roermond. In the evening they left in two police vans, one carrying thirteen and the other seventeen people. The destination was Amersfoort, but the driver missed his way and they did not arrive till three in the morning.[7]

Between Echt and Amersfoort the German SS were very obliging and friendly toward the prisoners, but in Amersfoort Camp they were treated very brutally, the SS prodding them on their backs with their rifle stocks, cursing and driving them with nothing to eat into a barrack where they had to sleep. The non-Catholic Jews appeased their hunger and then, after they had tried to sleep a little while in bunk beds, the prisoners were transported to Westerbork Camp near Hooghalen. Through the intervention of the Jewish Council that was looking after the prisoners, they were allowed to send telegrams. The Council is very kind, especially to Catholic Jews.[8] But the German Commandant of the camp ordered the Catholic Jews to be isolated from the rest. So now the Council can and may do nothing for them. They are all together in one barrack.

Sr. Benedicta told us all this calmly and composedly. In her eyes shone the mysterious radiance of a saintly Carmelite. Quietly and calmly she described everyone's troubles but her own. We were especially to remember to assure the Carmelites that she was still wearing the habit of the Order and that all the other nuns in the barrack – there were ten of them – intended to keep on wearing their habits.[G 1] She explained how glad everyone in the Camp had been to find Catholic nuns and priests there. These latter were the one hope and support of all the poor folk in camp who lacked everything, absolutely everything.

Sr. Benedicta was glad she was able to help with comforting words and prayers. Her deep faith created about her an atmosphere of heavenly life. Several times she assured us that, as far as she and her sister were concerned, Reverend Mother could set her mind completely at rest. The whole day was free for prayer[9] except for three breaks to collect their food. They had no complaint about the food, or about the soldiers' treatment of them. She did not know how long they would have to stay in the camp. There was a rumor that they would be leaving today (Friday 7 August) perhaps for Silesia, their homeland, but no one knew for certain.[G 2] Rumor had it that they were waiting for another transport of Jews from Amsterdam that had arrived the previous night (Thursday to Friday).[10] All was well for Fräulein Rosa too. She was greatly encouraged and strengthened by the example of Sr. Benedicta. If they had to leave, then no matter what kind of work she would be given (and this is still not known), nothing would be allowed to take precedence over prayer. Sr. Benedicta had written a short letter, but does not know if it arrived."[11]

Thus ends the account of their visit that the two good men wrote down in 1947, but one of the two messengers sent by the Ursulines from Venlo to Ruth Kantorowicz also made a report:

On Thursday, 6 August 1942, Mr. Jan Philipsen and I[12] set off loaded with cases for the Hooghalen Jewish Camp. On the way, after we made several changes; at one station I noticed two gentlemen and a nun who were always going the same way. At the end of the line we all saw one another again. The Sister was trying to find transportation for herself. The two men from Echt and we two had searched out the sand delivery situation between Westerbork and Hooghalen. The truck driver had already warned me that if the SS patrol discovered us we would never get the suitcases through. So we drove toward the camp with anxious hearts.

The truck stopped right outside a kind of pavilion, a glass house from which you had a clear view on all sides. These were the quarters of the Dutch police guards. The driver had revealed to us that we should try to get in there as quickly as possible because then we could count on success. It could not have worked out better. The police were visibly astonished to hear that the ones in the camp to whom we wished to speak were nuns.

They called in a little Jewish boy, some sort of orderly it seems, and explained our business to him. He knew at once in that barrack (No. 7, I believe) these people were billeted, and so he was sent off to fetch the persons asked for. Meanwhile the nun had arrived in a cab and we learned that she was the Mother Superior of a Community (Sisters of St. Joseph, Roermond, I think) seeking one of her nuns in the camp.[13] The boy returned with everyone we wanted.

Fräulein Ruth spotted me while they were still a long way off and she waved joyously. Each of them wore the Star of David. Fräulein Ruth was of course an old friend of the Carmelite, and they came to us together. But we arranged with the police to go with Fräulein Ruth to a bench behind the guard-house where we could talk to her privately and give her the parcels. As far as I know all the other visitors were allowed to get their packages

personally. Fräulein Ruth outlined for us the story of
the treatment they had had to endure so far. After their
arrest they were all delivered to Amersfoort, and then
shipped on a freight train to Hooghalen. But the train
stopped in an open stretch of country before Hooghalen
and they had to get out, after that they were herded across
fields, through the woods and hedges to the camp. Here
the Catholics had been isolated from the rest; that in one
way pleased Fräulein Ruth because she was now
amongst members of religious orders.

In the morning they would get up very early to say
their morning prayers together. There were also several
Trappist monks and lay-brothers, all siblings from the
same family, three or four of them.[G 3] They all came
to see the visitors, wearing their habits and the Star of
David. Whether they had their own visitors as well I
cannot say for certain.

Fräulein Ruth expressed the hope that they might
soon be allowed to have a Holy Mass celebrated every
morning. When the SS patrol with a shrill blast on their
whistles signaled the prisoners to go back to their barracks, Fräulein Ruth quickly called the Carmelite to
come across and introduced her to us. I was edified by
how composed and calm this Sister was.

When I offered her my sympathy, the brave Sister
said: "*Whatever happens I am prepared for it. The dear
Child Jesus is among us even here.*" With a firm handclasp she wished God's blessing on me and mine. When
I tried to express my own wishes she assured me we
need not worry about them, because they were all in
God's hands. When it came to bidding all the others
good-bye, the words just stuck in my throat. The prisoners walked away in a group to their barracks, but kept
turning to wave to us, all except Sr. Benedicta, who
went resolutely on her way.

Since we could not get back to Venlo that same day,
we preferred to stay overnight in Hooghalen. We were

on our feet early next morning. At the little railway station I noticed two men wearing the Star of David and said to Mr. Philipsen, "I'll have a word with them" and, though he thought it might be dangerous to talk to a Jew openly, I did so nevertheless. On my asking whether they came from the camp they said "Yes," and when I inquired if they knew Barracks 7 they informed me that all the Catholics, lay and religious, had been taken away during the night, apparently to the East.

These accounts are supplemented by a few lines that were written by a Jewish businessman from Cologne, Julius Markan. In the Westerbork Camp he had been put in charge of the prisoners and, along with his wife, had the good fortune to be spared deportation:

> Among the prisoners who were brought in on 5 August, Sr. Benedicta stood out on account of her great calmness and composure. The distress in the barracks, and the stir caused by the new arrivals, was indescribable. Sr. Benedicta was just like an angel, going around among the women, comforting them, helping them and calming them. Many of the mothers were near to distraction; they had not bothered about their children the whole day long, but just sat brooding in dumb despair. Sr. Benedicta took care of the little children, washed them and combed them, looked after their feeding and their other needs. During the whole of her stay there, she was so busy washing and cleaning as acts of lovingkindness that everyone was astonished.

This heroic performance of the spiritual and corporal works of mercy complete the portrait of this valiant woman who forgot her own plight because of the suffering of her neighbor and who was in every instance intent on being all things to all for the sake of Christ. Mr. Markan reports one conversation with Sr. Benedicta that, of course he is no longer able to recall in exact detail. He asked her: "What are you going to do now?" And she answered: "*So far I prayed and worked, from now on I will work and pray*."[14]

Their stay in Westerbork lasted from early on Wednesday, 5 August until the night of 6-7 August.[15] Altogether 1,200 Catholic Jews were interned in the barracks of whom ten to fifteen were members of religious orders. Together with Sr. Benedicta, a thousand Jews were deported during the night. Before leaving, however, Edith had managed to write [T 2] notes that eventually reached the Reverend Mother. [An analysis of this complicated series of messages from the transit camps and the texts can be found in [T 3] [G 4].]

[Another note]. . .took some days to arrive at Echt, and was written the same day that the messengers brought the articles asked for in the telegram.

> *J. M.*
> *Pax Xti!*
>
> > *Drente-Westerbork. Barracks 36. 6.VIII.42*
> > *Dear Mother, One Mother Superior from one of the convents arrived last evening with some suitcases for her child and now offers to take some short letters along. Early tomorrow a transport leaves (Silesia or Czechoslovakia?). What is most necessary: woolen stockings, two blankets. For Rosa all the warm underwear and whatever was in the laundry; for us both, towels and washcloths. Rosa also has no toothbrush, no cross and no rosary. I would like the next volume of the Breviary (so far I have been able to pray gloriously.) Our identity-cards, registration cards [as Jews] and ration cards.*
> > > *A thousand thanks and greetings to all,*
> > > *Y. R.'s grateful child, B.*
>
> *[PS] 1 Habit and aprons,*
> *1 small veil.* [G 5] [T 4]

News gradually filtered in that other convents had been the victims of the SS visitation on the same day; experiences were exchanged and so were the letters smuggled through by the abducted nuns.

The first note from Alice Reis was written after the whole group had been transferred from the barracks at Amersfoort to the Westerbork assembly camp, and it reached the Sisters of the Good Shepherd at Almelo on 6 August. Although she was not a religious she had worked at the convent as a lay helper. At five o'clock on the morning of 2 August, she had been carried off by the Gestapo, even though the superior protested vigorously and, pointing out that Alice suffered from severe asthma, tried by every means to prevent her arrest. In her note she asked them to send warm garments, bandages, and so forth, right away, because they had absolutely nothing. A telegram arrived at eight o'clock the same evening asking for the same articles, that the Sisters sent off by express delivery before nightfall. Alice had also informed them that the prisoners would not be kept in Holland but were to be transported farther away. Consequently the Sisters tried to find someone who could go personally the next morning to Westerbork or Assen in order to deliver the articles. But when the Dean of Almelo phoned the priest at Assen, he learned that the entire group had been transported to the East at half past three that very morning.

We can form an even clearer picture of this whole group from a letter that Fräulein Dr. Meirowsky addressed to her confessor in Tilburg, again on 6 August. Dr. Meirowsky and Sr. Benedicta had only been slightly acquainted previously, but during the first months of 1942 they had exchanged several letters.[16] Since 1940 Dr. Meirowsky had lived at the lodge of the Trappistine Abbey near Tilburg, acting as doorkeeper for the community besides rendering valuable service as the community-doctor. She was a member of the Dominican Third Order and regarded by the Trappistines as one of themselves. Her letter reads:

> *Transfiguratio, 6 August 42*
> You know already where we are, and that we are expecting to be sent to Poland. Tomorrow morning is the time fixed. There are two Trappistine nuns with me here, as well as two Trappist monks and a lay-brother from

the same abbey;[17] all of us were driven to the camp at Amersfoort on Sunday morning, before being brought to Westerbork Hooghalen on the Feast of our Holy Father, St. Dominic. I know, dear Father, that you're heart and soul in this with me, with us all. Your spiritual child, Sister Judith, is also here, and so is the Carmelite from Echt whom I met that time in Amsterdam. Now I want to send you my last greetings and to tell you that I have complete confidence in God and have surrendered myself entirely to His Will. Even more – I regard it as a grace and privilege to be driven along this road under these conditions, a witness to the words of our good fathers and shepherds in Christ.

If our sufferings have been increased somewhat then we have received a double portion of grace, and a glorious crown is being prepared for us in heaven. Rejoice with me. I am going forward unshaken, confidently and joyfully – like the Sisters who are with me – to testify to Jesus Christ, and to bear witness to the Truth in company with our bishops. We are going as children of Our Holy Mother, the Church; we will unite our suffering with the sufferings of our King, our Savior and our Bridegroom, sacrificing ourselves for the conversion of many, for the Jews, for those who persecute us, so that all may know the peace of Christ and His Kingdom.

In case I do not survive, would you please be so good as to write later on to my beloved parents and brothers, telling them that my life is being offered for them – may God grant them the light of faith and happiness both on earth and in heaven, if that is His Will. Pass on my love and gratitude to them and ask them to forgive me for any wrongs and sorrows I have caused them. Tell them also that my mother's sisters and my father's twin-sisters left here for Poland full of faith and trust, wholly given to the will of God. And send my best wishes to my sister-in-law and my little nieces – from the depths of my heart I pray for the good of their souls. Tell Fr. Stratman that he must not be troubled, but rather join me in thanking God for this great favor by singing an exultant Magnificat; the work that we started together [she refers to the Peace Movement] will only be fruitful when, where and how God wills. And this is the best and surest way for me to cooperate; either through my slight sufferings, that are not to be compared with the eternity of happiness that awaits us – or to continue by his side helping him from beyond the grave.

If you have the opportunity to visit Tilburg Abbey later on, please do so, or write to Father Willibrordus van Dyk that I gratefully pray for him always. I myself shall be writing to Mother Abbess and Father Rector, who was my confessor. All our good friends are brought into my prayers and sacrifice. Please write also to Frau Schmutzer in Utrecht; and please pray very hard for dear Dr. Lazarus, who has been imprisoned in Amersfoort Camp because he did not wear the Star. I am praying much for him.

And now I want to thank you from my heart for all your goodness toward me, for your compassionate brotherly love. How often you have given me courage.

Here our greatest trial is that we do not have Holy Mass and Communion; but if Jesus does not wish it, neither do I. He dwells in my heart, walks with me and gives me strength. He is my strength and my peace.

As soon as I can write again you shall hear from me. Would you also be so kind (if you think it advisable) to write to me on an international reply card (but not prepaid). May Mary protect you and God sanctify you with His Love. Once more I humbly ask for your prayers and your priestly blessing.

> In Jesus and Mary,
> Your Sister M. Magdalena Dominica
> (In the world Doctor Meirowsky) [G 6]

The community at Echt waited anxiously for some further communication, but the only news was of the deportation on the First Friday of all in the entire barracks to Poland. The vans were[18] full to the result that many of these poor creatures died on the journey. Moreover they were all reportedly dressed in prison uniform.[19] In Cologne they knew nothing at all of all of these events. Communication with Echt had necessarily been curtailed by the strict censorship imposed on foreign mail. The two sisters had been assigned to a group of forty Catholics that included some recently converted Jews. Perhaps they had already acquired their martyrs' crown before anything was heard of them in Cologne Carmel. The awful news eventually came in a few words written on a plain postcard from Echt: "B and R. taken away 2.VIII. Destination unknown. Probably to the East."[20]

What dreadful news! Shortly before, the Carmel at Le Pâquier had reported that all the passport difficulties had been surmounted, and Switzerland was now offering the two sisters refuge.[21] To their grief the Carmelites learned that all their trouble had been in vain. For a long time the cell set aside for Sr. Benedicta stood empty, awaiting her coming, but with heavy heart the Mother Prioress had to make the following entry in the Chapter book:

> Sister Teresia Benedicta, who with her sister Rosa had obtained an entry permit for Switzerland, thanks to the good offices of Mons. Etter, President of the Confederation, was suddenly (in ten minutes) abducted with her from the Carmel at Echt by the German police, and taken to an unknown destination in the East. We are making inquiries in various places to find her, but, alas, with no real hope.
>
> [Soeur Teresia Benedicta ayant obtenu, ainsi que sa soeur Rosa, l'entrée en Suisse, grâce à la bienveillante intervention de Mons. Etter, président de la Confédération, fut emmenée soudainement avec elle (en dix minutes) de son Carmel d'Echt par la police allemande pour destination inconnue vers l'est. Nous faisons des démarches de plusieurs cotés pour la retrouver, sans vrai espoir, hélas!][22]

22

The Last News

Now people began to inquire surreptitiously from many directions to find out the whereabouts of the missing women [Rosa and Edith Stein]. Yet these efforts had to be considered hopeless from the outset, for no one could name a specific concentration camp, and everything had to be done under cover. Various rumors circulated, but none proved reliable. Then just before Christmas 1942, Sister Bonaventura, from the monastery of St. Magdalena in Speyer visited the Cologne Carmel with a piece of information that she had not dared to send by mail. On 6 August (actually it must have been the 7th)[1] a newly married woman was standing on the platform at Schifferstadt, when she suddenly heard someone call her by her maiden name. On looking around, she recognized her former teacher, Fräulein Dr. Stein, in one of the trains at the station. Dr. Stein called to her, "*Give my love to the Sisters at St. Magdalena – I am on my way to the East.*" Despite tireless inquiries, this lady's name could not be discovered.[2] Valentin Fouqué,[3] the stationmaster at Schifferstadt, reports that, on the same day, a lady dressed in black, one of a group of prisoners being transported by train, introduced herself to him as a Carmelite named Sr. Benedicta, and asked whether by chance there happened to be a member of the Schwind family at the station.[G 1] [T 1] He replied that Dean Schwind from Frankenthal-Mörsch had been at the station just a few minutes before. Then she asked him to give him [Dean Schwind] her regards and tell him that she was en route to Poland.

Half an hour later the station master met Fräulein Schwind, the dean's sister, at the station and told her that a transport train had stopped there and a lady had sent her regards to the Schwind family.

It seems that the last word from Edith reached a St. Lioba Sister in Freiburg who received a small penciled note from an unknown quarter; it said no more than, *"Greetings from my trip to Poland. Sister Teresia Benedicta."*[G 2].

At first friends and Sisters of the beloved deportee cherished the hope that she was still alive and would come back. All kinds of rumors sprang up that no one could pursue, because most people had enough troubles of their own during those terrible years of bombardment. At one time Sr. Benedicta was reported to be in Auschwitz, on another occasion she was said to be in Theresienstadt. Others maintained that she had volunteered to go from there to Litzmannstadt (Lodz)[4] to work as a nurse. Last of all, a Jehovah's Witness [G 3] in Speyer, who had been released from concentration camp, claimed that she had seen Sr. Benedicta in Ravensbrück. Such news nourished the hopes of all who worried about the beloved Sr. Benedicta and prayed for her.

Meanwhile the Cologne Carmel had also met its doom. For four years the church and convent seemed to have been miraculously protected from the countless air raids that hit Cologne. Although it was hit time and again, no external damage could be seen; the Carmel still remained, like a peaceful oasis, in a desert of ruins. Then on the evening of 30 October 1944, came a sustained hour-long air attack that, in a powerful hail of bombs, reduced Lindenthal to a heap of rubble and ashes. The Carmel, too, was completely destroyed, except for a small room in the cellar, where the Sisters were huddled on their knees, sure that death was at hand. But the Lord was not in the earthquake that shook the foundations. He was not in the storm of bombs that swept away the house, nor in the fire that attacked them from all sides. He led them unharmed out of the place of horrors, out of the burning city into the welcoming peace of their sisters at Welden Carmel near Augsburg.

All contacts with the Carmel in Echt were broken off, as Holland was occupied by the Allies. Earlier, the Sisters in Echt had suffered a great deal during the defense of the town by German troops, and had to abandon their convent for a short time. Fortunately, they had previously put the papers left by Sr. Benedicta into good order and stored them away. Thus everything remained in safety until the Sisters were suddenly forced to flee from Echt, on 6 January 1945, before the wave of retreating troops. All of them were taken to Herkenbosch in German military vehicles. But three days later several Sisters managed to return to Echt to salvage some things. At that time they brought Sr. Benedicta's writings back with them in two bags.[5]

"We wanted to hide them in the cellar of the little convent, that resembled a house of cards and that had given us shelter," Mother Antonia recounted, "but the prioress did not permit it due to lack of space. So the bags were left upstairs. We asked at the big Franciscan house in Vlodrop whether we might store them there, but severe shelling prevented the request from getting attended to for three weeks. Long before this, we ourselves had been driven out of Herkenbosch, and although Sister Pia was left behind to look after Sister Francisca, who was wounded, she could do nothing. Danger and destruction were everywhere. Once we were in Leinarden, communication with the South was disrupted for months. We were powerless."

Eventually, in March 1945, a military vehicle, carrying Professor Father Hermann van Breda, O.F.M., director of the Husserl Archive and the Carmelite Prior of Geleen,[6] went from Leuven to Echt, where Sr. Pia and Sr. Francisca had returned. There they searched for the manuscripts. Since they could find nothing, they drove on to Herkenbosch in ice-cold winter weather. There they searched the tiny convent that was by now nothing more than a ruin, and they found, soiled, torn and scattered, about three quarters of [Sr. Benedicta's] papers. Later on, these were entrusted to the archivist of the Husserl-Archiv, Dr. L[ucy] Gelber, for restoration and scholarly evaluation.

In 1945 the country was beginning to return to some sort of order that enabled the Sisters to establish contact with America through the Red Cross, especially in order to inform Frau Dr. Biberstein of the forcible deportation of her sisters, Rosa and Edith. Knowing what such news meant, Dr. Biberstein also started making inquiries. Yet all was in vain.

Neither the office of the Father General of the Carmelite Order in Rome, nor the relatives in America, nor the Carmelite convents in either Germany, Holland or Switzerland were able to discover any trace of them. All the more startling, therefore, for everyone concerned was a notice that appeared in the *Osservatore Romano* in 1947, that reported the following news:

From Judaism to the University, and thence to Carmel

Before she entered life as a Religious, the Carmelite Sr. Benedicta a Cruce was known throughout Germany as Dr. Edith Stein, a woman philosopher and convert from Judaism to Catholicism.

Sr. Benedicta was born in 1875 [*sic*] and executed in 1945 [*sic*] by the Nazis. In October 1933 she entered the Carmelite convent at Lindenthal near Cologne, Germany. On account of her [Jewish] origins, she was secretly transferred to safety to the Carmel at Echt in Holland in 1938. One of her superiors testifies that she was as obedient as St. Thérèse of Lisieux. On 2 August 1945 [*sic*] a Nazi police-van drove up to the convent. Sr. Benedicta was given five minutes in which to get ready to leave. This delay was extended to ten minutes as a special favor. Then she was led away, together with a Sister Rosa [*sic*] and other unknown victims.

On arriving in Germany, she was beaten with cudgels, thrown into prison and then killed, either in a gas-chamber or, as some think, by being thrown down into a salt-mine.[G 4]

This newspaper notice was reprinted in Catholic diocesan newsletters both at home and abroad, despite the very obvious errors that it contains. It proved impossible to trace the source of this announcement. The only reliable news was a report sent from Echt to Cologne by one of the men who had taken the suitcases to Sr. Benedicta and

Rosa in the camp; [G 5] on 13 March 1947 he had received an official letter from the Joodsen Raad, [Jewish Council] Amsterdam, saying that none of those from the transport that contained the two sisters had ever returned.[7]

The letters sent to the Cologne Carmel, asking for more information, increased from day to day. (The community had returned to Cologne on 27 November 1945; it was housed temporarily in Junkersdorf and prepared to rebuild the convent Maria vom Frieden, Vor den Siebenburgen).[8] The only possible answer to all these questions was to send off a brief sketch of this great Carmelite's life, a hundred thousand copies of which went to all parts of the globe from 1946 on.[G 6] At the time this was very much a case of casting a fishing line out into uncertain waters, but it brought rich returns. Letters came pouring in from all over Germany as well as from abroad. The writers represented every profession, every age, every level of education, every conceivable grade of society, all with one voice acclaiming her as a venerable heroine, a shining example, a saint. One of the letters even contained a manuscript entitled, "Die ontische Struktur der Person und ihre erkenntnistheoretische Problematik" or *The Structure of Being of the Person and its Problematics Concerning its Theory of Knowledge*. It was a copy of lectures that Sr. Benedicta had delivered in Münster during the winter semester 1932-33; she had given the manuscript to Frau Dr. Schweitzer as a gift just before entering Carmel.[9]

Besides this precious find, the memorial leaflet unexpectedly brought about contact with the sole survivor who had witnessed Sr. Benedicta during the final days of her suffering.

In March [G 7] 1947 Professor Max Budde came across the life story of Edith Stein quite by accident and, with reference to it, wrote to say that his friend, Director General Doctor Lenig, had been interned in Amersfoort camp just about the same time and that he was the only one to escape from imprisonment, because, as a leader of the Resistance movement against the Third Reich, he received help from the outside. This internment in Amersfoort had been his third since the "Seizure of Power." Perhaps he could add some detail about Sr. Benedicta's fate.

Immediately, the Cologne Carmel sent a letter of inquiry to Dr. Lenig, from whom the following reply arrived on 27 March 1947:

> Reverend Mother Prioress,
> At the request of my dear friend, Professor Max Budde of Gelsenkirchen, I have the honor to inform you as follows: Time and again in their pastoral letters the Dutch archbishops[10] and bishops made vigorous, thoroughly justified attacks upon National Socialism. For a long time I had been aware of the danger threatening all Catholics who refused to fall into line with the political ideology of the new Greater German world view... But I must confine myself to details of personal interest to the Carmel Maria vom Frieden. I met Sister Teresia Benedicta a Cruce, known in the camp as Edith Stein, on the 2 August 1942, in the transit camp at Amersfoort, in barracks No. 9, if I am not mistaken.[11] On that Sunday all Catholics of Jewish, or partly Jewish, ancestry were arrested by the German hangmen's helpers as a reprisal for a pastoral letter that had been read from the pulpits of all Dutch churches the previous Sunday. They were taken away and at first assembled at Amersfoort before being deported from there to the gas chambers and crematoria... When your Sister, together with about three hundred men, women and children had been driven behind the barbed wire fence of the camp, they had to stand for hours on the barrack-square, where they could watch, just as a pleasant welcome, a roll call that had been in progress for two or three days. It was to punish the entire camp, so far as I remember – one of the starving internees had "stolen" some dry bread that had been thrown away. That is to say, some of them were still standing, the rest had collapsed and were being variously mishandled to get them on their feet again. Among those still standing I noticed an inflexible opponent of the

Third Reich, Ministerial Director Dr. Lazarus, who, like
the new arrivals, was a courageous and avowed Catholic.
Nor can I forget how the day was one long series of kick-
ings and beatings, although these were tolerable. More
upsetting was the condition of most of the women... It
was at this moment that Edith Stein courageously
showed her commitment. It must be mentioned that, to
begin with, all were released who had been brought in
by mistake, Protestants, Greek (Bulgarian) Orthodox,
etc., and then the monotony of camp life set in. Roll
calls and nightly deportations. With diligence, they read
the *Imitation of Christ*, that someone had smuggled in;
a Trappist faithfully said Holy Mass for them – his six[12]
brothers and sisters who had all joined the same Order
were with him, all prepared for transport.[G 8] Holy
Communion was distributed diligently, and despite the
harassment by the SS, everyone of this flock destined
for death steadfastly sang the *Confiteor* daily, until the
last of them had gone their way...

It was also very moving to see the response of this
brave flock of believers when they heard that there were
priests somewhere in the camp; immediately they gave
up some of their meager rations, their tobacco, their
money, etc., that were now useless to them but might
help the priests to placate their torturers and so hope to
experience the day of liberation.

Some of these night transports went to the death
camps[13] at Drente and others went straight to Auschwitz.
Mothers were permitted to request baby carriages from
home for their infants and to take them along as far as
the baggage car, that, alas! was always left behind. I
never heard anything more of any of them. There was
one lady of some religious order, who had been cleared
for immigration by the Swiss Consulate – and yet was
gassed. I would like to emphasize that the Dutch convents all took endless trouble to try to ease the lot of
their brothers and sisters. I myself, partly on my own

initiative, and partly at the request of different convents, including Echt, have been trying to discover the fate of all the deportees. Everywhere people tried to help me. I have never heard of any of the Religious, man or woman, nor of any woman or man, old or young, except that all their lives on earth ended within a few weeks.

Among the first to be carried off by night was your lamented Sister, Edith Stein. Like all of them, she went calmly to her death, fully assured of rising again to eternal life. It is impossible for me to say definitely whether the night of the deportation was on either 4 or 5 August. May God be merciful to her and all the victims of [Nazi] German "Race-Christianity"; may He grant them eternal peace and may His eternal light shine upon them. Amen.

> With my respectful regards,
> Yours,
> LENIG.

This terrifying picture raised some doubts in the Cologne Carmel about the accuracy of some of the facts mentioned in the published sketch of her life. Also the Sisters wondered whether the testimony sent by Dr. Lenig offered sufficient grounds for accepting Sr. Benedicta's death as certain. When these doubts were placed before him, Dr. Lenig replied again, on 8 April 1947:

> The statements on the memorial card are as accurate as human judgment allows. It is quite certain that some of the transports of the victims were directed through Schifferstadt. We know from accounts of other transports that such hapless persons sometimes managed to attract the attention of acquaintances whom they happened to see; consequently the possibility that your late Sister was seen and perhaps even heard definitely falls within the realm of possibility. Your Sister's death must be regarded as legally certain. And it is certain that she was murdered in Auschwitz, not in the Netherlands.

On the strength of this news, Sr. Benedicta was reported to the Father General in Rome as dead. From Rome the sad message was sent to all Carmelite houses, so that they might each offer to God the customary suffrages offered for all departed members of the Order.

In the little oratory of their temporary Carmel at Junkersdorf her Sisters sang a solemn Requiem for her. No one outside the community was present. No note of real mourning entered in, nor did bitterness cloud the holy sorrow and just anger that were called forth at the memory of the wrongs inflicted upon our dead Sister. It was Easter again, the high feast, the one that Sr. Benedicta had loved most of all the feasts in the Church calendar. And now she was singing her hallelujah to the Easter Lamb in heaven!

But the earth sounded with a chant of sadness: *Libera me Domine...dum veneris judicare saeculum per ignem.*

A word of Sr. Benedicta's, true to the spirit of one who had acquired so deep a vision into finite and eternal being, seemed to resonate with the Requiem:

> *Judge not lest you be judged in turn,*
> *Appearances cloud our view,*
> *We guess at the truth, but only learn*
> *God alone knows what is true.*[14]

23

Postscript

This little book was presented to the public on the feast of Christmas 1948 by Glock und Lutz, the Nuremberg publishers. The demand for it was so great that, already by the spring of 1950, the fifth edition had to be prepared, as well as translations into five foreign languages. But the present edition differs from previous versions. For we have been able to fill in and deepen this portrait of our beloved Sister, by quoting from her own valuable contributions, only recently and quite unexpectedly discovered, as well as from her friends' letters and reminiscences that have been received in recent years. But questions about the when, how, and where of her life's end remain unanswered, and this uncertainty has remained a constant, insistent spur that has driven her friends on to tireless investigations. So far these investigations have produced no indisputable results. Instead a number of stories and assertions, that sometimes contradict each other [G 1] are here informally presented, in the hope that they may yet provide clues to a reliable explanation.

In *Frauenland* (No. 3/4 1950) the Benedictine Lioba Sister, Sr. Placida Laubhardt writes that authentic witnesses prove that Edith Stein died a violent death in the gas chamber of the death camp Auschwitz on 9 August 1942. A similar assertion is found in the biographical sketch for the first volume of Edith Stein's works, *Kreuzeswissenschaft* or *The Science of the Cross)*: On 7 August 1942 she was deported to Auschwitz, where she was gassed, and her body was cremated.[T 1] [G 2] These details are based on an official document from the Dutch Red Cross. In answer to our request, we had received a printed form letter used to supply information about deportees who had not returned; because of its very general and imprecise wording it cannot be treated as authentic testimony. Therefore, as soon as a date of death had been stated, concerns were raised in regard to its accuracy.[1]

A lady from Berlin (formerly a prisoner in Ravensbrück-Auschwitz, viz., prisoner No. 279) writes:

Having read about Edith Stein, I feel in duty bound to give the following information: From the end of March 1942 (to be precise, 27 March 1942) about a thousand Jewish women used to come into the camp every day. The first transports came from Slovakia, Czechoslovakia and Hungary. Until the beginning of 1943, they came mainly from these countries. Afterward from Holland, Belgium, France, and Greece.

Not until the middle of 1943 did we get mixed Jewish transports (i.e., a mixture of German and others). The vast majority of these transports came from the camp of Theresienstadt.

According to my calculations, therefore, it is impossible that Edith Stein came to Auschwitz as early as 1942. If she had come to Auschwitz in 1942, it would be known for certain, since the writer of these lines was a prisoner in the women's camp of Auschwitz from 27 March 1942 until 18 January 1945, and was working until the end of 1943 in the Prisoners' Bureau at Auschwitz, and later also at Auschwitz-Birkenau. All the prisoners were registered there, and Edith Stein would have stood out immediately upon being asked about her denomination, if, as a Jew she would have stated that she was a Catholic.

Moreover there was a very active resistance movement in the women's camp at Auschwitz. They used to take almost all the German Jewish women upon arrival to barracks distant from Birkenau, where they would be in less danger. Those who survived in this way would be able to testify to that. I am certain Edith Stein was not one of them.[G 3]

If Edith Stein did not come directly to Auschwitz in 1942, where was she in the meantime? That will and can be determined by exact, detailed investigation.

A nurse writes:

> Unfortunately I cannot give you any definite informa-
> tion about Sr. Benedicta. But I can at least pass on to
> you what I have found out. For four years I worked as a
> nurse in a large factory at Augsburg (Michel- Factory).
> In October 1944, on instructions from the authorities,
> we had to convert one floor of the factory into a con-
> centration camp. On 5 September 1944 we received five
> hundred Jewish women from Hungary, who had come
> straight from Auschwitz. They were all cultured people,
> teachers, doctors, nurses and academics. Though it grieved
> me to do so, I refused at first to take charge of the health
> care, because many demands were made upon me that
> I, as a Catholic nurse, could not reconcile with my con-
> science. The supreme command of the camp forced me
> to do so, however, which meant that I could go in and
> out of the place regularly. Despite its many difficulties
> this task brought me great joy, because my charges soon
> discovered how tenderhearted I was. As soon as I knew
> that the SS bosses were out of the building we used to
> gather together and try to comfort one another. It was on
> one such occasion that a teacher talked about Edith Stein
> and, her eyes filled with tears, said to me: "She has al-
> ready trodden her way of the Cross; for on the day that
> she was called out of the ranks, gassings took place."
> There were many Catholics amongst those whom I had
> to look after. Whether it is 100 percent correct, I do not
> know. But one thing I can say for certain – that my charges
> and I would often pray for blessing and strength together
> to Christ, our Lord, who loved prisoners so much, and to
> our "Edithlein," as we used to call her. Those were hours
> of peace that gave us much inner strength. I would have
> preferred to accompany them further on their path of
> suffering. A fortnight before the Nazi collapse they were
> taken away to the collection camp at Kaufbeuren. Here
> most of them were shot, but a few managed to escape.
> Two later came to see me and told me, of course, of their

fate. One of them went to America, the other returned to Hungary. Unfortunately they never wrote to me after that. At one time I had occasion to go to Theresienstadt concentration camp, but there I never heard mention of Edith Stein. I am inclined to believe that she never got out of Auschwitz, because in October 1944 a great evacuation took place there. At that time, the camp was supposed to be cleared out entirely. That was the decision, though I do not know whether it was actually carried out. Actually one would think that "Edithlein" herself might give us a sign about the manner of her death. Certainly all those from Theresienstadt were taken to Auschwitz to be gassed. The gas oven in Theresienstadt, which I saw myself, was only completed a few days before the Russians arrived. All those killed in Theresienstadt were shot.

The third informative letter comes from a parish priest in Württemberg:

Yesterday I showed the picture of your dear Sr. Benedicta Teresia in her black veil to one of my parishioners who was a guard in Auschwitz. He insisted that he had seen that Sister there in the same habit. I contradicted him just as insistently, because he had admitted that he had only arrived there in October 1942. Yet he stuck to his original statement. Today he came back again and corrected the dates he had given for his stay there. According to his corrections, he had arrived in Auschwitz no later than the end of July 1942 and had stayed there about a year. He could just about swear that this Sister had looked intently at him and another guard as if she had realized that the two of them had just talked about her: "That one can't be mentally ill," they had said, in reference to the story the guards had been told, that the whole transport was mad.

Although I rather mistrust this fellow, because of his past and his family circumstances, I am very much inclined to accept his version as true, because he quite spontaneously claimed that he recognized the Sister the very moment I showed him her picture, and before I had explained my reason for showing it to him. He disputes that Sr. Benedicta must have been wearing prisoner's clothes when she arrived; that was not the case with any of the transports to Auschwitz. On the same day at the beginning of August – he cannot remember the exact date – two transports arrived from Holland, one of men in the morning and one of women after ten at night. Both transports were described to the guards as transports of mentally ill people. The SD sealed these transports off especially strictly, so that no one could speak to the victims.

The train tracks went further into the camp than he usually had access to in the course of his duties. Occasionally, and thus also on that day, he risked going further, and observed the Sister in the middle section of the train; around her were people who seemed to know her, but who were not wearing religious habits. Possibly there were more religious further forward. Otherwise selections for working parties had occurred, even from transports of women. But since the working parties noticed no one from this women's transport in the following days, he assumed that all these victims had stripped off their clothes at the usual spot and then been driven naked about 400 meters to the place of slaughter and cremated in the adjoining crematorium – immediately after they had arrived. He had not been aware that these victims had been Jews.

One might almost echo the sentiments of the writer who wished that Sr. Benedicta herself would give us some sign by which to clear up our suspicions. But she is content with her last recorded words, "*I am on my way to the East*," for they echo in our minds like words spoken from another world, recalling the *kalon to dynai* of Bishop Ignatius of Antioch. On his way West, with death before him, he found it so wonderful to sink pown

with Christ, the [setting] sun, in order to rise again with
Christ one day. Are the signs that Sr. Benedicta gives us
not proof of her renewed, transfigured life in Christ?

A great many letters have been received that tell of special protec-
tion and remarkable answers to prayers for her intercession. She especially helps those searching for jobs. The following letter from
Nijmegen gives an account of a cure attributed to her mediation:

> Nijmegen. S. Marcus 1950.
> Reverend Mother Prioress,
> I don't want to wait any longer to give you some news
> about the man for whom I asked you for a novena. This
> man was given up by the doctors who said he would only
> last another day or two. Then we prayed to Sr. Benedicta;
> and this is what happened. To everyone's amazement
> he has been discharged from the hospital and is back at
> work. He has already been home a week and feels fine.
> His one remaining kidney is functioning well, even bet-
> ter than before – normally, in fact. His love of life has
> returned, he eats well (though still on a diet); he goes
> for walks, and smokes, and everything agrees with him.
> All of this to everyone's astonishment, and to the great
> joy of his wife and his four little children, and everyone
> who knows him.
> But, of course, we want to be careful, i.e., he must go
> back to his doctor for another examination in a few weeks.
> I told him: You get the doctor to put it down in writing,
> what you were like at first, then a few weeks later, and
> now; because all this has to do with God's honor.

Edith Stein is the first witness of Israel, who has connected the
sufferings of her people with the crucifixion of Christ and transformed
it into reality.[2] Countless people are praying for her beatification, as
we are assured in many letters. The Order of Our Blessed Lady of
Mount Carmel has introduced the Informatory Process.[3] That is why
we ask for reports of answered prayers. But was Dom Raphael Walzer,

O.S.B., not right when he said: "We do not know what God's providence has in store for her now. Will she one day be raised to the altars
of the Church? Or will she only go down in history as an exemplary
personality? The latter would not surprise me. But one thing will remain forever: her image, her prayer and her works, her silence and
suffering, and her last journey to the East will not easily fade from the
memory of future generations. They will always radiate strength, and
will awaken the longing for ever deeper faith, hope, and love."

Cologne Carmel, Pentecost 1950

NOTES

Part 1

CHAPTER 1

1. Original text has "parents' house," but in fact Edith's mother purchased the house in 1910, long after she was widowed.
2. P's statement that Edith spent the greater part of her youth in this house is in error. Her mother purchased the house in 1910, when Edith was nineteen years old. She left home to study in Göttingen in 1913 and from then on only spent short periods of time and summer vacations there.
3. We have excised several sentences here that describe the interior as having had furnishings with biblical motifs and various Jewish artifacts. These statements do not reflect the facts. The inauthenticity of these statements is confirmed by Edith's sister Erna and her children, as well as several nephews and nieces who lived in this house for many years. See also Susanne Batzdorff, *Aunt Edith; the Jewish Heritage of a Catholic Saint,* (Springfield, IL: Templegate Publishers, 1998, 2nd rev. ed. 2003), 95. Hereafter cited as *"Aunt Edith."*
4. The author's description "lacking ornament and stucco," does not give an accurate picture of these rooms.
5. Again, a passage referring to the Stein family's religious observances in accordance with the Talmud, etc., has been omitted because it does not conform to the facts.
6. Edith was not quite two years old at the time of her father's death. She was born in October 1891, and Siegfried Stein died in July 1893.
7. Various sources refer to this person as either Ruben or Rubens.
8. In fact, Erna was twenty months older than Edith, having been born 11 February 1890, while Edith was born 12 October 1891.
9. Posselt note: "This was probably Edith's own name for herself, before she could speak properly. It was then adopted by her brothers and sisters, and persisted for a time."

   Editor's note: This footnote by P is based on a misconception. Actually, the word "Jitschel" is a dialect word meaning "little kid" probably from the area where the Courant family originated.
10. The apartment where the Stein family lived at that time was approximately 1.75 km northwest of the central square of the city (*Der Ring*).

11. He served an apprenticeship in a bookstore. See Edith Stein, *Life in a Jewish Family*, trans. Josephine Koeppel, O.C.D. (Washington, DC: ICS Publications, 1986), 43. The Collected Works of Edith Stein, 1. Hereafter cited as "*Life.*"

12. The original translation reads: "All her children, except the eldest boy, who was probably serving his apprenticeship, were still at school and of little help to her." However, actually, Else had to interrupt her schooling to look after the younger children and the household.

13. This was most likely the lumberyard on Matthiasstrasse. Auguste Stein's first lumberyard was on Schiessswerderstrasse, the second on Rosenstrasse, the third on Elbingstrasse. All these were rented. The largest one, that she purchased, was located on Matthiasstrasse.

14. An incorrect statement regarding the school Edith attended has been taken out [T 5]. All sisters attended Victoria School. (See *Life*, 48).

15. See also *Life,* 73.

16. This is confirmed in *Life,* 67.

17. These party games are also described in *Life,* 66-67. Mention is also made of occasional skits that Edith herself wrote and that were presented by siblings and friends.

18. At that time it was customary to rank students in order of their academic standing and assign them seats accordingly.

19. Rubens states: "We had moved to suburbs that lay in diametrically opposite directions." But in fact Edith never moved to the suburbs.

20. Posselt note: The house at Michaelisstrasse 38 came through World War II undamaged.

21. This bracketed passage is entirely absent from the German original text. We can only speculate about the reason for this omission. Evidently it was part of Mrs. Rubens' testimony. Another description of the Schiller prize episode can be found in Batzdorff, *Aunt Edith,* 123.

22. H/N erroneously translated the word "Silesia" as "Croatia."

23. See n. 8.

24. A card game with sets of four cards, dealing with authors and their works.

25. Breslau is located on the Oder, a major river.

26. Auguste Stein had jokingly reported that Else had failed her exam. Edith reacted with deep concern that Else had really failed and would now drown herself, while Erna was calm and was never fooled for a moment.

27. We can only guess which photograph is meant here. The well publicized photo of Erna and Edith in white dresses, probably dated 1897 or 1898 might be the one, especially since no other photo of the two sisters Erna and Edith has come to light.

28. Preussisch-Oderberg was a town located one-hundred seventy kilometers southwest of Breslau, in Upper Silesia, where the Oder crossed the border.

29. On Else's attachment to her little sisters, see also *Life*, 91-92.

30. This long passage of reminiscences by Else Gordon, Edith's eldest sister, is here being placed in its original position. The 1952 English translation of H/N had moved it to the end of Chap. 1.

31. H/N placed a quotation from Edith Stein's writings in their version, even though it was not given in the original German text of P. We reproduce it from the now published work Edith Stein, *Finite and Eternal Being, An Attempt at an Ascent to the Meaning of Being*, trans. Kurt Reinhardt (Washington, DC: ICS Publications, 2000), 113. Collected Works of Edith Stein, 9: *"Whatever did not fit in with my plans did lie within the plan of God. I have an ever deeper and firmer belief that nothing is merely an accident when seen in the sight of God, that my whole life down to its smallest details has been marked out for me in the plan of divine Providence, and has a completely coherent meaning in God's all-seeing eyes. And so I am beginning to rejoice in the light of glory wherein this meaning will be unveiled to me."* Hereafter cited as *"Finite and Eternal."*

CHAPTER 2

1. Posselt note: Frau Stein had fifteen brothers and sisters, whose names the children had to recite as if naming the twelve tribes of Israel. See Gleanings [G 1].

2. In preparation for writing this book P apparently asked Dr. Erna Biberstein to send her some reminiscences about her early years with her sister Edith. The text quoted here is almost word for word the same as was later included in the "Editor's Foreword" to *Life*, 14.

3. Professor Roehl was the Director of *Viktoriaschule* at the time. Edith's eldest sister Else Gordon apparently also contributed her reminiscences at the request of P.

4. Erna Stein-Biberstein erroneously states that Edith stayed in Hamburg for eight months. Edith herself tells in *Life,* 95-96 that she left school at Easter 1906 and went to live at her sister Else's in Hamburg for ten months.

5. Erna Biberstein's account is corroborated by Edith's own description of the entrance examination. Of the three candidates, she was the only one to qualify for admission to *Obersekunda.* See *Life,* 159.

6. *Abitur* is the final comprehensive examination given at the conclusion of the German high school (*Gymnasium*). The German school system at that time is explained in table form in *Life,* 471.

7. *Stein,* in German, means "stone."

8. Edith herself, in her autobiographical *Life,* recounts examples of the humorous verses and other writings that she contributed to class parties and celebrations. See, e.g., *Life,* 177.

CHAPTER 3

1. Richard Hönigswald (1875-1947). See also Gleanings [G 2].
2. William Stern (1871-1938). See also Gleanings [G 3].
3. *Life,* 186.
4. See the rhyme describing Edith as a suffragette, composed by her fellow-students for the comic program at their farewell party from Viktoria-schule, *Life,* 178.

CHAPTER 4

1. The "Würzburg Method," represented principally by Oswald Külpe (1862-1915), A. Messer and K. Buehler, studied the psychology of thought and thinking.
2. H/N note: A technical term of Husserl's phenomenological philosophy.
3. Editor's note: In this revised translation, the academic titles are given in the original German, with explanatory notes in English following in brackets, for example *Privatdozent, [Lecturer]* etc.
4. Posselt note: Daughter of her sister, Erika Tworoger [later Chanah Cohen (1911-1961)]. P misspelled the family name as "Tworoga."
5. Rose was the same age as Edith, about twenty-one years of age.
6. Edith was twenty-one at the time.
7. At this point begins Chap. VII of *Life.* See also Gleanings [G 1].

8. A plaque now marks the house where Edith Stein lived.

9. "The Göttingen Seven" were professors dismissed from that university in 1887 for their protest and refusal to take an oath prescribed by King Ernst August of Hannover. See also Gleanings [G 3].

10. *Maria Spring* named after a spring dedicated to the Virgin Mary, somewhat outside of Göttingen. At that time, a garden restaurant with dance hall was located there, today a *Heimvolkshochschule* (adult education academy).

11. *Rohns* and *Kehr* were two inns, the *Rohns* on the slope of the *Hainberg*, the *Kehr* on the mountain ridge. See also Gleanings [G 4].

12. Ludwig Richter (1803-1884), German painter.

13. Posselt note: He joined up in 1914 as a volunteer and in 1917 he died in battle. His wife and sister later became Catholics.
    Adolf Reinach (1883-1917). See also Gleanings [G 5].

14. Hans Theodor Conrad (1881-1969). See also Gleanings [G 6].

15. Moritz Geiger (1880-1937). See also Gleanings [G 7].

16. Posselt note: The first volume of the *Logische Untersuchungen* appeared in 1900 and proved epoch-making on account of its radical critique of the current psychologism and all other forms of relativism. The second volume followed the next year. Both in scope and importance it went far beyond the first volume: here, for the first time, logical problems were dealt with by means of that method that Husserl was later to perfect as the "phenomenological method" and apply to every province of philosophy.

17. H/N note: Usually referred to in German simply as *Ideen.*

18. Professors were paid a set amount per student attending. That is why they had to keep count.

19. Translator's [H/N] note. No attempt has been made, throughout this translation to reproduce the fine shades of meaning involved in such words as *Privatdozent, Dozent,* etc. that express academic gradings rather different from those common in Britain. Readers familiar with German academic life will appreciate the nuances without prompting; those unfamiliar with it would require an explanatory treatise for which this biography is not the place.

20. Dietrich von Hildebrand (1889-1977). See also Gleanings [G 8].
    Posselt note: Later a member of the Franciscan Third Order.

21. Alexandre Koyré (1892-1964) born in Russia, educated in Paris; from there he went to Göttingen and ended up teaching in Paris. See Chap. 12.

Posselt note: He and his wife later came very near to the Catholic Church.

22. Johannes (Jean) Hering (1890-1966) – one of the ablest interpreters of phenomenology to the French world.
    Posselt note: Later Professor of Protestant Theology in Strasburg.
23. Hans Lipps (1889-1941). See also Gleanings [G 9].
    Posselt note: Killed in the World War 1939-45.
24. Georg Simmel (1858-1918) was a pioneer in formal sociology.
25. Fritz Kaufmann (1891-1958). Gleanings [G 10].
26. Paul Natorp (1854-1924) specialized in social pedagogy and was a co-founder of the neo-Kantian Marburg Movement with Hermann Cohen (1842-1918).
27. Winthrop Pickard Bell (1884-1965). See also Gleanings [G 11].
28. Moritz Schlick (1882-1936) German philosopher who, with R. Carnap and O. Neurath, founded the Vienna Circle (1922-1936), the school of neo-positivism influenced by Ernst Mach and Ludwig Wittgenstein.
29. Max Scheler (1874-1928). See also Gleanings [G 12].
30. Edith Stein here refers to a passage in her autobiography, *Life,* 84-85.
31. Leonard Nelson (1882-1927) is known principally as the founder of the so-called Neo-Friesian School.
32. Jakob Friedrich Fries (1773-1843) was a philosopher who taught in Jena, Germany. He wrote on psychological and religio-philosophical themes; he was influenced by Kant and Jacobi.
33. Georg Elias Müller (1850-1934). See also Gleanings [G 13].
34. David Katz (1884-1953). See also Gleanings [G 14].
35. Baron Heinrich Friedrich Karl vom und zum Stein (1757-1831). See also Gleanings [G 15].
36. Leopold von Ranke (1795-1886), historian. Wrote extensively, treating among other subjects the Roman Papacy in the sixteenth and seventeenth centuries; German history during the time of the Reformation; the history of France and of England.
37. State Examination (Staatsexamen) was a comprehensive examination somewhat comparable to our State Boards. They are supervised and administered by the State and are required to qualify the individual to practice a profession.
38. Theodor Lipps (1851-1914), psychologist and philosopher. His students formed a club as early as 1901, and this led to their introduction to Husserl's work. By 1905 a steady stream of students went from Munich

to Göttingen, and vice versa. For her doctoral dissertation on empathy, Edith Stein had to review his teaching on it, at Husserl's direction.

CHAPTER 5

1. Translators Hastings and Nicholl consistently give her name as "Rese." We have substituted the correct name "Rose" throughout the text.
2. Posselt note: According to Edith herself her first encounter with Christianity was the Gothic Old High German "Our Father," that was then included in the basic German linguistics course. Afterwards, whenever she discussed this text with her students, she would always speak of the deep impression it had made on her.
3. See Edith Stein's reference to this "old group" as a four-leaf clover; it included Lilli Platau, Rose Guttmann, Erna and Edith Stein, *Life,* 122.
4. See Edith Stein, "How I came to the Cologne Carmel," *Selected Writings with Comments, Reminiscences and Translations of her Prayers and Poems by Her Niece,* trans. Susanne M. Batzdorff (Springfield, IL: Templegate Publishers, 1990), 13-30, and 22. Hereafter *"Selected Writings"* for the volume and "How I came" for the autobiographical sketch.
5. The reference, of course, is to World War I.
6. Edith needed to learn the Gabelsberger method of shorthand in order to decipher "the Master's" copious writings. See "Chronology, 1916-1942," *Life,* 416.
7. Edith Stein refers to her "philosophical kindergarten" in Letter 14 of *Self-Portrait in Letters,* trans. Josephine Koeppel, O.C.D. (Washington, DC: ICS Publications, 1993), 17. The Collected Works of Edith Stein, 5. Hereafter cited as *"Letters."*
8. For accuracy this sentence is being substituted for [T 2].
9. Original title in German: *Beiträge zur philosophischen Begründung der Psychologie und der Geisteswissenschaften.* Note that P errs in substituting the word "Philosophie" (philosophy) for "Psychologie (psychology). The error, then taken over into the H/R translation, is here corrected.
10. See the detailed account by Edith's sister Erna in Editor's Foreword, *Life,* 17, where she mentions visiting Edith, together with Rose Guttmann and Lilli Platau in 1916, and again by herself in 1917.
11. Also known as Lake Constance.

12. The priest in question, to whom these attributed words can be traced, was Fr. Johannes Hirschmann (1908-1981). He was a German Jesuit living in Holland near Echt during World War II. He even preached the last retreat that Sr. Benedicta attended before her death. His role as a witness to these sentiments supposedly confided to him was described in a booklet that P worked on (between June 1958 and her death in January 1961) as part of early examination of the cause for beatification of Sr. Benedicta. See *Kölner Selig- und Heiligsprechungsprozess der Dienerin Gottes Sr. Teresia Benedicta a Cruce (Edith Stein), Professae et Choristae Ordinis Beatae Mariae Viriginis de Monte Carmelo-Articuli pro construendo Processu Ordinario Informativo* (Cologne: private publication, 1962), 4-5. [text in German]

13. See, also, Chap. 7, "The Convert."

CHAPTER 6

1. Bienias, Maria: *Begegnung mit Edith Stein* (Leipzig: St. Benno-Verlag, 1965), 14. P misspelled her name as "Biennias."

2. See numerous anecdotes throughout *Life*.

3. The author again erroneously spells the family name "Tworoga" instead of "Tworoger" as it is here correctly rendered.

CHAPTER 7

1. See Edith Stein,, "VI. Die endlichen Dinge als stufenreich 'geformte Materie' durchgeführt in Auseinandersetzung mit H. Conrad-Martius' "*Metaphysische Gespräche*," *Potenz und Akt* (Freiburg: Herder, 1998), 158-283. "Edith Steins Werke," 18. Hereafter this series will be cited as "ESW."

   Also see Letter 135 where Edith mentions the 1921 *Metaphysische Gespräche* [Metaphysical Discourses] to its author, *Letters*, 134.

2. See par. 3 and *passim*, Chap. 40 of Teresa of Avila, *The Book of Her Life*, 2nd rev. ed., trans. Kavanaugh/Rodriguez (Washington: ICS Publications, 1987), 355.

3. Attested to by Amata Neyer, *Wie ich in den Kölner Karmel kam, mit Erläuterungen und Ergänzungen von Maria Amata Neyer* (Würzburg: Echter Verlag, 1994), 22. Hereafter cited as "*Kölner Karmel kam.*"

There is another version that claims Edith received the book as a gift from the Reinach family, before the summer of 1921, and so Edith would have *completed* her reading of it that night in Bad Bergzabern. The alternative explanation was asserted as early on as 1952 by Elisabeth de Mirabel, *Edith Stein, 1891-1942* (Paris: Eds. du Seuil, 1952), 60. More recently, Joachim Feldes supplies greater detail still in *"Diesen lieben Blick vergesse ich nie"*: *Edith Stein und der Liebfrauenberg* (private publication, 2000), 9-12. Feldes concurs with Neyer on the details of eventual return of the book to the town where it made such a significant difference in Edith's life. Cf. Uwe Müller and Maria Amata Neyer, *Edith Stein: Das Leben einer ungewöhnlichen Frau* (Zürich/Düsseldorf: Benziger, 1998), 149-50, n. 12. Hereafter cited as *"Das Leben."*

4. Posselt note: Breitling, Spiritual Advisor.

   See Amata Neyer, *Edith Stein: Her Life in Photos and Documents*, trans. Waltraut Stein (Washington, DC: ICS Publications, 1999), 35. Fr. Breitling was born in 1851 and died in 1931. Hereafter cited as *"Life in Photos."*

5. See baptismal register notation in *Life in Photos*, 35.

6. Reference to the reception of Holy Communion, imparted at a mass the next day (not along with the baptism ceremony), as asserted by Müller/Neyer, *Das Leben*, 149.

7. According to Amata Neyer in n. 3 to a letter from Edith to Fr. Breitling (Letter 37 in *Letters*) she went home to Breslau once in June, then later on in the year for a longer stay during fall and winter. See *Selbstbildnis in Briefen, erster Teil, vollständig neu bearbeitete und erweiterte Auflage* (Freiburg: Herder Verlag, 2000), 64. "Edith Stein Gesamtausgabe," 2. Hereafter "ESGA" (the up-to-date complete works German edition).

8. Locale for Edith's confirmation was in the private chapel of the bishop (not in "the great Cathedral at Speyer" as was erroneously rendered in the English translation of P's account). Bishop Ludwig Sebastian (1862-1943) was officiating prelate. Confirmations of converts as well as mixed marriage ceremonies in those days took place in more private surroundings. Candlemas day falls each year on February 2nd.

9. In 1921 Canon Joseph Schwind had reached his seventieth birthday. See Joachim Feldes, *Edith Stein und Schifferstadt* (Schifferstadt: Stadtsparkasse Schifferstadt, 1998), 92 pp. Hereafter cited as *"Edith Stein und Schifferstadt."*

10. Edith Stein, Letter 45, *Letters*, 54: "...*a good while after my conversion I was of the opinion*...*one had to give up all that was secular*...."

CHAPTER 8

1. Edith's time there has been studied by one of today's elder Dominican Sisters, someone who knew persons in contact with Edith while she lived in Speyer. See Maria Adele Herrmann OP, *Die Speyerer Jahre von Edith Stein: Aufzeichnungen zu ihrem 100. Geburtstag* (Speyer: Pilger Verlag, 1990). 212pp. Contains previously unedited texts and photos. Hereafter "*Speyerer Jahre*."

2. Photo in *Speyerer Jahre*, 59.

3. Fr. Erich Przywara, SJ was her counselor in this regard. For their working relationship see Marianne Sawicki, *Body, Text and Science: The Literacy of Investigative Practices and the Phenomenology of Edith Stein* (Dordrecht/London/Boston: Kluwer Academ. Publishers, 1997), 193-95. "Phaenomenologica," 144.

4. Photo in *Speyerer Jahre*, 167.

5. The fact that she ate "convent food" fits the other circumstances of her life that she led in close imitation of the Sisters. She even pronounced private vows of poverty, chastity and obedience, as indicated later on in her own description of how she entered Carmel. See Chap. 13 below.

6. Edith attests to certification of her specialization in German through success in the state board written and oral licensing exams in *Life*, 310-17.

7. See Letter 326, *Letters*, 338 about similar activity in behalf of her younger Sisters in Echt Carmel.

8. Several scholarly studies appeared in Husserl's *Jahrbuch für Philosophie u. phänomenologische Forschung* (1922, 1925, 1929); she published *John H. Kardinal Newman. Briefe und Tagebücher 1801-1845* (München: Theatinerverlag, 1928), but her translation of *The Idea of a University* has remained in manuscript form, can be consulted in the Cologne archives, and is awaited as a volume in the new ESGA; finally, the two volumes of her *Des hl. Thomas von Aquino Untersuchungen über die Wahrheit* (Breslau: Otto Borgmeyer, 1931). Edith herself lists the contributions to the *Husserl Jahrbuch* for us in Letter 138, *Letters*, 137-38. Hereafter cited as "*Jahrbuch*."

9. In contrast to P's almost smug conclusion that Edith "had become" a teacher see *Life*, passim for indicators of previous teaching stints by Edith, esp. p. 204 where, at the end of an English course conducted in "winter of 1912" her appreciative pupils present her with "a huge bouquet of roses and with a valuable book on the history of art. . ."

10. Letter 123, to Sr. Callista Kopf, 20 October 1932, *Letters*, 122 and 123.

11. In the latest German edition of Edith Stein's correspondence the editor, Sr. Amata Neyer, places this "fragment" at the end of the letters for 1930 and designates the person who received it as "unknown." There, in n. 1 for Brief 126, the editor comments about the practices of P in weaving such texts from the "Speyer period" into her biography of Stein. See *Selbstbildnis in Briefen,* ESGA, 2, 144. Hereafter we will cite the German volumes of correspondence as "ESGA 2" and "ESGA 3" respectively.

12. For a selection of some essay and class topics organized by Fräulein Doktor see section "Die Lehrordnung für Deutsch," *Speyerer Jahre,* 70-85; also Müller/Neyer, *Das Leben,* 177-78; and reference to the third theme by Berta Hümpfner in "II. A Great, Exceptional Personality: Edith Stein," *Never Forget, Christian and Jewish Perspectives on Edith Stein,* ed. Waltraud Herbstrith, O.C.D. and trans. Susanne Batzdorff (Washington, DC: ICS Publications, 1998), 214. "Carmelite Studies," 7. Hereafter cited as *"Never Forget."*

13. Cf. Müller/Neyer, *Das Leben,* 178.

14. See section "Edith's Loyal Love for Germany" in "Translator's [Josephine Koeppel] Afterword," *Life,* 444-47.

15. Charitable beneficence on her part was learned in her family, as she indicates in numerous passages in her *Life.* See especially *Life,* 309-10 for a description of some parallel wrapping of Christmas packages destined for the troops during World War I.

16. Papal decree ordered the last Sunday in October to be observed as the liturgical feast of Christ the King, and it was celebrated for the first time in 1925.

17. Posselt note: Edith Stein asked to be admitted to the Carmel *Himmelspforten* ["Gate of Heaven"] in Würzburg but was refused.

This attempted entrance might have occurred with the encouragement of friends of the Mission Institute in that city. See Müller/Neyer, *Das Leben,* 212. [Editor's note.]

18. We have restored the original order to the parts of Edith's letter to her friend Sr. Callista Kopf that P had edited. The current translation follows layout found at Letter 45, to Sr. Callista Kopf, 12 February 1928, *Letters*, 54.

19. The expression in parentheses comes from the fifth-sixth century Church writer Dionysius the Areopagite, *De Divinis Nominibus*, Chap. 4, par. 13, Patrologia Graeca 3:711f, some of whose teachings she expounds in her "Ways to Know God," *Knowledge and Faith*, trans. Walter Redmond (Washington, DC: ICS Publications, 2000), 83-134. The Collected Works of Edith Stein, 8. Hereafter cited as "*Knowledge and Faith.*"

20. This article now appears as "Husserl and Aquinas, A Comparison," (first part of) *Knowledge and Faith*, 1-62.

21. The quotation, according to n. 2 at ESGA, 2, 109, is a Latin translation of Aesop's Fable 203 and means "seize the opportunity, and act!"

22. Letter 52 to Sr. Adelgundis Jaegerschmid, 16 February 1930, *Letters*, 60. Editorializing by P led her to insert an ellipsis at the end that we have supplied in brackets. Italics in Edith's original text. The first sentence, out of place in the ICS translation, has been restored to where it belongs.

23. Posselt note: To be found in Edmund Husserl's *Yearbook for Philosophy and Phenomenological Research*. [See our n. 8 above.]

24. Given on 12 April 1928 and published in English as "The Significance of Woman's Intrinsic Value in National Life," in *Essays on Woman*, trans. Freda Mary Oben (Washington, DC: ICS Publications, 1996, 2nd rev. and corrected ed.), 253-65. The Collected Works of Edith Stein, 2. Hereafter cited as "*Woman.*"

25. See the very informative study about this period of lecture tours by Amata Neyer, "Die Vorträge Edith Steins aus den Jahren 1926-30," *Edith-Stein-Jahrbuch* 6 (2000): 410-36, esp. pp. 428-29 for the Heidelberg speech titled "The Intellect and Intellectuals"; see also Letter 66 to Emil Vierneisel, 9 October 1930, *Letters*, 70. The date of the talk turned out to be 2 December 1930 and it took place in Aula 13 of the famous university (at that time the largest auditorium on campus). This was not the talk she had intended to give "to Heidelberg's Catholic community" to help celebrate the jubilee of St. Elisabeth of Thuringia on 22 November 1931 but never gave. See Letters 95 and 106, *Letters*, 95 and 106. Hereafter we cite the *Edith-Stein-Jahrbuch* as "*ESJ.*"

26. One concludes P erroneously included Prague, in the light of the conclusions of Amata Neyer's, "Die Vorträge Edith Steins aus den Jahren 1926-1930," *ESJ* 6 (2000): 426.

27. Given on 1 September 1930 and published in English as "The Ethos of Women's Professions," *Woman*, 43-57.

28. She wrote three letters to Peter Wust and mentioned him in as many others, worried over the throat cancer he ultimately died from in 1940. See the recent study "Edith Stein und Peter Wust," of Elisabeth Lammers, *Als die Zukunft noch offen war: Edith Stein, das entscheidende Jahr in Münster* (Münster: Dialogvertrag, 2003), 192-203.

29. P's reckoning of Edith's age at the time of the Salzburg lecture ought to be corrected to thirty-nine years of age.

30. Sentence removed because of its obviously gratuitous and prejudiced nature.

31. It is difficult to intuit what "danger" might have lurked in the publicity gained from Edith's lecturing, so one sentence has been deleted and has become [T 3].

32. Date of his death was 17 September 1927, about two months short of his seventy-fifth birthday.

33. "Obituary by Dr. Edith Stein for her Spiritual Director, Canon Joseph Schwind." Original in *Korrespondenzblatt des Priestergebetsvereins im theologischen Konvikte zu Innsbruck* 62 (1927): 6-9.

CHAPTER 9

1. See John Sullivan, "Liturgical Creativity from Edith Stein," *Teresianum* 49 (1998): 165.

2. Archabbot Raphael Walzer was born just three years before Edith, and died in Neuburg Abbey near Heidelberg in 1966 (with a period of surveillance by the Nazis aided by a fellow monk of his Order in the 1940s). Unfortunately there is no full-fledged biography of him available in English. See Joachim Koehler, "Companion in Human Fate," *Never Forget*, 145 and Chap. 15 below where he likens Edith to St. Benedict with the words *"fuit et quietus"* [he was tranquil]. The newly-named Sr. Teresa Benedicta of the Cross took particular joy in telling some persons not present at her Clothing as a novice that "Everything went smoothly and Fr. Archabbot [Walzer] was able to be here by Saturday afternoon." See Letter 171, *Letters*, 174 and Letter

172 for a description of the ceremony conducted by Walzer, *Letters*, 176.

3. This segment of personal testimony, as well as the longer segment below, are found in the Edith Stein Archives, Cologne.

4. See Edith's own use of the Latin phrase "*in desiderio vitae monasticae*" [in the (same) desire for monastic life] in Letter 51 written on 26 January 1930, *Letters*, 59 or the remark in n. 17 below. Significantly, the present chapter was joined to the previous chapter in the German original and both parts bore the title "*Klostersehnsucht*" that translates literally as "longing for the monastery." The extra prominence given to the abbey of Beuron by the English language edition is justified, since Edith came to rely significantly on this place and on its spiritual leader (Dom Raphael).

5. It is worth noting she chose a Benedictine journal to publish "Problems of Women's Education," a series of lectures she gave at that time. See "Editor's Introduction to the First Edition," *Woman*, 35-36. Years later she would choose the name "Benedicta" in Carmel to go along with "Teresa," in the astute play-on-words most people are now familiar with. She affirmed, in fact, *"You asked me about my name-patron. Of course it is holy Father Benedict."* (!) See Letter 178, *Letters*, 182.

6. Beyond her contacts in Beuron Edith drew on a "support system" of other Benedictine religious and houses: on her way to Beuron from Speyer or elsewhere she would often stay overnight at the St. Lioba priory of Benedictine nuns where she gladly visited with a phenomenologist friend from student days, Sr. Adelgundis Jaegerschmid, O.S.B. and another acquaintance, Sr. Placida Laubhardt, O.S.B. See *Letters*, passim.

7. Letter 69, *Letters*, 72. ICS text slightly altered.

8. Letter 45, *Letters*, 54-55.

9. Usual translation by liturgists of this ancient phrase is "the Church at prayer."

10. Biblical quote from Jn 17:19. See Edith's lively description of the setting of the Beuron church alluded to by Fr. Damasus in Letter 90, *Letters*, 88. See, also, the recent volume of studies by Jakobus Kaffanke and Katharina Oost eds., "*Wie der Vorhof des Himmels*": *Edith Stein und Beuron*" (Beuron: Beuroner Kunstverlag, 2003), 208pp.

11. Text in Edith Stein, *The Hidden Life*, trans. Waltraut Stein (Washington, DC: ICS Publications, 1992), 7-17. The Collected Works of Edith

Stein, 4. Hereafter cited as "*Hidden Life*." She did not attend the symposium due to her observance of enclosure as a Carmelite nun.

12. Rom 8:26.

13. 1Cor 12:3.

14. *Hidden Life*, 15-16. We have supplied the first sentence, left out by H/N.

15. Here P is alluding to formal, communal praying of the psalms in the Liturgy of the Hours on one hand, and to individual, silent and reflective prayer on the other.

16. Cf. John Sullivan, "Edith Stein Carmelite, Pt. II: Why did Stein enter the Carmelite Order?" *Studies in Spirituality* 10 (2000): 277-86.

17. Striking words like the following illustrate this penchant of hers: "*I had another chance to spend almost two weeks as a 'happy monk' in Beuron*." See Letter 115, *Letters*, 112.

18. See n. 21 below, with its remarks about *compassio*.

19. Translated text by Sr. M. Julian, R.S.M. "Edith Stein and the Mother of God," *Cross and Crown* 8 (1956): 423-24.

20. What is witnessed to here is developed at length by Edith in her own text "Death and Resurrection," *The Science of the Cross,* trans. Josephine Koeppel (Washington, DC: ICS Publications, 2002), 181-93. The Collected Works of Edith Stein, 6. Hereafter cited as "*The Science*."

21. The thought of this Latin word captures the whole thrust of the poem above where Edith invites herself and others to stand "*with* You at the Cross," that is, with the suffering mother of Jesus, unjustly condemned to death by the Roman Procurator, Pontius Pilate.

22. Maria Schäfer was a young woman Edith met at St. Lioba Benedictine priory in Günterstal. While we have no extant letters from Edith to her, there is a letter to Edith in Carmel from her found in the new German edition of Edith's correspondence. See Maria Schäfer an Edith Stein, 14 April 1934, ESGA 2, 49-50. The text evokes their celebration of Easter together in Beuron. Redolent of the changed times, however, is the sender's address at "Adolf Hitler Strasse, 15" in Freiburg-im-Breisgau. The psalm quoted by Maria in P's text is Ps 83 [84]:2 as found in the Vulgate version.

23. Letter 74, *Letters*, 75. [Slightly amended.]

24. Cf. Letter 74, *Letters*, 76. The Beuron baptismal register reveals that the person to be baptized, and for whom Edith was godmother, was Alice Reis. The same register shows 27 December 1930 as the baptismal day.

Alice died alongside Edith in Auschwitz twelve years later. See A. Neyer, ESGA 2, 151, n. 10.

25. Letter 89, *Letters*, 86. This description shows there were no reasons adduced by school authorities either persuading her to leave or terminating her service. She donated her manuscript of the translation of St. Thomas Aquinas' *Disputed Questions on Truth* to the nuns as a token of appreciation. See *Speyerer Jahre*, 108; also details of her departure with three photos taken on the very day she left in Chap. VIII "Der Abschied von Speyerer," *Speyerer Jahre*, 131-41.

26. Letter 89, *Letters,* 86-87.

27. Letter 87, *Letters*, 85. [Slight modification of ICS translation.] The date would be 26 March, not the 27th, as time references in the letter itself allow us to deduce, and she wanted to start her Easter retreat on the Thursday before Holy Thursday that fell on 31 March that year. She goes on to indicate that another "big project" was intended by her – a *Habilitationsschrift* or thesis for submission to obtain a university teaching position (her second such thesis). See her letter to Hedwig Conrad Martius on 24 February 1933 where she mentions the "*paper on* Act and Potency *that I wrote in the summer of 1931*," *Letters*, 134. Edith frequently referred to the title of this work in reverse order.

28. See Carla Jungels, "Rosa Stein," *ESJ* 5 (1999): 399. (Sr. Carla Jungels, O.C.D. bases her research on direct contact with archival material, in her capacity of assistant to Sr. Maria Amata Neyer in the Edith Stein archive at Cologne Carmel.)

CHAPTER 10

1. H/N note [excerpted from P's paragraph]: Recently reprinted by the Wissenschaftliche Buchgemeinde, Tübingen. [This must have been previous to 1950 – editor's note].

    Borgmeyer publishers of Breslau issued volume 1 in 1931 and volume 2 in 1932. Finally, the series of "Edith Steins Werke" brought out two volumes, the first in 1952, the second in 1955 (see n. 3 below). The full history of the edition deserves a monographic presentation of its own.

    Unfortunately, P is mistaken in her claim here that the *Quaestiones Disputatae* volumes were the "major work" hinted at by Edith at the end of the last chapter. Actually, Edith was going to spend time in Breslau to deepen her research and drafting of *Potenz und Akt, Studien zu einer Philosophie des Seins* [Potency and Act: Studies for a Philosophy of Being]. See the introductory remarks in the first edition of this work by Hans Rainer Sepp ed. "Zur Textgeschichte," *Potenz und Akt* (Freiburg: Verlag Herder, 1998), 11-21, ESW, 18. See our remarks in [G 5] for further information about *Potency and Act.*

2. Cf. J. Morrison, "Martin Grabmann," *New Catholic Encyclopedia* 6: 657.

3. Edith Stein, *Des hl. Thomas von Aquino Untersuchungen über die Wahrheit*, Band I, Quaestio 1-13 (Louvain/Freiburg: E.Nauwelaerts/ Verlag Herder, 1952), xiv + 348; Band II, Quaestio 14-29 (1955), xi + 518. "Edith Stein Werke," 3-4.

4. See review "Thomas von Aquin deutsch" in *Stimmen der Zeit* 121 (1931): 385-86.

5. Neither of her letters from Beuron at Christmas 1930 reveal this possibility to her correspondents. See *Letters*, 78. Her correspondence with Roman Ingarden is helpful in following events as they unfolded at this time. See Briefe 151-153, Edith Stein, *Selbstbildnis in Briefen: Briefe an Roman Ingarden*, ESGA 4 (Freiburg: Herder Verlag, 2001), 222-26. Hereafter cited as "ESGA 4."

6. Heinrich Finke was professor of philosophy at Freiburg University, and he co-signed Edith's doctoral "sheepskin" in 1917. See *Life in Photos*, 29.

7. Letter 83, *Letters*, 82.

8. Heidegger's oldest son Jorg was eleven years old when he welcomed Fräulein Stein to his family's house. The future rector of the university at this point in his career was already a professor since 1928 when he received "his appointment to the chair of the retiring Husserl." Obtaining his support would be important for anyone's attempt to gain a position on the faculty whether they knew him, as was the case for Edith, or not. He had also published her revised comparison of Husserl and St. Thomas Aquinas in the *Jahrbuch* the year previous to their interview in his house. See English translation Edith Stein, "Husserl and Aquinas, A Comparison," *Knowledge and Faith*, 1-62.

9. Letter 85, *Letters*, 83-84. [ICS text slightly amended.]

10. Reference by P to *Potenz und Akt*, the second "Habilitationschrift" or dissertation required for admission to the faculty. It would turn out to be a preliminary elaboration of thoughts later to appear in *Finite and*

Eternal Being. Edith announced inception of work on *Potenz und Akt* in a letter written on 28 March 1931 – see Letter 87, *Letters*, 85 – and refers to it off and on until she arrives at Münster to take up teaching duties there.

11. Johann Peter Steffes (1883-1955) headed the "German Institute of Scientific Pedagogy," the more common way of designating the specialized school Edith would lecture at. He wrote a personal catch-up note to his former colleague, Sr. Teresa Benedicta, in the winter of 1934-35. See Brief 360 (14 January 1935), ESGA 3, 97. For a photo portrait see *Als die Zukunft*, 154.

12. Maria Schmitz (1875-1962) was a co-founder of the Münster Pedagogy Institute. See note 1 of Brief 312 sent by her to Cologne Carmel accepting its invitation to Edith Stein's clothing as a novice in ESGA 3, 47.

13. The abbreviation, according to Amata Neyer, refers to an *academy* (not the Münster Institute) located at Spandau in the Berlin area. See Brief 150, ESGA, 2, 165, n. 5. Edith gives her own description of Spandau within the system of "Akademie" to Roman Ingarden, in Brief 149, ESGA 4, 223.

14. Letter 89, *Letters*, 87.

15. Joseph Koch (1885-1967) was professor of Catholic theology both in Breslau and Cologne. By "Salzburg" she meant the lecture she gave there on 1 September 1930 titled "The Ethos of Women's Professions."

16. Reference to her translation of the *Disputed Questions on Truth* of St. Thomas Aquinas.

17. Ludwig Bauer (1871-1943) had been a professor at Breslau since 1925. P at times spells his name Baur.

18. Latest indications of Amata Neyer say the last word on this speaking tour is yet to be pronounced. That is, one does not always find traces left from speaking appearances in all the places cited in advance of the tour itself. As well as the usual article already cited, i.e., Amata Neyer, "Die Vorträge 1926-1930," (in Chap. 8, n. 25) see Amata Neyer, "Die Vorträge Edith Steins aus den Jahren 1931-32," *ESJ* 7 (2001): 318-37. See also ESGA 3, 179, n. 14.

19. Letter 95, 28 June 1931, *Letters*, 94-95. [ICS text slightly amended.]

20. See Jan Nota, "Edith Stein and Martin Heidegger," *Carmelite Studies* 4 (1987): 50-73.

CHAPTER 11

1. Reference to Rosa Stein. See Jungels, *Rosa Stein*, 397-403.
2. Letter 87, *Letters*, 85.
3. As already stated in Chap. 1, Dr. Rubens, nee Katharina (Käthe) Kleemann, went to Breslau's Viktoriaschule with Edith. See a lengthy sketch of Käthe and her family in Edith's *Life*, 146-47.
4. Several instances of Frau Stein's respect for other religions, coexistent with zeal for her own, can be documented, such as Edith's own words in *Life*, 56-57 where she points to her mother's gestures of kindness at Christmas and of visiting one of her sick workers in a sanitarium on Sundays. Dr. Rubens bases her opinion on a point of view derived from the cases she would have noticed with her own eyes or by hearsay.
5. This is a useful testimony to the process of erosion of religious conviction in the young Edith. It tends to confirm the opinion that poor quality of the religious training available to Edith in public school would have had a deleterious influence on her religious convictions and rendered her "indifferent to religious matters." See Batzdorff, *Aunt Edith*, 191.
6. The later date is the more accurate of the two, judging from the information found in Amata Neyer's n. 4 accompanying Brief 217 "Jan Hering an Edith Stein," 4 September 1932, ESGA 2, 231.
7. In the summer of 1931 Frau Stein was eighty-one years old.
8. Edith, not long after they met again in Würzburg, wrote in *Life*, 147 that as schoolgirls she and Käthe "*often discussed questions that were ignored in school; a serious search for truth had begun for her as for me.*"
9. These letters to Africa have not come down to us; nor are there any to Edith from either Käthe Rubens or her husband.
10. The details given by Dr. Rubens are borne out by Amata Neyer in her note to Brief 217, cited above in our n. 6.
11. Edith was a postulant at the time, and would have worn dark clothes, resembling street clothing, over whiich she'd put an overcoat to protect her against the cold encountered in monastic houses.
12. At the time indicated, Frau Stein had just about four years left to live, before a stomach tumor would take her, the date of death being 14 September 1936. Cf. Letter 239, *Letters*, 251 where Edith herself confirms the date and Letter 227, *Letters*, 238 where she speaks of the cause.
13. See the first note of this chapter above for an article noting Rosa's baptism in Cologne.

14. Letter 74 (10 December 1930), *Letters*, 75. P mistakes the date of this letter as 10 December *1931* in the German edition.
15. Title of the talk, given on 30 May 1931, was "St. Elizabeth: Nature and Supernature in the Formation of a Saint." Not yet translated, it has been published in the 1990 volume, *Ganzheitliches Leben* (ESW, 12).
16. Dr. Rudolf Allers, who was teaching and leading research projects at the Medical School of the University of Vienna at that time, subsequently played an important role in making the thought of Edith Stein known to English-speaking readers. He published her study "Ways to Know God," in *The Thomist* (Washington, DC) in 1946. For details see "Foreword to the I.C.S. Edition" by Steven Payne, O.C.D. in *Knowledge and Faith*, xv-xvii.
17. Exact dates for this stay are difficult to determine. According to Amata Neyer "Edith Stein probably left Bonn for Freiburg on 13 November because there are indications she obtained an appointment with Edmund Husserl for 14 November." See n. 4, Brief 178, ESGA 2, 194. Edith writes from St. Lioba (to her friend Sr. Callista Kopf) on 14 January 1932, Brief 187, ESGA 2, 200-01. In her note to Brief 188, sent from Zürich, Amata Neyer fills out the chronology with this remark: "Early in February she traveled back to St. Lioba/Freiburg-Günterstal and [from there] on 29 February she went to Münster to take up her position as a Lecturer at the German Institute of Pedagogy."
18. Letter 95 (28 June 1931), *Letters*, 94.
19. Edith identifies her for us as the cousin of a colleague on the faculty at St. Magdalena's in Letter 57, *Letters*, 65.
20. See Chap. 9, n. 22.
21. First of the "Essays on Woman" to be found as "The Ethos of Women's Professions," in *Woman*, 43-57. This is the text of the noted lecture she gave in Salzburg on 1 September 1930 and the one mentioned in the final lines of this chapter of P's biography.
22. *The Song at the Scaffold* [Letzte am Schafott] is a novella about the Carmelite Martyrs of Compiègne. The previous spring Edith Stein met, for the first time, its author Gertrude von le Fort at the Easter Congress in Munich of the Young Bavarian Catholic Teachers Association. See *Das Leben*, 201-02.
23. See Amata Neyer, "Die Vorträge 1931-1932,": 325-26.
24. Septuagesima Sunday that year fell on 24 January.

25. English translation found in *Woman*, 143-45 and dated 12 January 1932.
26. This last sentence, omitted in P's book, is being supplied from *Woman*. 145.
27. These words were added by the author.
28. Letter 89, *Letters*, 87.
29. The next few lines, a portion of an entirely different letter, Letter 57, *Letters*, 64-65, apparently have no bearing on the fragment from Letter 89 dealing with the supernatural, so we have placed it among the "Take-Out" texts as [T 3].

CHAPTER 12

1. [T 1] is not found in P's German text.
2. Date of arrival in Münster was 29 February 1932; the first class given at the Institute took place on 23 April that year. See *Das Leben*, 205. As with [T 1], [T 2] is not found in P's German text either.
3. The Marianum was a residence that offered room and board to Catholics studying in the city, most of whom were women religious. The building where Edith lived still stands, even after damage sustained in World War II, and a bronze memorial to her was erected in one of the inner courtyards. Other details appear in the eyewitness testimonies of people who were in residence there in 1932-33 with Edith. See Lammers, "Das Collegium Marianum," *Als die Zukunft*, 35-36.
4. The size of this accommodation matches the space available to Edith in her years at St. Magdalena's in Speyer.
5. Confirmation of this is found in A. Neyer, "Münster, Where my Limits Lie," *Life in Photos,* 52 (photo caption).
6. The "at that time" phrase is a reference to the meatless diet she accepted upon entrance into Carmel. Apparently no health considerations influenced her choice, and severe health problems had not emerged at that time in her life.
7. As an example of the themes she treated, the title of a course given twice monthly in the first semester was "Problems of Modern Girls' Education." See *Kölner Karmel kam,* 10.
8. From this period comes the letter she wrote to her teaching Sister friend Callista Kopf, Letter 123 (20 October 1932) in *Letters,* 122-23 quoted in Chap. 8 above and commented upon in John Sullivan, "Edith Stein Challenges Catholics," *Teresianum* 50 (1999): 342-43.

9. Contrary to the impression given by this statement of Edith as someone unconcerned with communication techniques, she even used the medium of radio and appeared on "The Woman's Hour" to give an address about "Questions about the Maternal Art of Rearing Children" on 1 April of that same year, 1932. See *Das Leben*, 206. Also Lammers, "Vortrag im Bayerischen Rundfunk 'Mütterliche Erziehungskunst,'" *Als die Zunkunft*, 64-65.

10. See Edith's own opening words below of the encounter she had in Münster with a "Catholic teacher" (name unknown) in her autobiographical narrative "How I came," in *Selected Writings*, 16: "*True, I had heard of rigorous measures against the Jews before.*"

11. P is mistaken in the numbering she provides for the age of Edith's mother, viz., "eightieth." The eightieth birthday of Frau Stein would have occurred in October of 1929 (i.e. before Edith moved from Speyer to Münster). Actual birth date of Frau Stein was 4 October 1849.

12. Fragment from Letter 120 (from Breslau dated 28 August 1932), *Letters*, 118.

13. Letter 116 (from Münster dated 9 June 1932), *Letters*, 113-14.

14. Letter 120 (from Breslau dated 28 August 1932), *Letters*, 117-18. [ICS text slightly altered.] See Edith Stein, Chap. VI "The Church, Woman, and Youth," *Woman*, 237-51.

15. This visit returned the compliment to Alexandre Koyré who had visited Edith earlier that year "on Corpus Christi." See Letter 116, *Letters*, 114.

16. Müller/Neyer feel this was "**probably** the most important of Edith's projects" for 1932. See *Das Leben*, 212-13; quote taken from Edith's Letter 120, *Letters*, 118.

17. Gottlieb Sölingen (1892-1971) was a philosopher-theologian, also prelate in Munich and lies buried in Cologne.

18. The acts of the conference, with segments in both French and German, were published as *La Phénoménologie, Juvisy, 12 septembre 1932* (Juvisy: Editions du Cerf:, 1932), 115pp. "Journées d'études de la Société Thomiste," 1. See pages 101-03, 104-05, and 109-11 for transcripts of Edith's words in German.

19. Daniel Feuling, O.S.B. (1882-1947) was an expert in spirituality and Aquinas, and a professor of theology and philosophy in Salzburg. See his "Short Biographical Sketch of Edith Stein," in *Never Forget*, 260-63.

20. The text in "[T 3]" was not found in P's German text.

21. Four years later Edith refers to Aloys Dempf (born, like her, in 1891) in correspondence with Hedwig Conrad-Martius. See Letter 224, *Letters*, 234.

22. Annie Bender was almost the same age as Edith, having been born on 21 May 1890. She died in Cologne on 9 December 1973.

23. A reference to her lecture "Fundamental Principles of Women's Education," in *Woman*, 129-42.

24. Letter 121 (dated 11 October 1932), *Letters*, 119-20. [ICS version slightly corrected according to ESGA 3, 240-41.]

25. Published subsequently as *Der Aufbau der menschlichen Person* (Freiburg: Herder Verlag, 1994), 200pp. ESW, 16.

26. Dorsten lies forty-one miles southwest of Münster. Mother Petra Brüning, according to the edition of *Letters*, received thirty-two letters in all from Edith between 1933-41. See n. 1 to Letter 130, *Letters*, 130 for an explanation of how their friendship began at Christmas 1932.

27. Actual date of departure from Münster, however, was later on in the year, on 15 July 1933, because maneuvers took place to try to secure a research position for her in the orbit of the Pedagogical Institute. Edith captures the events of her last days in Münster (April through mid-July) in "How I came to Carmel" in the next chapter below. See *Selected Writings*, 18-23.

CHAPTER 13

1. Posselt note: The following account was given as a Christmas gift on Christmas Eve 1938 by Sr. Teresa Benedicta to her prioress in Lindenthal. [rendered by H/N as: Edith Stein's own account of her entry into the Carmel of Cologne.]

    Editor's note: The translation of this chapter is Susanne Batzdorff's version in *Selected Writings*, 15-30. See also Gleanings [G 1].

2. Dr. Raphael Josef Walzer (1888-1966). See also Gleanings [G 2].

3. 1933 was considered the 1900th anniversary year of the death of Jesus Christ. Thus this year was singled out for pilgrimages to Rome and other holy places, e.g., the Cathedral of Trier.

4. We have retained this spelling, since Edith herself used it in her handwritten text, although the spelling "Lindenthal" appears to be the one generally accepted and is therefore adopted elsewhere in this text.

5. Hubert Wüsten (1891-1962) was Curate at the Cologne Cathedral from 1926 to 1935.
6. Pater Aloys Mager, O.S.B. (1883-1946). See also Gleanings [G 3].
7. Pope Pius XI (Ambrogio Damiano Achille Ratti) pontificate 6 February 1922-10 February 1939.
8. H/N note: It was transmitted to the Holy See by the Lord Abbot of Beuron, with a letter of his own warmly recommending the writer and stressing the menace of National Socialism to Christianity. This was in April 1933, before the signing of the new Concordat. Editor's note: See [G 4] for full text of the letter.
9. See Chap. 12, n. 27 above.
10. Maria Schmitz (1875-1962) was the first chairperson of the Society of German Catholic Women Teachers and had arranged for Edith Stein's appointment as an instructor to the German Institute for Scientific Pedagogy in Münster. See *Kölner Karmel kam,* 17.
11. No details are known about this offer.
12. The denial probably originated with her spiritual advisor Archabbot Raphael Walzer.
13. See also *Das Leben,* 225.
14. A small plaque now marks this incident of Edith Stein's visit.
15. Hedwig Spiegel, née Hess, who was baptized on 1 August 1933.
16. Dr. Elisabeth Cosack (1885-1936) was editor of *Frauenland,* a magazine of the Catholic German Women's Organization. See *Kölner Karmel kam,* 25.
17. Edith received the letter on 20 May 1933 and traveled to Cologne the following day, Sunday 21 May. See *Das Leben,* 225.
18. A well-known family of nobility in Silesia. Their forebears founded a monastery of Carmelite friars in Silesia.
19. Sr. Teresia Renata (1891-1961). For a two-part biographical sketch of her life see Maria Amata Neyer, "Teresia Renata Posselt ocd: Ein Beitrag zur Chronik des Kölner Carmel," *ESJ* 8 (2002): 319-33 and "Teresia Renata Posselt ocd: Ein Beitrag zur Chronik des Kölner Carmel," *ESJ* 9 (2003): 447-87. See also Gleanings [G 6].
20. Posselt note: A remark intended to remind the postulant that she should not count on being able to continue her intellectual work in Carmel. To this she gave the beautiful answer: *"It is not human activity that can help us but the Passion of Christ. It is a share in that, that I desire."*

21. Johannes von Poggenburg (1862-1933) was Bishop of Münster from 1913 to 1933.

22. The distance between Breslau and Cologne was more than 800 km, and at the time surely a full day's train trip.

23. Small town on the Moselle River, now spelled Kordel. Because of almost constant flood conditions, the Kordel Carmel has been moved to Anderath-Waldfrieden.

24. Erna, Edith's sister, was married to Dr. Hans Biberstein.

25. See Chap. I "My Mother Remembers" in *Life.*

26. H/N note: Countess Stolberg, d. 1948.

27. An article by historian Franz Heiduk of Würzburg, formerly a resident of Silesia, explores the identity of this "head pastor" and concludes that it must have been Stadtdekan Walther Lierse (1873-1957). For Heiduk's interesting description of the negotiations between Auguste Stein and the prospective tenants, most likely the Elftausend-Jugfrauenkirche (Church of the Eleven Thousand Virgins), see "Edith Steins Begegnungen mit dem Stadtdekan von Breslau, *Schlesien,* 33 (1988): 129-135. (The building where Edith went to speak with Rev. Lierse has changed hands and become a local monastery of the Discalced Carmelites Friars.)

28. For "Susel's" perspective, see "Prologue," *Aunt Edith,* 23-25.

29. Yitzhak Heinemann (1876-1957) was a professor of philosophy at the Breslau Rabbinical Seminary from 1919-1939, when he emigrated to Palestine.

Part 2

CHAPTER 14

1. The sentence was penned by Edith in her statement "How I came to Carmel:" found in the previous chapter.

2. Franziska Ernst entered the Cologne Carmel the evening of 7 December 1933. She received the name Maria de Deo [Maria of God]. The text of the letter mentioned by P was not found for inclusion in ESGA 3, nor is it in the English collection of *Letters.*

3. From 1935 to 1945 German youths between the ages of eighteen and twenty-five were obliged to do a six-month period of compulsory "work service."

4. Hans Brunnengräber, PhD, M.D., (1902-1961) taught at the Pedagogical Institute in Münster alongside Edith. Cf. Letter 161, 20 November 1933, *Letters,* 164.

5. Letter 152 to Sr. Adelgundis Jaegerschmid, 27 August 1933, *Letters,* 154.

6. The "clapper" was a hand-held contraption of two small wooden rectangles fastened by a knotted cord to the front and back of a paddle. When shaken, the boards made a clapping sound, hence the name. It served to call the nuns to prayer in the morning. and also was sounded each hour of the day, when the nuns would recollect themselves and say a "Hail Mary."

7. The final sentence is found before the rest of the quoted words in the middle of Brief 300 to Margarete Günther, 11 December 1933, ESGA 3, 33. (There is no letter of that date in the ICS edition of *Letters.*) Edith, in writing to Günther, refers to herself and Sr. Maria de Deo, Franziska Ernst, identified in the second note of this chapter above.

8. This letter is found neither in the German nor English-language edition of the correspondence.

CHAPTER 15

1. In the original German, this chapter bears the title "The Postulant." The time period covered justifies retention of the English title "Novitiate," however.

2. This vestment survived the bombing of the Cologne-Lindenthal monastery. For the Beatification Ceremony, held in Cologne on 1 May 1987, the vestment was worn by Pope John Paul II.

3. As Edith attested, ". . . *I brought my religious name with me into the house as a postulant. I received it exactly as I requested it.*" See Letter 287, *Letters,* 295.

4. At the entrance of the monastery there were rooms assigned to the portress or "extern Sister" who answered the door and led visitors to the "speakroom" – literally: a room in which persons spoke to one another. The Sister was inside and separated from the visitors by a double grille. Speakrooms are not then "guest rooms," the term rendered by H/N.

5. This use of double negatives occurs extensively in Edith's writing and accordingly they have been preserved in translation. Quite possibly, it was a literary device in vogue at the time in Germany.

6. This is a kneeling bench – its purpose is given in its name "pray to God."

7. Rev. Theodore [George] Rauch [of St. Francis of Assisi, O.C.D.], b. 22 August 1890 in Altegloffsheim, d. 15 September 1972 in Regensburg. From 1933 to 1936 he was Provincial of the Bavarian Province of the Discalced Carmelites.

8. "O glorious Lady," a hymn in honor of the Virgin Mary.

9. The original translators here changed more than half of this paragraph without explanation. We have supplied the correct text from "looked and listened" through to the end of the paragraph. The incorrect version has been removed, see [T 3].

10. This refers to Husserl's return to his former views, that Edith and others of his followers could not accept.

11. His reference here is to a chapter in the Rule of St. Benedict, not of Carmel.

12. "Love for Love – The Life and Works of St. Teresa of Jesus" can be found in *Hidden Life*, 29-66.

13. "St. Teresa Margaret of the Sacred Heart," is also found in *Hidden Life*, 67-75.

14. Brief 368, ESGA 3, 106 to Margarete Günther Schweitzer (1904-1988). The correspondence with Margarete will appear translated in future volumes of *Letters*.

15. This refers to St. Teresa of Avila, who founded the Reform of Carmel.

16. These two paragraphs are taken from Letter 164, 11 January 1934, to Sr. Adelgundis Jaegerschmid, O.S.B., *Letters*, 164. P has reversed the order of the paragraphs she excerpts from this letter.

17. This is from Brief 368 to Margarete Günther, ESGA 3, 106. Sr. Teresa Benedicta shows her gratitude for the impressions about Gertrude von le Fort shared by Margarete. We have corrected and extended the truncated text provided by H/R. Correct dating for this letter is 7 February 1935, not the "7 March 1935" indicated by P.

18. Letter 194, 11 February 1935, *Letters*, 199.

19. From "The Ethos of Women's Professions," *Woman*, 51-52 in the 1996 rev. ed. Since this was the famous Salzburg lecture of 1930, the audience were the members of the Association of Catholic Academics meeting at their annual convention. Presumably there were some "nuns" (according to P's assertion) among them.

When reading the excerpt one is reminded of Edith's Letter 19 of 19 February 1918 to Roman Ingarden, *Letters*, 22 in which she stated she could not accept a situation in which she would be at some person's disposition.

20. H/N note [excerpted from P's paragraph]: Letter to Heliodor[us].
21. The meeting of all the nuns in which community matters were treated is simply called "Chapter."
22. H/N note: The form of address from one Carmelite to another.
23. Ordinarily a Sister who had visitors in the speakroom lowered her veil to cover her face but on the occasion of a profession or veiling, the veil was folded back, as it was at all times for one's immediate family.
24. The person attributing these words to Sr. Teresa Benedicta was Elisabeth Kramer. She offered her account to the Cologne Carmel and it was reproduced in the beatification booklet of 1962. See *Kölner Selig- und Heiligsprechungsprozess*, 17.

CHAPTER 16

1. Sr. Teresa Renata of the Holy Spirit, O.C.D., or P.
2. St. Thérèse of Lisieux, *Story of a Soul*, trans. John Clarke, O.C.D. (Washington, DC: ICS Publications, 3rd. ed. 1996), Ms A, fol. 69r, 147. The experience is necessary to understand the reference. St. Teresa of Avila felt as though the pain of leaving her home and father was tearing her apart.
3. Ruth Kantorowicz, b. 7 January 1901 in Hamburg, Germany, d. in Auschwitz 9 August 1942 in the same transport as Edith and Rosa. Ruth was baptized on 8 September 1934. She typed most of Edith's works from the handwritten manuscripts and so earned the gratitude of all who read Edith's writings.
4. Brief 450, 19 April 1936 to Margarete Günther, ESGA 3, 198. Our translation follows the text published in 2000. "G.K." = Gerta Krabbel, editor of *Die Christliche Frau*. P's text used the impersonal "*man*" in German, that H/N rendered "the editors," but Edith's original carried the abbreviated name.
5. This remark of oral tradition, "and said," stands against what Sr. Teresa Benedicta wrote in Letter 226 on 3 October 1936, *Letters*, 237: ". . .I

can hope with confidence that God took her to Himself very quickly and that today she is able to celebrate her **eighty-seventh** *birthday with our dear Sister Thérèse."* [emphasis added]

6. Letter 227, 4 October 1936, *Letters*, 238.
7. Confirmation of the simultaneity in timeframe is given in both Letter 239 and 262, *Letters*, p. 251 and p. 275.
8. Letter 227, *Letters*, 238.
9. Heinrich Spaemann, "Witness to the Presence of God: A Portrait of Edith Stein," *Never Forget*, 207.
10. Hildegard Domizlaff, b. 21 January 1898, d. 22 February 1987.
11. P fails to indicate the locale for Rosa's first Holy Communion. It was in the Cologne-Lindenthal conventual chapel. See Jungels, *Rosa Stein*, 399; also Letter 239, *Letters*, 252 ". . .*and received her first Holy Communion at the High Mass* **here** *on that Holy Night. . .*" [emphasis added]
12. Part of the ritual at a baptism is the lighting of a candle signifying the faith of the person receiving the sacrament. The candles were often beautifully decorated, and were kept as a memento of the ceremony.
13. Posselt note: The church at Hohenlind had been brightly decorated with flowers known as "Christmas Stars." [probably poinsettias]
14. The double baptismal name Rosa accepted was Maria Agnes, placed between her two given names as a child, viz., Rosa Adelheid. See photostatic copy of her baptismal certificate in *Life in Photos*, 61.
15. Letter 238, *Letters*, 250-51. We have added the opening sentence to frame the events, although P did not include it. The sentence removed as [T 3] was added in by H/N.

CHAPTER 17

1. See Chap. 10, nn. 1 and 3 above.
2. Two versions of a subtitle exist. See R. Leuven and L. Gelber, "Editors' Appendix to First German Edition," *Finite and Eternal Being*, 529-31.
3. See "Editor's Introduction" by Marianne Sawicki in Edith Stein, *Philosophy of Psychology and the Humanities*, trans. M.C. Baseheart and M. Sawicki (Washington, D.C.: ICS Publications, 2000), xi-xxiii, esp. xix-xx. The Collected Works of Edith Stein, 7. Hereafter cited as "*Psychology and the Humanities*."
4. This was St. Thomas Aquinas' "Disputed Questions on Truth."

5. See Edith Stein, "Husserl and Aquinas: A Comparison," Pt. 1 of *Knowledge and Faith*, 1-63.

6. The preliminary study has been subsequently published as vol. 18 of ESW. See Edith Stein, *Potenz und Akt: Studien zu einer Philosophie des Seins* (Freiburg: Herder Verlag, 1998). Prof. Walter Redmond is preparing a translation into English for publication in the ICS series.

7. It was at this time that Edith stopped teaching in Speyer, then began to lecture at Münster until she was finally able to pursue her vocation for Carmel.

8. See Edith Stein, "Preface of the Author," *Finite and Eternal*, xxvii-xxviii.

9. Alexander Koyré, Jewish fellow student with Edith of Edmund Husserl, was born 29 August 1892 at Odessa in the Ukraine on the Black Sea, and died on 28 April 1964 in Paris. He taught at the Universities of Montpellier, Cairo, and Paris. He and Do, his wife, visited Edith in the Carmel of Cologne, in August 1935.

10. It was known that Edith Stein was of Jewish birth, and anyone printing a work of hers would run the risk of incurring serious consequences from the Nazi authorities.

11. These appendices were, in the end, not printed. The first was a compilation of the thought of St. Teresa of Avila from her *Interior Castle*. The second appendix had reference to the work of Martin Heidegger and to have included it with the first edition would have required extensive revision by the time the work could be printed, so the appendices have not been included in the editions of *Finite and Eternal Being* available to date. See the editors' (of the German editions) explanation in *Finite and Eternal*, 542. Subsequently, the Appendices on St. Teresa and on Martin Heidegger were issued in ESW 6 in 1962.

12. This sad story is recounted by Sr. Teresa Benedicta in a letter sent from Echt, Holland to the U.S. See Brief 664 to Marvin Farber, ESGA 3, 445-46 and in English translation in *Finite and Eternal*, xvi. She told him that "*I would like to mention also that the publisher has repeatedly suggested an alternative proposal: that the book be brought out under another's name, preferably the name of the prioress of the Carmelite Monastery in Cologne (to which I formerly belonged); she it is who signed the contract for the publication. I decidedly turned down that suggestion, not only for reasons of truthfulness, but as well for fear of putting the convent or the order in jeopardy.*"

On another occasion she explained the authorship and the history of the printing of the work *Endliches und Ewiges Sein* in Brief 659, 29 February 1940, to Malvine Husserl (Edmund Husserl's widow, at that time in Belgium) in ESGA 3, 434-35.

13. P adds the following parenthetical remark "(she referred to the violent struggle for the schools then in progress [in Germany])". P's text sewed together Edith's narrative, thereafter, with a later letter. Before the parenthetical remark, then, we have Letter 238, 7 May 1937, *Letters*, 250; after the parentheses Letter 246, 15 October 1937, *Letters*, 259, both written to Sr. Callista Kopf.

14. See Letter 244, 4 September 1937 to Mother Petra Brüning, *Letters*, 257 that writes of *"our good Sr. Clara, the oldest lay Sister in the house."* According to biographical information found there (n. 5) Sr. Clara died the next year in Cologne.

15. We have reinstated the following final clause "and who were devoted to her like children," left out by H/N.

In addition, we have taken out an extra two sentences introduced only in the H/N version, [T4]. They give, for no apparent reason, an erroneous title to *Finite and Eternal Being* (with the terms "Finite" and "Eternal" backwards.)

CHAPTER 18

1. Now begins the last part of Chap. IV in Pt. II of the 1952 H/N translation. We have made it a chapter with a name of its own to conform to the German 5th edition. The numbering of subsequent chapters will change accordingly.

2. H/N in error called Bishop Stockums the friend of Edith rather than of the Vicar.

3. Part of the "Prayer of a Soul Taken with Love," no. 27 of the Sayings of Light and Love in the Minor Works of St. John of the Cross, *The Collected Works of St. John of the Cross*, trans. Kavanaugh/Rodriguez (Washington, DC: ICS Publications, 1991), 87-88.

4. Hedwig (called Hede) Spiegel, b. 5 July 1900 in Waldorf/Baden, d. 4 Feb 1981 in Heidelberg, was baptized 1 August 1933. Edith was her baptismal sponsor and gave her as a gift a small crucifix that was a reliquary. The Spiegels suffered a great deal as a result of the persecution of the Jews by the Nazis. They emigrated to the U.S. but later

returned to Germany. Mrs. Spiegel deeded the crucifix to the Cologne nuns, and handsomely mounted, it served as the processional-cross at the Beatification of Edith Stein on 1 May 1987 in Cologne.

5. See next chapter for a listing of four German Carmels that in fact experienced closure and the expulsion of their nuns.

6. Paul Strerath was born 4 July 1880 in Schlebusch and died 5 March 1945. Late in the afternoon of 31 December 1938, he and a friend of his drove Sr. Benedicta from Cologne to the Carmel of Echt. Accounts of their roles in the trip are found in *Never Forget*, 247-48.

CHAPTER 19

1. Original German title that was rendered by H/N as "Echt."

2. Ottilia Thannisch, O.C.D., b. 29 July 1878, d. 15 May 1958.

3. Ambrosia Antonia Engelmann, O.C.D., b. 31 March 1975, d. 30 April 1972.

4. See Chap. 17 above.

5. The family name of Fr. Rhabanus was Laubenthal. He was born in 1905 and died in 1980. After surviving the war he was active in missionary work.

6. See remarks of L. Gelber and R. Leuven in *Life*, 11-12.

7. Sr. Maria Pia of St. Joseph, O.C.D., b. Regina Nüschen in 1885, d. 4 February 1971. Westphalia is the region of western Germany that borders on the Netherlands east of the Rhine River. It includes the Ruhr Valley; and from 1816 to 1945 was a province of Prussia.

8. See "Erna Biberstein, née Stein, Reminiscences, (New York, 1949)," in *Life*, 18.

9. Letter 294 in *Letters*, 302 has Edith commenting that "*My sisters and brothers cannot visit me here. Erna sailed from Bremerhaven to the United States yesterday with her children; she could say farewell only by letter. Only persons who permanently immigrate to Holland or use a Dutch steamship line have the possibility [to enter the country].*"

10. See Jungels, *Rosa Stein*, 401.

11. Exact dates of the two German aggressions were 1 September 1939 and 10 May 1940.

12. Essays one, four, five, and six are available in *Hidden Life* (Collected Works 4); the others will appear in translation after they have been published in a future ESGA volume.

13. See fifth part "Ways to Know God: The 'Symbolic Theology of Dionysius the Areopagite' and Its Objective Presuppositions," of *Knowledge and Faith* (Collected Works 7), 83-134 for text/notes, and ii-xvii for the story of her placing it in the United States for English-language publication.
14. St. Teresa of Avila, also known as Teresa of Jesus, who, like St. John of the Cross, has been named a Doctor of the Church. Although she founded the reform of Carmel and recruited St. John to help her, she herself said she was his "spiritual daughter."
15. *The Science*, 5.
16. Posselt note: *Kreuzeswissenschaft*, published 1950 by Nauwelaerts of Louvain as Vol. 1 of Edith Stein's Collected Works; ed. P. Romaeus Leuven, O.C.D. and Dr. L. Gelber.
17. See Edith's own use of the term late in her life in Letter 330: "*A scientia crucis <knowledge of the Cross> can be gained only when one comes to feel the Cross radically*," *Letters*, 341.
18. See Kieran Kavanaugh, "A Completed Work," in "I.C.S. Introduction," in *The Science*, xxxvii.
19. H/N note: League of German Girls [or Bund deutscher Mädchen].
20. Text now known as "Exaltation of the Cross" and included, not among the letters, but in the spiritual writings of *Hidden Life*, 102-03.
21. This letter (number 320) was sent to Cologne to Sr. Maria of God, O.C.D. (Franziska Ernst, b. 21 December 1904, d. 7 February 1981), *Letters*, 330-31. As explained in the Gleanings for Chap. 5, "Y.C." stands for Your Charity as a form of personal address between nuns.
22. The story of how Sr. Teresa Benedicta composed a new Latin stanza for this ancient Carmelite hymn is told by Sullivan, *Liturgical Creativity from Edith Stein*, 165-85 (with a more popular synthesis of the story called "Edith Stein's Flower of Peace," *Spiritual Life* 45 (1999): 199-205).

CHAPTER 20

1. She did write to Carmelite authorities in Rome about profession of solemn vows, and she chose English to draft her letter. See *Life in Documents*, back cover (for photostatic copy of the 18 November 1939 missive to Fr. Baptista Pozzi).
2. See John Sullivan, "Newly Refound Transfer Document of Edith Stein," *Catholic Historical Review* 81 (1995): 398-402.

3. Recently a Swiss Stein scholar has published the story of the failed attempt at bringing Sr. Teresa Benedicta and Rosa Stein to safety. See Philibert Secretan, *Edith Stein et la Suisse: chronique d'un asile manqué* (Genève: Ad Solem, 1998), 61pp. For his exposition Prof. Secretan had access to documents that he cites but without reproducing in extenso or indicating their location at the present time.

4. Eyewitness summary of her own efforts to help the Stein sisters was left by Hilde Vérène Borsinger, "Attempt to Bring Edith Stein Safely in Switzerland in 1942," *Never Forget*, 268-71.

5. Nothing explicit about life in Carmel appears in the Zurich speech. See "Spirituality of the Christian Woman," *Woman*, 87-128; and no trace of a speech given in Geneva has been found, not even in the latest collection of writings on women, i.e., *Die Frau* or volume 13 in ESGA.

6. For a copy of a letter sent to Dr. Borsinger on 28 January 1942 by Bishop Marius Besson, indicating the willingness of the nuns in Le Pâquier and the Secular Order Sisters to receive Sr. Teresa Benedicta and Rosa respectively see *Kölner Karmel kam*, 124. But, according to Secretan, *Edith Stein et la Suisse*, 39 the bishop did not grant full permission until 30 July.

7. Difficulties in Switzerland were listed by the prioress of Le Pâquier monastery to the Prioress of Echt in a letter sent six months after the initial contact, revealing she was caught up in what appears to be a glacial pace of efforts. See Marie Agnes de Wolff, O.C.D. to Antonia Engelmann, O.C.D., 30 June 1942, Brief 747, ESGA 3, 558-559.

8. Background information on the congregation of religious approached, including location in France of the motherhouse P alludes to, as well to the name of the village where Rosa would stay (i.e., in Seedorf, one hour away from her sister), is found in note 1 of Brief 756, ESGA 3, 571-72.

9. Secretan places the brunt of the problem at the doorstep of the Swiss bureaucratic bodies, with their multiple levels of responsibility and power. See "Les chemins de l'administration," *Edith Stein et la Suisse*, 35-40; also a revelatory note on p.12.

10. For more information on Fr. Cornelius Leunissen, O.C.D. see n. 3 to Letter 337, *Letters*, 348. A 1939 letter from him to Edith Stein, written in English, was found and recently included in the latest German edition of her correspondence. See Brief 628, ESGA 3, 397-98.

11. H/N note: *Gelobt sei Jesus Christus*, a form of greeting in Catholic Germany, expecting the response *In Ewigkeit* (To all eternity).

12. According to "Zwitserland en de Vluchelingen," in *Als een Brandende toorts: Documentaire Getuigenissen over Dr. Edith Stein (Zr. Teresia Benedicta a Cruce) en medeslachtoffers* (Echt: private publication by "Vrienden van Dr. Edith Stein," 1967) 63 the inaugural date for use of the odious "J" mark was 4 October 1938; and Amata Neyer in n. 4 to Brief 580 in ESGA 3, 339 says effective date was 1 January 1939 so Edith's departure from Germany on the last day of 1938 enabled her not to have the mark placed in her passport. Hereafter cited as *"Als een brandende toorts."*

A different version of the measures imposed on Jews in Germany indicates that "a decree came out on 17 August 1938 stipulating that all Jewish women had to adopt the middle name "Sara" and all Jewish men that of "Israel." This law took effect on 1 January 1939. As far as passports issued to Jews, they were supposed to become invalid after 5 October 1938 unless stamped with a "J" indicating the Jewish origin of the bearer. See *The Holocaust Chronicle* (Publications International: 2000), 154; 155.

13. Edith herself attests to the kindliness of the people serving the Jewish Council in contrast to the German occupying authorities when she writes to a Carmelite nun in nearby Beek Carmel (a mere thirteen miles south of Echt) *"an invitation. . .that will not take us to the* **benevolent** *Joodsen Raad but to the SS."* See Letter 333, *Letters*, 344. [Emphasis added]

14. Letter 336, *Letters*, 346-47.

15. This piece of information given them leads one to concur with P as she dates their Amsterdam stay early in May 1942, or from 29 April onward at the earliest.

16. See biographical sketch of Alice Reis. "Muß ich auch wandern in finsterer Schlucht, ich fürchte kein Unheil; denn du bist bei mir (Ps 23:4)," *Passion im August (2-9 August 1942)*, eds. Anne Mohr u. Elisabeth Prégardier (Annweiler: Plöger Verlag, 1995), 131-35. Coll. "Zeugen der Zeitgeschichte," 5. Alice Reis' work for the Sisters of the Good Shepherd paralleled the service rendered by the lay convert, Rosa Stein, at the Echt Carmel.

17. *"In the meantime, I have also received a letter from a Spanish Carmel urging me to come there, but that would be impossible now."* See Letter

337 to Hilde Borsinger, 9 April 1942, *Letters*, 348. In the same letter she writes that *". . .entering Switzerland is impossible. . .So we. . .leave the future to Him who alone knows anything about it."*

18. Mt 10:23 is as follows: "When they persecute you in one town, flee to the next; for truly I say to you, you will not have gone through all the towns of Israel before the Son of Man comes." No trace of this letter, nor of the slip of paper, has ever been found.

19. See, however, n. 6 above and Brief 761, ESGA 3, 578 for the "declaration" sent to Edith Stein by the bishop finally allowing her and her sister to find sanctuary in his diocese issued on 30 July 1942.

20. The vote was taken the day after the matter was submitted to the nuns in their Chapter meeting, according to usual canonical and monastic usage of observing a "twenty-four hour" rule. Our text corrects the mistaken translation of H/N that said the votation took place on the "fifth Sunday of the same month" – July that year had only four Sundays.

21. Confirmation to Edith Stein of the community's decision, sent in French to her, is found in ESGA 3, 574 as Brief 758 dated 25 July 1942.

22. There is no trace left of the letter P says Dr. Borsinger sent to "Reverend Mother." On 3 August she wrote from Zermatt to Edith Stein Brief 764, ESGA 3, 580-81 and indicated she would be staying in Aargau (not Bern, the capital) until 1 October. The purpose of the letter was to inform Sr. Benedicta, inter alia, that one week previous she had "phoned Bern. . .and taken further steps. . ." to assure that Sr. Benedicta would be able to leave the Netherlands with Rosa Stein.

23. Arthur Seyss-Inquart (1892-1946) was rewarded by Hitler for achieving the absorption of Austria into the Third Reich by being made the highest Nazi official in the Netherlands. Hitler hoped Seyss-Inquart could achieve there the same success he had had in Austria. Not wishing the SS to play the dominant role, Seyss-Inquart became more and more personally involved in the persecution of the Jews. He was sentenced to death in 1946.

24. Jan Cardinal de Jong, Archbishop of Utrecht, b. 10 September 1885, was made archbishop of Utrecht in 1935. His was a leading role in the protest of 26 July 1942, as a result of which Edith and her companions were arrested and killed. The Cardinal died in 1955.

25. Bishop J.H.G. Lemmens is described by Edith in a letter she sent to another Carmelite nun in Holland. See Letter 314, *Letters*, 324-25, esp.

n. 3. The Carmel of Echt was in his diocese, the diocese of Roermond. What he "wrote at once" has not been preserved.

26. "Ds." is the Dutch equivalent for Rev. and here the head of the Netherlands Reformed Church is named.

27. Posselt note: Taken from the book: *Het verzet van de Nederlandsche Bischoppen tegen National-Socialisme en Duitsche Tyrannie* by Dr. Stockman, O.F.M., Utrecht 1945.

28. No traces of immediate reaction by Sr. Teresa Benedicta have remained.

29. Letter 57 in *Letters*, 64, presumably from July 1930, was written to Sr. Adelgundis Jaegerschmid O.S.B. three years before Edith entered Carmel. It ended with the wry comment *"One must not meddle in the angels' business!"*

30. 700 Catholic Jews were registered in the Netherlands, of these 212 from the district of The Hague and 44 from Amsterdam were arrested on 2 August 1942.

31. The reader or a Sister appointed, in this instance it was Edith, reads a paragraph or two from a meditation manual for the Sisters to use, if they so wish, for their meditation at that time.

32. This was not actually the case, but the Rev. Mother could not have known the exact state of the appeal. In fact, according to Secretan, at first a denial of entry permits was issued by Swiss officials on 3 August (see ESGA 3, 579-80), then they reversed themselves and issued a concession of entry visas dated 9 September (see ESGA 3, 591-92) a full month after the deaths at Auschwitz-Birkenau of both sisters and their companions.

33. She actually wrote out the address of the Consul in Amsterdam. See [G5] [T4] in the next chapter. For a photographic reproduction of the original see *Life in Photos*, 77.

34. These were Annemarie Goldschmidt (20) and her sister Elfriede (19), who came from Munich. They were killed, like Edith, on 9 August 1942. See *Als een brandende toorts*, 30.

35. See "Secret Order of the Commandant of the Security Police of S.D. (Security Service) of 30 July 1942," in *Edith Stein, Documents Concerning Her Life and Death*, ed. Jakob Schlafke, trans. S. Batzdorff (New York: Edith Stein Guild, 1984), 24-26.

   Posselt note: *De Tijd*, 3 August 1942 (Holland's daily Catholic newspaper).

36. See "Secret Order of the Reich Kommissar for the Occupied Territories of the Netherlands, 31 July 1942," in Schlafke, *Documents Concerning Her Life and Death*, 29-30: "3. Furthermore the public is informed of the concession made by the Reich Kommissar in answer to the telegram, namely that all Jews converted prior to 1 January 1941 are to be exempt from this measure."
37. Pater Heinrich Horster, S.V.D., served the Ursuline nuns in Venlo as confessor. He came weekly from the S.V.D. Missionhouse in Steyl, Netherlands to the convent at Venlo where Ruth Kantorowicz lived. The spelling "Hopster" originated with P, then was simply copied by H/R.
38. Alternate Latin term for the one given here is "*in odium fidei*," or out of hate for the faith. How this later affected the memory of Edith Stein is indicated by Ambrosius Eszer, "Edith Stein, Jewish-Catholic Martyr," *Carmelite Studies* 4 (1987): 314-19.

CHAPTER 21

1. Westerbork Camp lay in the northeastern Dutch Province of Drente. Not far from the German border, i.e., only thirty miles from the town of Emerlichen to the east, it was eighty-six miles north-northeast from Amersfoort Camp, and a hundred seventy miles north northeast from Echt.
2. This is numbered Letter 296, directed to Mother Ottilia Thannisch, O.C.D., prioress of the Carmel in Echt and dated "Passion Sunday, 26 March 1939." It is found at *Letters*, 305. Unlike the supposed "small picture" that went lost once it was sent to her, a photostatic reproduction of Letter 296 is available in *Kölner Karmel kam*, 111.

    Also in the first half of 1939 (on 9 June, to be exact) Edith drafted a Last Will and Testament after she destroyed the one she made before her profession of vows as a safety measure when she left Germany for the Netherlands.
3. Translations of their accounts of that eventful meeting with Sr. Teresa Benedicta and Rosa Stein are found in *Never Forget* by Piet O. van Kempen at 272-76 and by Pierre Cuypers at 277-78 (with original texts found in *Als een brandende toorts*). The text by Pierre Cuypers is the one that P places in her book.

    An incomplete, and sometimes inaccurate (see n. 15 below) chronology at best is what one derives from P's interspersed time references to the captivity of Sr. Teresa Benedicta, Rosa Stein, and their companions. The following chart is an attempt to clarify what is known of their movements from place to place under arrest:

SUNDAY   2

   Arrest

     to Roermond;

     to Amersfoort

MONDAY   3

   3 a.m. arrival at Amersfoort transit camp

TUESDAY   4

   early morning arrival in Westerbork

WEDNESDAY   5

   Westerbork transit camp

THURSDAY   6

   Westerbork

FRIDAY   7

   3:30 a.m. *ca.* departure "to the East"

   noontime stop at Schifferstadt

SATURDAY   8

   by train

     to Auschwitz–Birkenau

SUNDAY   9

   arrival early in day;

   gassing in "White House" gas chamber;

   cremation in open field

4. A photo of Piet van Kempen on the site of Barrack 36 (number given by Edith herself) in Westerbork, taken in the Spring of 1987, is found in *Passion im August*, 96.

5. Available visual documentation of the Westerbork Camp shows fewer than one hundred buildings within the perimeter of the camp. Edith and Rosa's barrack had the relatively low number of 36. This leads to the need for [T 1].

6. This remark could have been about other prisoners who had arrived at the same time as the two from Echt. No record exists of relatives of the Steins at Amersfoort.

7. Posselt note: Usually this journey takes three to four hours. Apparently the driver took the good road through Nijmegen, Arnhem, and then followed the main road from Utrecht to The Hague. Between Arnhem and

Utrecht they left the main road and did not get back again, that is understandable enough in view of the blackout. The prisoners remained in the Amersfoort Camp from early on Monday until Tuesday evening. Then they set off for Westerbork, where they arrived in the night. The transport went through Apeldoorn, Zwolle, Meppel, Hogeveen, Hooghalen. Westerbork lies to the side of the Hooghalen station.

8. See Chap. 20, n. 13 above.

9. Compare her succinct claim written on 6 August, her last day in the transit camp *"so far I've been able to pray gloriously,"* in Letter 342, *Letters,* 353.

10. Postwar testimony from an Auschwitz survivor bears out this occurrence. See Josef van Rijk in Amsterdam, "Protokoll vom 29. Mai 1964 über die Ankunft in Auschwitz-Birkenau am 9. August 1942," *Passion im August,* 301. Through this sentence P appears to add to knowledge of events, though it is a statement additional to the narrative given by the narrator, Pierre Cuypens, in his remarks recorded in *Als een brandende toorts,* later translated in *Never Forget,* 278.

11. See [G 4] regarding the "short letter."

12. Posselt note: Mr. [Alois] Schlütter.

13. Sr. Hieronyma Weinforth traveled to see the prisoner Sr. Miriam Michaelis. See n. 3 to Brief 768 in ESGA 3, 585 where, in spite of the rich data she assembled, the devoted editor, Sr. Amata Neyer, apologizes over how "very difficult it is to reconstruct all details."[!]

14. We have supplied this paragraph from P's original German – the H/N translation did not include it.

15. P asserts the stay in Westerbork began "early on Wednesday 5 August" – it actually began early on Tuesday 4 August. She was, however, correct in stating it lasted "until the night of 6-7 August, the time the transport left for Auschwitz. See chart in n. 3 above.

16. Nothing remains of this correspondence. Two letters from Dr. Meirowsky to Edith Stein, written in the second half of that month of July 1942, have been found and are included as Brief 754 and Brief 759 in ESGA 3, 569-70 and 575-77.

17. Posselt note: These five brothers and sisters were children of Dr. Löb, a lecturer in mining at Bergen op Zoom.

18. P curiously uses the German word "Autos," but transport away from Westerbork was by train and overcrowded conditions in the freight cars did induce death by suffocation.

19. This assertion about prison garb is hardly upheld by the eyewitness account of Valentin Fouquet who saw Sr. Benedicta on the train as it stopped in Schifferstadt station. He testifies in *Never Forget*, 264 that "From this car [attached to the express train], a lady in dark clothes spoke to me. . . ." The dark clothes were in all likelihood her religious habit.

20. No further identification (sender? signature?) of this postcard has been reported. It would have arrived some time before the letter from the Swiss Carmel. See next note.

21. Brief 758 is an attestation by the prioress of Le Pâquier sent on 25 July 1942 that her Carmel's Chapter voted on 5 July to admit Sr. Teresa Benedicta for "an unlimited period of time." See ESGA 3, 574-75. No indication is given as to when this communication reached Echt, nor does the editor of the German correspondence surmise about the twenty-day lapse of time between the favorable vote and the sending of the notification.

22. Order changed in text for clarity's sake: P ended this chapter with the French version of this notation in the Chapter book and H/N placed their translation in a footnote. This notation would have taken its place in the same book of acts following upon the chapter act alluded to in the 25 July letter mentioned in the previous note above.

CHAPTER 22

1. See table that reconstructs position of the people in the station on 7 August in *Edith Stein und Schifferstadt*, 75.

2. According to J. Feldes the young woman would have been Emma Jöckle. See ibid, 64-66.

3. In other sources the name appears as Fouquet.

4. Lodz, the second largest city in Poland, was occupied by the Germans on 8 September 1939 and was officially renamed Litzmannstadt.

5. See also Maria Amata Neyer, "Geschichte des Edith-Stein-Archivs," ("History of the Edith Stein Archive"), *ESJ* 4 (1998): 549-575, also Michael Linssen, "Das Archivum Carmelitanum Edith Stein," *ESJ* 5 (1999): 405-422.

6. According to Michael Linssen, *Das Archivum Carmelitanum Edith Stein*, 408, the prior of the Carmelite monastery in Geleen was Fr. Bruno a Cruce (Joseph Heunen, 1908-1979). The Geleen friary (like the monastery of nuns in Beek) lay to the south and a little to the southeast of

Echt, and was only thirteen miles distant from Edith Stein's monastery there.

7. Three survivors (Josef van Rijk, Jesaya Veffer, and Maurice Schellekes) subsequently gave testimony in 1964 about some aspects of their travel in that transport to Auschwitz. See "Berichte von Überlebenden des Transportes vom 7. August 1942," *Passion im August*, 301-08.

8. Nothing remains of the monastery in Köln-Lindenthal. Only a memorial plaque marks the site among new buildings erected on the spot.

9. See ESW 6, 137-97 for the edited version of those five lectures.

10. In fact, in 1942 there was one (1) archbishop and four (4) bishops and one (1) co-adjutor bishop actively working in the Catholic dioceses of the Netherlands.

11. He must have seen her from Monday 3 August onward, since her group arrived at the early morning hour of 3 a.m. in Amersfoort.

12. This should read "five brothers and sisters." Of the Löb family, six members were deported at the same time, Hedwig, Ignatius, Linus, Veronica, Maria Theresia, and Nivardus.

13. Lenig's reference to Westerbork Camp ought to have qualified it as a "transit" not "death" camp.

14. Translation of this verse is taken from "Aphorisms in the Month of June 1940," *Selected Writings*, 75.

CHAPTER 23

1. See *Life in Photos*, 78-79 for a Dutch Red Cross attestation giving corrections to the earlier communication issued in 1950.

2. The opening sentence of this paragraph was omitted by H/N.

3. For a succinct listing of the efforts to have Sr. Benedicta beatified see John Sullivan, "The Path to Beatification," *Never Forget*, 7-14.

GLEANINGS

Part 1

CHAPTER 1

[G 1] Sr. Teresia Renata Posselt OCD, or P, wrote this first biographical account of Edith Stein based on her own recollection of their conversations as well as accounts by various people who had known her. Her book was first published at Christmas 1948, and a copy with a personal dedication by the author, dated 30 January 1949 was sent to my mother in New York. From a handwritten letter, dated 5 April 1949 by Sr. Teresia Renata, it is evident that Erna Biberstein, née Stein, thanked her; but she also listed some errors that she had found in the text, requesting the author to correct them in subsequent editions of the book. Paragraph one of the letter foresaw changes in the following terms: "I thank you very much for your kind reaction to the little book, but even more for pointing out the small errors that it contains and that I hope to correct in the third edition." The text of that significant letter is worth reporting in full:

> Junkersdorf, 5 April 1949
> My Dear Dr. Biberstein,
> I conclude from your cordial letter that the book about our Edith, beloved by both of us, has brought us closer to each other, even though it must have been painful for you. I thank you for your kind reaction to the little book, but even more for pointing out the small errors that it contains and that I hope to correct in the third edition.
>
> I am happy to have known Edith and to have been loved by her, and I believe the same about you, dear Frau Doctor. You should feel greater happiness at having had such a noble person in your family than you should mourn at having lost her. We ourselves have suffered so much that we always think of you all with

deepest sympathy. And how often do we speak of you, who are all so familiar to us from Edith's stories. Therefore, remember us fondly to all your loved ones, especially your husband and the dear children.

Your devoted Sr. Teresia Renata

My mother's chagrin at the failure of Sr. Teresia Renata to keep that promise is still fresh in my mind. Between 1948 and 1963, the book appeared in nine editions, but the errors that my mother had pointed out at the very beginning remained. It was painful for my mother to note how in subsequent years these errors were picked up and repeated as proven facts by numerous writers. For example, the statement that Edith Stein came from an Orthodox Jewish family even found its way into the respected *Encyclopedia Britannica*.

In 1987, prior to the beatification of Edith Stein, my brother, Dr. Ernst Ludwig Biberstein contributed the following comments to a radio broadcast of the *Deutsche Welle*: ". . .Corrections were never made, and in the end we could no longer get rid of the suspicion that such a 'retouching' of history, or at least its persistent maintenance despite being aware of the truth, could not be coincidence but. . .[evoked] once again. . .the tableau at the portal of the Notre Dame Cathedral: On one side the Church triumphant, on the other the defeated, broken Synagogue. Unfortunately the fact is that in Edith's array of sculptures, the niche of the synagogue always stood vacant and nothing existed to dispute either her adolescent atheism or thereafter the Catholic Church."

[G 2] We have no evidence to characterize the marriage as "very happy," though that may have been the case. Neither is there any evidence to say that it was particularly unhappy. Some sources, e.g., Edith Stein's own *Life in a Jewish Family,* 41 (Hereafter cited as *"Life"*), as well as a diary of Sigmund Courant, a brother of Auguste, raise the possibility that there may have been difficulties. We have therefore omitted these words. Since the marriage lasted from 1870 to Siegfried's sudden death in 1893, it cannot be called "of short duration."

[G 3] The status of a widow with a large brood of children was precarious at that time. Society offered limited opportunities for women to earn a living. It is characteristic of the thinking then prevalent that Auguste Stein's family advised her to "*sell the debt-ridden business, perhaps take a larger apartment and sublet furnished rooms. The brothers would contribute whatever was lacking.*" See Edith Stein, *Life,* 42. Typically the status of women at the time would have been first, as dependents of their fathers, then as wives of their husbands, and uncertain if they became widowed. All the more remarkable is the determination of Edith's mother to take over the management of a debt-ridden business and resolutely maintain her independence and that of her children. It is evident that she had the confidence in her own abilities to return the lumber business to profitability and keep her family intact.

[G 4] It is highly unlikely that Else ever got involved with the sales in the lumberyard. She was fully occupied with the care of her younger sisters and with her studies.

[G 5] Examples of Edith Stein's "deeds of lovingkindness" in Hebrew *g'milut hassadim*, to use a phrase common to Jewish teachings, can be found later in Chap. 8, "Fräulein Doktor" and in Chap. 12, "Lecturer in Münster." These habits of finding ways to help those in need, without even being asked, were surely inculcated at an early age by the example of her mother.

CHAPTER 2

[G 1] While the original German footnote correctly stated "fifteen siblings," the translators H/N give "twelve brothers and sisters" that is incorrect.

[G 2] The entire second paragraph on this page has been taken out because it is an inaccurate translation of the German text. A correct translation has been substituted.

[G 3] This passage is quoted as part of a statement by "a girl who was at school with her," but P does not give her name. Part of the sentence has been omitted, inasmuch as it would sound offensive to present-day readers. Still it has been retained verbatim in the "Take-Outs" in order to show how pervasive such bigoted views were at the time when P was gathering material for her biography. We may assume that P would have omitted this remark if she herself had found it problematic.

CHAPTER 3

[G 1] Most of the information about faculty and students in Göttingen is taken from the endnotes painstakingly assembled by Sr. Josephine Koeppel, O.C.D., that can be found in the Notes at the end of her translation of *Life*. For dates and brief annotations, see endnotes. For additional detail, see Gleanings.

Historical background on various sites in Göttingen and environs was furnished by Dr. Marianne Zingel, Göttingen, Germany.

[G 2] Richard Hönigswald (1875-1947) His writings on philosophy and philosophers, on the theory of knowledge, on Ernst Haeckel, on Kant, on psychology and languages, are listed in the National Union Catalog of pre-1956 imprints. His archive is located in the philosophy seminar of the University of Bonn, Germany.

[G 3] William Stern (1871-1938), a German philosopher, better known as pioneer in child and adolescent psychology. He developed testing by cloud pictures, and his formula for measuring the I. Q. is still used as he developed it in 1911. Edith visited him in Hamburg in 1919. Stern is one of the many brilliant Germans who found refuge abroad when the Hitler regime ended their careers in the universities of Germany, where they had made great contributions. Stern died in America in 1938.

[G4] This statement seems to be derived from Edith Stein's assertion in *Life*, 148, *"Deliberately and consciously, I gave up praying here* (in Hamburg)." This seems to this editor a rather weak basis on which to build a judgment of non-belief. The fact that she gave up praying in her teens does not necessarily imply that she had ceased believing in God. What's more, this statement by P, labeling Edith as an atheist from adolescence to age twenty-one has been quoted and used as evidence innumerable times. In addition, we learn from Edith's own statements that at the age of twenty-one she was a student in Göttingen and had not yet resolved her search for truth. Her conversion to Catholicism would not happen until 1922, at the age of thirty-one.

[G 5] What Frau Stein may have feared, can only be speculative, since she never spoke about it. Our only clue is that Edith mentions how much sadder her mother appeared than would seem warranted by a projected separation of one semester.

CHAPTER 4

[G 1] Almost the entire chapter consists of Edith Stein's chapter "Mein erstes Göttinger Semester" ("My First Semester in Göttingen") that later became part of her book "*Aus dem Leben einer jüdischen Familie*" ("*Life in a Jewish Family*"). We have attempted to ascertain how P came into possession of the then as yet unpublished manuscript of Edith Stein. We acknowledge the indispensable assistance of Sr. Maria Amata Neyer, Archivist of the Edith-Stein-Archiv in the Carmel Maria vom Frieden in Cologne, who writes, in a letter dated 5 June 2001:

> "*Ruth Kantorowicz [who had typed several manuscripts for Edith Stein] had already begun to type the manuscript of* Aus dem Leben einer jüdischen Familie (Life in a Jewish Family) *while she was still in Cologne. She always made several carbon copies... I seem to recall that Edith gave away several copies of this chapter to friends, I seem to remember Archabbot Walzer being one of them...*"

Thus it is likely that one of the copies of this chapter existed in the Cologne Carmel and served as a basis for this chapter in the fifth edition as well as all subsequent editions of P's book *Edith Stein*. We have shown her text in indented form and italicized type to distinguish it from the text original to P, as with other texts of Edith later on in this book.

[G 2] "Die Mütze," a house with the date 1547 is actually called *Junkernschänke* (Squires' Inn). In Edith Stein's days, its owner was Hermann Mütze. Dr. Marianne Zingel was researching the identity of this building when she came upon a book *Göttingen in alten Ansichtskarten (Göttingen in Old Picture Postcards)* that contained a picture of the *Junkernschänke* with a sign *Weinhandlung Herm. Mütze (Wineshop Herm. Mütze)* Thus the connection between the *Junkernschänke* and the nickname for the building "die Mütze."

[G 3] The Göttingen Seven. Among them were: Jacob Grimm (1785-1863) and his brother Wilhelm (1786-1859), who are better known for their compilation of fairy- and folktales; Wilhelm Eduard Weber (1804-1891), pioneer in telegraphy; Friedrich Christoph Dahlmann (1785-1866), a liberal historian and politician; and the historian Georg Gottfried Gervinus (1805-1871).

[G 4] The *Rohns* and the *Kehr*, the former was then visible on the slope of the Hainberg from the Husserl home in the valley. Only the main building remains today, but it is no longer a restaurant. Rohns is actually the name of the builder. The *Kehr* is on the mountain ridge and is still a restaurant. Its actual name is *Hainholzhof*. The nickname *Kehr* (not *Kehrs*, as Edith Stein refers to it) probably refers to it as a place where one enters (*einkehren*) and also where one turns around (*umkehren*). (I am indebted to Dr. Marianne Zingel of Göttingen for this explanation.)

[G 5] Adolf Reinach (1883-1917) has been called the phenomenologist *par excellence* and he was valued as teacher by the earliest students of Husserl. Reinach's version of early phenomenology was simpler and clearer in form and more concrete and suggestive in content than that of the "Master." Husserl himself saw in the clear-headed, warmhearted and widely read Reinach a philosopher who had thoroughly understood and assimilated the phenomenological method in the sense of the *Logische Untersuchungen*. He joined up in 1914 as a volunteer and died in battle in 1917. Reinach's death in action cut short not only his promise but that of the Göttingen Philosophical Society. His wife and sister later became Catholics.

[G 6] Hans Theodor Conrad (1881-1969) was one of the earliest Göttingen students of Husserl. He married Hedwig Martius (1881-1966), another of Husserl's students. Both taught philosophy in Munich and influenced the generation of phenomenologists who followed them, including Edith Stein. It was at their home in Bergzabern that Edith read the *Book of her Life*, by Teresa of Jesus and was led to become a Catholic.

[G 7] Moritz Geiger (1880-1937) was first of the early phenomenologists to come into direct contact with American philosophy. He met James and Royce in 1907, when he studied at Harvard for a year. He was a guest professor at Stanford University in 1926. As a Jew he lost his chair at the University of Göttingen in 1933. He subsequently became chairman of the Department of Philosophy at Vassar College.

[G 8] Dietrich von Hildebrand (1889-1977) studied in Göttingen, then taught philosophy at the University of Munich, until the advent of the Nazis forced him to leave Germany. He became a professor of philosophy at Fordham University and remained there for life. He had been born a Protestant and was one of the earliest of several phenomenologists whose study led them to become Catholics. He died in New Rochelle, NY in 1977.

[G 9] Hans Lipps (1889-1941) was born in Pirna, south of Dresden. As professor of philosophy in Frankfurt/Main, he published phenomenology of a highly personal type, as for instance two volumes on *Phenomenologie der Erkenntnis (Phenomenology of Knowledge)* 1927-28, leading in the direction of "Hermeneutic Anthropology." Lipps also occupied himself with the phenomenology of language. He died of a head wound while serving with the German army on the Russian front in World War II, in 1941.

[G 10] Fritz Kaufmann (1891-1958) was born in Leipzig. Fellow student and close friend of Edith Stein, he served in World War I, studied in Freiburg and began his teaching career there. From 1933 to 1936 he taught at the Academy for the Study of Judaism in Berlin; from 1936 to 1938 he had a research grant in London, England; between 1938 and 1956 at Northwestern University and the University of Buffalo. He taught History of Philosophy, Ethics, the Great Philosophical Poets, and Philosophy of Religion. His friendship with Edith Stein, begun during their student years in Göttingen, endured until her death. A large number of her letters to him were preserved by him and later donated to the Archivum Carmelitanum Edith Stein. Professor Kaufmann died in Zürich in 1958.

[G 11] Winthrop Pickard Bell (1884-1965) was born in Halifax, Canada and died in Chester, Nova Scotia. He studied at Harvard under Josiah Royce, then in Göttingen under Husserl between 1911 and 1914. Husserl had Bell write a highly critical thesis on Royce's theory of knowledge. This thesis was printed in Göttingen University Yearbook 1922. During World War I, Bell, as a Canadian national, was interned at Ruhleben, Döberitz until 1918. Bell died in Nova Scotia in 1965.

[G 12] Max Scheler (1874-1928), philosopher and sociologist, conceived phenomenology as the concerted effort to go from symbols back to the things themselves; he advocated giving attention to the "what" (the *essentia*) while suspending the question of the "that" (the *existentia*); he held that attention was to be given to the *a priori*, i.e., to the essential connections that exist between these "whats."

During World War I, Scheler served semi-officially on diplomatic missions for Germany to Switzerland and the Netherlands. After the war, Scheler returned to the academic life; he held a special chair for philosophy and sociology at the University of Cologne and taught there from 1919 until his death in 1928.

[G 13] Georg Elias Müller (1850-1934) made a traditional application of the psychology of associations; he produced a monumental work on the role of associations in the learning process; and he made a study regarding raising the sensitivity of parts of the brain to stimuli. Müller developed and taught theories regarding perception of color;

he formulated five well-known "psycho-physical axioms for empirical psychology."

[G 14] David Katz (1884-1953) was born in Kassel, Germany and died in Stockholm, Sweden. For a time he studied under Theodor Lipps, but Katz did not find Lipps's lectures to his taste. He spent several months at Külpe's Institute in Würzburg. After 1907 he became Georg Elias Müller's assistant in Göttingen. Katz wrote an account of his academic career for *A History of Psychology in Autobiography,* v. 4, Clark University Pr., Worcester, MA, 1952.

Katz married Rosa Heine in 1919. As a Jew in Nazi Germany, he lost his job after 1933 and emigrated to Scotland.

[G 15] Baron Heinrich Friedrich Karl vom und zum Stein (1757-1831), Prussian statesman dismissed and proscribed in 1808 by Napoleon, he organized the East Prussian rebellion in 1813. In 1819 he founded a society for the preservation of German historical material and the collection of artifacts relating to the years 500-1500 that is known as the *Monumenta Germaniae Historica.*

CHAPTER 5

[G 1] Edith's sister Erna Biberstein, confirms this in her reminiscences written in 1949:

> For me, my work as a doctor changed only in that I moved to a different hospital, while Edith felt obliged to interrupt her studies to go to a field hospital in Mährisch-Weisskirchen as a volunteer Red Cross aide." (*Life,* 16). Edith served as a Red Cross aide from April 1915 until 1 September of the same year.

[G 2] In the original text, there follows an account of a visit to Frau Reinach. This sequence has been relocated to its proper chronological place at the end of this chapter. Edith Stein became Husserl's assistant in 1916. Adolf Reinach was killed in action 16 November 1917. See ESW 8 (1998 ed.), 20, n. 2 by Sr. A. Neyer. The funeral did not take place until 31 December 1917. Edith was among those attending. In a letter of 20 May 1918, written from Freiburg, Edith writes:

> *I have only been back here for three weeks. Before that, I spent a full month in Göttingen and looked over the entire literary legacy with Frau Reinach.* (Letter 22, *Letters,* 24)

[G 3] The collaboration between Professor Husserl, the "Master," and his assistant Edith Stein did not prove to be mutually satisfactory, as evidenced by her letter to Roman Ingarden, dated 19 February 1918 in that she laments *"...to be at the service of a person, in short, to obey, is something I cannot do. And if Husserl will not accustom himself once more to treat me as a collaborator in the work – as I have always considered our situation to be and he, in theory, did likewise – then we shall have to part company. I would regret that, for I believe there would then be even less hope of a connection between himself and "youth."* (Letter 19, *Letters,* 22)

And later that month (in a letter dated 28 February) she reports *"...The Master has graciously accepted my resignation. His letter was most friendly – though not without a somewhat reproachful undertone. So now I am free, and I believe it is good that I am, even if, for the moment, I am not exactly happy."* (Letter 21, *Letters,* 23)

Her letter to Fritz Kaufmann (No. 21, p. 23) also reveals that she bristled under the type of work that Husserl assigned to and expected from her, namely *"putting manuscripts in order,"* without the opportunity to do some independent work also.

[G 4] The statement "Besides her strenuous work...for her own work" has been omitted, because Edith Stein's constant complaint, while in Prof. Husserl's employ, was that she had no time for her own work. We can infer from Letter 22, dated 20 May 1918, that Edith Stein was no longer working as Husserl's assistant when she prepared her contributions to a *Festschrift* for Husserl's sixtieth birthday, that would take place in April 1919. Husserl, in a letter of recommendation dated 6 February 1919, (No. 15) states that Edith Stein had obtained her doctor's degree in the summer semester of 1916 and "after that worked for more than one-and-a-half years as my assistant ..." Thus, her employment with Husserl would have terminated about the end of 1917 or early in 1918. Only after that would she have had time to devote to her own research and writing.

[G 5] A mistranslation of the German word "Heuen" as "woodcutting" has been corrected to "haying."

[G 6] "The Belchen"(1414m) and "the Blauen"(1165m) are two of the highest mountains in the Black Forest. Both are part of the Black Forest mountain range south of Freiburg and parallel to the Rhine valley in the direction toward Basel and are favorite destinations for hikers. Information about mountains in the Black Forest has been kindly furnished by Karl and Heidi Spenner of Freiburg, Germany.

[G 7] H/N combined Chaps. 5 and 6 in the German edition into a single Chap. 4, "Assistant to Husserl."

CHAPTER 6

[G 1] The phrase "When Erna got married in the summer of 1920," that appears in the original, has been corrected, because the wedding date was 5 December 1920.

CHAPTER 7

[G 1] P's allusion to an essay that was an "ascent, an acknowledgment of God" containing a section on "Plant soul – animal soul – human soul" is a reference to Chap. 6 of *Potenz und Akt*. Hedwig Conrad-Martius was herself a communicant of the Lutheran Church, as was her husband Hans Theodor Conrad. The precise time ("at this time") of her suggestion to Edith to develop this particular topic is hard to determine. Edith's reflections were a reply to what Dr. Hedwig

Conrad-Martius published in 1921 in her opus *Metaphysische Gespräche*.

[G 2] P's own remark joined to the frequently quoted one-liner "My longing for truth was a prayer in itself" deserves comment. Stirrings in Edith toward the acceptance of belief in Jesus Christ with entrance into a Christian church are traceable to several influences she noticed already years before the 1921 conversion high point in the home of her friends. ("*Gradually*" is the very word used by Edith to describe her discernment away from an atheistic outlook to a life of belief in *Life*, 261.) In the previous chapter P described the encounter with Anna, the widow of Adolf Reinach. In related fashion Edith herself expressed keen interest in the religious writings of A. Reinach (in Letter 21 written in the same timeframe of 1918). More direct evidence of the "longing for truth [as] a prayer in itself," that is, beyond what we here receive from P's pen, is not available, but the thought itself does not, for all that, seem foreign to Edith's attitudes nor her remarks on belief and unbelief in some of her writings from that period.(for instance, in her thesis *Problem of Empathy*, 50; 117-18).

[G 3] Edith gladly stayed at the Conrad-Martius' two-story house in Bad Bergzabern, a small town about 24 miles southwest of Speyer in the Pfalzer Wald region, not far from the French border. The house's address today is Neubergstrasse 16 (privately owned). The orchard's extent at that time is unknown, so it is difficult to tell whether fruit gathering was from a sizable fruit-farm.

[G 4] P's direct quotation of Edith's description of what occurred during one of the summer nights in 1921 that so radically changed her life cannot be traced to any written account. As elsewhere, P claims that "Edith tells us," and it seems she is quoting from memory by harking back to words uttered afterward by Sr. Teresa Benedicta in the Cologne Carmel. The sequence of events given indicates completion of Edith's reading of St. Teresa's *Life* at Bad Bergzabern. There is no reason not to accept as authentic the famous and oft-quoted accolade "That is the truth" applied by Edith to what she read in St. Teresa's account of "the mercies of God." Internal evidence in St. Teresa's book shows there is a "vision of the truth" in its final chapter (especially in paragraph 22). This would have left a poignant impression on Edith as she was bringing her reading to a close. St. Teresa's use of the four-waters metaphor to explain prayer elsewhere in her *Life* (well water, water wheel, stream, downpour of rain) could also have made a distinct appeal to Edith's phenomenological sensitivities, thus adding to her admiration for the first woman Doctor of the Church. After a peripatetic destiny once she finished reading it, the actual book read by Edith has come back to Bad Bergzabern and can be viewed there in the parish church.

[G 5] The purchase of both a "Catholic catechism and a missal" sounds characteristic of Edith: not just as a sequel to her reading a book that contained mystical teaching on prayer and the truth, but as vehicles of the official texts of the church she decided she would join in order to be a Catholic like St. Teresa. It is difficult to calculate how much time elapsed between her purchase of these sources of both information and devotion, and her attending mass in the church of Bad Bergzabern.

[G 6] The pastor of that church was Fr. Eugen Breitling, seventy years old at the time. He initiated her steps toward baptism. Most likely there would have been more than one session between the Fräulein Doktor and the pastor of Bad Bergzabern in their "discussion ranging over the entire doctrine of the Catholic Church." No less than a comprehensive examination of the tenets of that faith would have been expected of her, and her own thoroughgoing honesty would have spurred Edith on to a full perusal with Fr. Breitling of all she intended to embrace.

The direct quotation "Nothing was strange to me. . .my knowledge," is owed exclusively to P as one can surmise from the phrase "said Edith later." Nothing in the description sounds implausible: the eagerness Edith showed to receive the sacrament(s) of initiation is shared by other converts. Fr. Breitling's cautious reply that "one had to be prepared before being received into the church" reflects usual pastoral practices. It is interesting to note there is no mention of the Jewish origins of Edith in this respect, since the docudrama "Stations of an Exceptional Life" (U.S. video vers. 1996) puts words in the mouth of the priest to that effect.

[G 7] As P indicates, Edith received the sacrament of baptism on 1 January 1922 (a Sunday that year), and the next day she received there her first Holy Communion. Regarding the formalities of the baptism itself some details can be added to what P gives: a dispensation for a Protestant Christian godmother was foreseen by Canon Law, thus admitting Hedwig Conrad-Martius to the ceremony; Edith, in Letter 105 to Erna Hermann, says she wore Conrad-Martius' white (wedding) cloak to imitate the white garments worn by ancient catechumens on the day of their baptism. Finally, the parish records show she took the Christian names of Teresa Hedwig, in acknowledgment of the special soul-bonding she had with St. Teresa of Avila, whose autobiography led the way to the ritual of entrance into the Catholic church, as well as with her philosopher friend. The baptismal font can still be seen in the main aisle of the recently renovated church interior.

[G 8] P's dramatic and somewhat overwrought account of how Edith informed her mother of her baptism has recently received an alternate version. At *Aunt Edith*, 83-84 S. Batzdorff draws on her mother Erna Stein Biberstein's firsthand experience of the tense days that descended upon the Breslau household in the summer of 1921. In place of the direct dialogue between Frau Stein and Edith, relying on her own mother's advisement, Susanne has her aunt Edith asking Erna to play the role of intermediary in breaking the news. She chose to entrust to her favorite sister Erna the tension-laden task of telling their mother she had moved away from her atheistic attitude and from Judaism to Catholicism. Aside from P's five succinct (and according to S. Batzdorff "surely apocryphal") words "Mother, I am a Catholic," we do not have other witnesses close to Edith revealing what she might have said to inform Auguste Stein of her conversion.

[G 9] Since the statements of two persons used by P are not identified and cannot be substantiated, we place them among the Take-Outs.

In the first of them, the term "East-Schleswig" is a mistaken rendering of the original German's text's "East-Silesian" where Breslau was located. The claim supposedly made by the second of the paragraphs that Edith's fidelity to her family remained unflagging (". . .she clung to her people with as much love as before. . .") is undeniable, and it is affirmed by family members like Susanne Batzdorff.

[G 10] That Frau Stein would have noticed intensity of prayer in Edith, and at synagogue services too, is not implausible; that she would actually have stated "I never have seen such prayer as Edith's. . ." to "an intimate friend" is not so easy to confirm. Nor can one lightly agree with P's assertion that Edith brought "her breviary" to pray the psalms at the same time as her mother at services. (The "breviary" is the daily prayer book of the Church that, according to liturgical practice of Edith's times, contained psalms, prayers, hymns and readings both scriptural and patristic. P indicated it was a "catechism and a missal" that she purchased in Bad Bergzabern, not a breviary, although in the chapter about Beuron Abbey she does note that Edith "recited the Office daily from the time of her conversion" and for this she would have needed a breviary.) Even with Edith's re-found religious devotion for prayer to God, it is more likely she would have avoided overzealous eagerness to pray à la Catholique when she attended synagogue with her mother, especially on the Day of Atonement (Yom Kippur). "She was far too decent and respectful to do such a thing," tells us Erna, her sister, in words relayed by S. Batzdorff, *Aunt Edith,* 199.

Equally unlikely is P's claim that Frau Stein "clasped" her thirty-one year old "child" to whisper in "distressed tones" the words of the beloved *Sh'ma Israel* prayer: "Do you hear: Thy God is but one!"

The subsequent report of Frau Stein about acquisition of a grave must be equally considered a possible confidence shared in Cologne Carmel, between Sr. Teresa Benedicta and P. Frau Stein's grave, not far from her husband's, may be visited today in the Jewish cemetery of Wroclaw on the southern side of the capital city of Silesia.

[G 11] Canon Joseph Schwind (b. 28 Nov. 1851 - d. 17 Sep. 1927) had a distinctly formative influence on her from the time he made her acquaintance. As indicated by a recent monograph on Edith's relationship to his birthplace Schifferstadt, not far from Speyer, he also introduced her to his family who lived in that nearby village (see Chap. 8 below). Schwind, though "learned" and holding the position of Curator of the Speyer Cathedral, said he needed to consult other priests about many of the deep theological questions raised by Edith. His bishop called Canon Schwind "a God-gifted director [of souls]" in his obituary (see pp. 74-77 below).

[G 12] Vocational discernment became a major concern for the duo, viz., Edith and Canon Schwind: Moved by the zeal that so often marks a convert, Edith wanted to contribute to the Church's life so she looked to him for advice about the future. She did contemplate strict separation from secular pursuits. Schwind recommended a *via media*, as it were, by preparing for her a teaching position in a local Catholic normal school. The convent school was St. Magdalena's, it was run by Dominican sisters, and it would become her home for the ensuing decade.

CHAPTER 8

[G 1] To link this chapter to the previous one's praise of truth found and embraced (through reading St. Teresa's autobiography) P begins with the Latin word for "truth" emblazoned over the gate to St. Magdalena's convent at Hasenpfuhlstrasse, Speyer, where it still stands today. A book-length study of Edith's years there was published in 1990 by a contemporary elder Dominican sister, Sr. Adele Herrmann, someone who knew persons in contact with Edith while she lived there. P's claim that Edith wanted to strike a balance between devotion and scholarship is borne out by the many eyewitness accounts of her flourishing prayer life, especially at her kneeling bench near the main altar of the chapel. The approximate day of arrival at St. Magdalena's was around Easter 1923 in time for the spring semester (and the day of her departure came on 26 March 1931 as indicated in her Letter 87).

[G 2] Her studies on Thomas Aquinas produced a major translation of Aquinas' Latin text, the *Quaestiones Disputatae de Veritate* [i.e., "Disputed Questions on the Truth"]. Strong point of the translation was the way it gave a modern phraseology to the thoughts of the leading light of Catholic theology in the thirteenth century. The Dominican Sisters today place the manuscript of this extensive opus on display in an interesting exhibit of many Steiniana objects (making this manuscript the only major one of Edith not found in the Cologne monastery's specialized archive.)

[G 3] The private room obtained from the superior is modest in size, with a view on the inner cloister garden, and facing other wings of the convent where her students had their rooms at the time. Since the beatification in 1987 this room serves as a meditation chapel, displaying mementos of Edith, including an urn that contains soil from Auschwitz.

The fact she ate "convent food" fits the other circumstances of her life that she led in close imitation of the Sisters.

[G 4] Assuming the duty of giving classes in German could not have been difficult for Edith, since her state board exams for a teaching license tested her on German as her main subject along with History and Philosophical Propaedeutics (Introduction to Philosophy) at Göttingen in 1915 (earning her the distinction "Passed with Highest Honors").

Later on in the Echt Carmelite monastery she gave classes in Latin to the younger Sisters in formation, too.

[G 5] The "scholarly work" she kept "always busy" at included readings of leading Catholic authors, essays written for publication and some translations, especially those of Cardinal Newman and St. Thomas Aquinas that P specifically mentions later on in this chapter.

[G 6] The first eyewitness account shows perspicacity in the remark that Dr. Stein's correspondence "was very extensive." In spite of the loss of many copies of letters from her because of World War II we now count over 600 letters published in different volumes of her works.

[G 7] Kindliness surely impelled her to assist the "maids" in their menial kitchen tasks on holidays but, here, too, one notices she did not shy away from, or demonstrate inability for, housework.

[G 8] When P enthusiastically writes that Edith "then, had become a teacher" she might have underestimated other allied accomplishments already logged earlier on, as a replacement instructor in Breslau in 1912; then again in 1915; or in Freiburg where she conducted a "philosophical kindergarten" (the term is her own) as Husserl's assistant in order to introduce his students to the rudiments of his new, intricate philosophical system and method.

[G 9] The essay subjects listed are themes derived from a variety of sources: 1) "First weigh, then dare," a popular folk proverb; 2) "Character is Destiny" from Heraclitus; and 3) "I am not a book to be read and understood, I am a human being with all his contradictions" from the nineteenth century Swiss author Konrad Ferdinand Meyer's poem "*Homo Sum*." The use of Shakespeare as an introduction of her students to theater fits her own high regard for the "Bard of Avon."

[G 10] The *Eck Bible* was a "German-dialect version of the Bible for Catholic use" produced in 1537 to counter the popularity of the vernacular translations of the Protestants. It derives its name from Johann Eck, Roman Catholic theologian and principal polemicist in the public debates with the chief German and Swiss Reformers.

[G 11] She gave a life of a saint, St. Aloysius Gonzaga reputed to be a fine exemplar for youth since he died very young of the plague, and the *Taugenichts* novella (Engl. trans. *Memoirs of a Good-for-Nothing* and considered "a high point of Romantic fiction" published originally in 1826).

[G 12] The concluding remark of the fourth student expressing the wish that Edith, now gone, "pray for. . .our unhappy Fatherland, that she loved truly with all her heart" is not an opportunistic absolution of Germany from the tragedy its leaders imposed on her, rather, a tribute to her undying sense of patriotism. From the short "bio" she drafted for her doctoral thesis (it asserts she is a Prussian citizen); to her [Last Will and] Testament in which she offers herself for, inter alia, the "safety of Germany"; through her generous Red Cross volunteer service in World War I, she gave ample evidence of being a true German patriot. In return for her generous devotion to her country she was cruelly eliminated by the Nazi government, like so many others who had contributed significantly to their homeland.

[G 13] For Edith, assuming the stance of a student, through planned readings of Catholic thinkers like St. Thomas Aquinas and John H. Newman whetted her appetite for serious investigation of new sources of learning. Even if she did not pursue the production of entirely technical phenomenological disquisitions, she still managed to contribute to the *Husserl Jahrbuch* and was pleased with a personal visit to her "Master" that seemed to have a confirmatory effect on her, both as Christian convert and as an intellectual – "*he responded with such depth and beauty.*" (Letter 52, *Letters*, 60)

Then came the shift, through the lectures she gave in several countries of the German-speaking world, to assuming the function of an admired expert consultant for Catholic women's organizations. Her audiences could see, not just imagine, someone who held out to them proof positive of a rich, productive life of the mind and spirit. She spoke about professionalism and an adequate formation necessary to exercise it; but she also demonstrated by her bearing and the clarity of her delivery that women were quite capable of holding their own in promoting their due role in society.

[G 14] From P's account of Edith's acceptance of Canon Schwind's lead one realizes how relationships between a spiritual director and the person he was assisting in that period were based on implicit respect for the former's judgment. It always carried the day and, to a great extent, it prevailed precisely because the director was an ordained cleric. Catholic laypersons would readily go along with the advice they received. So, Edith should not be scored on excessive passivity by leaving "her direction in his hands." She was simply following the *règle du jeu* current then and lent herself to assimilating practical methods of Catholic spirituality. (Today, like some other devout Catholic laywomen, she very well could be giving formal spiritual direction to priests.)

[G 15] Noteworthy elements in the text of the obituary tribute for Canon Schwind may be further explored by consulting the following literature: Biographical details of Canon Schwind's life are in the monograph by J. Feldes, "Edith Stein und ihr Seelenführer Joseph Schwind," *Edith Stein und Schifferstadt,* 9-27; the main fruits of Edith's translation work, especially of Cardinal Newman whom she alludes to in the obituary, are listed in the eighth note of this chapter and H. Grisar, *Martin Luther: His Life and Work,* ed. F. J. Eble and A. Preuss (2nd ed. St. Louis; reprint Westminster MD: Newman Press, 1950).

CHAPTER 9

[G 1] Although Edith's relationship with Canon Schwind had been quite intense, it is probable that P wishes to indicate by her remarks "childlike openness" that a shift had occurred with her acceptance of Dom Raphael's direction. She was perhaps moving away from a phase of demanding intellectual inquiry to intense spiritual questing.

[G 2] Dom Walzer's desire to see Edith at work devoting the "rich talents" God had given her for the benefit of others through direct contact with them in intellectual exchange is a sign of his own erudite view about Church outreach. Like the title of a book written several decades later by the late great Benedictine scholar, Dom Jean Leclerq, he conceived of the monastic vocation as a "Love of Learning and Desire for God," or a melding of scholarly investigation and the cultivation of spirituality. But he could also see that both the acute, empathic mind of someone like Edith Stein's, joined to her ability to intervene in current events, would help offer antidotes to the crisis-laden society Germany had become in the post-World War I years.

Not unlike the parallel relationship of St. Teresa and St. John of the Cross, the Archabbot and "Fräulein Doktor" outdid each other in mutual respect and esteem. St. Teresa called the younger friar "father of my soul," so one sees Edith adopt the stance of daughter to Dom Raphael in a natural way, and as an extension of her previous relationship with Canon Schwind. More remarks by Dom Raphael are found in the second chapter of pt. 2 of P's text, "The Novitiate."

[G 3] The idea that we are "instruments" for God is frequently propounded by Edith, as in her 12 February 1928 letter to Sr. Callista Kopf. She seemed to enjoy alluding to it to stress a collaborative role for us all in God's gracious plan for humankind. Another way of expressing this occurs later in this chapter in the term *"causa secunda"* or secondary cause, i.e., an intermediary cause in the chain of causality that links us to God, the ultimate and first cause.

[G 4] P offers some helpful words of contextualization about the "Prayer of the Church" essay. For Catholics today a dichotomy between individual and communal prayer seems strange, given the benefits reaped from Vatican II's teaching on the liturgy. At the time Edith wrote, however, tensions were running high and she was courageous in her own way to offer a position that presented a conciliatory solution for opposed views. One recent commentator notes the obvious pride Edith took in displaying the spiritual beauty and richness of Jewish worship in her little treatise: "Stein's reaffirmation of her own Jewish tradition is particularly conspicuous in *The Prayer of the Church*. . .This liturgy, Stein notes, served as a prototype for that of the Catholic church."

[G 5] The Swiss lady's puzzled remark regarding the evident devotion of Fräulein Doktor for the suffering mother of God at Beuron can be answered plausibly from a knowledge of the church there. The Pietà statue in the abbey church stands in a side chapel above the tabernacle of reposition for the Blessed Sacrament. Edith would then have two potent points of attraction to keep her focused in prayer. One would be free to believe, as a result, that she was not drawn to pray before the statue of Mary only but also before what was to her the "living bread" and, in the words of her dear master St. Thomas Aquinas, a "gage of future glory."

[G 6] The querulous words in Maria Schäfer's quote deserve a reply, too. Those persons who thought Dr. Stein maintained strict silence "out of pride" certainly did not appreciate how appealing a strict observance of Holy Week must have been for someone like her whose life could be overloaded with interviews, dialogues, and meetings of all kinds back at St. Magdalena's school. For her the abbey was an oasis of silence, not a stage for extending social or professional contacts. To be a "happy monk" was to know when to draw aside, like both Moses and Elijah on Mount Horeb, and listen to the voice of God in the "little whisper" surrounded by silence.

[G 7] Edith was baptismal sponsor, or "godmother" for several Jewish converts. Among them were Alice Reis (baptized in Beuron), Hedwig (Hede) Spiegel, and others mentioned by P in Chap. 11 of the first part of this biography. She advised others in their steps toward entering the Catholic Church without adopting the liturgical role of sponsor. A memorable in-between presence she enjoyed was attendance, even though a cloistered nun, at her sister Rosa's baptism in Cologne on Christmas Eve 1936. A hospital stay made it possible for her to be on hand (due to some fractured bones from a fall on 14 December) as Rosa was baptized. Edith even wrote a poem, "For Rosa's Baptism, Holy Night," to mark the event. See pt. 2, Chap. 16 below for text of the poem.

[G 8] In the face of the apparent heedlessness involved in not announcing her departure from St. Magdalena's to some persons "until the last day," it seems safe to assume Edith felt herself on solid ground with her employers, the Dominican nuns there. She felt encumbered by the hard job of translating St. Thomas Aquinas' great work on truth, but she could at the same time remind the Sisters she wanted to make their Dominican Brother's thought better known to the German public and receive appreciative assent.

[G 9] The final sentence of this chapter is an indicator that probably in 1931 Rosa was continuing to consider a change in religious allegiance; though, as already noticed, she did not act on this until a few months after their mother's death in Breslau on 14 September 1936.

CHAPTER 10

[G 1] As premise to this entire chapter it must be pointed out that P mistakes one major published work of Edith for another. That is, at the beginning P considers the two-volume translation of St. Thomas Aquinas' *Quaestiones Disputatae de Veritate* [Disputed Questions on Truth] as being the "major work" Edith was drafting in the summer months of 1931, when actually she was writing *Potency and Act* as her second attempt to secure a university teaching position. However, P devotes this chapter to describing both books, so a reworking of her text would be both superfluous and disruptive. We thus think it preferable in this case to maintain the order P chose to develop her explanation. Through our notes the reader will be able to recognize the flow of events as they actually happened. One reason for such a mix-up derives from the fact that Edith could not publish *Potency and Act* at all during her lifetime.

[G 2] She produced a translation in two volumes of *The Disputed Questions on Truth* of St. Thomas Aquinas, but in a novel way. She set out in her two volumes both a modern German rendition of the work of the medieval giant in philosophy, inserted many of her own interlinear notes, and added a list (fifty pages long in the 1950s ESW edition) of useful terms she translated to assist modern readers in understanding and rendering better the thought of St. Thomas. By creating it, she built a bridge to more modern philosophical terminology. Not all Thomists were pleased with her rendition, and the Dominican Order organized another translation by some of its scholars (even with Edith teaching in a Dominican Sisters' school).

[G 3] The table of contents of St. Thomas Aquinas' work serves as an indicator of how much Edith would have fairly enjoyed, or at least benefited personally from, her translation work. Many of Aquinas' themes would have appealed to her, as a new Christian who had abandoned an atheistic world-view only about a decade before starting her work: They would have offered deeper knowledge of her recently new-found Christian faith-life. To choose just some such themes out of the twenty-nine chapters, one imagines the significance of chapters like "Truth"(1), "Providence"(5), "The Book of Life"(7), "The Teacher"(11), "Ecstasy"(13), "Faith"(14), "Knowledge of Christ's Soul"(20), "God's Will"(23), and "The Grace of Christ"(29). She found in those and the other reflections of the "Angelic Doctor" a veritable manual of Christian theology, one well-suited to extend her grasp of theology through the arguments of the acknowledged authoritative master of Catholic doctrine. As was the case with her association with Husserl, the best proponent in Germany of her profession of philosophy, she delved into Thomas Aquinas because she always worked to assimilate the "top" proponents of intellectual systems in her quest for excellence.

[G 4] The two assessments of Edith's first project incorporated by P in this chapter come from individuals personally acquainted with Edith and thus more sympathetic to her overall effort, although they were respected scholars in their own right with reputations to uphold. Martin Grabmann (b. 1 May 1875, d. 1 Sept. 1949) was a leading "theologian and historian of Scholasticism" whose endorsement would have contributed much to sales of Edith's translation. Professor of dogma at Munich when Edith published her translation, he would have had ample opportunity to meet Erich Przywara who also lived in the Bavarian capital at that time. Fr. Przywara was a Jesuit (b. 12 Oct. 1889 – he had the same birth date as Edith – d. 28 Sept. 1972) who guided Fräulein Doktor Stein through an intellectual apprenticeship in Catholic thought a few years after her conversion. As a collaborator of Dietrich von Hildebrand and Daniel Feuling he "commissioned" her to translate the *Letters and Journals before His Entry into the Catholic Church* of

Cardinal Newman for inclusion in a critical German edition of Newman's Collected Works. It was published by Theatiner Verlag, Munich in 1928. Also at Przywara's invitation, she completed, but never published, Newman's *Idea of a University*.

[G 5] The second text she wrote was *Potenz und Akt*. It was a by-product of an attempt to obtain *Habilitation*, or a teaching position as a philosopher in a university. P gives, in outline format, the back and forth of Edith's efforts. From indications she herself has left behind in her correspondence, the intensity and demands of a university position might have had only a weak appeal for her (in fact, she admits humbly in Letter 116: *"I have put up quite a struggle to justify my scholarly existence - not with any of the people, since they do all they possibly can to help me - but with the situation created by my ten-year exclusion from the continuity of [academic] work and the lack, rooted so deeply within me, of contact with the contemporary scene."*)

[G 6] Eventually she would accept an offer to serve as an instructor at the Catholic Pedagogical Institute in Münster. She felt the surroundings would seem closer in spirit and religious atmosphere to what she had at Sankt Magdalena's in Speyer; and she was scheduled to teach precisely a subject that flowed logically out of all the lectures she had been giving toward the end of the 1920s and beginning of the 1930s, i.e., 'problems of modern education of girls" and related questions concerning women (Brief 153 to Ingarden, ESGA 4, 227). In all (see next chapter), she would spend merely sixteen months here from "the Spring [semester] of 1932," having arrived in Münster in the leap year of 1932 on 29 February, to June 1933 (the last class she gave was on 2 February), but the duties involved in teaching would exercise a favorable influence on her to the extent they started calling her back to a higher level of academic output than what she had grown accustomed to at Sankt Magdalena's.

[G 7] The passing chance of her obtaining a teaching position at the Breslau university, with the help of Professor Koch, who knew her brother-in-law Hans Biberstein, never materialized. What seems significant in the motivation attracting her toward her first alma mater was her mother's green light in spite of the fact she would be teaching there as a Catholic faculty member. Mother Stein showed a distinct preference for any activities that would bring her youngest daughter, her Benjamin, closer to her, as a later occurrence showed. In fact Edith writes (in her brief account "The Road to Carmel" – see pp. 100-115 below.) about choices to be made after leaving Münster in 1933 that "*surely my mother would prefer me to be in a convent in Germany rather than a school in South America.*"

[G 8] Professor Koch's lapidary summation of Edith's judgment of Martin Heidegger's philosophy as "the philosophy of a bad conscience" was borne out by a text of Edith's drafted as part of her manuscript of *Finite and Eternal Being*: She included a 66-page appendix that expressed her misgivings about several of Heidegger's insights.

CHAPTER 11

[G 1] This chapter shows P stressing how keenly Edith affirmed the faith she was growing in by passing on its benefits to other individuals. Whether by identifying a group of several women of her acquaintance who became Catholics, or by re-introducing her elder sister Rosa (the only member of her immediate family to follow in her footsteps), P devotes almost half of the chapter to a description of religious "generativity" on Edith's part, as she shares her religious experience with others.

[G 2] Phraseology used here sounds somewhat exaggerated if one were to take the term "abundant" literally, and further listing of persons who were actual godchildren shows there was only a modest quartet. In private correspondence Sr. Maria Amata Neyer confirmed this on 6 June 2001.

In the case of her own sister Rosa, Edith did not serve as preparatory sponsor for baptism due to her monastic enclosure during the years of immediate preparation. However, she indicates in Letter 231, *Letters*, 243 that, thanks to an accident in the cloister she was admitted to a hospital at the very time Rosa came to Cologne to be baptized and, so, was able to be physically present at the ceremony, without serving as godmother.

[G 3] We learn about the adolescent Edith through the eyes of Käthe Kleemann Rubens. P uses the latter's remark about the "exceedingly bad quality" of the "religion classes" provided in public school and attended by her and Edith as a counterpoint to the transformed state of the matured convert whom she met as an adult years later. But the comparison also evokes sympathy for any and all teachers of religion who shoulder the task of re-enforcing the faith of their young pupils.

[G 4] It is worth noting efforts by Edith to weigh the effects of her Christian faith on her family. P shows how Rosa benefited from this sensitivity and the author makes another reference to family tensions for Rosa in the next chapter, through a quote from Letter 116, *Letters*, 113, sent by Edith on 9 June 1932. In yet another missive, Letter 231, *Letters*, 243, sent on 13 January 1937, Edith explains that her niece Erika acted positively, along with her aunt Erna, as "intermediary" between her family and Rosa, to accommodate Rosa's new behavior patterns as a Catholic living within the family circle.

[G 5] Through all the events described in this first part of the chapter Edith appears to encourage others, though oftentimes from the distance her professional teaching duties required of her, to continue their travel along a path of conversion similar to her own. As [T 2] shows, she did not exercise the technical role of catechist of the Christian faith in an organized and surely not in an overbearing fashion. Her prudent tolerance of religious practice flourishing under the influence of God's grace kept her from exerting pressure or voicing strong expectations. Again, later on in that decade (23 March 1938), from her monastery in Cologne, she expressed the healthy cautionary conviction in a letter that *"It has always been far from me to think that God's mercy allows itself to be circumscribed by the visible church's boundaries. God is truth. All who seek truth seek God, whether this is clear to them or not."* (Letter 259, *Letters* 272)

[G 6] The second part of the chapter makes a bow to the activities forming part of Edith's contribution as a professional woman, viz., lectures given outside Germany, counseling others, conferring with colleagues, shared readings, interest in literature; and it also betrays her personal investment in the deeper dimension that today would go by the name "spiritual development."

[G 7] The influence of the Benedictine lifestyle is highlighted by P as she describes Edith's stay at St. Lioba monastery in Günterstal, Freiburg. The personality details given by two eyewitnesses to Edith's 1932 visit there – openness to others, balance between intense devotion for God and the "greatest gentleness" toward others, quietude, ascetical simplicity – confirm other previous descriptions and set the stage for the text of *Ways to Interior Silence*.

[G 8] The "Marie de la Trinité," whose name gave the title to the book Edith and Maria Schäfer read together, was a seventeenth-century Discalced Carmelite nun from France.

[G 9] *Ways to Interior Silence* was a written reflection, not previously given as a lecture although evocative of the speech delivered several years previously in November 1930 at Bendorf ("Fundamental Principles of Women's Education"). In it Edith gives advice to cope with the "duties and cares of the day" in the framework of a dedicated life in many settings, such as the "teaching profession" and at "office work," and not just in monastic solitude and silence.

[G 10] As final quote in the chapter, the letter fragment introduces a note of contrast that doubles as a transition to P's next chapter. Here Edith points to the overarching keynote of her lecturing; there, for however short a period of time it was, Edith was a "Lecturer" in Münster's pedagogical institute.

CHAPTER 12

[G 1] The limited stay at Münster (in all, only ten months teaching, and *ca.* sixteen months' residence) provided Edith with her final professional placement as a layperson. Her own words, confiding to friends in her letters (besides the one used in this chapter by P, one could quote Letters 126, 128, 133, 135, 139), occasionally attest to the effort she was expending to "get up to speed" as a lecturer in the university-level world of the German Pedagogical Institute there. P's numerous eyewitness testimonies show Edith's ever-diligent strivings to fulfill satisfactorily her teaching duties. The key position of librarian allowed frequent contacts with Edith to one of the onlookers: Edith "stood head and shoulders above the other tutors on account of her incisive thought, her broad culture, her masterly exposition and her self-assurance. . ." P gives other positive indicators that tend to demonstrate a creative tension was at work between Edith's felt need to overcome rustiness in the intellectual realm (due to the interval away from teaching philosophical topics) and her newly assumed duties. The years in Speyer devoted to teaching fundamentals of linguistics and history to younger women intervened between her "philosophical kindergarten" exercises as Husserl's assistant in Freiburg on the one hand and the Münster stint on the other.

[G 2] In spite of the work entailed in bridging the gap, she resolutely kept up a regimen of accepting invitations to speak in public (at Augsburg and Berlin); once, even, to deliver a talk on the radio (Munich). Attendance at a dialogue among leading philosophers near Paris was nigh unto a triumph for her, as the published records of the meeting shows (pagination in n. 18 of Chap. 12). She not only gave succinct summaries, she offered accurate translations in both French and German of oftentimes intricate philosophical terminology. She attended conferences on professional topics (Aachen), and kept up contacts with other philosophers, as when she went to visit the ailing Hedwig Conrad-Martius in Heidelberg. If there seemed to be a gap between her readiness to contribute to the programs of the Pedagogical Institute and her actual output, one thinks this could have been a projection of her own never-failing desire to excel in positions of trust. This did not force her to lead the life of a hermit while in Münster:

She planned and carried out travels back to Breslau for vacation both in summer and at New Year's 1933, went for Christmas to Dorsten; mentioned visits to the Benedictine abbey at Gerleve "*three times*"; and did what she could to assist with kindness the people with whom she lived in the Marianum residence (the strawberries to the students, and warm clothing through them to a struggling village being two prominent cases of her charitable gestures).

[G 3] For a detailed account of this incident, see Edith Milz, "My Encounter with Edith Stein," *Never Forget*, 228-30.

P uses this chapter to begin describing some instances of Edith's reactions to Nazism and Nazi sympathizers. (Every chapter from here on out refers in some way or other to the "storm raging" in Germany, and later in the countries its "masters," the Nazis, occupied.) During her Münster stay Hitler's party seized power in Germany officially, climaxing years of agitation, as it took over the levers of political decision-making. While P's intention was primarily a biographical sketch of Edith herself, she included several references to the turmoil that affected her destiny. The terminology we have grown accustomed to nowadays, such as "genocide," "Holocaust" or "Shoah," and "Final Solution" are missing, but signs of their reality show through the author's narrative. Like other eyewitness accounts (and P's first edition came out three years after the cessation of hostilities), she expresses observations from her own viewpoint, and a limited one at that, since she lived a secluded life in a cloister. One can derive some real information from her reminiscences, but for confirmation of that viewpoint, cross-referencing to other sources is oftentimes necessary.

[G 4] However droll and ad hominem the description of the student zealot who "smoked like a chimney," the testimony of one of her co-students presents a useful insight into Edith's desire to send a signal to a dupe of Nazi propaganda. On the other hand, her less-than-stirring intervention in a debate betrays not so much a lack of zeal in rebutting the tenets of that same propaganda, as an instance of her relying on calm exposition of the truth as the best way to state her mind. As P indicates, one important reason Edith was attending in the first place was the scope of the assembly itself: It was a student meeting organized "*against* the 'A.N.S.T.' or 'Study Group of National Social-ist Women Students.' " And Edith did not dissimulate, she got up and said what she judged suitable.

[G 5] The closest Edith came to expressing sentiments like the ones attributed to her here sounded much milder in formulation. In the previously cited short narrative (found in the next chapter below) she looks back from late 1938 to her letter to Pope Pius XI written in 1933 "about the Jewish question" and closes her remarks with the rueful, but not emotion-laden, words "*For what I predicted about the future of Catholics in Germany was fulfilled step by step in the follow-ing years.*"

[G 6] She showed resilience or initiative so long as she felt she could make a difference. Then she relied on foresight when doors started to close, excluding her from her lecturer's position at the Insti-tute. She thought things over carefully and moved toward another realm where she felt she could rely on "weapons of the spirit" (name of a film about a village full of Holocaust rescuers in France) as a suitable response. The faith vision that had been inspiring her since the early 1920s would bring her from lecture halls to the chapel and cell of a contemplative monastery. Fortunately for us and all generations, the next chapter explains, in her own words, the transition that occurred from her last months in Münster to her arrival in the Cologne Carmel.

CHAPTER 13

[G 1] The editor used a photocopy of the original account in the handwriting of St. Edith Stein as basis for this translation. The origi-nal is in the Edith-Stein Archiv of the Carmel Maria vom Frieden in Cologne. It was written about two weeks prior to her transfer from Cologne to Echt and presented by Edith Stein to her prioress, Sr. Teresia Renata de Spiritu Sancto or P.

[G 2] Dr. Raphael Josef Walzer (1888-1966), Archabbot of the Benedictine monastery of Beuron. Abbot Walzer had to flee from the Nazis and spent many years abroad, in the United States, North Africa and elsewhere. He returned to Germany after World War II and resided in the Abbey of Neuburg near Heidelberg. He died in Heidelberg.

[G 3] Fr. Aloys Mager, known as an outstanding teacher and author, was a member of the Benedictine Order. A professor of philosophy and experimental psychology, he acquired some renown through his research on the psychology of mysticism, with special emphasis on Teresa of Avila.

[G 4] The original text of her letter became available from the Vatican archives in February 2003. We give here the English translation devised by the three editors of this new edition of P's biography of Edith Stein:

> *Holy Father!*
>
> *As a child of the Jewish people who, by the grace of God, for the past eleven years has also been a child of the Catholic Church, I dare to speak to the Father of Christendom about that which oppresses millions of Germans. For weeks we have seen deeds perpetrated in Germany that mock any sense of justice and humanity, not to mention love of neighbor. For years the leaders of National Socialism have been preaching hatred of the Jews. Now that they have seized the power of government and armed their followers, among them proven criminal elements, this seed of hatred has germinated. The government has only recently admitted that excesses have occurred. To what extent, we cannot tell, because public opinion is being gagged. However, judging by what I have learned from personal relations, it is in no way a matter of singular exceptional cases. Under pressure from reactions abroad, the government has turned to "milder" methods. It has issued the watchword "no Jew shall have even one hair on his head harmed." But through boycott measures – by robbing people of their livelihood, civic honor and*

fatherland – it drives many to desperation; within the last week, through private reports I was informed of five cases of suicide as a consequence of these hostilities. I am convinced that this is a general condition that will claim many more victims. One may regret that these unhappy people do not have greater inner strength to bear their misfortune. But the responsibility must fall, after all, on those who brought them to this point and it also falls on those who keep silent in the face of such happenings.

Everything that happened and continues to happen on a daily basis originates with a government that calls itself "Christian." For weeks not only Jews but also thousands of faithful Catholics in Germany, and, I believe, all over the world, have been waiting and hoping for the Church of Christ to raise its voice to put a stop to this abuse of Christ's name. Is not this idolization of race and governmental power that is being pounded into the public consciousness by the radio open heresy? Isn't the effort to destroy Jewish blood an abuse of the holiest humanity of our Savior, of the most blessed Virgin and the apostles? Is not all this diametrically opposed to the conduct of our Lord and Savior, who, even on the Cross, still prayed for his persecutors? And isn't this a black mark on the record of this Holy Year that was intended to be a year of peace and reconciliation?

We all, who are faithful children of the Church and who see the conditions in Germany with open eyes, fear the worst for the prestige of the Church, if the silence continues any longer. We are convinced that this silence will not be able in the long run to purchase peace with the present German government. For the time being, the fight against Catholicism will be conducted quietly and less brutally than against Jewry, but no less systematically. It won't take long before no Catholic will be able to hold office in Germany unless he dedicates himself unconditionally to the new course of action.

At the feet of your Holiness, requesting your apostolic blessing,

(Signed) Dr. Edith Stein, Instructor at the German Institute for Scientific Pedagogy, Münster in Westphalia. Collegium Marianum.

[G 5] This appears to have been a severe miscalculation on the part of Edith Stein. Her mother was devastated by her entry into Carmel, a further step toward total immersion in a faith that represented everything that was "alien" and incomprehensible to her mother.

[G 6] P was a remarkable woman. As prioress of the Carmel "Maria vom Frieden" in Cologne she experienced the destruction of the monastery of Köln-Lindenthal by bombs in an October 1944 air raid and oversaw the rebuilding of the monastery on its former site after the end of World War II.

[G 7] This cross is at present in the Edith-Stein-Archiv, Carmel "Maria vom Frieden," Cologne. Edith Stein gave it to her friend Hedwig Spiegel on the occasion of her baptism. Mrs. Spiegel left it to the Cologne Carmel in her will. It was used in Edith Stein's beatification ceremony, 1 May 1987.

[G 8] The Holy Robe is an ancient, seamless garment purported to be the robe worn by Jesus of Nazareth. After the crucifixion, the Roman soldiers drew lots to decide who should get it. Bloody battles have been fought over it, though its authenticity is at best doubtful. It has been the object of veneration over the centuries and is carefully preserved in a chapel in the Cathedral of Trier and occasionally on view to the faithful. Because the garment is all of one piece, it assumes a symbolic significance, standing for unity not only of all Christians, but also of the nations of the world.

[G 9] The distance between her home and the Bibersteins' new apartment, approximately 4 km, could be covered in about 25 minutes by trolley or 1 hour on foot. Yet, even if that distance would have been shorter, the fact was that they no longer lived in the same house. Auguste Stein suffered at the thought that she would no longer see these two grandchildren on a daily basis.

Part 2

CHAPTER 14

[G 1] The expression "Circumscribed by two words the 'Nothing' and the 'All'" comes from P. H/N rendered it as "summed up by the two words 'all' and 'nothing.'" The latter more familiar formulation misses P's intended emphasis on the word "nothing."

[G 2] Edith's daily schedule at Speyer included the hours of prayer, recitation of the breviary, and fasting similar to Carmel's daily regimen. It is obvious that Edith bore sole responsibility for scheduling her activities, both by day and night during those years, and enjoyed greater flexibility to arrange for hours of prayer than she would have in Carmel where she followed a schedule that was not of her own making.

[G 3] At the end of this paragraph P's original offers: "the Lord called her into his solitude where, *at His feet* with Mary [actually, Mary *of Bethany* mentioned in Luke's gospel 10:42], she might find that better part that would never be taken from her." H/N indicated mistakenly "with Mary [*His Mother* – in John's gospel 19:25] at the foot of the Cross."

[G 4] By using the expression "God had *shown* her, etc.", P here adopts her own subjective interpretation of Edith's detailed account of an incident described in this book (see p. 132 above). Comparison of the two references shows how P was inclined to call *a vision* what Edith described in her "How I Came To Carmel" as *an insight*. P qualifies her interpretation by saying "we may infer," but Edith had described her experience clearly. P says the Lord "*showed her* His Cross," but Edith wrote that "I told Him *I knew that it was His Cross* that was now being placed upon the Jewish people." She *volunteered* to take it freely upon herself, but P more dramatically writes "He requested her to carry her allotted share of this Cross." Edith states at this point that those who understood what was offered here had an obligation to accept the Cross in the name of those who were totally unaware of any connection between their suffering and that which Jesus had borne. Nowhere does Edith intimate she had a vision.

Whenever Edith alludes to the Cross with "the people" and with herself, she evidently wishes that for her to carry it symbolically would in some way remove it from "the people." This wish, in complete conformity with the Catholic teaching that intercessory prayer and vicarious reparation are possible, is not shared by Jewish theology.

[G 5] What Edith really gave up upon entering the Cologne Carmel was the ease with which she could quietly go about her free time. Previously she was under obligation to no one and was able to go about her way unobtrusively. What was difficult was, at the age of forty-two, to learn a whole array of ceremonial practices. These exercises were taxing for anyone coming into Carmel. The youthful postulants, not long out of school, almost expected this list of "ceremonial practices." How one took part in the Divine Office; how to comport oneself in the refectory; even spending time together in recreation had regulations that needed to be learned and observed before one could simply and spontaneously merge with the community.

[G 6] This paragraph reflects more on the community Edith had joined than on her. Sewing and cleaning were the activities that laid real claim to most of the nuns' time outside the hours of prayer. Sewing was the principal means of earning income, and they took pride in turning out excellent work whether in altar linens, albs or in handmade articles of clothing. Even in American Carmels in the same 30s and early 40s, a postulant would be evaluated with the same criteria. As for cleaning, monastery standards for housekeeping were nearly excessive compared to those of even the most careful homemaker. The recounting of Edith's reputed ineptitude in these two "monastic accomplishments" should by this time be discontinued. It was merely a one-day's wonder, and deserves to be forgotten. She was not the only one ever to be awkward. Only, the others have no biographers.

[G 7] Sentiments of condescension or feelings of superiority over the Sisters, because of their lack of higher education, was altogether foreign to her.

[G 8] Carmelites were in the time of their foundress, St. Teresa of Avila, admitted to the community either as "choir nuns" or "lay sisters."

Choir nuns belonged to the Chapter of the Carmel and they elected from among themselves in triennial elections a Prioress, a Sub-prioress and three Council Sisters who saw to the administration of the community. These nuns had a strict obligation to recite all the hours of the Divine Office found in the breviary. They were also to work to earn their livelihood. These daily duties in the sixteenth century consumed much of the day, and some of them, especially cooking and housework when neither of these chores were made easier with electric appliances, called for long hours of attention.

To enable the choir nuns to give priority of attention to their spiritual exercises without encroaching on them for manual tasks, additional members were admitted to the community who were not bound by "choir duties" – they were called "lay sisters," and they gave priority to fulfilling the household tasks. Since Vatican Council II most Carmelite communities no longer have "lay" Sisters.

[G 9] When Edith was accepted as a postulant, she expected the community would send her on to Breslau to the foundation made there in 1933. That this did not happen may indicate that upon acquaintance they recognized her qualities and were reluctant to let her go. There is also a poignant human interest angle to be considered. By their rule, Carmelite nuns live on alms that most often come in the form of small donations of home grown vegetables, or homemade bread and pastries. Many of these come from relatives of the Sisters if they are anywhere in their vicinity. It has been suggested that in light of the growing oppression from the Nazis, the nuns in the foundation in Breslau may have been reluctant to risk the attention that would be given to frequent visits from Edith's relatives if she were transferred to Breslau. Such an interpretation could presume fear underlying such caution, if indeed it was true.

[G 10] This was the conflict between the Catholic Church in Germany and the civil government under Chancellor Bismarck that began in 1871 and only slowly started to reverse itself by 1887. Religious congregations were either disbanded or went into exile. The nuns of Cologne went to Echt in the Netherlands. Gradually they were allowed to return from exile, but the Jesuits were forbidden until 1904 to reestablish themselves.

[G 11] On 30 October 1944 the community sustained an hourlong air raid and sought refuge, as always, in the shelter in the monastery basement. The monastery was hit by "a hail of bombs," and an incendiary bomb scored a direct hit, setting the building on fire. When the nuns ventured out of the shelter the whole upper floor was fully engulfed in flames, and the entire building burned down.

[G 12] Strictly speaking, after their first profession, these two Sisters were no longer "novices." Those who had made temporary profession remained with postulants and novices under the direction of the formation directress.

[G 13] This "cell" is no "place of confinement as in a prison," but the nun's room. For a Carmelite this "cell" is a true place of refreshing solitude where she can pray, work or simply *be* in the presence of God.

[G 14] P's description of Christmas may be confirmed as a time of unique joy in Carmel. Although some of the customs have changed, the spirit of Carmel, with the decorations and the singing, remain a tradition. Edith's joyousness and laughter have been echoed in the lives of many a newcomer to Carmel. Edith showed increased joy over having Fränzi Ernst with her in the novitiate from 7 December onward.

[G 15] The letter quoted here is not identified by name or date, nor is it included in the complete edition of letters. P quotes several times from letters that must have been loaned to her at the time she wrote the memoir. Unfortunately she did not always identify the person who supplied the information: Regrettably, today's definitive collection shows no trace of several letters cited. It is easy to understand how persons in possession of a note or letter from Edith would have wished to keep them. A few that remain unidentified were not included in the most recent collection of correspondence but, consequently, they make this biography all the richer.

[G 16] The ceremonial Edith described here - kneeling to ask for the grace to be received into the Order - is another custom that has changed since Vatican II. It was purely symbolic and it emphasized the really personal choice to follow a vocation to Carmel. The choice is never imposed, and there have been times when the request made in this ceremonial form was not granted. The joy Edith felt was more than enough compensation for the eleven years she had waited, in obedience, before seeking to follow her star to Carmel.

[G 17] Carmelite rules called for the habit. Other clothing, like the white tunic and homemade handkerchiefs of 100 percent wool, were, at the time of St. Teresa of Avila, materials used by the poor in Spain, spun by them from wool shorn from their sheep. Custom changes in Carmel since Vatican II have substituted modern textiles for expensive present-day wool.

CHAPTER 15

[G 1] The practical foresight of the nuns is responsible for an unusual sartorial note regarding the bridal dress Edith wore. The community had made a new foundation in Breslau/Pawelwitz and, in sharing with the "daughter" house their own small supply of liturgical vestments, they were aware that new white ones would need to be made. When Rosa Stein generously supplied beautiful material for a gown to be made for Edith's clothing ceremony, the sacristan saw to it that the pattern used would have as many generous folds as possible. That way, after Edith wore the gown for the two-three hour ceremony, it could be restored to practical dimensions, allowing the vestment pattern to be cut with a minimum of seams and with as little piecing as possible.

[G 2] Many Sisters in Carmel at that time took the name of St. Teresa of Avila as part of their religious name, as U.S. custom led religious women to include Mary as part of their name or title. Edith chose to add "Benedicta" to honor St. Benedict of Nursia since, in her own words, "He adopted me and gave me the rights of home in his Order [at Beuron] even though I was not even an Oblate since I always had the Mount of Carmel before my eyes." (Letter 178, *Letters*, 182)

[G 3] What has been frequently referred to as a "parlor" was more often a reception hall where visitors were received by the extern Sister who then gave a signal at the "turn," summoning the nun who had visitors. Some monasteries had the custom, before a Clothing Ceremony, to allow the Sister to go for a last meeting with family and friends outside the "enclosure." (Today, in many Carmels there is no longer a "material barrier" separating the nuns from their visitors.)

[G 4] Edith told Frau Conrad-Martius as early as 31 October 1933 that she hoped her godmother would be present at the Clothing Ceremony. (Letter 160, *Letters*, 163).

[G 5] Persons who had studied with Edith were on hand as well as others whom Edith taught. Her friends remained interested in her, even when they seldom heard from her.

[G 6] The ceremonial of the Carmelite nuns instructs the nuns to ring the "lesser and the greater bell." These bells contribute significantly to the silent order in Carmel, calling all the nuns to the various community acts.

[G 7] The habit according to the rules of the Discalced Carmelite nuns was made of 100 percent wool, that in comparison with textiles used for clothing by 1933 could be called coarse. The Carmelite clothing ceremonial calls for the "habit made of coarse cloth" to be placed on the new novice's shoulders. So it was not, as H/N stated here, "a penitential hair-cloth."

[G 8] The sandals were made by the nuns themselves of hempen rope braided and laboriously sewn together for soles, and then woven into a band that "finished" what was called an "alpargate."

[G 9] The cincture is a term widely used to describe the belt in a religious habit.

[G 10] The quotation refers to the religious' promise of obedience. Originally, it was the statement made to Peter to predict his martyrdom. See Jn 21:18.

[G 11] The second promise of a religious is poverty, and the third, chastity. They are all symbolized in the habit, but only at the time of profession does the religious make a vow of each of these virtues.

[G 12] Two or four nuns, depending on the degree of solemnity of the event, are designated as chantresses (feminine form of the word "cantor") for the recitation of the Divine Office, and in public ceremonies. They intone the psalms and hymns. There were also two versiclers who announced the antiphons before the psalms.

[G 13] In Prof. Wust's article many words and phrases were not literally translated by H/N; as a result the article is here retranslated. The substitutions or insertions were so numerous that it would be counterproductive to reprint in the Take-Outs section the entire text; the same holds for the commentary by Archabbot Walzer that follows.

[G 14] In Germany in Edith's time, the nuns were under the jurisdiction of the friars, and their Father Provincial was the competent authority to conduct a "visitation," the inspection that he usually conducted every three years at the time of their election of a prioress. When a monastery receives a "canonical visitation" each of the community's members is interviewed individually and privately, so that each has an opportunity to discuss with the visitator any questions, complaints, or difficulties. The bishop who has jurisdiction of a Carmel may appoint a Vicar for Religious, either male or female, who then presides in his place at elections and conducts visitations.

[G 15] Katharina Esser (1804-1866) in 1848 successfully overcame tremendous obstacles to refound the Cologne Carmel. Papal enclosure was established in the monastery on 3 June 1850; and on 7 June, Feast of the Sacred Heart, four postulants were clothed in the brown Carmelite habit. Katharina Esser was one of the four and she received the name of Sr. Frances of the Infinite Merits of Jesus Christ. She would play a key role in getting the Carmel of Cologne firmly established. Elected prioress because the two foundresses who had come from the Carmel of Liège, Belgium, to help train the new German community had to return to their home Carmel due to illness, she became the first prioress of St. Joseph's Carmel, Cologne at the age of fifty in June of 1854. She worked valiantly at assisting a Carmel in Aachen (founded by Belgian Carmelites) by sending some of her nuns from Cologne. The reward for this generosity came later when a prioress of Aachen was able to repatriate the Cologne nuns from Echt in the Netherlands in 1894 after the *Kulturkampf*. Mother Frances died on 11 February 1866, the Feast of Our Lady of Lourdes. Edith Stein's account of Katharine Esser's life was published in *Ganzheitliches Leben* [Wholeness of Life] in 1990 in *ESW* 12. This volume has not yet been translated into English.

[G16] *"Horarium"* is the monastic term for schedule and is used by German- and English-speaking Carmelites alike. Edith gives a detailed account of the schedule in Letter 171, *Letters,* 174. There one can see that the hours for work were quite short.

[G 17] There is no record of any visit to Edith's family in Breslau by either Gertrud von le Fort, or Fr. Jon Svensson, S.J.

Fr. Svensson was well known as "Nonni," author of popular books for youth. Born in Iceland in 1857, he died and was buried in Cologne in October 1944. A convert from Protestantism, he studied in France, England, and the Netherlands. As Edith mentions, he was a visitor at Carmel in Cologne. Iceland issued a commemorative stamp to honor him in 1980.

[G 18] In most monasteries of Discalced Carmelite nuns there was a tabernacle built into the wall between the nuns' choir and the public chapel. In a monstrance in this tabernacle, the Blessed Sacrament was reserved, with a glass separation permanently fixed between the monstrance and the choir so that the nuns inside could experience the continual presence of the Blessed Sacrament. The prioress could open the door of the tabernacle so that the nuns could recite the Divine Office with Exposition, or have the Exposition for adoration on First Fridays or on other occasions when customs of the monastery or the Order called for it.

[G 19] The nuns processed throughout the monastery, stopping at improvised altars in three places called "stations" for a reading and response. The fourth or last one was at the so-called "tomb." It was the custom for the sub-prioress to construct a replica of the empty tomb, beautifully decorated with flowers and candles. Its location was a secret. It was hidden in some corner of the enclosure, the nuns vied with each other to be the first to discover it on Easter morning.

[G 20] By custom the nuns did not address one another as "you" but as "your charity." This was more significant in the European countries where, in ordinary circumstances, one was addressed either formally as "Sie," in German, or familiarly as "Du." Using "your charity" or "Euer Lieb" in German seemed to create an impersonal distance and a certain equality between persons by avoiding any semblance of either familiarity or formality.

CHAPTER 16

[G 1] Edith's relatives to whom Frau Stein said nothing about such a visit were inclined to doubt it had happened. Recent scholarship has uncovered a text where Edith, in a postscript to Brief 420, dated 5 October 1935 and addressed to Margarete Günther, remarks: *"You will rejoice with me when I tell you that now, every week, we receive a few lines from my Mother, and that last Wednesday she gave her daughters the slip and paid a visit to Pawelwitz.* See ESGA 3,165.

Pawelwitz is a suburb of Breslau where the new Carmel was located. This change of heart, after presumably meeting a Sister or Sisters from the foundation, is not surprising. A family can oppose the entrance into Carmel of a young woman before they have ever seen or met a Carmelite nun. After meeting some of the Sisters, their preconceived fears and prejudices oftentimes disappear.

[G 2] In Carmel, the chapter nuns of the community elect the prioress for a term of three years. She may be re-elected for one term by a vote of two-thirds of the community.

[G 3] The novices could have been either choir or lay Sisters since only the postulant is identified as a "choir" aspirant. Those designated "choir" belong to the body of the Chapter after final profession but remain in the novitiate during the three years of temporary profession.

[G 4] Margarete Günther (m. Schweitzer) was a library assistant in the Pedagogical Institute in Münster when Edith met her. She was born in Hamm 29 August 1904 and died in Brombach/Odenwald 19 February 1988. (No letters of hers were included in the earlier German editions of Edith's correspondence, so there are none in the English edition.)

For whatever reason, there are no letters from Margarete after her marriage. It is said of one correspondent that once she married she no longer wrote to Edith nor wished to have letters from her, and that this was at the request of the husband who feared for his new wife's safety. Should the correspondence with a Jewish friend be discovered at that time – even though the friend were a Catholic nun – it might cause her trouble. Although Edith understood the different reactions to situations that arose for her friends and acquaintances and never complained or let them know if she was hurt, one can easily imagine how much pain such repercussions caused her.

[G 5] From this time on, in all her letters, Edith commends her mother to the prayers of her friends, along with the nuns in her community who were, naturally, most faithful in their prayers for Frau Stein. The quote is from Letter 227 sent 4 October 1936 to Sister Callista Kopf, O.P., *Letters*, 238.

[G 6] This paragraph regarding her book was not included at this point in the H/N translation. We supply our version of the seven lines of German text.

[G 7] As stated here, the monastic fast observed in Carmel begins on the Feast of the Exaltation of the Cross 14 September, intensifies on Ash Wednesday, and lasts all of Lent. A much more severe fast began on Ash Wednesday – no milk, butter, eggs, or dairy products were taken.

[G 8] In imitation of family relationships, it was a custom at that time (since abandoned) to speak of the Sisters in the novitiate as "the children" or "the little ones," whereas the finally professed Sisters were the "grown-ups" – the "adults."

[G 9] The nuns were under the jurisdiction of the Cardinal Bishop of Cologne and would need his permission to leave the cloister for a stay in the hospital. The cardinal's vicar for religious could grant this. In an emergency there is no delay, that is, one need not wait until it has been granted before getting medical attention for a Sister.

[G 10] P called Edith Rosa's "religious" or "spiritual" sister (an adjective omitted by H/N that could lend itself to misinterpretation). They related very much as loving blood sisters. But, since Rosa's visits were not simply social and intended by Edith and Rosa to deepen the latter's knowledge of the faith and thus better prepare her for baptism, their conversations treated of spiritual matters.

[G 11] Rosa waited until after her mother's death to begin preparations for her reception into the Catholic Church. She had received instructions from Fr. Zephyrin Franz, a Franciscan priest in Breslau, and needed only some final reviews before being baptized in Cologne. Heinrich Spaemann was not yet ordained to the priesthood at the time he helped to make arrangements for Rosa Stein's baptism. There are no more details about the sculptress, Hildegard Domizlaff.

[G 12] There was *no* Frau Hantelmann at the baptism, as indicated. That a third person named Frau Hantelmann was not present is verification that the book of P depended a great deal on the recollections of a large number of persons, and so, it sometimes carries mistakes that appear as such when the circumstances are known.

[G 13] The sentence placed in [T 3] is not found in Edith's German text of this letter.

[G 14] The next seven (7) paragraphs of this edition, found at the beginning of the next (and fourth) chapter of Pt. 2 in the German edition had been placed by H/N at the end of the present chapter. We have restored them to the place they occupied in P's original disposition of her narrative. There they appear more suitable to the subject matter dictated by Chap. 17's title, "Learning and Service of Love" (see [G 1] there).

CHAPTER 17

[G 1] The current title is a more literal rendering of P's terminology *"Wissenschaft und Liebesdienst."*

[G 2] Two subtitles are possible for the opus Edith completed in 1936, both the ones we know can be derived from manuscript evidence. P here supplies the words: "a survey of the *philosophia perennis."* It differs from the one found in the published German version (ESW 2) and in most of the translations into modern languages, namely *"An Attempt at an Ascent to the Meaning of Being."*

[G 3] The related treatises *Sentient Causality* and *Individual and Community* appeared in the Husserl *Festschrift,* that Edith prepared and dedicated to him on his sixtieth birthday, 8 April 1919. Because of the poor economic situation at the time, the volume in tribute to Husserl did not get into print until 1922.

[G 4] The expression "tabula rasa" is defined by Webster as "the mind in its hypothetical primary blank or empty state before receiving outside impressions." It may be in doubt whether there is any such state in reality.

[G 5] Sr. Benedicta, who had taken a final vow of poverty by this time did not sign the contract personally. Mother P, as superior of the community, signed it (see n. 12, this chapter).

[G 6] "Not allowed" meant "impossible to print" if Edith were named as author. As has been mentioned, the Sister whom Borgmeyer proposed to name as author was P, Edith's superior in the Cologne Carmel, who was known as an author in her own right.

[G 7] Although it was suggested that P be named as author to get around the anti-Semitic Nazi discriminatory laws, neither she nor Sr. Benedicta was willing to take such a step. Not only would Edith have considered a maneuver like this deceitful, she was also keenly aware of the price Mother Renata would pay were such a ruse ever detected.

[G 8] Later on in early 1940 Edith was doing her utmost to find a way of putting to full use the 3000 kilograms (or 6,600 pounds) of lead type, costing 3000 Reichsmarks paid for by her community and already set by Borgmeyer. She even suggested to philosophers in Buffalo, N.Y., that they have her work printed in Germany under U.S. (not yet a belligerent in World War II) auspices. See Brief 664, 4 April 1940 to Marvin Farber, ESGA 3, 445.

[G 9] Webster defines a "festschrift" as a volume of writings by different authors presented as a tribute to a scholar for a special event. The one prepared here by P with Edith's help was a 200-page illustrated book entitled "Under the Scepter of the Queen of Peace." In three sections, it told the colorful history of the monastery church, something that amounted to a small history of the Catholic church in Cologne and Germany. The first part tells of Carmel's early history in Cologne from 1637 to 1802. The second picks up the history of the church and Carmel in 1850, until the beginning of the exile in 1875 during the *Kulturkampf*. The final section describes the foundations made after the restoration of Carmel in Cologne from 1890 to 1937, the third centenary of the monastery's foundation.

[G 10] The politics of the first Chancellor of Germany, Prince Otto von Bismarck (1871-1890), had long-range repercussions in the story of St. Edith Stein. The nuns banished from Cologne by Bismarck founded the Carmel of Echt in the Netherlands that became Edith's refuge. To it she took along two books of the treasured objects here mentioned in order to return them to the Sisters at Echt.

[G 11] On 24 July 1936, at Guadalajara, Spain, three young Discalced Carmelite Nuns, Sisters Maria Pilar, Teresa, and Maria Angeles, were killed for their fidelity to the faith. All three were proclaimed Blesseds of the Church.

[G 12] The Turn Sister received that name because the room in which the "turn" was situated was her office. It usually consisted of a barrel-like cupboard set in the wall between two rooms that could be turned around in a circular motion. It had an opening to allow persons to lay in the barrel packages, donations, etc. that would pass from the extern quarters to the Sister inside the enclosure.

[G 13] An entire chapter, the fifth of Pt. 2, from P's original was fused to the fourth chapter in the H/N English translation and its title was thereby suppressed. We end this chapter at this point where it ends in the German 5th edition and restore Chap. 5 with its title as the following chapter.

The affirmation about completion of *Finite and Eternal Being* (although accurate about timing) has been taken out [T4], because it was introduced by H/N but not translated from P's German.

CHAPTER 18

[G 1] Before final vows were taken, the Sister wore a white veil and remained with the other younger religious in the novitiate under the supervision of the Directress of Formation who in Edith's time was called the Mistress of Novices.

[G 2] H/N added a sentence not in the German (= [T 1]). Still more inexplicable is the omission by them of almost the entire paragraph on the death of Edmund Husserl that we include in the present text.

The former student of Edith, Sr. Adelgundis Jaegerschmid, O.S.B., was helping Frau Husserl take care of her invalid husband, and she kept Edith informed about his final days. Frau Husserl also wrote an account of his last hours, repeating some of the details alluded to here. See Brief 547 in the collected letters in ESGA 3, along with numerous valuable letters to Edith from others.

It was at this point that P inserted her comment that Edith's profession and Husserl's death both occurred on 21 April. The biographical sketch of Husserl written by Prof. Ludwig Landgrebe for the *Encyclopaedia Britannica,* affirming that date, clashes with the eyewitness notification of Brief 543, dated 27 April, from Sr. Adelgundis to Edith Stein in that she describes Husserl's peaceful death at a quarter-of-six *that* morning. Edith assumes as much when, in Brief 560 to Prof. Rudolf Allers in the U.S., she mentions he must have read in the papers of Husserl's death on "27 April."

[G 3] To vote in the monastery Chapter involves two modes: using "active" voice means the ability to cast a vote; having "passive" voice means the person has a right to be voted for, as for instance, a right to be elected to any of the offices in the community.

[G 4] This letter may not have been preserved after P used it in her book. Many of the artifacts loaned to her at the time she wrote this first biography were returned to their owners, some of whom were no longer living when materials were being collected for the canonization process. Mother Renata was not as exact as one could wish in recording either the dates or names of the recipients of letters and both are missing from this excerpt. Although the volumes of letters by and to Edith Stein have been greatly expanded in the most recent ESGA series volumes, so far this letter has not surfaced again. All the same, the sentiments expressed are echoed in a few other instances, so the excerpt is retained here in its unspecified state.

[G 5] In the monastery, Edith would have been wearing the *alpargates,* the sandals woven and braided from hempen cord. To go out as for voting here, the nuns had leather shoes.

[G 6] The nuns depended on friends and possibly relatives to keep them au courant of the topics to be voted on, and these people did not expect the nuns to have any special, much less vested, interest in the elections and so gave the poor advice that roused Edith to protest to her Sisters that they had a responsibility to vote against Hitler even if the election was rigged.

[G 7] Reference to Blessed Mary of Jesus Crucified (Mirjam Baouardy), the Discalced Carmelite nun known sometimes as "The Little Arab." She was born in 1846 at Abellin in Galilee. At the age of twenty-one, she entered Carmel at Pau in France and from there she went to help found a Carmel in Mangalore, India, where she was professed in 1870.

She returned to France in 1872, then three years later went to the Holy Land where she built a monastery in Bethlehem and began planning for another at Nazareth. She died in Bethlehem in 1878.

[G 8] This is the infamous and dreadful "Kristallnacht," the night between November 9 and 10, 1938 when the Nazis burned synagogues and destroyed the shops, homes and properties of the Jews and arrested many Jewish men. The Shoah continued steadily until the end of World War II in 1945.

[G 9] These grief-inspired words attributed to Edith evoke sympathy. Regardless of who may have made, at the time of Jesus' trial before the Roman Procurator (see Mt 27:20), any statement such as "His blood be upon us," it is certain that in the eyes of God the Almighty the prayer or wish of Jesus on the cross would have outweighed any rash statements prompted by mob psychology claiming responsibility for his death. By saying "Father, forgive them for they know not what they do" Jesus surely meant to include every person in every phase of those last days of his life.

After Kristallnacht Edith could indeed have made this the topic of her meditation and prayer. Her closing statement at this time about what would result for those who were perpetrating such inhuman crimes, that is, "woe to" the city and country who would experience the wrath of God, could be interpreted as a conviction that God would not abandon her people. In the final analysis, both these assertions are reminiscences of P, and are expressed in her own terms.

[G 10] When Teresa of Avila established the first Carmelite Monasteries of nuns in Spain in the mid 1500s many young women of the nobility joined her. These women were known by their titles, but Teresa ordered the cessation of calling any woman by the title she had from birth. There was to be neither formality nor familiarity; all were to address one another as "your charity," no longer as "your ladyship" or similar secular titles of honor. H/N did not use the Carmelite expression in this instance; it has been restored in the text.

[G 11] The present-day monastery at Cologne has the address "vor den Siebenburgen 6." During the night of 28 April 1942, Allied bombing attacks were so fierce that the interior of the church as well as the treasured statue of Mary, Queen of Peace, burned completely. Only the shell of the church remained standing. As the next chapter attests, Edith and Rosa had confirmation of the destruction suffered by the church during an interview at the Nazi headquarters in Holland. Edith had visited the church briefly the evening she left Germany in December 1938. The nuns at that date were living in their monastery in the Lindenthal sector of Cologne: their home underwent total destruction on the night of 30-31 October 1944.

CHAPTER 19

[G 1] This indicates the province of Limburg in the Netherlands. The village lies just 71.5 miles from Cologne over modern highways: tantalizingly close to her home monastery, and maybe chosen with hopes for an eventual return to that great metropolis on the Rhine.

[G 2] P's count of the languages Edith "mastered" seems generous. First comes German; then, Edith translated from Latin and English; studied Greek in the university; and taught French at Speyer. It seems safe to presume she had a passing familiarity of Italian and she did study Spanish when she worked on St. John of the Cross's writings. Her close friendship with Roman Ingarden may have led to a knowledge of some Polish. Her stay at the Lazaretto in Mährisch-Weisskirchen (long description in Chap. VIII of *Life*) garnered many phrases from the tongues of the Austro-Hungarian Empire.

[G 3] Rosa had hoped she would be able to enter the community. Again because of the times, this was more and more difficult and Rosa served both in Cologne and later in Echt as extern by taking care of many indispensable duties in service to the community. As a result of her willing readiness to help where she could, Rosa was much loved both in Cologne and Echt and won many friends for the community and for herself among the visitors to the Carmel.

[G 4] It was often almost legendary in monasteries that whenever anything had to be found or some necessary service rendered to either the community or one of the nuns, the portresses would produce marvels. They invariably knew someone who could arrange what was impossible for someone else to achieve, and so these Cologne portresses managed to call on individuals on both sides of the border to assist Rosa. Their names were kept from the public by P out of respect for their privacy.

[G 5] A large part of the refectorian's duties was to keep the room where the nuns took their meals clean and the tables set with all the necessary dishes and utensils. Preparing for meals and cleaning up after them kept a refectorian very busy most of the time.

[G 6] *Ways to Know God,* a small study of the "symbolic theology" of Dionysius the Areopagite, was sent as a contribution to the *Journal of Philosophy and Phenomenological Research* published by the newly founded philosophical group in Buffalo, N.Y. Edith was invited to join the group, but when she explained her situation as a contemplative nun with a vow of poverty, she made it clear that her participation would be very limited. Marvin Farber had been in Göttingen and knew of her background with Husserl and invited her to write an article for their publication. Edith chose something that had a religious flavor. When it was received in Buffalo it was judged to be outside the scope of the philosophy magazine and Farber sent it to Washington, D.C. to Prof. Rudolf Allers, a friend of Edith's. He translated it and submitted it to *The Thomist* where it appeared in the July 1946 issue.

[G 7] It was indeed the last day Edith worked at the manuscript of *The Science of the Cross,* but it is not likely that "the last pages were written" on 2 August 1942, the day Edith was arrested. The manuscript was on her desk and she had done work on it, but most probably she was editing and rearranging some of the last pages. Seen this way, the book should no longer be called "unfinished."

[G 8] Like all professed choir-nuns Sr. Benedicta was obliged to recite all the hours of the Divine Office daily. The time for the choral recitation of these "hours" was spaced throughout the day and, as she mentioned elsewhere, this caused the work time to be broken up into periods of hardly more than two-and-a-half hours at one time.

[G 9] The reflections on enclosure were written for the ceremony of the renewal of vows on the Feast of the Exaltation of the Cross on 14 September 1941 in the Carmel of Echt, and published subsequently. If Edith sent a copy of her reflections to P in Cologne, the latter therefore characterizes the quoted lines as "a letter early in September 1941."

[G 10] Edith closes her letter to Sr. Maria with the Latin words "In the Heart of Jesus and the Queen of Carmel." She added the customary mention in the complimentary closing of "the least," a phrase used so constantly by the nuns out of humility.

CHAPTER 20

[G 1] When a nun transferred to another Carmel she frequently had to spend three years in the new community before she could both vote and be voted for, i.e., have active and passive voice. To grant Edith this so very early on in Echt was a sign of how much she was accepted there.

[G 2] Edith herself never belonged to the Third Order of Carmel since, from her baptism onward, she felt the day when she could enter a monastery would come quickly. Nevertheless, her love of Carmel led her to speak of it and to encourage others to become lay members of the Order – now called the "Secular Order."

[G 3] Church regulations required the permission of the "local Ordinary." In other words the permission of the bishop of the diocese to which the Carmel of Le Pâquier belonged was required to receive a transfer to the community.

[G 4] Carmels were restricted to twenty-one members. Once that number was reached, it was customary to refer an applicant to another Carmel. There were at this time only two Carmels in Switzerland.

[G 5] These "Third Order Carmelites" were a congregation of Sisters who followed the Carmelite Rule and Constitutions, but were so-called "active" religious, not cloistered contemplatives. Edith could not have gone to them, but Rosa was grateful for their willingness to have her join them. Unfortunately, it was too late – she was unable to go to Switzerland.

[G 6] One report said they taunted him because of his American citizenship: "What! You, a Yankee, represent a Jew!" His action called attention to him and he narrowly escaped being arrested. Some loyal friends in the Dutch police prevailed on him, against his will, to flee. He made his way south through Europe and managed to get back to the United States.

[G 7] It was a custom in all Carmels for this greeting to be used any time two Sisters passed one another in the halls of the monasteries. The junior would say "Praised be Jesus Christ!" and the other would reply "Now and forever." The same "Praised be Jesus Christ" was used in religious services when the reply could be a simple "Amen."

[G 8] Three weeks for a letter to reach Echt demonstrates how difficult communication between the Carmels had become.

[G 9] Edith was at work writing *The Science of the Cross* and she next mentions that St. John of the Cross helped her by letting her have new insights about symbols.

In this letter she clearly indicates wishing to send a "German" copy of the manuscript to the Fr. Provincial. That might only imply that there would be a subsequent manuscript in some other language. Edith possibly intended, once she had completed writing it in German, to translate the work into Dutch. Her aim was to write it for the Sisters in her Carmel and they did not all read German. It was only practical to write in German, since the main source of her quotes from St. John was also German, but she also was getting to be fluent in Dutch and it would be good exercise then to translate her work on St. John for her Sisters.

[G 10] Inquiries at the present time have not turned up any Spanish Carmel that has a record of either an offer or an inquiry. This has been explained by saying any prioress receiving such a request would keep it confidential, even from her own community, in order to safeguard the petitioner.

Anna Reinach did find refuge in Spain, so speculation occurs sometimes as to whether she attempted to find a place for Edith or tried to encourage Edith to seek one. The Dutch provincial, Fr. Leunissen, O.C.D., passed through Spain when he made his way to the U.S., and he might have inquired at some Carmel there whether they could receive Edith.

[G11] "Ember" Days were days of fast and abstinence observed at the beginning of each of the four seasons of the year to seek God's blessing for that period. On Wednesday, Friday, and Saturday, Catholics fasted and abstained from eating meat.

[G12] By Carmelite legislation, membership in Carmels could not exceed twenty-one, eighteen choir nuns and three lay sisters. Edith would have transferred as a choir nun.

[G13] An indult from the highest authority in the Order had to be obtained for a transfer from one community to another, but it was not necessary to wait for it to be granted before the person could go to the new community. The Rule of Carmel contains a provision to cover such contingencies: Necessity has no rule.

[G14] "Clavary" comes from *clavis*, the Latin word for key or one who has a key. Here it is an obsolete term for a Council Sister in a Carmel – one of the three community officials who had a key to open the money chest for business needs.

[G15] Sr. Teresa Benedicta's practical gestures of taking some food and then (in the next sentence) of attempting to enlighten the SS man fit well her personality of attentiveness to details, especially when the details had practical import for her colleagues (in this case her own sister, Rosa). The Prioress's narrative does not indicate she lost contact with her surroundings, or strike some pious pose aside from her request "Pray, Sisters."

[G 16] The friend indicated by the narrative could quite possibly be Maria Delsing. Her presence as a witness underscores the significance of the lack of any direct quotations from either Edith or Rosa on the sidewalk as they exited the monastery. Neither here nor in later editions did P place on the record any words exchanged by Edith either with her sister Rosa or the nuns or the people outside the monastery.

No indication comes to us, then, of the now legendary sentence people think she uttered, at that very moment, to Rosa, "Come, we go for our people." The legendary phrase does not have P as its source.

[G 17] The description "van" for the SS vehicle is the best description of the round-up truck sent to pick up Edith and Rosa. Later on, in the next chapter, such "vans" conveyed "eleven" and "seventeen" persons. Sometimes depictions of the scene, be they verbal or visual, indicate a passenger car – too small, in all events.

CHAPTER 21

[G 1] Arrested the same day as Edith and Rosa were: Alice Reis, Ruth Kantorowicz, Sr. Aloysia Löwenfels, Sr. Mirjam Michaelis, the Löb blood-sisters (Sr. Hedwige and Sr. Maria-Thérèse), Sr. Charitas Böck, Sr. Judith Mendes da Costa. Rosa, Alice and Ruth, though not members of any religious order or congregation, were closely attached to the communities with whom they lived, and may have been wearing some kind of habit.

[G 2] The words "today (Friday 7 August)" attributed to Pierre Cuypers by P's text tends to skewer the chronology, giving the impression the departure was during the day while it occurred sometime in the night hours between 6 and 7 August. Compare the English translation of his account found in *Never Forget*, 278: "Rumor had it that on *that day* (on August 7, a Friday) they might leave. . ." (emphasis added)

[G 3] A reference to the members of the Löb family, all arrested on the same day: the male religious were Frs. Ignatius and Nivard, and Br. Linus, all Trappists from the Abbey of Koningshoven by Tilburg; their sisters are mentioned in [G 1] above.

[G 4] Actually Sister Benedicta managed to write three (3) notes while detained at Westerbork, 4, 5, and 6 August, i.e., they are Letters 340, 341, and 342 (see *Letters*, 350-53).

To assure flow in P's account we will retain in the text only the third of them, viz., Letter 342, transcribing in this Gleaning the other two in order. We also have put among the Takeouts [T 3] a letter given by P at this point that recent scholarship places late in the year of 1941, several months before her deportation to Auschwitz.

Letter 340 was started on 4 August but sent only on 5 August to her prioress Mother Ambrosia Antonia Engelmann, OCD. The ICS translation used here is taken from *Letters*, 350-51:

> *Drente-Westerbork, Barracks 36, August 4, 1942*
> *Dear Mother and Sisters,*
> *During the past night we left the transit-station A.*
> *[Amersfoort] and landed here early this morning. [We*
> *were given a very friendly reception here.] They intend*
> *to do everything possible to enable us to be freed or at*
> *least that we may remain here.+* In the margin near +
> is written: *Aug. 5 – (this) is no longer possible.*
>
> *All the Catholics are together and in our dormitory*
> *we have all the nuns (two Trappistines, one Domini-*
> *can) Ruth, Alice, Dr. M. and others are here. Two Trap-*
> *pist Fathers from T. [see G 3] are also with us. In any*
> *case, it will be necessary for you to send us our per-*
> *sonal credentials, our ID cards, and our ration cards.*
> *So far we have lived entirely on the generosity of the*
> *others. We hope you have found the address of the Con-*
> *sul and have been in touch with him. We have asked many*
> *people to relay news to you. The two dear children from*
> *Koningsbosch* [Annemarie and Elfriede Goldschmidt,
> only twenty and nineteen years old then] *are with us.*

We are very calm and cheerful. Of course, so far there
has been no Mass and Communion; maybe that will come
later. Now we have a chance to experience a little how
to live purely from within. Sincerest greetings to all. We
will probably write again soon.

In Corde Jesu, your B.
When you write, please do not mention you received this.

[From Rosa:]

Sincerest greetings to all. We are very sorry not to have
seen Mother Ottilia any more. In this brief time we have
experienced a great deal; one lives together with the
others and everywhere people help each other. We have
slept very little, but have had a lot of good air and much
traveling. Many greetings to Sophie, Maria too, and to
everyone; they were so upset; we not at all.

In Corde Jesu we all find ourselves in gratitude,
Rosa

(Edith's ending remark asking for silence about the note could have
flowed from either fears over her entrusting it to someone who had to
smuggle it out of camp, or simply because she mentions several individuals, including the [Swiss] Consul.)

Letter 341, also sent to Mother Ambrosia Antonia Engelmann, OCD
reads in *Letters*, 352:

August 5 [1942]

My dear Ones,
A R[ed] C[ross] nurse from A[msterdam] intends to speak
today with the Consul. Here, every petition on behalf
of fully Jewish Catholics has been forbidden since yes-
terday. Outside [the camp] an attempt can still be made,
but with extremely little prospect. According to plans, a
transport will leave on Friday. Could you possibly write
to Mother Claire in Venlo, Kaldenkerkeweg 185, [the
Ursuline Convent] *to ask for my manuscript if they have*
not already sent it. We count on your prayers. There are

*so many persons here who need some consolation and
they expect it from the Sisters.*

In Corde Jesu, your grateful
B

[G 5] Yet another note, placed by P in the third position of her listing, has been identified as a piece of paper ("a leaf torn out of a small calendar booklet") on which Edith jotted down a brief message and left it behind in the Echt monastery in all haste to satisfy the SS demand to leave quickly. It was an instruction to her prioress to obtain official intervention by the Swiss Consul. Today it is numbered in the German edition as Brief 762, ESGA 3, 579. See Chap. 20, n. 33 above.

We have placed P's reference to it among the Takeouts [T 4], since it was not among the three notes drafted in and sent from Westerbork. We have included a paragraph after the text of the note in [T 4] to simplify the flow of P's inventory of epistolary contacts en route to Auschwitz.

The text of the hurried note is found translated in *Letters*, 351. It reads:

Carmelite Monastery Echt
Bovenstraat 48
Sister Teresia Benedicta a Cruce (Edith Stein)
Rosa Stein,
Swiss Consulate, Amsterdam C., Heerengracht 545,
*Enable us as soon as possible to cross the border. Our
monastery will take care of travel expenses.*

[G 6] The letter by Doctor Meirowsky is a precious eyewitness account by a person who, like the other Catholic converts arrested on 2 August, underwent the same imprisonment and fate as Edith Stein. From within the mechanism of the "Final Solution" she describes, not unlike Julius Markan who is cited in this chapter, conditions confronted by Edith Stein.

What we know from eyewitness sources either during or after the war is confirmed by another contemporary eyewitness, Etty Hillesum, who wrote correspondence later collected into the book *Letters from Westerbork*. The arrival of Edith Stein's group in the transit camp is in fact described by this woman working for the Jewish Council and pressed into concentration camp service by the Nazis to induce a semblance of order and thus exclude any chance of rebellion from the prisoners. (See Etty Hillesum, *Letters from Westerbork*, trans. Arnold J. Pomerans, New York: Pantheon Books, 1986, 28-30.)

CHAPTER 22

[G 1] Two half-sentences have been rephrased and the H/N text placed among the Take-Outs. They did not correspond to the original German text. The version supplanting them follows P's text in the fifth edition more closely.

[G 2] The Sister here referred to was most likely Sr. Placida Laubhardt OSB (1904-1998). (See Hugo Ott, "Edith Stein and Freiburg," *Never Forget,* 138) who was a good friend of Edith Stein and a member of St. Lioba Benedictine community in Günterstal, outside of Freiburg. Being "non-Aryan" according to the Nazi definition – her father had been Jewish – she was later interned in Ravensbrück. Prior to her own deportation, Sr. Placida had destroyed all the letters she had received from Edith Stein. So we must assume that this note, too, was among them. J. Feldes reports that, in a conversation with Sr. Placida on 21 January 1998, she told him she had received the note; that it was unmistakably in Edith's handwriting; and that she burned it a few days before her own arrest, to protect her community. The actual wording, according to Sr. Placida, was "Grüße von Schwester Teresia Benedicta a Cruce. Unterwegs *ad orientem*" or "Greetings from Sr. Teresia Benedicta a Cruce. En route to the East." (See Feldes, *Edith Stein und Schifferstadt,* 74) and more recently confirmed by Renate Hegeman, "Sr. Placida Laubhardt (1904-1998)," *St. Lioba, 1927-2002: Die Föderation der Benediktinerinnen von der hl. Lioba, Dokumentation* (Friedrichshafen: Verlag Robert Geseter, 2002). This formulation is different from the one given by P.

[G 3] The word "Bibelforscherin" was translated by H/N as "Quaker," but it means "Jehovah's Witness."

[G 4] Several errors appear in this news report. For accuracy's sake we stress: Edith Stein was *born in 1891* and *killed in 1942.* The "Karmel Maria vom Frieden" was located *in Köln-Lindenthal.* The date of her arrest was 2 August *1942.* She was arrested with *her sister* Rosa. The last sentence has no basis in fact. She was arrested in Echt, Holland, taken via Amersfoort to Hooghalen, the train station closest to the transit camp Westerbork, and from there by train to Auschwitz. She was never in a German prison. Finally, the mention of "being thrown into a salt-mine" is not corroborated anywhere.

[G 5] For more about the two men here referred to, P[iet] O. Van Kempen and Pierre Cuypers see Chap. 21, nn. 3 and 4 and *Never Forget*, 272-278. The two men were witnesses for Edith Stein's beatification process in Cologne in 1963.

[G 6] The brief sketch mentioned here cannot be the biography *Edith Stein* by P (not published until 1948). It is referred to in German as a *Gedenkblatt* (memorial leaflet) or *kurzgefaßtes Lebensbild* (a brief biographical sketch) and might have been anything from a single sheet to a short brochure.

On 7 July 2001, Sr. Amata Neyer OCD, sent this editor a leaflet that, Sr. Amata believes, is the one mentioned here by P. Assuming this text to be the announcement of the death of Edith Stein/Sr. Teresia Benedicta a Cruce, sent out by the Pater General of the Carmelite Order in Rome in 1947, we are reproducing it here for the first time in English and will place some specific corrections at its conclusion below:

> God has put them to the test
> And proved them worthy to be with Him;
> He has tested them like gold in a furnace
> and accepted them as a holocaust.
> ...and the Lord will be their king forever. (Ws 3: 5-8)
> (Trans. *Jerusalem Bible*, Doubleday, 1966)

Edith Stein was born on 12 October 1891, God's gift to her Jewish parents Siegfried Stein and Auguste Courant. She attended the humanistic gymnasium in the city of her birth and, after passing her final examinations with highest honors in 1909, she attended the universities of Breslau, Berlin, and Göttingen. At first she devoted herself to the study of philology and German literature, that she concluded with the State Examination *summa cum laude*. The outbreak of the First World War caused her to interrupt her studies. Her patriotic enthusiasm made it impossible for her to watch Germany's battle as an idle bystander. She volunteered for the Red Cross and, after some brief training, was assigned to an Austrian military hospital for contagious diseases. There she nursed the suffering soldiers with heroic selflessness. A Red Cross Medal was her thanks from the fatherland.

After the end of the war, she went to Freiburg, where Professor Husserl, the founder of phenomenology, accepted her among his students. She soon surpassed the others by her extraordinary intelligence and tenacious diligence, so that she was able to assist her famous Master in a spirit of camaraderie. In his behalf, she lectured at philosophical conferences inside and outside of Germany, in order to introduce scholars to Husserl's system.

God rewarded her sincere search for wisdom with her discovery of truth. On New Year's Day, 1922 she was admitted into the Catholic Church. At her baptism she received the name Theresia, because the study of the works of this seraphic saint had given the impetus to her conversion.

From Freiburg she withdrew to Speyer where she taught at the Lyceum of the Dominican Nuns of St. Magdalena. She lived there among the nuns like one of them, in fact, according to their testimony, as a role model for all. In this quiet period that was solely dedicated to prayer and scholarship, she produced a masterful translation of John Henry Newman's *Letters and Diaries up to his Conversion to the [Catholic] Church* as volume 1 of his *Collected Works,* Theatinerverlag, Munich, 1928. In 1930 her translation of Thomas Aquinas's *Quaestiones de veritate* was published in two volumes by Otto Borgmeyer, Breslau, [Editor's comment: publication dates were 1931 and 1932] a celebrated work that made her name known far beyond the borders of her homeland.

Neither fame nor honor could detract from her modesty. The celebrated philosopher longed for the solitude of a cell in Carmel. But her admirers tried in every possible way to retain a talent such as hers in the secular world. In 1932 she was appointed to the faculty of the German Institute for Scientific Pedagogy in Münster. At that time she published an excellent short paper about *The Ethos of Women's Professions* and in the Benedictine monthly journal a series of contributions on the problem of modern education for young girls.

The outbreak of the persecution of Jews put a sudden end to her public activities. In this development she recognized the door that opened to her long-held desire, but at the same time the impetus for her to offer herself to God for the salvation of her people. With touching humility she pleaded for admission to the Order of Our Lady of Mount Carmel, and it was granted to her on 14 October 1933 in Köln-Lindenthal. At her clothing ceremony on 15 April 1934 by the Most Reverend Archabbot of Beuron – that abbey had been her spiritual home – she received the name Teresia Benedicta a Cruce. On Easter Sunday, 21 April 1935, she dedicated herself to Christ, her divine bridegroom, by profession of holy vows.

Hidden from the world, she revealed the wealth of her virtues, without being aware of it, a spectacle for heaven and earth. She welcomed the opportunity to perform the most humble services and, at the direction of her superiors, she wrote her most important work, *Ewiges und endliches Sein (Eternal and Finite Being)*, an analysis of modern philosophy from Descartes to Heidegger.

This two-volume work was printed, though with difficulty, by Otto Borgmeyer in Breslau, but could not be published because of the laws then prevailing that prohibited the publication of all writings by non-Aryans.

With far-sightedness she anticipated the intensifying persecution and recognized the danger that her presence represented for the community that was so dear to her. With a heavy heart she pleaded for her transfer to a Carmel abroad. During the night of New Year's Eve 1938, a friend, the physician Dr. Paul Strerath, took her across the Dutch border, where she found a loving welcome in the Carmel of Echt. There she wrote her last major work about her seraphic Carmelite Father and Doctor of the Church St. John of the Cross. In this work she set forth his teachings with the clarity and precision of thought and expression that were typical of her. Before she could complete the manuscript, she was coerced by the German state police on 2 August 1942, to leave the Carmel of Echt and was led away by force. On 6 August, one of her former students recognized Edith Stein at the train station in Schifferstadt, as she stood at the window of a locked compartment. A brief word was her last message: "Tell my Sisters, I am en route to the East" – *Ad orientem.* Yes, the last phase of her sacrificial ascent, toward the light, had begun. We do not know when, where and how she reached her destination. Many rumors, including that of her murder by gas in Auschwitz, have reached us, but not one confirmed reliable report.

We no longer seek her in this world, but with God, who has accepted her sacrifice and who gives its fruit to the people for whom she prayed, suffered and died, in the fullest sense of the word.

Benedicta a Cruce.

The above text is filled with errors. We can only assume that it was prepared in haste, without giving sufficient attention to the details of Edith Stein's life. We offer correction to some of these errors.

She did not attend a humanistic gymnasium, but a so-called "Realgymnasium," for the simple reason that a humanistic gymnasium for girls did not exist in Breslau. She passed her final examinations *(Abitur)* in 1911. She never studied in Berlin. Among the subjects she studied in Breslau were not only philology and German literature, but also history, philosophy and psychology. Her service as a Red Cross aide in Mährisch-Weißkirchen lasted from April to September 1915. In September, the hospital in which she worked was closed, and Edith was never called back or re-assigned to duty elsewhere. No documentary proof is available to confirm she received a medal as an award for her nursing service. She returned to Breslau, where she substituted for a teacher (who was absent due to a prolonged illness, at *Viktoriaschule*, the school she herself had attended). When school closed for the summer vacation, she went to Freiburg to take her doctorate with Prof. Husserl, earning her degree in August 1916. In the Fall of 1916, she became Prof. Husserl's assistant and remained in that position until early 1918. Edith had first become a student of Edmund Husserl in Göttingen. When she was ready for her doctoral examination, she followed him to Freiburg, where he had joined the faculty in 1916.

Her activities as a lecturer did not start until 1923, during the years when she taught at the Dominican girls school of St. Magdalena in Speyer. Betwcen 1919 and 1923 Edith was busy with a variety of scholarly research projects, lived in Breslau, and still hoped for a university position. Her conversion to Roman Catholicism occurred on 1 January 1922, and it was only the next year that she took a teaching position in Speyer.

The correct title of the two-volume work that could not be published during her lifetime is: *Endliches und ewiges Sein* or *Finite and Eternal Being.*

To the lay reader, it may also be surprising to find in this biographical sketch no mention of the courageous protest of the clergy in the Netherlands that precipitated the arrest of hundreds of Jewish-born

Catholics in August 1942, nor of the fact that Edith shared her fate of deportation and death with her sister Rosa.

[G 7] We have changed "February 1947" to "March 1947" in agreement with the German original.

[G 8] The family mentioned here is undoubtedly the Löb family. The members arrested on 2 August 1942 in the action of vengeance against the Dutch Catholic church have already been named in the previous chapter; another brother Hans, who had not entered an order also perished in the Holocaust. Only the youngest sister Paula survived. See *Passion im August*, 209-227.

CHAPTER 23

[G 1] On P's own admission this final section of her biographical account adopts a somewhat unusual approach, viz., a stimulus to submission to her monastery of further eyewitness accounts, even though the ones included might present "contradictory" assertions. Further editions of P's book tended to lengthen this "postscript" feature. Because of the details that sometimes clash not only among themselves, but with previous passages of the book we will limit corrections to a minimum and retain the section in order to present the outline of the volume as the author intended.

[G 2] Auschwitz (Oswiecim) was and is located in Poland, not in Silesia. Silesia did not become Polish until after World War II. Death occurred for the prisoners from Holland in the Birkenau part of the concentration camp and very likely on 9 August.

[G 3] It is now assumed that the transport with which Edith and Rosa Stein arrived in Auschwitz went directly to the gas chamber, possibly without being registered. Hence the survivor from Ravensbrück and Auschwitz (these were two totally different camps, and therefore should not be hyphenated) might never have encountered these deportees, even though she worked in the "Häftlingsschreibstube" or prisoners' registration office.

TAKE-OUTS

Part 1

CHAPTER 1

[T 1] If you knocked at the door and stepped into the large hall, you were at once surrounded by the atmosphere peculiar to years of a consciously cultivated Jewish tradition. Big engravings, illustrating scenes from the history of Israel, beautiful carving on cupboards and chests displaying exclusively biblical motifs, gave one a sense of having been carried back into the Old Testament.

[T 2] But everything was attuned to a dominantly religious note, so that one might have thought oneself in the house of a devout Rabbi. The vast spaces of the living rooms also, lacking ornament or stucco, and too big to be really comfortable, were all arranged in accordance with this same Hebrew pattern. They would be best compared to some of Rembrandt's interiors.

[T 3] For instance, grace was said in Hebrew, and every appropriate ceremonial prescription of the Talmud was precisely carried out.

[T 4] Her very happy marriage with Siegfried Stein had been of short duration.

[T 5] Frau Stein's three elder daughters had gone to a private school, but she sent the two youngest to the town's Viktoriaschule, that was considered much better but meant a quite considerable journey to school, on which they had to cross a long bridge.

[T 6] ... including even the sales in the lumberyard.

CHAPTER 2

[T 1] ...her sixth birthday, when she hoped to get permission to go to school. Chance was on her side. Out walking one day with her eldest sister Else she met one of the teachers. He took a fancy to the intelligent child, and Else told him her small sister's birthday wish. The good man gave her an examination on the spot, and found her perfectly fit to go to school. Edith was thrilled. Though she was exceptionally small and often taken for less than her six years, the Head Master of the Breslau *Viktoriaschule,* that Erna was already attending, gave in to her earnest request.

[T 2] Even then she already possessed great modesty, which is not a characteristic typical of the Jewish people as a whole.

CHAPTER 5

[T 1] However, before following Husserl's invitation to Freiburg, Edith Stein had another duty of a sad nature to fulfill. [The passage that follows this sentence has been relocated to its proper chronological place in this narrative at the end of the chapter.]

[T 2] Besides her strenuous service as an assistant Edith Stein managed to find time and energy for her own work.

CHAPTER 7

[T 1] Kneeling before her mother, looking her in the face, she said gently but firmly: "Mother, I am a Catholic." And the woman who had mastered her difficult lot with truly biblical heroism, and had by her own labor won security for herself and her children, felt the strength go out of her; she wept. This was something Edith had not expected. Never had she seen her mother in tears. She had nerved herself for insult and abuse, she had even reckoned with the possibility of being cast out of the family; she knew the righteous anger of which her mother was capable. Yet this strong woman wept! Edith wept with her. These two great souls, knowing that they were intimately bound together by flesh and blood, yet parted, rose up, each in the strength of her faith, to lay before God on the altar of her heart the victim demanded by His immutable laws.

[T 2] A member of the family states: "We were all dumbfounded by the news and did not know whether to be more astonished at Edith or at our mother's behavior. Edith's step was incomprehensible to us all. We knew Catholicism only as it was to be found in the lowest social class in our East-Schleswig [mistranslation of East-Silesian], home and thought Catholicism merely consisted in groveling on one's knees and kissing the priest's toe. We simply could not conceive how our Edith's lofty spirit could demean itself to this superstitious sect."

But a Catholic acquaintance of the Steins gives a further explanation, saying: "I am convinced that the change that had taken place in Edith, and that lit up her whole being with supernatural radiance, disarmed Frau Stein. As a God-fearing woman, she sensed, without realizing it, the holiness radiating from her daughter, and though her suffering was excruciating she clearly recognized her helplessness before the mystery of grace. We could all see at a glance that Edith had become another person, though she clung to her people with as much love as before and did everything possible to prevent any alteration in their relationships."

[T 3] Her mother gazed with astonishment on her (as she thought) perverse daughter. To an intimate friend she confided, "I have never seen such prayer as Edith's and the strangest thing is that she could pray with us out of her own book, and found it all there!" Edith had in fact brought her Breviary with her and prayed the Psalms with them. And when the Rabbi in ringing tones read out the words "Hear, O Israel, Thy God is *one!*" her mother in her distress and love clasped her child and whispered, "Do you hear? Thy God is but one!"

Poor mother! She saw that her efforts were useless and yet could not desist from them. One day, when she came home from the town, she said softly to Edith, "Well, I have chosen my burial place!" These words were her last appeal to the tenderness of her child's heart. But against all these trials Edith stood unshaken as a courageous soldier of Christ.

CHAPTER 8

[T 1] . . .and Prague.

[T 2] Nothing in her features betrayed her Jewish origin.

[T 3] Sometimes her success was overwhelming and the publicity that surrounded her almost dangerous.

CHAPTER 11

[T 1] . . . of translating St. Thomas, . . .

[T 2] . . . instructing catechumens and then . . .

[T 3] *My presentation in Salzburg will treat of "Das Ethos der Frauenberufe" [The Ethos of Women's Professions]. Originally I was scheduled to present the basic theme [of the conference], "The Ethos of Christian Professions," and actually I had accepted only because, at the time, that topic particularly attracted me. But then the people in Salzburg decided it was essential to address the women's theme separately, so I consented to change. [Dietrich von] Hildebrand has taken over the other topic.*

CHAPTER 12

[T 1] Various colleges had offered Edith Stein tutorial positions.

[T 2] . . .where she went in the spring of 1932, after spending Easter at Beuron.

[T 3] During her time at Münster Dr. Edith Stein was called upon just as frequently as ever to give addresses and conferences. Here is an account of one such event, as reported by herself in early October 1932.

Part 2

CHAPTER 14

[T 1] . . .where with Mary at the foot of the Cross. . .

CHAPTER 15

[T 1] And yet she did not allow this demonstration of universal admiration to disturb her soul even for a minute.

[T 2] . . .the penitential haircloth. . .

[T 3] Those outside the grille continued looking and listening until at last they moved out again into their everyday life; they had said good-bye to one who had won the pearl of great price by surrendering herself freely to the truth.

[T 4] When I asked her if the lecture that evening had made a good impression she simply said 'Yes.'

[T 5] After Mass, however, she had to wait a whole day before being allowed to communicate her joy to her sisters. . .

CHAPTER 16

[T 1] . . .Frau Hantelmann. . .

[T 2] *After leaving a mother's womb?*

[T 3] *Rosa lives peacefully within the family, though naturally she is very lonesome interiorly.*

CHAPTER 17

[T 1] The Way of Love and Knowledge

[T 2] . . .was not going to appear under her name but would be issued. . .

[T 3] . . .of thanksgiving. . .since. . .

[T 4] Yet in spite of such calls upon her from all sides her great philosophical work was now completed. It was entitled *Ewiges und Endliches Sein* (Eternal and Finite Being).

CHAPTER 18

[T 1] Her happiness this day was very great. [and] It is true that no one could foresee the future calamity, but everyone had uneasy suspicions of its imminence.

[T 2] . . .the day of the going to rest of Edmund Husserl.

CHAPTER 20

[T 1] . . .at Geneva. . .

CHAPTER 21

[T 1] . . .that consisted of thousands and thousands of. . .
[T 2] . . .two. . .
[T 3] The first, with no identification of either date or place, runs [text transcribed as translated by H/N] :

> *Dear Mother*
> *If Your Reverence has been allowed to see Fr. [Hirschmann's*
> *– the name is illegible] letter you will know what he*
> *thinks. There is nothing more for me to do in the matter.*
> *I leave it all in the hands of Y. R. to decide whether Y. R.*
> *should do anything about it. I am quite content in any*
> *case. One can only learn a* Scientia Crucis *if one feels*
> *the Cross in one's own person. I was convinced of this*
> *from the very first and have said with all my heart:*
> 'Ave crux, spes unica!'
>
> Y.R.'s grateful child. B.

The second note. . .
[T 4] The third note, to the Swiss Consul at the Hague, merely contains her address and a few words: *"Try to have us taken out as soon as possible. Our convent will pay for the tickets."*

How deep is the desire, expressed in the second letter, to continue living the life to which she was dedicated, as far as possible. The third was intended, perhaps, as an S.O.S. to be telegraphed to the Consul. A letter from Rosa to the Prioress at Echt was unfortunately lost.

CHAPTER 22

[T 1] . . .priest on the station. He was sorry, but there wasn't; having learned this she simply asked him to give her regards to the parish priest. . .

CHAPTER 23

[T 1] . . .(Silesia). . .about 10 August 1942 in or near Auschwitz.

FREQUENTLY CONSULTED WORKS

ICS Publications' Translations
of Edith Stein's Works

Life in a Jewish Family, trans. of *Aus dem Leben einer jüdischen Familie* by Josephine Koeppel. Washington, DC: ICS Publications, 1986. ICS, 1.

Essays on Woman, trans of *Die Frau* by Freda Mary Oben. Washington, DC: ICS Publications, 1987; rev. ed. 1997. ICS, 2.

On the Problem of Empathy, trans. of *Zum Problem der Einfühlung* by Waltraut Stein. The Hague: Martinus Nijhoff, 2nd ed., 1970. Rev. ed. Washington, DC: ICS Publications, 1989. ICS, 3.

The Hidden Life, Essays, Meditations, Spiritual Texts, trans. of *Verborgenes Leben* by Waltraut Stein. Washington, DC: ICS Publications, 1992. ICS, 4.

Self-Portrait in Letters, trans. of *Selbstbildnis in Briefen* by Josephine Koeppel. Washington, DC: ICS Publications, 1993. ICS, 5.

The Science of the Cross, trans. of *Kreuzeswissenschaft* by Josephine Koeppel. Washington, DC: ICS Publications, 2002. ICS, 6.

Philosophy of Psychology and the Humanities, trans. of *Beiträge zur philosophischen Begründung der Psychologie und der Geisteswissenschaften* by Mary Catherine Baseheart and Marianne Sawicki. Washington, DC: ICS Publications, 2000. ICS, 7.

Knowledge and Faith, trans. of *Erkenntnis und Glauben* by Walter Redmond. Washington, DC: ICS Publications, 2000. ICS, 8.

Finite and Eternal Being: An Attempt at an Ascent to the Meaning of Being, trans. of *Endliches und Ewiges Sein* by Kurt F. Reinhardt. Washington, DC: ICS Publications, 2002. ICS, 9.

Other Editions of Texts by Edith Stein

Letter to Pope Pius XI. Trans. Batzdorff, Koeppel, and Sullivan in Susanne M. Batzdorff, *Aunt Edith, The Jewish Heritage of a Catholic Saint.* 2nd rev. ed. Springfield, IL: Templegate publishers, 2003, pp. 226-27.

The Mystery of Christmas, trans. of *Das Weihnachtsgeheimnis* by Josephine Rucker. Darlington, England: Carmelite Press, 1985.

Edith Stein, An Edith Stein Daybook; To Live at the Hand of the Lord. Trans. Susanne M. Batzdorff. Springfield, IL: Templegate Publishers, 1994.

Edith Stein (St. Teresa Benedicta of the Cross, O.C.D.) Essential Writings. Comp. and Intro. by John Sullivan. Maryknoll, NY: Orbis Books, 2002. "Modern Spiritual Masters Series."

Edith Stein, Selected Writings. With Comments, Reminiscences and Translations of her Prayers and Poems by her Niece Susanne M. Batzdorff. Springfield, IL: Templegate Publishers, 1990. (Includes 1938 autobiographical account by Edith Stein, "How I Came to the Cologne Carmel.")

The Works of Edith Stein, New German Edition

Aus dem Leben einer jüdischen Familie und weitere autobiographische Beiträge. Eds. Amata Neyer and Hanna-Barbara Gerl-Falkovitz. Freiburg: Verlag Herder, 2002. (New edition containing numerous detailed footnotes that provide data previously unavailable or incomplete.) ESGA, 1.

Selbstbildnis in Briefen: Erster Teil, 1916-1933. Ed. Amata Neyer, Intro. Hanna-Barbara Gerl-Falkovitz. Freiburg: Verlag Herder, 2000. ESGA, 2.

Selbstbildnis in Briefen: Zweiter Teil, 1933-1942. Ed. Amata Neyer, Intro. Hanna-Barbara Gerl-Falkovitz. Freiburg: Verlag Herder, 2000. ESGA, 3.

Selbstbildnis in Briefen: Briefe an Roman Ingarden. Eds. Amata Neyer and Eberhard Avé-Lallemant, Intro. Hanna-Barbara Gerl-Falkovitz. Freiburg: Verlag Herder, 2001. ESGA, 4.

Studies

Batzdorff, Susanne M. *Aunt Edith, The Jewish Heritage of a Catholic Saint.* 2nd rev. ed. Springfield, IL: Templegate Publishers, 2003.

Feldes, Joachim. *Edith Stein und Schifferstadt.* Schifferstadt: Stadtsparkasse Schifferstadt, 1998.

Herbstrith, Waltraud, ed. *Never Forget, Christian and Jewish Perspectives on Edith Stein.* Trans. Susanne M. Batzdorff. Washington, DC: ICS Publications, 1998. "Carmelite Studies," 7.

Hermann, Maria Adele. *Die Speyerer Jahre von Edith Stein: Aufzeichnungen zu ihrem 100. Geburtstag.* Speyer: Pilger Verlag, 1990.

Koeppel, Josephine. *Edith Stein, Philosopher and Mystic.* Collegeville, MN: Liturgical Press, 1990. "The Way of the Christian Mystics," 12.

Krusenotto, Wolfram. *Die letzten Tage im Leben der seligen Schwester Teresia Benedicta vom Kreuz.* Liegburg: Rheinlandia Verlag, 1991.

Lammers, Elisabeth. *Als die Zukunft noch offen war: Edith Stein, das entscheidende Jahr in Münster.* Münster: Dialogvertrag, 2003.

Mohr, Anne u. Prégardier, Elisabeth, eds. *Passion im August. 2-9 August 1942.* Annweiler: Plöger Verlag, 1995.

Müller, Andreas Uwe and Neyer, Amata. *Edith Stein: Das Leben einer ungewöhnlichen Frau.* Zürich/Düsseldorf: Benziger, 1998.

Neyer, Amata. *Edith Stein: Her Life in Photos and Documents.* Trans. Waltraut Stein. Washington, DC: ICS Publications, 1999.

_____. *Wie ich in den Kölner Karmel kam, mit Erläuterungen und Ergänzungen von Maria Amata Neyer.* Würzburg: Echter Verlag, 1994.

Schlafke, Jakob, ed. *Edith Stein, Documents Concerning Her Life and Death.* Trans. Susanne M. Batzdorff. New York: Edith Stein Guild, 1984.

Sullivan, John, ed. *Holiness Befits Your House: Canonization of Edith Stein, A Documentation.* Washington, DC: ICS Publications, 2000.

[Vrienden van Dr. Edith Stein] *Als een brandende toorts: Documentaire Getuigenissen over Dr. Edith Stein (Zr. Teresia Benedicta a Cruce) en medeslachtoffers.* Echt: private publication by "Vrienden van Dr. Edith Stein," 1967.

INDEX

List of Places

The **bold** print used for eleven places indicates that Edith lived there for a time. The SMALL CAPITALS mark five stations on her way of the Cross from Echt to Auschwitz.

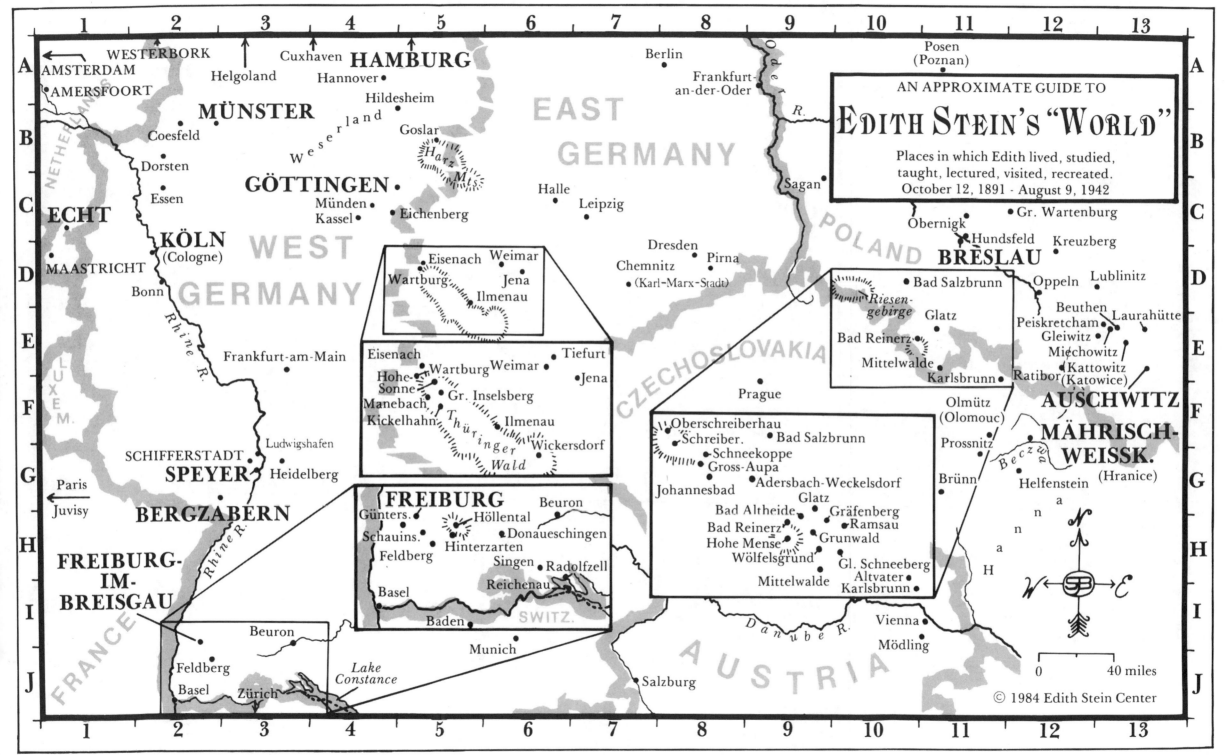

AN APPROXIMATE GUIDE TO

EDITH STEIN'S "WORLD"

Places in which Edith lived, studied,
taught, lectured, visited, recreated.
October 12, 1891 - August 9, 1942

© 1984 Edith Stein Center

Note: National borders reflect political entities as of 1984.